Praise for *The Birming*

The writers' views about the effects of the Trojan Horse affair, drawn together by Colin Diamond, are a reminder of the damage wreaked upon the reputation of a city and a part of its community by some politicians and a section of the press determined to find radicalised violent extremism where there was none. *The Birmingham Book* reveals a deeper and disturbing truth which forces one to consider why it is we have failed to encourage, mentor and promote sufficient numbers of teachers of the Muslim faith to become future leaders in our British schools.

Ian Kershaw, Independent Chief Adviser to Birmingham City Council

Colin Diamond, and those he persuaded to write these always illuminating chapters from the viewpoints of community and professional leaders, deserves our deepest thanks as he calmly sets out the key issues which arose from the extraordinary affair of the Trojan Horse letter – in its way more damaging than the other notorious fake Zinoviev letter ninety years earlier. That one affected politics while this one damaged children's futures in vulnerable parts of a great city. It's harder to forgive. Diamond's book – always calm, generous and informed – reveals the issues which beset that shifting mix of diverse communities, rival faiths and the interplay of professional commitment and parental ambition – or lack of it – which is veiled under the easy heading of 'urban education'. Those who engage with it will find plenty of stimulus from these pages.

Tim Brighouse, former Commissioner for London Schools

Diamond's book is very relevant and has implications beyond Birmingham. It sheds light onto how the needs of the largest minority group in England – Muslims – are or are not being met and the reaction by authorities to alarmist levels, escalating prejudice, fear and mistrust despite it resulting in no criminal charges whatsoever. His privileged position to bring together many of the key actors in the Trojan Horse affair allows a focus on the causes of the series of incidents. His reference to Holmwood provides an apt interjection in the discourse. The subsequent effects on the professional lives of many are alluded to in an authentic narrative by Campbell-Stephens. With this, the book leaves the reader wanting to ask more questions – four of which I allude to here: how can the mistrust amongst the Muslim community be repaired with an authentic voice? How can pupil outcomes be regained to the high levels of attainment pre-Trojan Horse? What is the accountability of governance across all multi-academy trusts in England? Lastly, how can barriers be removed for aspiring Muslim school leaders in their career progression who are still in the shadow of the incidents from 2013–2014?

Kausor Amin-Ali, author of *A-Z School Leadership: A Guide For New School Leaders*, founder of All Children Read, experienced Head Teacher

The Birmingham Book is not just a book about Birmingham. There are warnings here – and lessons aplenty – for school leaders, administrators and governors everywhere. And, of course, for local and national politicians. More than a book about what happened in Birmingham, this is a book about politics, religion, equality, tolerance and intolerance, about the politicisation of education, abuses of power at local and national level and the ability of ethical school leaders to do what needs to be done, despite enormous pressure, wherever they may be.

There are many lessons to be learnt by unpicking the debacle that was Birmingham's sorry Trojan Horse scandal. One is about the uses and abuses of power in the education system at school, local and national level. Another asks us to reflect how far we have genuinely come as a society in matters of tolerance, acceptance and equity. And among many takeaways from the inspiring education leaders in this book, it is clear that 'community, community, community' will always be at the heart of all great schools.

Ian Gilbert, founder of Independent Thinking Ltd, education writer, editor of *The Working Class*

The Trojan Horse affair in Birmingham, as it is popularly referred to, was a watershed moment for the way educationalists, community leaders and politicians, both locally and nationally, perceived the local Muslim communities in this great city. In the three decades from the end of the 1950s to the end of the 1980s, Muslims from the predominately rural areas of Kashmir, Pakistan and Bangladesh came and settled in the highly urbanised city of Birmingham. Uppermost in their minds is to live a better quality of life than that which they came from; one route in achieving this is through the education of their children. This book of essays is a must-read for those wishing to understand the important underlying dynamic between Muslims considering the education of their children, and the educational establishment's quest for a quality education based on British values. The Trojan Horse affair provides the fertile context for drawing together those issues. The contributors provide serious and authentic perspectives on the systemic issues of structural racism, Islamophobia, class and cultural imperialism that gave rise to the hysterical response to an unsubstantiated letter. This is excellently achieved by many of the authors giving candid biographical accounts of their own personal experience growing up in Birmingham schools and then of their professional experience as educators. This is balanced by well-researched evidence-based contributions on future policy and lessons for contemporary urban school leadership. The book is the first opportunity for those in the mix of the Trojan Horse affair to give a sober and thoughtful appreciation of the events and of the lessons learnt.

Dr. Muhammad Mashuq Ally, Chair of Governors, Bordesley Green Girls' School and Sixth Form

Professor Colin Diamond presides over a cornucopia of authentic and inspiring, hitherto untold stories from school leaders; stories of recovery that offer an alternative lens through which to view the kaleidoscope that embodied the Trojan Horse affair.

Refreshing and vividly personal accounts of recovery – the existential angst that refines the compassion that inspires motivational leadership – are woven through every chapter and each one offers alternative dimensions through which schools can work relationally with communities.

The most compelling takeaways from this book are offered by Reza Gholami and Joy Warmington; a reminder of the importance of preparing and equipping teachers and school leaders to work in intersectional spaces, to develop the critical social awareness and cultural humility that enable all learners to flourish.

Razia Butt, MBE, Isonomy Education

Chapter 12 is a go-to for all educationalists from teachers to leaders as it inspires and is part of the book that is the phoenix rising from the ashes of the Trojan Horse debacle.

Colin takes us on a roller coaster of a journey, sequencing the historical political contexts from Labour's high investment and equally high accountability to Gove's vision of leadership encapsulating low investment and high accountability with 'corporate management' approaches to educational leadership. Amazingly well researched, Colin has collated the historical and present-day theories of school leadership from all angles. He then brings all these vividly to life though citing the lived narratives of exemplary school leaders he has worked alongside in the urban Birmingham context. He sums up what works simply as 'a combination of adaptive leadership and pragmatic interpretation of government education policy from a secure base in the community, driven by a passion for Birmingham's children'.

Colin rightly stresses the unique challenges these leaders face and analyses their commonality of moral purpose, values and character – 'quiet leadership at the heart of the moral compass'. The matrix of the three characteristics is key for any aspiring or established leader. Best of all, Colin has distilled the experiences of the urban leaders into ten wise takeaways for the 'survive to thrive' journey. These are the valuable diamonds of wisdom (deliberate pun intended!) such as 'roots to grow and wings to fly' and 'YNWA' (you never work alone) and the superb UNICEF RRSA as a framework for a diverse, equitable and inclusive curriculum.

Meena Wood, international Edu-speaker, trainer, author and leadership coach

The **Birmingham Book**

Lessons in urban education leadership and policy from the Trojan Horse affair

Edited by
Colin Diamond

Foreword by Mick Waters

Crown House Publishing Limited
www.crownhouse.co.uk

First published by
Crown House Publishing Limited
Crown Buildings, Bancyfelin, Carmarthen, Wales, SA33 5ND, UK
www.crownhouse.co.uk

and

Crown House Publishing Company LLC
PO Box 2223, Williston, VT 05495, USA
www.crownhousepublishing.com

First published 2022.

Cover image © Ewan White.

British Library Cataloguing-in-Publication Data
A catalogue entry for this book is available from the British Library.

Print ISBN 978-178583592-6
Mobi ISBN 978-178583608-4
ePub ISBN 978-178583609-1
ePDF ISBN 978-178583610-7

LCCN

Printed and bound in the UK by
CPi Antony Rowe, Chippenham, Wiltshire

To Birmingham school leaders who quietly
transform children's lives every day.

Foreword

I remember my feelings as I drove away from Park View Academy in November 2012. I had visited at the invitation of the head teacher, Lindsey Clark, ten years after her appointment. She had written to me following her attendance at a conference at which I had spoken:

> After your presentation I came back to work refreshed and excited as you made sense about what matters in education. I am writing to invite you to visit Park View School, a school that I know you knew. I would be interested in your observations about the journey we have travelled and suggestions about what we need to do to keep on the right tracks. I am also interested in a conversation regarding multi-academy trusts – if you are willing. Park View is now an academy and is sponsoring Nansen Primary School. We want to do it 'right' and in a way that lasts, but making sure that each and every child gets the best possible deal.

The academy had been judged outstanding following an Ofsted inspection on the new and more demanding framework introduced by Sir Michael Wilshaw in January that year.

I was in the school for an hour and a half, so I gained only a snapshot. Lindsey showed me around some classrooms and I talked with an enthusiastic team of teachers in the mathematics department, committed to teaching maths and teaching it well, inspiring children towards the joy and intrigue of the discipline. I talked with a few pupils and with Lindsey and the chair of governors, Tahir Alam. The Park View Academy Trust was thinking of expanding, and we shared an open debate about the benefits or otherwise of becoming further engaged in the national schooling development that had so few clear organisational guidelines.

I remember raising questions, in the way I do, about the rather subdued nature of several classrooms, the subtle difference between rigour and suppression. I felt there was an uneasy discipline based more on external control than self-control. I wondered whether it was me: whether children had been told to show their best image and had overcooked it. We talked about the very clerical nature of every lesson we had visited and, as in many schools, the feeling of anticlimax that many pupils must experience at not doing what it 'says on the door': science or design technology, for example, and instead doing writing. I raised the issue of single-gender classes, but only tentatively, as I know it is a personal view that single-gender teaching in a mixed school is unsatisfactory. I am tentative because I am aware that the city prizes its single-gender foundation schools, and most of our esteemed public schools are also single-gender entry. Each of my reservations or questions was met with the trump card so often played: 'Ofsted says we are outstanding.' I sensed it wasn't, but who would I be to judge based on just a short time in the school?

As I drove away, I reflected that the school was infinitely improved from the one I had last visited in 2002. That was the day when I had been part of the panel that had appointed Lindsey Clark as head teacher. Whilst the school had been improving in the period at the start of the new millennium, it was still struggling when Lindsey took over. Now, the tone of the school was controlled as opposed to unpredictable. Building Schools for the Future had transformed the environment and created a business-like environment compared with the previously shabby secondary modern atmosphere. I respected Lindsey's efforts and assumed that Tahir would be proud of his contribution after the previous frustrations over the poor performance of the school and others in the area. I didn't think it was superb, but it had improved certainly and significantly.

I was not as effusive as I felt both Lindsey and Tahir probably wanted me to be, especially since Sir Michael Wilshaw, Her Majesty's Chief Inspector, had visited earlier in the year and used the school as a benchmark for others.

Just over a year after my visit, the Trojan Horse row broke. It is hard to believe that such a small piece of paper with no signature could cause such turmoil in a school, community and city – and even central government. The fallout was significant: a swathe of schools subject to inspection, previous success obliterated, individuals ostracised, court cases that collapsed through lack of authoritative evidence, and a confused community once more doubting its schools, its city and itself. When I was invited to contribute to this book, I was intrigued to know whether I was going to understand the events which had caused such upset and which I had watched from a distance.

However, this book does far more than revisit the turmoil and tread again the complexity explored in two major enquiries. Some of the issues are contentious, and many people tend to overlook their complexity or have simplistic views on them. This book avoids pointing the finger and raking up bad blood. It doesn't settle scores, but nor does it turn a blind eye to the uncomfortable.

Colin Diamond offers an excellent analysis of the turbulent period that engulfed the schools, as parallel enquiries did their work against a background of political point-scoring. His introduction is followed by first-hand accounts of the efforts to rebuild both the schools and the community's belief in its schools. There are personal accounts of a harrowing time for a community alongside life stories of awareness of unfairness and underestimation. There are examples of responsibility and accountability being shifted and responsibility and accountability being accepted. It is a book about rights and wrongs that avoids recrimination and blame, and instead relates stories of hope, ambition and collaborative partnership.

This book offers a fascinating read; it is informative and revealing whilst at the same time unsettling, salutary and uplifting. The recollections in each chapter are vivid. Images of childhood half a century ago sit alongside the reflections of head teachers working to establish trust against a backdrop of suspicion. Frustration comes through the feeling of the unfulfilled potential of communities and young people, now adults, subject to historic under-expectation and underachievement within a school system unprepared for their arrival from abroad, slow to adjust and quick to rationalise shortcomings.

Reading this book, it is easy to imagine the screenplay for a film of the 'feel-good' genre. The vignettes appear so often. With the right music, a cinema audience would be carried along with a story offering an emotional switchback: funny, poignant and homely scenes set against confused and angry images of injustice, interspersed with the order and certainty of officialdom. The clichés would be there, along with a musical score and settings that would drift from the tension and wrath of the period to the rise of a community, and particularly its schools, and which would highlight certain individuals who would be overstated and over-characterised. Of course, even in this harmless observation there is an irony, for some of the main protagonists and some of those involved in the story would not want the music and would not tolerate a film.

What the book reveals is the outcome of a managerial age where organisations such as Ofsted and the Department for Education applied themselves to the challenge of their targets, tick-lists and risk assessments without looking closely enough at the reality in front of them.

Academy trusts were created to accelerate the number of academies in the education system but with little regard as to how they would work in practice. Schools were allowed to be classified as 'outstanding' and then 'fail' within a very short time, seemingly without turning the mirror to question the processes of inspection itself. The academy regime had played into the hands of people who wanted the best for their own children and had taken at face value Michael Gove's offer of autonomy at school level.

It is easy to forget that the crisis arose at a time of a tightening screw. We had a prime minister and an education secretary who had announced that they were 'declaring war' on coasting schools (*Daily Mail*, 2010) and referring to people who questioned policy as 'enemies of promise' (Gove, 2013). Gove's review of curriculum and qualifications was emphasising an intellectually demanding approach at the expense of vocational and practical aspects. The English Baccalaureate, which Gove had admitted the previous year was a 'bridge too far',[1] was becoming the currency of approach through the Progress 8 measure and schools were looking over their shoulders at the newly invigorated Ofsted. Inspectors were fixated by data to the extent that struggling schools were being visited by Her Majesty's Inspectors half-termly to look at data drops and expecting to see 'spikes' of improvement. For a community previously disappointed and frustrated with the schooling of their children, these sorts of standpoints would have convinced those involved that they were on the right path, and the political zeal would have been welcomed and used as a spur. Governors were being urged to exert influence on their schools. Would these criticised governing bodies have compared unfavourably in their determination for success with other dominating governing bodies driving their own agenda within their own community elsewhere? Don't most multi-academy trusts seek to appoint trustees who accord with their outlook?

It was also the time of the Prevent agenda, which at the time asked schools to 'respect' fundamental British values. There was a sense of contradiction for professionals, with an evolving shift away from the community cohesion agenda that schools had been expected to address in previous years.

---

1 See Hansard, HC Deb vol. 558, col. 441 (7 February 2013). Available at: https://hansard.parliament.uk/Commons/2013-02-07/debates/13020759000004/CurriculumAndExamReform.

The label of 'social deprivation', along with the accompanying poor results at GCSE and low positions in league tables, was distorting the way that children in schools in such areas had been treated. Someone else had decided they were socially deprived and that they were inadequate in terms of results. Yet, when those results had been addressed, the schools initially acclaimed by inspection were now seen to be not addressing the right issues.

Much was made of the lack of cultural opportunities for these pupils, and that a narrowed curriculum restricted opportunity for the arts. It is easy to forget that, at the time, it would have been relatively easy to find a school where the curriculum focus was on a narrowing range of supposedly academic subjects, to the detriment of arts and culturally based disciplines. There is considerable reference to the work done by school leaders in encouraging communities to embrace a wider landscape, as well as examples of teenagers who had never ventured into their city centre. Head teachers elsewhere could provide examples (even now) of youngsters reluctant to leave their estate or postcode, but, against a backdrop of political rhetoric, changing this became a priority and a 'measurable' for these communities in a way that it did not for others under scrutiny.

The vital importance of place runs throughout the story; people leaving their place, mainly Pakistan, from the late 1960s and making a home in a new place – in a community within a city which welcomed them by default rather than with a warm embrace. There are stories of the efforts to be taken seriously, to secure some sort of equality and then equity; stories of a community bringing its traditions, routines and religious practices; stories of people dissatisfied with authority, trying to exert influence on those in charge and eventually seeking to use the government's own policies to secure the best interests for their young people and a sense of self-esteem for their community.

Adrian Packer (Chapter 7), who picked up the mantle of headship at Park View Academy, the school at the centre of Trojan Horse, describes that confusion finding its way into the whole school community, not least the pupils who appeared bemused at the way they had become the centre of a crisis. He communicates the loyalty to an ideal achieved through a homemade recipe, yet turned to dust after such short-lived success.

Whilst Packer moved in from elsewhere with fresh eyes, others were working at the heart of a community they knew well. Sajid Gulzar

(Chapter 8), CEO of Prince Albert Community Trust, was in the unique position of trying to support Highfield Junior and Infant School, which he had attended as a child. Building upon previous experience of helping schools to lift themselves, he knew there was no blueprint. Adrian Packer describes the way he had to resist urgings to impose a new regime to replace the discredited one. Professionalism shines through his description of a desire to build community, and through Azita Zohhadi's (Chapter 6) commitment to bold spirit and purpose at Nelson Mandela Primary School. There is a recognition that the crisis presented a wider challenge to the city and to people such as Pat Smart – mentioned several times for her contribution – who epitomises all those head teachers and teachers across the city who have, over time, committed themselves to making Birmingham the best place it can be for children in schools.

Much of the book is also about the way schools relate to their parent community. Joy Warmington's (Chapter 13) analysis of the more recent dispute at nearby Parkfield Community School, which centred on the No Outsiders programme, goes below the surface and looks first at the reasons for the protests and then the way forward. She explores the detail of larger tensions, the lack of clarity in law and the importance of each side listening to the other and working towards compromise. She describes a situation where parents 'trusted' their school because it secured good results and was deemed outstanding and, as a result, both school and parents accepted a relationship that was muted.

Azita Zohhadi proposes that better futures for children rely on trust (there is an irony in the use of that word) and tells of the early days in her headship as parents viewed with suspicion the steps that she was taking to move the school forward. As parents bought into the developments and saw evidence of the children achieving, that trust became the fuel for an immensely positive relationship. Similarly, Herminder Channa (Chapter 10) portrays her leadership role at Ark Boulton Academy being built upon a rejection of draconian approaches of 'zero tolerance' regimes in favour of listening to pupils and parents as they considered what their school could offer them.

It is the need to address that 'muted' relationship between school and parents that comes through as a message that is applicable to schools elsewhere and in other aspects of schooling. Do parents accept too easily the reassurances, rules and expectations of schools? Perhaps Trojan

Horse was simply an example of members of a community taking a form of direct action as opposed to undermining or plotting anything sinister.

Kamal Hanif (Chapter 2) brings a fascinating perspective on the world beyond schooling. He traces developments using milestones such as the murder of Stephen Lawrence, the Swann Report on multiracial education, the impact of the Rushdie episode and the events of 9/11. The tension associated with being a British Muslim and recognising the perceptions of Islam beyond the community was significant – and not relieved by the response of ministers. There are fascinating and at times upsetting reflections on incidents in school staffrooms. Coming through so much of the book is a sense of a community lacking insight about how to influence.

Karamat Iqbal (Chapter 3) questions systemic issues which result in the continuing lack of representation of the Pakistani community in decision-making roles in the city and delves into questions of competence in bureaucracy at the highest level. This is also picked up by Thomas Perry (Chapter 4) from the University of Warwick who provides an analysis of national and school-level data and poses many important questions for policy-makers and school leaders about differential performance and educational inequalities by ethnicity, gender, English language status and socio-economic status. He acknowledges the unique position of school leaders to respond to need, but asserts that government and community should not shirk from their responsibility to address social problems, and nor should the accountability system be excused from its wilful blindness to school context and (dis)advantage.

Nearly all the writers based in schools saw recognition of their quality through inspection as important in terms of acknowledging that the schools had a clean bill of health. This was surprising given that, at least in part, Ofsted had been a cause of the turmoil wrought upon the community and its schools. Several contributors express doubt about the validity and integrity of the inspection agency in the twenty-one inspections commissioned by the secretary of state. Perhaps this is because many of the writers saw the events from the perspective of arriving on the scene after the negative judgement, and perhaps also there is something about recognition from outside seeming like validation.

Ultimately, *The Birmingham Book* is a kaleidoscope of relationships and values: trust, belief, tolerance, professionalism. It is about a community and its shared commitment to making childhood the very best it can be for all its children and seeing schools as a vital part of that process. It always was.

Professor Mick Waters

References

Daily Mail (2010) Gove Declares War on Failure in Our Schools (25 November). Available at: https://www.dailymail.co.uk/debate/article-1332891/Michael-Gove-declares-war-failure-schools.html.

Gove, Michael (2013) I Refuse to Surrender to the Marxist Teachers Hell-Bent on Destroying Our Schools: Education Secretary Berates 'The New Enemies of Promise' for Opposing His Plans, *Daily Mail* (23 March). Available at: https://www.dailymail.co.uk/debate/article-2298146/I-refuse-surrender-Marxist-teachers-hell-bent-destroying-schools-Education-Secretary-berates-new-enemies-promise-opposing-plans.html.

Swann, Michael (1985) *Education for All: Report of the Committee of Enquiry into the Education of Children from Ethnic Minority Groups* [Swann Report]. London: HMSO. Available at: http://www.educationengland.org.uk/documents/swann/swann1985.html.

Provenance –
a personal journey

Colin Diamond

It is important to explain the origins of this book. First, I need to confess my affection for Birmingham. I often describe the city as England's best-kept secret because, whilst Brummies are immensely proud people, they keep it to themselves and are generally self-effacing about their achievements. As a professor at the University of Birmingham, my colleagues would expect me to be upfront about conscious bias – and probe my unconscious bias too. I like working in the city and feel at home. I have even been conferred the status of 'honorary Brummie' on a few occasions. There, I have said it. Make of it what you will.

An urban educationalist at heart, with my own schooling in downtown Liverpool and teaching career in inner London, working in Birmingham felt natural from the outset. Twenty years ago, the city's schools were recognised for their cutting-edge innovation and transcending the social disadvantage of the children and families they served. The commitment to Birmingham's children continues. Every day, thousands of miracles occur in the city's classrooms against a backdrop of severe socio-economic deprivation. In communities that are on the bottom rung of the ladder in English society, schools work to give those children a foothold, and they begin to climb. It isn't glamorous work and it is well known that the school inspectorate is less likely to judge inner-city schools to be outstanding, no matter what the quality of the education. Walk the streets just beyond the magnificent civic piazza and Victorian municipal buildings and you will find schools that are beacons of hope amid the urban jumble of roads, dilapidated factories and housing estates. It was always a privilege to visit and celebrate their achievements.

When I left Birmingham City Council in summer 2018 to take up a post at the university, it provided me with the opportunity to reflect on four intense years. Starting with little knowledge of the city and its communities, it had been a crash-course induction. Working initially for the

Department for Education and then moving to the council in 2015, the pace was relentless. Trojan Horse and its legacy dominated those years.

I needed to make sense of what had happened, and there is no greater discipline than writing a book to create a framework for reflection and learning. My understanding has deepened during the process of writing and editing. This book became possible when all of the authors agreed to tell their stories. I asked them to imagine we were in a cafe or pub and to describe their journeys through the Trojan Horse era. Francis Bacon's quotation, 'Reading maketh a Full man, Conference a Ready man & Writing an Exact man', which sits above the entrance to Kensington public library in Liverpool, has been my lodestar.

The strength of the book lies in the integrity of its authors, who have lived and breathed Birmingham education for many years. There is a range of experiences and perspectives defined by each author's position as school leader, academic or their leadership of related organisations such as brap (formerly Birmingham Race Action Partnership) and the National Governance Association. I deliberately set wide parameters for the authors and trusted their judgement and scholarship. Each contributor read near-final drafts of my introduction and early chapters and agreed to write, knowing my take on events.

The result is a rich brew of powerful accounts which dispels the myth that there is a single version of 'the truth' about Trojan Horse. This is the opposite of a simplistic and convenient single-line narrative that some commentators prefer. It is easy to take a position that supports Michael Gove's paranoia about supposed Islamic extremism infiltrating schools or to create a hagiography that beatifies the principal players at Park View Education Trust (PVET). The multi-layered perspectives found in this book reveal a complex intersectional landscape that continues to evolve.

What took you so long to get here?

By April 2014, it had become apparent to ministers and officials in the Department for Education that something really serious had gone wrong in Birmingham. I was asked to pull together a team drawn from the department's official education adviser team (experienced school leaders and former Ofsted inspectors) who would work with Education Funding

Agency staff to find out what was really going on in the PVET academies and in Oldknow Junior School following the Ofsted inspection judgements. It was meant to be a six-week assignment.

I am still working in Birmingham eight years later. It wasn't the chaos and dysfunction that detained me, and nor was it the immediate task of getting two damaged academy trusts into safe hands. It was an invitation from Pat Smart, at that time executive head teacher of the Greet Federation, to come and see her primary school in Sparkhill that hadn't been directly caught up in Trojan Horse but had experienced some of the behaviours aimed at its leadership.

Sir Mike Tomlinson, the education commissioner for Birmingham, and I visited Greet and were seriously impressed by the standards that pupils achieved. Here was an inner-city primary with almost 100% Muslim children, of whom the majority were of British Pakistani Mirpuri heritage, achieving brilliant results. The Year 6 pupils' books contained writing of sophistication and maturity, testimony to the progress they had made at Greet. And yet many of those pupils, high achievers in Year 6, went on to the neighbouring Golden Hillock secondary school where by 2014 their progress was being halted abruptly.

It was the generosity of Birmingham's head teachers that I found most compelling. The sense of family and loyalty to the city was palpable. Many heads were asked to step up to the plate to remedy what had gone badly wrong because of Trojan Horse. None refused. They wanted to purge the damage to the reputation of Birmingham's education system. And they all asked, 'What took you so long to get here?' In other words, why had the Department for Education ignored all the warning signs that we now call 'Trojan-type behaviours' over many years?

Ministers took some convincing that the solution to most of the problems identified were already on the doorstep in Birmingham. Their instincts were to invite national academy chains to take over this group of rudderless schools. And in the case of the Ark multi-academy trust, already established in the city, this worked out well. It adopted Golden Hillock secondary and Oldknow junior (renamed as Ark Boulton and Ark Victoria respectively). For the other schools, local solutions were found. As a result of exceptional leadership, most of these schools – whether in local or national trusts – have since thrived. It is important to state that many Birmingham City Council-maintained schools that had managed to avoid serious Trojan incursions into their governing bodies continued to provide high-quality education in spite of the turbulence that surrounded them.

The full weight of what had become a national education crisis was felt most acutely in Birmingham's east end. The mood was febrile in summer 2014. Cab drivers lectured me on the calumny that Michael Gove had visited on Park View and Golden Hillock schools once they knew my destination from New Street station. It was a hot summer. The Intifada was raging in the Gaza Strip and Palestinian flags were on display along the Alum Rock Road. The sense of injustice locally and internationally towards Muslims found voice across the community.

Colleagues at the Department for Education in London were worried, needlessly, about my safety in the city. Their understanding had been shaped by the creation of a narrative with incendiary ingredients: the flagship academy programme had apparently been hijacked and become an incubator for Islamist extremist behaviour. This fed Gove's worst imaginings. Of course, there was anger and confusion in abundance and intense curiosity about what was going to happen to the local schools that had been plummeted into special measures. There were hostile, shouty meetings. There was despair and suspicion in equal measure from everyone involved. Some school staff requested meetings in neutral venues at night and passed information containing school documents to me literally under the table. They feared that once the investigation into Trojan Horse was over and the Department for Education left town, there would be retribution and the termination of careers.

Events were chaotic, with governors locked out of one school by senior leaders as the summer term ended. One parent-governor of two secondary school-aged children caught up in Trojan Horse told me, in tears, that when he was at school in Birmingham, he was informed by the careers teacher that his future would consist of 'driving cabs or cooking kebabs'. Now, all those years later, it looked like a new generation of the community, including his own children, was being failed by that very same school.

Yet, under the circumstances, on a personal level, the reception I received was always polite and very reasonable. Hospitality was invariably offered and accepted. Trust was at a premium. Events over summer 2014 continued to destabilise until new leadership was installed in the academy trusts and schools for the autumn term. And, always, the invitation was to come and talk things through in the homes of local families, mosques and cafes, with everyone having a view on how to sort things out.

In autumn 2014, work continued at the top level of the Department for Education, with Sir Mike Tomlinson, former Her Majesty's Chief Inspector, appointed as education commissioner by the secretary of state with the remit of getting the city's education back on track. I was appointed as his deputy and embedded in the council's education offices. An education improvement plan was needed to get the basic elements of the council's duties back in good working order. They included school improvement, safeguarding and governance. Communications with schools were broken and needed to be restored. By January 2015, the improvement plan had been approved by the secretary of state for education and the journey to rebuild relationships and trust had begun.

My move from the Department for Education to the city council was seamless in that, broadly, I was working with the same people as the recovery plans gained momentum. I wasn't 'changing sides', as my loyalty lay with the children and families in the city, not the infrastructure – whether in Whitehall or Birmingham. At school level, exactly as foretold by the city's most successful education leader, Sir Tim Brighouse, the real deals were sealed in pubs or curry houses in the evening. The Birmingham education community rightly expects total commitment from its leaders and that involves 24/7 engagement far from the council building and its civic formalities.

Being director of education in Birmingham is an all-consuming job, with around 450 state schools and roughly 205,000 pupils to oversee. The post-Trojan Horse improvement plan had staunched the immediate damage found by the Clarke and Kershaw investigations (see Timeline). However, as I advised Ofsted and the Department for Education in 2015, the biggest risk sector was then to be found within the city's independent schools, which ranged from King Edward's School (founded in 1552 with a civic roll of honour amongst its alumni) through to start-up schools in the east end that could not pass the most basic of safeguarding tests.

At the same time, the number of families resorting to elective home education was increasing rapidly, partly as a result of displacement when Trojan Horse activities stopped in state schools. Families were persuaded that a better, more Islamic education was on offer in these backstreet operations. A number of them were educating children illegally, never having registered with the Department for Education. Ofsted created a specialist team of inspectors to investigate independent schools where risk was evident, and I joined them on one visit. Everything about this 'school' was appalling. The thirty children sat passively in tiny classrooms receiving poor teaching and were making no progress. The premises were unsafe on every level. The lead inspector warned the proprietor that she was running a school unlawfully and it would be reported to the Department for Education. I informed her that fire safety breaches, insanitary conditions and rodent infection were all major issues that would be reported immediately to the relevant authorities. The real tragedy was that cash-poor families had been conned into paying fees for a substandard education in the name of their faith, whilst places were available in a good community school a few hundred metres away. The proprietor closed the 'school' a few days later.

2015 – turning the corner

By 2015, things were starting to fall into place. One feature of Trojan Horse had been the pressure to narrow the curriculum and remove or reduce subjects such as sex education, mixed physical education, citizenship, music and the humanities. In its revived leadership role, Birmingham's cabinet member for children's services, Brigid Jones, and for inclusion and community safety, James McKay, signed the Birmingham Curriculum Statement in September 2015. It stated unequivocally that 'ALL children in Birmingham will experience a broad and balanced curriculum enabling them to grow and learn in an environment without prejudice or inequality' (Birmingham City Council, 2015, p. 1). It was explicit about the place of arts, physical activities, music and social, moral, spiritual and cultural education.

This simple statement, underpinned by a raft of educational legislation, was a crucial ingredient that affirmed Birmingham City Council's moral authority in education. It has been used extensively by head teachers and governing bodies as the touchstone for curriculum planning. It was reissued in 2019 to bring it up to date with legislation and to ensure that it was fit for purpose with the advent of compulsory relationships, health and sex education in all schools in England from 2020 (Birmingham City Council, 2019). The Birmingham Curriculum Statement was subsequently recognised as an example of good practice by the Department for

Education. Moving from national opprobrium to approbation in a year demonstrated how well Birmingham City Council was motoring once more. In August 2016, the secretary of state for education, Nicky Morgan, stood down the commissioner because solid progress was evident in the outcomes of the improvement plan. This was the beginning of the recovery journey that continues today.

At the University of Birmingham, a number of the authors now share their experiences with master's students in education leadership. Seminars led by Herminder Channa, Sajid Gulzar and Bev Mabey have been well received because of their authenticity and impact. These leaders know how to turn around schools in the city by dropping anchor in the community, building relational trust and then turning up the school improvement repertoire. Prior to working with the university, they had not been asked to write down their leadership journeys. It was a natural next step to bring everything together in this book. It has made me reflect on how few of our school leaders capture their contributions and pass them on to their peers and the next generation of leaders. We are doing that now constantly at the university's Education Leadership Academy.[2]

References

Birmingham City Council (2015) Birmingham Curriculum Statement. Available at: https://www.stedmund.bham.sch.uk/images/Documents/birmingham-curriculum-statement.pdf

Birmingham City Council (2019) Birmingham Curriculum Statement. Available at: https://www.birmingham.gov.uk/downloads/file/1491/birmingham_curriculum_statement.

Clarke, Peter (2014) *Report into Allegations Concerning Birmingham Schools Arising from the 'Trojan Horse' Letter* (HC 576). Available at: https://assets.publishing.service.gov.uk/government/uploads/system/uploads/attachment_data/file/340526/HC_576_accessible_-.pdf.

Kershaw, Ian (2014) *Investigation Report: Trojan Horse Letter* [Kershaw Report]. Available at: https://www.birmingham.gov.uk/downloads/file/1579/investigation_report_trojan_horse_letter_the_kershaw_report.

---

2   See https://www.birmingham.ac.uk/schools/education/ela/index.aspx.

Trojan Horse timeline

November 2013	Trojan Horse letter sent to the leader of Birmingham City Council.
February 2014	Reports of the Trojan Horse letter being sent to fourteen schools in the city.
March 2014	First major media reports of the letter. Ofsted mobilised to undertake twenty-one inspections by Secretary of State for Education Michael Gove.
April 2014	Outstanding flagship academy Park View judged to require special measures by Ofsted, plus three more academies and one maintained school.
April/May 2014	Department for Education/Education Funding Agency investigations into what has gone wrong in the academies.
April 2014	Gove appoints former Metropolitan Police Head of Counter-Terrorism Peter Clarke to investigate what happened.
April 2014	Birmingham City Council appoints Northern Education Associates (Managing Director Ian Kershaw) to conduct its own investigation into what happened.
April 2014	The secretary of state for communities and local government and Birmingham City Council ask Sir Bob Kerslake to carry out an independent review of the governance and organisational capabilities of the council.
July 2014	Clarke reports to the secretary of state and Kershaw reports to Birmingham City Council. Many parallels between their findings.
July 2014	Park View Educational Trust members resign.

August 2014	Sir Mike Tomlinson appointed as education commissioner for Birmingham by new Secretary of State Nicky Morgan. Colin Diamond is appointed as his deputy. Birmingham City Council in formal Department for Education intervention.
January 2015	Birmingham City Council's education improvement plan approved by the secretary of state.
August 2016	Department for Education intervention ends and the education commissioner is stood down in view of the progress made. Trojan Horse activity had ceased following the implementation of the education improvement plan and national changes to the governance of academies and free schools made by the Department for Education.
August 2016	Trojan-type activities move from undermining schools from within to undermining them from the outside.
2019	Resurgence of Trojan-type activities as the Department for Education plans to introduce compulsory health, sex and relationships education in all English schools.

Map – key schools

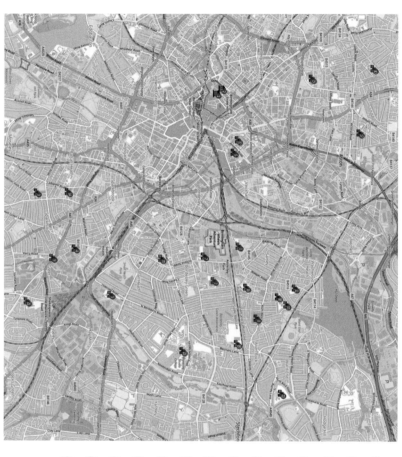

SCHOOLS

1 Adderley Primary School
2 Al-Hijrah School
3 Anderton Park Primary School
4 Ark Boulton Academy (formerly Golden Hillock)
5 Ark Victoria Academy, (formerly Oldknow Junior)
6 Birmingham Ormiston Academy
7 Bordesley Green Girls' School & Sixth Form
8 Eden Boys Leadership Academy
9 Greet Primary School
10 Heathfield Primary School
11 Highfield Junior & Infant School
12 Matthew Boulton College
13 Nansen Primary School

10 Nelson Mandela School
15 Nisham High School
16 Parkfield Community School
17 Prince Albert Junior & Infant School
18 Rockwood Academy (formerly Park View)
19 Saltley Academy
20 Small Heath Leadership Academy
21 The Olive School
22 Washwood Heath Academy
23 Waverley School

BUILDINGS

1 Birmingham Council House
2 National Governance Association

Birmingham – fact check

Birmingham has a population of 1.14 million (2018) projected to grow to 1.31 million in 2039. It is the most deprived local authority area in the West Midlands and the sixth most deprived in England. 41% of the population and 50% of the children live in the most deprived decile. Over one in three children live in poverty, with Ladywood constituency having the third highest level in the UK and Sutton Coldfield the fifteenth lowest (Birmingham City Council, 2018). Birmingham is 'super diverse' with people from nearly 200 countries having made their homes in the city. The 2011 Census revealed that 42.1% of the population classify themselves as within an ethnic group other than White British (compared to 30% in 2001). Over 60% of the under-18 population was from a non-White British background in 2011, compared to 44% in 2001. The largest ethnic groups of young people are Asian (with British Pakistanis being the largest Asian group), White British, Black and mixed race.

There were approximately 450 state schools and approximately fifty independent schools in the city in 2018. Precise numbers cannot be provided as the number and status of state schools now changes within the school year and independent schools are opening and closing frequently. There were 205,867 pupils in schools with 82% of state schools rated good or outstanding in 2017.

References

Birmingham City Council (2011) Census 2011. Available at: https://www.birmingham.gov.uk/directory/35/population_and_census/category/447.

Birmingham City Council (2016) Life in the Most Deprived Decile [infographic]. Available at: https://www.birmingham.gov.uk/downloads/file/7921/infographic_life_in_the_most_deprived_decile.

Birmingham City Council (2018) [Infographic]. Online. No longer available.

Birmingham City Council (2019) Birmingham Health Profile 2019. Available at: https://www.birmingham.gov.uk/downloads/file/11845/birmingham_health_profile_2019.

Acknowledgements

Professors Julie Allan and Deborah Youdell, my bosses at university, for unswerving support and encouragement throughout.

The chapter authors for their wonderful writing, profound insights and infinite patience as the book came together.

Pat Smart for showing how good Birmingham's primary education is.

Sir Mike Tomlinson – mentor and coach, and the best HMCI ever.

David McVean – my colleague from the Education Funding Agency.

Mark Rogers, former CEO at Birmingham City Council, whose watch was far too brief.

Everyone at Birmingham City Council who helped to 'get the basics back in place' in the education improvement plan.

Saleem Quazi, MBE – my first wing man in Birmingham from the Department for Education days.

Safi Bi – my PA at the Department for Education and former Bordesley Green Girls' School pupil who really helped out at Alum Rock back in 2014.

Amarjot Butcher and Emma Tuck – without whose diligence and editing skills there would be no book.

And, finally, my family for their great support along the way since Birmingham loomed large in our lives.

Contents

Foreword by Professor Mick Waters .... *i*

Provenance – a personal journey .... *ix*

Trojan Horse timeline .... *xvi*

Map – key schools .... *xviii*

Birmingham – fact check .... *xix*

Acknowledgements .... *xxi*

List of contributors .... *xxv*

Introduction 1

Part I: Setting the Scene – What Took You So Long to Get Here? **5**

Chapter 1   Shame visited on Birmingham: publication of the Trojan
             Horse letter and its consequences, 2013–2014
             Colin Diamond 7

Chapter 2   Growing up in Birmingham: place and identity
             Kamal Hanif 31

Chapter 3   Unrepresentative and ill-equipped education bureaucracy
             Karamat Iqbal 51

Chapter 4   The educational achievement of Birmingham's children,
             2002–2018
             Thomas Perry 73

Chapter 5   Learning for governance from Trojan Horse
             Emma Knights 99

**Part II: We Educate Birmingham Children – Case Studies in Urban
School Improvement** **127**

Chapter 6   The pedagogy of equality: the role of the UNICEF Rights
             Respecting Schools Award in making schools safer and
             more inclusive
             Azita Zohhadi 129

Chapter 7   One love: the creation of the CORE MAT
             Adrian Packer 165

Chapter 8   I went to Highfield Junior and Infant School as a kid
             Sajid Gulzar 183

Chapter 9   We are family: creating social capital in Hodge Hill
             Bev Mabey 201

Chapter 10   It takes a whole community to bring up a child.
             From Golden Hillock to Ark Boulton: a case study in
             transformative leadership
             Herminder Channa 213

Chapter 11   Healing wounds, building trust and bridging communities:
             Birmingham's post-Trojan Horse challenge
             Sir Mufti Hamid Patel 227

**Part III: Policy Implications – What Can Be Learnt from Birmingham's
Experience?** **243**

Chapter 12   Lessons for contemporary urban school leadership:
             where the rubber meets the road
             Colin Diamond 245

Chapter 13   Opposition to LGBT awareness teaching: no outsiders,
             but what was it like on the inside?
             Joy Warmington 273

Chapter 14   Reflections on the impact and legacy of Trojan Horse: an
             intersectional view
             Reza Gholami 289

Chapter 15   Trojan Horse and aspiring Asian leaders: the impact on
             development programmes intended to change the face
             and heart of leadership
             Rosemary Campbell-Stephens 313

Chapter 16   Urban education policy: it takes a city to raise a child
             Colin Diamond 327

Final thoughts *357*
Postscript 2021 .... *367*

List of contributors

Rosemary Campbell-Stephens, MBE

Rosemary Campbell-Stephens is a veteran educator who grew up, went to school and trained as a teacher of English in Birmingham. Rosemary is a visiting fellow at the Institute of Education, University College London and an associate at Leeds Beckett University. Her leadership work as part of the London Challenge (2003–2011) was in developing a programme focused on increasing the numbers of Black and Asian leaders in London schools. Investing in Diversity became the catalyst for subsequent programmes in the schools sector across the UK. Rosemary is an anti-racist practitioner who frames her work through a critical race lens. She provides bespoke leadership training and coaching internationally and is a sought-after keynote speaker in her areas of expertise and passion, namely anti-racist decolonising practice. In 2016, Rosemary was awarded an MBE for thirty-five years' service to education in the UK. She was honoured to accept the award as recognition by peers of her activism in education. As a junior elder, she embraces the label 'disruptor' and is rarely in her lane. Her latest book, *Educational Leadership and the Global Majority: Decolonising Narratives*, was published in 2021. Rosemary lives with her husband in Jamaica.

Herminder Channa, OBE JP

Herminder Channa is currently an executive principal at Ark Schools, a lead Ofsted inspector, a local leader of education and a magistrate. Herminder chose teaching as a profession as she is driven by the idea that access to an excellent standard of education is a birth right for all. Herminder, who was born locally in Sandwell, helped to found Nishkam High School in Birmingham in 2012, one of the first Sikh multi-faith free schools. Under her headship it gained Ofsted outstanding status in just eighteen months. Herminder left Nishkam for Ark because she wanted to work with children in disadvantaged areas and where she felt she could make a difference. In 2015, she took over Golden Hillock School, one of the schools at the centre of the Trojan Horse affair, which had seen a decade of underachievement, re-brokerage to two different academy chains, high levels of supply staff and judged as an inadequate academy by Ofsted, twice. In the Queen's Birthday Honours List 2020, Herminder was awarded an OBE for her services to education. When asked how she transformed the school she replied, 'We did it with love!' Herminder is proud to serve her community as a magistrate.

Professor Colin Diamond, CBE

Colin Diamond has worked in education leadership roles for forty years. He started his career in inner-London secondary schools as a humanities teacher and soon began to specialise in working with pupils with additional needs. He became a local authority adviser for special educational needs and disabilities and an associate head teacher in Hackney and Tower Hamlets. His career then took him to jobs in North East England and then the South West, where he has lived for over twenty years. En route he trained as an Ofsted inspector. He became director of education in North Somerset when it was in intervention from the then Department for Education and Employment and led its improvement journey until it gained outstanding judgements from Ofsted. He then worked for the Department for Education as director for children and learners based in Bristol and Plymouth, holding seventeen local authorities to account for their value-added performance. In 2011, he returned to the Department for Education in London to head up the academies and free schools education adviser team.

In 2014, he was asked by the Department for Education to lead the team that went to Birmingham in the wake of the Trojan Horse crisis. This led, in the short term, to the re-brokerage of the academies damaged by Trojan Horse. In the longer term, it led to his appointment as deputy education commissioner for Birmingham. In 2015, he was appointed as executive director of education in Birmingham to deliver the Education Improvement Plan signed off by the secretary of state.

In September 2018, Colin took up the new post of professor of educational leadership at the University of Birmingham. His main tasks are to create greater engagement between schools and the university and to establish an Education Leadership Academy. He is driven by the power of education to transform the lives of working-class children and wants them all to have the same opportunities that he was lucky enough to get from going to brilliant schools in Liverpool.

He is a member of the Liverpool Education Improvement Board and chair of the West Somerset Opportunity Area. In 2018, he received a CBE in the Queen's Birthday Honours for services to education.

He is a lifelong supporter of Liverpool Football Club and Anfield is his spiritual home. He used to play in blues and rock and roll bands until Birmingham took over his life.

Dr Reza Gholami

Reza Gholami is a reader in sociology of education at the University of Birmingham where he is also the deputy director of the Centre for Research in Race and Education. His research interests are Islamophobia and racism in education as well as community-based forms of education. He is a Fellow of the Royal Society of Arts and an honorary senior research associate at the University College London Institute of Education. He earned his Doctor of Philosophy in the Department of Anthropology and Sociology at the School of Oriental and African Studies, University of London, where he also conducted postdoctoral research funded by the Arts and Humanities Research Council, working with diverse youth and community organisations in London to improve educational and citizenship outcomes for young people. Currently, he is leading an Economic and Social Research Council-funded project working with non-formal educators in Birmingham to develop innovative educational materials to foster inter-communal learning. Reza is the author of numerous books and articles in his field, including co-editing the book *Education and Extremisms: Re-Thinking Liberal Pedagogies in the Contemporary World* (2018). He regularly appears in national and international media, including featuring in the BBC Radio 4 documentary *The Corrections* about the Birmingham Trojan Horse affair.

Sajid Gulzar, OBE

Sajid Gulzar is the founding CEO of the Prince Albert Community Trust. The trust currently consists of five primary schools and a new secondary free school which opened in September 2021. Sajid has led the trust in operating a 'turn-around' model, taking on failing schools and improving them markedly. He is passionate about improving the life chances of children, especially those raised in challenging circumstances. Sajid was born, raised and educated in Birmingham. The son of first-generation immigrants from Pakistani-administered Kashmir, he was taught the value and life-changing impact of education from a young age. He is a national leader of education, has previously inspected for Ofsted and has worked internationally on behalf of the National Association of Special Educational Needs and Cambridge Education. Sajid is a guest lecturer at the University of Birmingham's Education Leadership Academy and has served as a regional schools commissioner on the West Midlands advisory head teacher board since 2017. In June 2019, Sajid was awarded an OBE for services to education.

Kamal Hanif, OBE

Kamal Hanif is a former CEO of the Waverley Education Foundation Trust. He has successfully engaged in various roles in education since 1992, supported the Department for Education to resolve issues around schools in the city during the Trojan Horse episode and was on the Kershaw review group. As a national leader of education, Kamal has supported a number of schools. He is also a trustee of the charity SINCE 9/11 and sits on various working groups, such as the Department for Education's Due Diligence and Countering Extremism Group, and was on the Association of School and College Leader Council. Kamal has been involved as a Stonewall School Champion and training partner. In his spare time, Kamal enjoys restoration projects, gardening and swimming.

Dr Karamat Iqbal

Karamat Iqbal has been associated with Birmingham since his father came to the city in 1957. He himself arrived in 1970. Karamat received his upper secondary, college and university education locally. He began his public sector work (as an informal educator and then secondary school teacher) serving the diverse local communities. He spent fifteen years in Wolverhampton, first as a community relations officer, challenging racism and promoting multicultural education. This was followed by his role as deputy director of the Equal Rights and Opportunities Management Unit and later as head of the supported learning department at Bilston Community College. After this, Karamat spent ten years as a schools adviser in Birmingham. Since 2000, as a director of the Forward Partnership consultancy, he has undertaken numerous consultancies in education and diversity. His clients have included local and national organisations in the public, private and third sectors, including several government departments. He is the author of *Dear Birmingham: A Conversation with My Hometown* (2013), *A Biography of the Word*

'Paki' (2017); *British Pakistani Boys, Education and the Role of Religion: In the Land of the Trojan Horse* (2018) and *Educating Brummies* (edited with Tahir Abbas; forthcoming). He blogs on education and diversity, including for Optimus Education.

Emma Knights, OBE

Emma Knights is the chief executive of the National Governance Association (NGA), which provides guidance, advice, research and professional development for school governors, trustees and governance professionals in state schools in England. NGA's charitable objective is to improve the educational welfare of pupils by improving governance. Emma has particular interests in vision, culture and strategy; accountability; stakeholder engagement; disadvantage; ethical leadership; diversity, inclusion and staff development. She is the author of the NGA's *The Chair's Handbook* (now in its eighth edition) and edited the association's magazine *Governing Matters* for seven years. She is co-author of many other publications on welfare rights, child support, legal services, early years and, of course, most recently, governance, including *MATs Moving Forward: The Power of Governance* (2021). Prior to joining the NGA in 2010, Emma was joint CEO of the Daycare Trust, and before that, worked in a number of roles in the voluntary sector, including the Child Poverty Action Group and Citizens Advice, and then at the Local Government Association and the Legal Services Commission. She was a governor at a secondary school in Warwickshire for eight years, and earlier set up an after-school club at her children's middle school in Norfolk. Emma was awarded an OBE in the New Year Honours List in 2018 for services to education.

Dr Bev Mabey

Bev Mabey has worked in education for over thirty years and as a head teacher in Birmingham for over ten years. She led the academisation of Washwood Heath Technology College in 2013. Bev has been chair of the Secondary Heads Forum for the city. She was chair of the city/police panels and vice-chair of the east local policing unit independent advisory group. She was awarded an honorary doctorate by Aston University in 2018 in recognition of her contribution to education in Birmingham.

Adrian Packer, CBE

Adrian Packer was appointed executive principal of Park View Educational Trust (now CORE Education Trust) in 2014. He was also principal of Park View School (now Rockwood Academy) at that time. He is currently CEO of CORE Education Trust. Prior to this, in 2012, Adrian was the founding principal of Everton Alternative Provision Free School and Sixth Form College, the first free school set up by a Premier League football club. From 2010, Adrian was part of the founding team of Birmingham Ormiston Academy, an arts academy partnered with the BRIT School. Adrian was a senior artistic director at the BRIT School for twelve years and taught some of the country's highest profile, award-winning talent in the music, theatre, film and television industries during that time. He is currently a member of the Liverpool Institute for Performing Arts (LIPA) Council and director and governor of the LIPA sixth form. Adrian is an independent non-executive director of ukactive and chair of the ukactive Kids Council. In 2018, Adrian conceived the Echo Eternal project, a commemorative arts participation project which brings together groups of schools with different characteristics and uses Holocaust survivor testimony to inspire community integration and empathy. In 2019, he was awarded a Points of Light award from the prime minister for this work. In March 2021, Adrian became a board-appointed Lawn Tennis Association councillor.

Sir Mufti Hamid Patel, CBE

Mufti Hamid Patel has been the chief executive of Star Academies since its inception. The multi-academy trust currently comprises thirty schools and was named as the top-performing trust in the Department for Education performance tables published in 2018 and 2019.

Previously, Hamid was executive principal of the trust's founder school, Tauheedul Islam Girls' High School (TIGHS), which has consistently secured the best Progress 8 score in the country since this measure was introduced. TIGHS, and thirteen of the Star Academies schools, have been judged by Ofsted to be outstanding.

Hamid's knowledge and experience of the education sector is extensive. He was formerly the director of strategy, change and external relations at Bradford College, leading on one of the most ambitious change programmes in further education. As a national leader of education, Hamid has contributed to the development of strategies and programmes as diverse as teacher training, leadership development, community cohesion, curriculum reform and social mobility. He is committed to the development of a strong, world-class academy sector.

Through his membership of several Department for Education expert groups, Hamid influences national policy development. As chair of the Grants and Evaluation Committee of the Youth Endowment Fund, he leads a team of experts on the evaluation of initiatives to prevent serious youth crime and violence. He also serves as a member of the Ofsted board and is a board member of the Confederation of School Trusts.

Hamid's uncompromising vision is to ensure the success of disadvantaged pupils. His commitment to securing excellent academic outcomes through the provision of a knowledge-rich curriculum is mirrored by his drive to nurture the philanthropic leaders of tomorrow.

Hamid's contribution to education was recognised by the award of a CBE in 2015 and knighthood in 2021.

Dr Thomas Perry

Thomas Perry is an assistant professor in the Department of Education Studies at the University of Warwick. He is a former lecturer in education at the University of Birmingham, programme leader for educational leadership masters programmes, and head of research and knowledge transfer in the Department for Teacher Education. Tom's research and teaching are focused on supporting students, school leaders and policy-makers to improve education through research- and evidence-informed policy and practice. He has specialist methodological expertise relating to research synthesis and review, quantitative methods and secondary data analysis, educational evaluation and improvement, social research methodology, and knowledge mobilisation, exchange and use. His work has been cited widely and internationally, including a UK Parliament Briefing, the United Nations Educational, Scientific and Cultural Organization, the Young Lives international study, FFT Education Datalab, and has featured in national news media, including the *TES*, *Schools Week* and BBC Radio 4.

Professor Mick Waters

Mick Waters has a deep affection for Birmingham and its schools, having worked for the city around the turn of the millennium as what was, at the time, called chief adviser for schools. He has a wide experience of the world of education in schools, higher education and local authorities. Mick has also worked with central government on curriculum development and supported governments in different parts of the world on aspects of teaching and leadership. He has written and contributed to many books and is much in demand as a conference speaker. He enjoys spending time in classrooms, asking adults to look at learning through the eyes of the pupil.

Joy Warmington, MBE

Joy Warmington began her leadership career over thirty years ago designing groundbreaking learning programmes for marginalised communities. Then came senior leadership roles in education, local authority and civil society, including nineteen years as the CEO of brap, one of the UK's most progressive equality and human rights charities. brap seeks to rethink our approach to equality and progress our learning, use of evidence and innovation to make sustainable change. brap's impressive work portfolio covers research, evaluation, organisational and individual development, and community support. Joy's insights into making equity a reality are sought after by organisations seeking real solutions to exclusion and inequity. In 2019, Joy was awarded an MBE and named one of fifty 'Women to Watch' by Cranfield University. As a lifelong learner and recent graduate in process work – a psycho-social method to democratise spaces and address conflict – Joy brings her unerring curiosity and appetite for change and creativity to her work.

Azita Zohhadi

Azita Zohhadi was born and brought up in west London and graduated from Kingston University, Surrey in 1989. Her first teaching post was in Kingston upon Thames at a small one-form entry primary school where she became the literacy lead in her newly qualified teacher year. In her desire to understand education at all levels she became the staff governor in that same year. In 1990, she became the deputy head of a school in Hammersmith and Fulham where she later took on her first headship. In 2008, Azita moved to Birmingham, remaining as the head teacher of Nelson Mandela School until November 2021, where she sadly finished her final months of headship away from her school community due to self-isolating because of the COVID-19 pandemic. Since leaving Nelson Mandela School, Azita has worked as a consultant developing local provision for special educational needs and disabilities across Birmingham's primary schools, contributed to the Durham Commission's second report on creativity and education, and worked as an education adviser with the Rosie Kay Dance Company and Royal Shakespeare Company.

Introduction

Colin Diamond

The purpose of the book is to share the learning that has arisen from the experience of the Trojan Horse affair and extract the implications for school leadership, governance and education policy. It is not a post-mortem on Trojan Horse, but it does seek to contextualise the major events that occurred in 2014–2015 in order to understand the school leadership journeys in some of the schools most affected.

The majority of contributors to this book have first-hand experience of living and working in Birmingham for many years. Four of the authors picked up the pieces at schools that were in bad shape by summer 2014 and led the improvement journeys in unique circumstances. Two of the authors grew up in Birmingham as members of the British Pakistani community and went on to become chief executives of multi-academy trusts, honoured by Her Majesty for their contributions to education. Others have worked across the community and have been embedded in the rich, complex inner-city cultures, which enabled them to support school leaders and governors authentically. The book is about their authentic experiences and perspectives. Colleagues from the University of Birmingham School of Education have contributed critical analysis of the educational performance of children in the city and the complex intersectional social environment in which these events took place.

The book does not examine forensically all of the schools caught up in Trojan Horse or those on the periphery. Neither does it dwell on the actions of protagonists named in the Clarke (2014) and Kershaw (2014) reports. And nor does it attempt to record a comprehensive history of events. Rather, it seeks to learn from history, so the catalogue of events that led to Trojan Horse and were acted out in high drama in 2014 are never repeated.

Trojan Horse remains a hotly contested narrative with entrenched positions on both sides of the debate. As a BBC journalist commented recently, 'reading the Guardian and Telegraph articles, you would think that you were reading different stories' (Fidgen, 2020). For some, it will remain a hoax based on an anonymous letter which fuelled a witch-hunt against Muslim school governors in Birmingham. For them, Secretary of State for Education Michael Gove weaponised the letter and unleashed the power of the state against a group of governors who had been attempting to improve the life chances of inner-city Muslim children over many years. Her Majesty's Chief Inspector Sir Michael Wilshaw is forever cast in the role of attack dog because he did a U-turn on Park View. In 2012, he had lavished praise on the secondary school, celebrating its success and outstanding judgement from his own inspectors. In 2014, with nothing fundamental having changed in respect of leadership or governance, his inspectors produced a damning report that pitched Park View into requiring special measures.

For others in Birmingham, the arrival of Ofsted inspectors and the follow-up investigations by the Department for Education and Education Funding Agency marked liberation from the suffocating control and coercion that had gradually extended over a number of schools – and latterly academies – in the city. As one primary school head teacher told me, 'I can breathe again.' It was an open secret in Birmingham that school leaders had been undermined by factions within their governing bodies for years. The tactics were unsavoury and went largely unchallenged by the city council, as its own report confirmed (Kershaw, 2014). Unofficial meetings were held between civil servants and heads, senior staff, school administrators and governors to share the experience of working in these schools. Documents were passed to officials under the table. Witnesses to the Clarke and Kershaw inquiries were guaranteed anonymity because many involved with the schools were fearful for their futures. The biggest anxiety was that things would be allowed to return to 'normal' and nothing would really change for the future.

The reality is that there is no single narrative or 'truth', as the contributors to this book explain. There are multiple, overlapping perspectives that jigsaw together into a three-dimensional picture. However, there are themes that have emerged from the experience which are examined by the authors from their different perspectives, and they will be familiar to all those in education leadership roles in inner cities:

- The challenge of 'getting it right' – that is, getting the balance right in schools that serve communities in complex, urban, multi-faith and multiracial societies.

- How to work with socially conservative religious cultures and faiths alongside more established cultural norms without imposing what were termed 'fundamental British values' by the government in response to Trojan Horse.

- Socio-economic status remaining the biggest determinant of school outcomes but with the overlay of what that means in different sections of a city's community – factoring in the performance of White working-class children in relation to children from the British Mirpuri or Somali communities and how this should influence education policy.

- Local politics, with councils dominated by White elected members and chief officers who are uncertain about how to create policy for fear of being seen to be racist.

In summary, when all the intersectional elements within a city's education community align, they create learning power with the heat of phosphorus; when they clash, that same heat can be destructive and leave lasting damage.

More broadly, Trojan Horse threw into sharp relief:

- The relationship between the state, education and faith.

- Importance of place and social capital versus the de facto and de jure nationalisation of the English education system since the Academies Act 2010.

- The fragility of the academies and free schools programmes.

- How a neoliberal government opportunistically used the less than edifying behaviours of some governors in Birmingham to create an Islamophobic narrative for its own ends. Let us be clear: Trojan Horse was never about Islamic extremism, as Baroness Warsi (2017) expressed so succinctly in *The Enemy Within: A Tale of Muslim Britain*.

Part I of the book sets the scene with a combination of narrated events, first-hand accounts of growing up and working in education in Birmingham, and data harvested from the Office for National Statistics on what was really happening in schools during those years. The lessons for governance at local and national level are explored. Part II contains six values-driven education leadership journeys that have enabled pupils to achieve against the odds in the east end of Birmingham. Each chapter has a list of 'takeaways' for school leaders. Part III pulls things together with lessons for school leaders and education policy-makers in complex urban environments. It also contains perspectives on the protests against teaching lesbian, gay, bisexual, transgender and queer awareness in primary schools, the media coverage about Trojan Horse and the impact it had on career progression for Asian school leaders. It concludes that urban education leadership is a neglected area of development and research, long abandoned by English education policy. However, there are some fine examples of community-based, innovative practice that yield excellent results. The postscript brings things up to date as the pandemic, the Black Lives Matters movement and the climate crisis all impact on urban school leadership with unrelenting pressure and growing impact.

References

Clarke, Peter (2014) *Report into Allegations Concerning Birmingham Schools Arising from the 'Trojan Horse' Letter* (HC 576). Available at: https://assets.publishing.service.gov.uk/government/uploads/system/uploads/attachment_data/file/340526/HC_576_accessible_-.pdf.

Fidgen, Jo (2020) *The Corrections: Trojan Horse* [radio programme], BBC Radio 4 (6, 13 and 20 November).

Kershaw, Ian (2014) *Investigation Report: Trojan Horse Letter* [Kershaw Report]. Available at: https://www.birmingham.gov.uk/downloads/file/1579/investigation_report_trojan_horse_letter_the_kershaw_report.

Warsi, Sayeeda (2017) *The Enemy Within: A Tale of Muslim Britain*. London: Penguin Random House.

Part I
Setting the Scene: What Took You So Long to Get Here?

Chapter 1

Shame visited on Birmingham: publication of the Trojan Horse letter and its consequences, 2013-2014

Colin Diamond

Introduction

Chapter 1 takes us through an overview of events in 2014 which cast a long shadow over Birmingham's reputation. They influenced the direction of national education policy with the introduction of the duty to promote fundamental British values in all English schools (DfE, 2014) and the arrival of the Counter-Terrorism and Security Act 2015. This new legislation made Prevent a legal duty in schools (and all public authorities). Later, in 2015, Tahir Alam became the first person to be banned from governance of any schools in England under powers set out in the Education and Skills Act 2008. The direction stated that he had engaged in 'Conduct aimed at undermining the fundamental British values of democracy, the rule of law, individual liberty, and mutual respect and tolerance of those with different faiths and beliefs' (Taylor, 2015).

The combination of new duties on schools and the use of longstanding regulations firmed up the government's position towards what it perceived to be the threat of extremism from principally Muslim sectors of the community. The impact in English inner cities has largely been compliance teaching of the Prevent duty and the flowering of Union Jack displays in schools to ensure they pass muster with Ofsted. The real risk was not stopping the tide of extremism. In fact, swathes of the Muslim community became alienated because they considered that the government response to Trojan Horse had been disproportionate (Hughes, 2014).

This chapter includes two case studies that exemplify the real nature of Trojan Horse-style subversion of school leaders in the name of what a few governors believed was right for young Muslims educated in English schools. Equally, they reveal that such events had nothing to do with Islamism, the gateway drug to the Caliphate or any other conspiracy theory fantasy. Adderley Primary School suffered from interference for many years, which diverted its leaders from improving the life chances of its mainly Muslim pupils. Al-Madinah School, a Muslim free school in Derby, was all but destroyed by such activities within a matter of months. It is sad to reflect on how much positive energy, purpose and commitment to the local communities served by both schools was undermined by governors from inside their own schools.

2014 – shame visited on Birmingham

Publication of the Trojan Horse letter in February 2014 led to a chain of events that unfolded rapidly and generated huge turbulence in Birmingham's schools. In March, at the request of Secretary of State for Education Michael Gove, Ofsted inspected twenty-one schools in the city and catapulted two showcase academies (Park View and Oldknow) from outstanding judgements to requiring special measures. The subsequent Education Funding Agency investigations, carried out by teams of education advisers and officials, exposed multiple breaches in academy trusts' funding agreements (the legal contract between the secretary of state and the academies) and equally serious breaches of the Independent Schools Standards regulations.[1] In 2013, the Al-Madinah free school in Derby, which had opened in 2012, was found to have a similar set of failings in its governance following whistle-blowing and follow-up inspections. The academy and free school programmes were in crisis due to a volatile combination of significant failings at a local level and the perception within the Department for Education that these events were linked to Islamic extremism.

Two major investigations were commissioned into Trojan Horse. Michael Gove asked Peter Clarke, the former head of counter-terrorism at the Metropolitan Police, to lead his investigation. Birmingham City Council wanted to collaborate with the Department for Education and conduct one joint inquiry. That approach was rejected by the Department for Education, so Birmingham City Council commissioned Northern Education,

---

1   See https://www.legislation.gov.uk/uksi/2014/3283/schedule/made.

chaired by the former secretary of state for education Baroness Morris of Yardley, with chief executive officer Les Walton, former head of the Education Funding Agency, to lead its investigation. Ian Kershaw, managing director of Northern Education, ran the team and wrote the report.

The two investigations ran in parallel over early summer 2014 and reported within weeks of each other in July. Both were required to move quickly as the Trojan Horse narrative had taken off in the media with extensive coverage in the newspapers and on TV. For the Department for Education, and Gove in particular, this was an existential crisis. He had authored *Celsius 7/7*, published in 2006, which set out his views on the 'hellish violence and oppression' of Islamism (p. vii) and compared it with Nazism and Communism. It now appeared to Gove that a version of Islamism was infiltrating schools in Birmingham. It was a short stop from that assumption to appointing a former head of counter-terrorism to find out what was happening as quickly as possible. For Birmingham City Council, the Trojan Horse letter stated that the subversive activities had been 'tried and tested' and were well established – in effect, it had begun before the Academies Act 2010 began to fragment the English school system. The council needed to find out quickly why there had been a serious breakdown in its custodianship of local schools and how to remedy things.

Clarke and Kershaw did cooperate with each other as far as was practicable and shared some witness interviews. There are different emphases and somewhat different conclusions to the reports, but both stated that the intimidation and undermining of school heads and governors was a reality. Gove never got the opportunity to follow up on the findings of the Clarke report himself as he was demoted to become chief whip by David Cameron on 15 July 2014 and was replaced by Nicky Morgan. She described to the House of Commons Clarke's findings and how they were to be followed up (DfE and Morgan, 2014). It was evident that Trojan Horse was symptomatic of deep historic failings in Birmingham City Council's discharge of its duties and powers in relation to schools.

Morgan set in train a formal intervention, appointing Sir Mike Tomlinson, former Her Majesty's Chief Inspector (HMCI) at Ofsted, as education commissioner. Birmingham City Council was required to produce an improvement plan which addressed all the recommendations of the Clarke report. The plan incorporated the recommendations of both Clarke and Kershaw's reports and was approved by the secretary of state for education in January 2015. The core of the plan addressed what was termed 'getting the basics back in place'. Major gaps in the council's discharge of its duties on safeguarding, governance and school improvement needed remedying. Relationships and communication with schools needed rebuilding. Above all – but not written down – the city's education system needed to believe in itself once more.

On the same day that Gove was removed from his role as secretary of state, Tahir Alam resigned as chair of Park View Educational Trust. Alam had attended Park View School as a pupil, became a governor and eventually chair of governors. By 2012, Park View had risen from requiring special measures to outstanding in Ofsted's judgement. Its GCSE examination results and pupil progress were stellar under the leadership of head teacher Lindsey Clarke. In 2012, it had featured in an article in *The Guardian* (Vasagar, 2012) with praise lavished on its leadership by the newly appointed HMCI, Sir Michael Wilshaw, during an informal visit. Two years later, Wilshaw's inspectors had judged Park View inadequate following a full inspection, and once again it was facing special measures.

A host of safeguarding, leadership and governance issues were identified with the overall message that Park View was not preparing its pupils for life in modern Britain. The Ofsted inspection was followed up by an investigation by a joint Department for Education and Education Funding Agency team which found multiple breaches in the funding agreements. This picture was compounded by the headline conclusions from the Clarke report in early July which described an 'aggressive Islamist ethos' afoot in some schools in the city (Clarke, 2014, p. 96). In the light of the reports from Ofsted, the Education Funding Agency and Clarke, new members of the trust were installed following negotiations between Tahir Alam and the Department for Education. Alam, as the Clarke report illustrates, had been at the centre of a large network in Birmingham and had been an influential player in many of the schools damaged by Trojan Horse activities.

Birmingham has a proud education history. The leadership of Sir Tim Brighouse, chief education officer at Birmingham City Council (1993–2002) and his team, had created a superb local education authority in which pupils' achievement was rising against the social odds. It had embraced multiculturalism and worked with the grain of the local, diverse communities (see Diamond, 2020, p. 123). It was recognised internationally for its innovation and empowerment of school leaders. During my years working for Birmingham City Council, visiting schools every week, Brighouse's name was mentioned regularly and his contribution is still revered today. It was also said to me by many head teachers that no chief officer from the city had visited their school since Brighouse's tenure. That sadly illustrated the gap that had been allowed to grow between the city council and its schools.

'We educate Birmingham children'

I heard this said many times by head teachers back in 2014. It resonates still because of its unqualified generosity and inclusiveness at a time when Birmingham's education system was in crisis. In spite of all that was happening, head teachers' loyalty to and compassion for the children across the city shone through. They wanted to find positive ways forward after Trojan Horse had brought national shame on the city's schools and Birmingham City Council.

Trojan Horse was a damaging, scarring episode that had profound consequences for education in Birmingham. It was symptomatic of how Birmingham City Council's custodianship of its schools had deteriorated from being recognised as national best in class by Ofsted in 2002 under the leadership of Sir Tim Brighouse (Ofsted, 2002) to being placed in formal intervention by the Department for Education and requiring an education commissioner, Sir Mike Tomlinson, in 2014 (Ofsted, 2014a).

The twelve years between 2002 and 2014 had witnessed many changes in national education policy, a reduction in the power of local government and the arrival of austerity in 2009 (Smith, 2014). The combination of these developments seriously reduced the role and influence of all English local education authorities.

For many local authorities, including Birmingham, the pressures of budget reductions, the national policy emphasis on school autonomy and the challenge of poor children's social care provision resulted in a downgrading of education as a local priority. In Birmingham's case, the urgent need to improve the quality of children's social care became the number one priority when Ofsted judged it to be inadequate in the annual performance assessment (Ofsted, 2008a). The subsequent ten-year improvement journey dominated the council's focus and resources.

By comparison, education in the city was in rude health to judge by the accolades received from Ofsted (2002). In the last decade of the twentieth century, the collective power of schools was galvanised by the inspirational leadership of the local education authority's senior officers. Initiatives flourished, successes were celebrated and standards rose as a result of innovative, transformational approaches that brought schools together in new 'families' with similar socio-economic characteristics (Brighouse and Woods, 1999, 2008, 2013).

That era produced a generation of school leaders who had self-belief because they knew their contribution was valued by the city and celebrated nationally:

> the leadership provided by the Chief Education Officer is outstanding, and has contributed significantly to the 'can do' and aspirational culture demonstrated by headteachers and others interviewed during the inspection, without which such a good rate of improvement is unlikely to have been achieved. (Select Committee on Education and Skills, 2002: para. 8)

It is easy to portray these years as the Camelot era in Birmingham, and it is true that respect for Brighouse and his team remains as high today in 2021. The legacy from this period can be divided into national and local influences. Nationally, the London Challenge (with Brighouse and David Woods as its architects) deployed school improvement strategies developed in Birmingham and adapted them for the capital with great success. The secretary of state for education and skills, Estelle Morris, then MP for Yardley, had seen first-hand how schools in Birmingham had improved, and invited Brighouse to become the London Challenge's chief adviser (Kidson and Norris, 2011). This model, in turn, was the template for other challenge areas set up by the department. The University of the First Age, founded by Brighouse, engaged with a wide range of adults including teachers, parents, carers and community organisations. It trained them, based around change theory, to offer extracurricular activities as a way of closing the achievement gap between young people from disadvantaged and affluent backgrounds.

For the reasons explained above, education was not the council's priority and the need to focus on children's social care and implement the Children Act 2004 prevailed. Welding together an outstanding education service with an inadequate children's social care service in the largest urban authority in England was always going to be a challenge. The broad result was that school leaders carried the torch themselves for many years, as the council no longer had the resources to shape the city educationally.

The head teachers knew what best practice looked like and how to continue its traditions. Birmingham City Council was then hit by austerity measures in 2009 and wound down its education services whilst ramping up investment in children's social care. Spending on school improvement was reduced to less than £1 million per annum by 2014.

Unsurprisingly, the number of academies and free schools increased quickly in Birmingham following implementation of the Academies Act 2010. The strongest performing schools were allowed to convert to academy status, with plenty of financial inducements to do so in the early years of the programme. The weaker performing schools were either persuaded or compelled to join a multi-academy trust. The fragmentation of a formerly united civic education system was driven through in the name of neoliberal education policy with no regard whatsoever for the wider social consequences.

In response to the atrophying of local authority influence and the creation of so many semi-autonomous academies and free schools, Birmingham's head teachers joined together and formed the Birmingham Education Partnership (BEP) in 2013 with the direct aim to 'harness our collective strengths and to support partnership working'.[2] It had explicit encouragement from the city council, which recognised its limited capacity and role in the education and local government policy landscapes.

BEP's core mission is neatly summarised by another quote from its website: 'Recognising that it takes a whole city to raise a child and that schools need to be rooted in locality, BEP champions working with all those who support and develop Birmingham's young people.' With around 450 state schools in the city, the partnership clearly had good potential to pick up where the council had left off.

---

2   See https://bep.education/about.

The Trojan Horse letter[3]

It was against this complex background that the episode subsequently known as Trojan Horse gathered momentum. At its most basic, Trojan Horse was summarised by Peter Clarke (2014, p. 14) as a 'co-ordinated, deliberate and sustained action, carried out by a number of associated individuals, to introduce an intolerant and aggressive Islamic ethos' into schools with a majority Muslim student population in Birmingham. The Trojan Horse letter set out a five-step plan that allegedly would ensure that schools were run on Islamic principles. Salafi parents and a governor specially installed for this purpose would put unreasonable pressure on the head teacher to adopt Islamic practices until they gave up. In spite of all the evidence that Ian Kershaw (2014) found for Birmingham City Council about long-running Trojan Horse activities, events remain hotly contested. The debate has generated more heat than light, with some still claiming that the letter was a hoax. The interpretation of events, from the emergence of the Trojan Horse letter in late 2013 onwards and culminating in the publication of two major reports from the Department for Education and Birmingham City Council in mid-2014, has been polarised.

Academic analysis has portrayed Trojan Horse as a miscarriage of justice which destroyed the reputation of the Park View Educational Trust, its leaders and chair. In the only book on the subject published to date, John Holmwood and Therese O'Toole (2018) reject the notion of a plot to Islamicise schools. They rightly locate poor aspiration for and dissatisfaction with educational outcomes for Muslim young people in the east of the city as the drivers from within the community to improve schools (see also Iqbal, 2013). They correctly reject the idea that Islamic extremism was the motivation to become involved in school governance and leadership, and they explore how the Trojan Horse narrative was hijacked by Michael Gove's longstanding suspicion of and ambivalence towards Islam, which was set out in his polemic *Celsius 7/7* (2006).

It was Gove's paranoia about the supposed scale of 'rejectionist' views within Britain's Muslim communities that led to the commissioning of twenty-one snap school inspections of Birmingham schools by Ofsted. In turn, the inspections led to the three schools within the Park View Educational Trust (Park View, Nansen and Golden Hillock) being placed in special measures along with Oldknow primary school and Saltley

---

3 A copy of the Trojan Horse letter can be found in Annex 2 of the Clarke report (2014, pp. 108–112).

secondary school. The school that attracted most attention was Park View as it had previously been rated outstanding by Ofsted in 2012, feted by HMCI Sir Michael Wilshaw who said, 'all schools should be like this' (Adams, 2014), and allowed to convert to academy status by the Department for Education and establish the Park View Educational Trust in 2012.

Holmwood and O'Toole state that Park View was 'both mainstream and exemplary' (2018, p. 20), but subsequent investigations by officials from the Education Funding Agency and Department for Education into Park View, Golden Hillock and Nansen found that there were major issues, including inadequate governance, with the chair of the trust involved in day-to-day running of the schools. Safeguarding was also inconsistent.

Some aspects of the curriculum were 'restricted to a conservative Islamic perspective' (Education Funding Agency, 2014, p. 3) and the national guidance on sex and relationships education had not been considered. Staffing structures were unclear, with staff appointed to some posts with little experience and no external validation. At Park View, specifically, there was gender segregation in some classes which had 'boys sitting at the front of the class and girls around the edges' (p. 10). Schemes of work for personal, social, health and economic education, biology, and sex and relationships education 'had been restricted to comply with a conservative Islamic teaching. In Biology, GCSE year 11, discussion with pupils indicated that the teacher briefly delivered the theory of evolution to comply with the syllabus, but had told students that "This is not what we believe" ' (p. 11). Topics such as body structure and the menstrual cycle were not covered in class.

The Department for Education (Nash, 2014) wrote to Tahir Alam stating that in the light of both Ofsted's and the Education Funding Agency's findings it was giving notice of the secretary of state's intention to terminate the funding agreements for the three schools. New members and school leaders were in place by September 2014. The same process took place at Oldknow junior school, although over a longer period. Saltley secondary school joined the local Washwood Heath Multi-Academy Trust.

The views of school leaders and governors who were directly affected by Trojan Horse differed significantly from the conclusions of the academics. Many times I was asked, 'What took you (the Department for Education) so long to get here?' Heads and chairs of governors had been on the end of unacceptable pressures to introduce socially conservative Muslim practices into their schools for many years. Their experiences are more accurately reflected by the perhaps unusual combination of words from the former chair of the Conservative Party Baroness Warsi and journalist Andrew Gilligan.

Warsi (2017, p. 150) described the main Trojan Horse actors as 'a bunch of blokes with pretty misogynistic, conservative and intolerant views [who had] decided that they were right and everyone else was wrong, that their vision of the world was going to trump others and through the brown boys' network had managed to keep power in the hands of themselves and their mates'.

Gilligan (2014), writing in *The Telegraph*, commented that 'the employment of relatives, the bullying and other dubious practices show how another strand is simple old-fashioned power-grabbing and nepotism'.

In early summer 2014, Clarke and Kershaw obtained evidence from a wide range of people who had direct involvement in Birmingham's schools over many years. Kershaw's team collated 24,300 pages of evidence. The sources were documents from schools and Birmingham City Council and seventy-six witness interviews (eighteen interviewed jointly with Clarke). Clarke had the full power of the secretary of state's powers behind him and the council had a duty to disclose any information that he considered relevant. He interviewed over fifty witnesses, many of whom were frightened for their careers and reputations within the community.

In summary, both reports found overwhelming evidence of activities designed to influence and subvert governing bodies, undermine head teachers and run schools along Islamic principles. Kershaw (2014, p. 4) did not find evidence of 'a conspiracy to promote an anti-British agenda, violent extremism or radicalisation in schools in East Birmingham'. Clarke (2014, p. 14) concluded that 'there has been co-ordinated, deliberate and sustained action, carried out by a number of associated individuals, to introduce an intolerant and aggressive Islamic ethos into a few schools in Birmingham', although he was clear that there was no evidence of 'terrorism, radicalisation or violent extremism in the schools of concern' (p. 95). In other words, both reports found substantial evidence of low-level Trojan behaviours, but more along the lines described by Warsi and Gilligan rather than Gove's grim caliphate fantasies in *Celsius 7/7*.

The damage caused to Birmingham cannot be overstated. Its fall from being England's leading local education authority in 2002 to the humiliation of being under the Department for Education's direction and monitored by a commissioner was demoralising for educationalists. The city they loved, and in which they had worked tirelessly to transform children's lives, was a national disgrace. The social capital, so hard won in previous years, had been dissipated.

Why was this allowed to happen under the noses of Birmingham City Council's officers and politicians, and go on for so long? Why were the warnings made by so many heads not heeded? Both Clarke and Kershaw were withering in their criticisms of the council. It is apparent that schools and the education service had been allowed to drift for the reasons stated previously. Kershaw (2014, p. 12) reported that operationally there was 'no systematic approach to filtering intelligence or data about the conduct of schools or governing bodies' and 'numerous instances where issues about the conduct of some governing bodies have gone without investigation or challenge' (p. 56). Tim Boyes, currently CEO of BEP and former secondary head teacher, had raised alarm about what was happening locally at a national level. In 2010, he had briefed the parliamentary under-secretary of state for schools, Lord Hill, about destabilisation tactics in several schools (Oldham, 2014). More recently he told The Guardian, 'Alam caused me concern over many years … He was very deliberately and strategically looking for people to be embedded in the education system' (Shackle, 2017).

At a deeper level, a culture had developed whereby, in the name of community cohesion and a desire not to rock the political boat, there was no challenge of unacceptable behaviour from some governing bodies. The then leader of Birmingham City Council, Sir Albert Bore, admitted in July 2014, 'We have previously shied away from tackling this problem out of a misguided fear of being accused of racism' (Elkes, 2014). The silo working reported by Clarke, Kershaw and subsequently Sir Bob (now Lord) Kerslake (2014) had resulted in no meaningful connections between education and community cohesion, including Prevent. At a strategic level, there was no city vision for education and one group of governors had wrought havoc in the vacuum.

Adderley Primary School:
Trojan Horse exemplified

If you travel to Birmingham by train from London, just before the historic Curzon Street Station, in the midst of scrapyards and the freightliner depot, you will see Adderley Primary School. Before getting to know the city I had wondered if the building still functioned as a school. Its Victorian provenance is clear, the original building having been erected by the Aston School Board in 1897. Surely, such a dilapidated site was no place for a school in the early twenty-first century, with high levels of air pollution, noisy freight traffic passing all day long and a neighbouring park often strewn with rubbish and graffiti? But, no – behind those nineteenth-century walls you will find a school whose journey exemplifies the best and worst of education in Birmingham; a story of how the school's current leadership overcame years of Trojan Horse-style disruption which was aimed at unseating the head teacher and her team.

Visit now and you will find a school that drips ambition for its pupils and looks out beyond its postcode towards the city, country and the world. Pupils visit the Warwickshire County Cricket Club at Edgbaston, Westminster Abbey, the Houses of Parliament, Oxford and Cambridge universities. All major religious festivals are celebrated. It is a United Nations Children's Fund (UNICEF) Rights Respecting School, having received its gold award in July 2018. A quick glance at its Twitter feed tells you all you need to know about its vibrant DNA. I have taken senior guests from the Department for Education and UNICEF UK to see for themselves a quintessentially successful inner-city primary school that overcomes enormous challenges on a daily basis.

Adderley's pupils are typical of schools in this area of the city: currently 83% do not have English as their first language and 47% are eligible for free school meals (compared with the national averages of 21% and 23%) (DfE, 2020). The majority of the pupils were of Pakistani heritage when Ofsted last inspected in 2016 with a ringing endorsement for outstanding 'Leaders' promotion of pupils' spiritual, moral, social and cultural education' (Ofsted, 2016, p. 1) and praise that 'leaders have created a distinctive culture, in which all pupils feel valued and which celebrates their diversity' (p. 13). It hasn't always been like that.

Prior to Rizvana 'Riz' Darr taking over as head teacher in 2009 there had been nine heads in seven years. There had been periodic episodes of breakdowns between school leaders, governors and a small minority of parents and staff. As far back as 2004, Ofsted reported that 'The head-teacher has made a satisfactory start in improving the quality of teaching and learning, and the pupils' standards, which were in the lowest five percent nationally when she came to the school', but 'The time expended in dealing with a mutual lack of confidence between the headteacher and governors, and between a significant minority of parents and the school, has deflected the focus off raising standards. Governors are not totally clear about their role and responsibilities' (Ofsted, 2004, p. 6).

In 2008, Ofsted commented:

> the school has been through a very difficult period over the past sixteen months. November 2006 onwards saw a period of real difficulty where tensions between top management and gover-nors resulted in a number of teachers resigning, including the headteacher, in December 2007. Severe staffing disruption since autumn 2006 has adversely affected the continuity and coherence of pupils' learning and lowered staff morale. Resources were not always used effectively and efficiently to achieve value for money. When staff left, leaders had difficulty recruiting suitable replace-ments and pupils' education suffered. Consequently, standards fell, with many pupils making insufficient progress because too much teaching was ineffective. (Ofsted, 2008, p. 4)

The themes of internal dissent and a series of head teachers being undermined by elements within the parent, governors and staff groups continued for many years.

When I first visited in 2015, it took Darr two hours to explain the extraor-dinary sequence of events that would have pulled down most heads. Her resilience is astounding. The negative impact of such subversive behav-iour from a few staff working in cahoots with a small group of parents cannot be overstated. It is demoralising, destructive and has defeated a number of heads in the city. Some heads, like her, survived and eventually thrived but at enormous personal cost. Others were broken by attritional attacks, similar in format to those experienced at Adderley.

Having witnessed Trojan-type behaviours at various governing body meetings in Birmingham in 2014 and 2015, I could see how they sucked the energy out of a school and undermined its leaders. The base note discourse was always that the school wasn't meeting the true needs of 'the Muslim community' – as expressed via a small number of activists who claimed to be its true representatives. The tactics were to grind down the head teacher and their team through well-rehearsed ploys, including placing inappropriate demands on heads to modify the curriculum, requesting unreasonable amounts of information, interfering in operational matters, the inappropriate appointment of friends and relatives, and undermining heads during Ofsted inspections (Kershaw, 2014).

Adderley had been targeted as a poorly performing school, governors had been installed to encourage Islamic ideals, key staff had been identified to disrupt from within and campaigns had been mounted against heads at a number of schools, including Adderley.

The full chronology of events during Darr's headship up to 2015 is set out in the unlikely form of an Employment Tribunal judgment.[4] On the face of it, this should have been a straightforward case where four former teaching assistants claimed unfair dismissal. But, as the judgment states, 'the wider context is the so-called "Operation Trojan Horse plot"; said to be an attempt by individuals to oust school leaders in Birmingham and replace them with leaders who would introduce a stronger Islamist, or Salafist, ethos' (p. 7, s. 31).

Prior to Darr's appointment, 'all four claimants had run-ins with the senior leadership team of the school' (p. 21, s. 109) involving, at different times, warnings about potential disciplinary action, lodging grievances and generally being at odds with whomever was in charge. Darr stated during the employment tribunal that she was warned that two of the claimants 'have the capacity to make your life very difficult and will not hesitate to use dishonest means to rally parents' (p. 22, s. 117). There was a turbulent atmosphere in the school with claims and counterclaims that some of the claimants were working in league with a small group of parents from the local Salafi community.

Darr herself was 'castigated for not being "a good Muslim"' (p. 23, s. 121) as she did not cover her head and was not married at the time. There was criticism of music being played at school, unisex PE lessons and a curriculum that included non-Muslim religious festivals such as Christmas and

---

4   Mrs R. Khanom, Miss Y. Akhtar, Miss S. Bibi and Miss H. C. Owens v The Governing body of Adderley Primary School. Cases: 1308248/2013, 1305579/2013, 1308373/2013, 1308454/2013. Employment Tribunal Judgment. Held at Birmingham (1–22 December 2015).

Diwali. The claimants denied any involvement with or knowledge of the parental complaints, even denying that they knew what Salafism was. This stretched their credibility, as one of the claimant's husbands is Salafi and was the head teacher of the Salafi Independent School in Birmingham. The nephew of another claimant had attended the Salafi school for four years. The judgment concluded that three of the claimants knew about the parental complaints and played a part in them.

Ironically, Darr was also accused by three of the claimants of Islamifying the school across a range of fronts including, for example, removing images of pigs from books and furniture and not allowing Muslim pupils to make Easter baskets or receive Easter eggs. Ever under scrutiny from Ofsted due to a stream of parental grievances, inspectors 'praised the schools' commitment to diversity and inclusivity' (p. 32, s. 173) – a far cry from what was alleged.

In this Kafkaesque theatre of the absurd, Darr took a further step and introduced pork sausages into the canteen and arranged for pupils to visit farms where pigs were reared. A bold gesture in this part of Birmingham with its overwhelmingly Muslim population, and certainly not the action of a head teacher who was Islamifying her school.

Fractious events rolled on, distracting Darr and her leadership team from the basic job of running the school and raising standards. In December 2012, it was claimed that Darr had forged the resignations of the claimants who were arrested by West Midlands Police with several computers that had been removed from the school. No charges were brought due to 'insufficient evidence' (BBC News, 2015). The subsequent employment tribunal ran across most of December 2015 – a full three years having elapsed since the alleged forgeries and during which the shadow of these events hung over Darr and her team. The unfair dismissal claims of the three former teaching assistants were rejected, although the claim of the fourth was upheld.

In November 2013, in the middle of the unfair dismissals saga, the anonymous Trojan Horse letter – clearly authored by a person or people with detailed knowledge of events at Adderley – was sent to the leader of Birmingham City Council. It precipitated a chain of events that had consequences which are still unfolding for the city, its schools and national education policy.

The authorship of the Trojan Horse letter continues to be a matter for speculation. For some commentators it will remain a hoax designed to discredit Muslims in Birmingham and which was used subsequently to create an extremist narrative by the Department for Education and Ofsted. For others, it shone a light on unsavoury practices that had dogged schools for over a decade at the expense of many head teachers.

Al-Madinah: the experiment that went wrong

By March 2014, it had become apparent to ministers and officials in the Department for Education that something really serious had gone wrong in Birmingham. However, there had been warning signs from elsewhere that academies and free schools, operating largely outside local authority jurisdiction, could go wrong quickly.

The Al-Madinah Muslim-ethos free school opened in Derby in 2012, but within 15 months it had descended into chaos revealing the fragility of an ideologically driven education policy. And to the horror of Secretary of State Michael Gove, it also showed what could happen when a group of Muslim governors turned an English state school, according to an anonymous member of staff, into 'like being in Pakistan' (Bains and Spencer, 2013).

This felt like a dress rehearsal for the events that unfolded in Birmingham in early 2014, and is significant because it appeared to prove to Gove that there was indeed a thin line between the political Islamism advocated by a minority of the Muslim population and the views of the overall Muslim population in the UK (Gove, 2006). If this was what could happen when a group of Muslims had been running a state school for just a year, what might happen over the long term? Fortunately, Gove's pessimistic prognosis was not borne out by other Muslim faith-based schools in the free schools programme, but there can be no doubt that Al-Madinah's plunge into 'dysfunction' influenced his handling of Trojan Horse. As former Conservative MP Matthew Parris said of Gove, 'something in his brain flips when Islamic extremism is mentioned' (Faux, 2017).

Al-Madinah was part of the second wave of free schools to open in England. The free school programme had been announced by Gove whilst still in opposition and ahead of the general election in 2010. Its aims were to tackle the attainment gap in England by giving schools a higher degree of autonomy. Applications would be invited from teachers, parent groups, charities and philanthropists. Free schools would be about 'liberating teachers' and 'extend[ing] the choice that parents have' (Gabbatt, 2010), heedless of the Swedish experience which indicated that standards would not be raised (Sahlin, 2010).

All free school proposals and plans were stress-tested by officials from the Department for Education Free Schools Group and the Education Funding Agency. Expert educational advice was provided by the department's team of education advisers who were, at the time, mainly former Her Majesty's Inspectors or successful heads with national leader of education status. The due diligence process of approval, readiness for opening status, pre-registration inspections by Ofsted and actual opening would take over a year. All free school applications were assessed and scored, with only a minority of proposals taken forward for interview. Plans were scrutinised in fine detail by teams of civil servants who had been re-brigaded into the new Free Schools Group as the former Department for Children, Schools and Families was reorganised to drive implementation of the new legislation.

Al-Madinah opened in September 2012 led by head teacher Andy Cutts-McKay, whose career had included spells as a production line manager with Ford. He had dealt with industrial relations issues in the tough environment of the motor industry, but nothing could have prepared him for the way he was undermined by his own school trustees and governors. A school that had got off to a brilliant start during its first term was judged to be in the deepest of special measures by October 2013 (Ofsted, 2013).

A series of whistle-blowing complaints had emerged during the summer term. They included discrimination against girl pupils and women teachers. It was alleged that girls were instructed to sit at the back of the classroom and wait until boys had been served first at lunchtime. Non-Muslim women members of staff were told that they must wear headscarves in school. Cutts-McKay told *The Guardian* that he had been a whistle-blower after resigning with stress and diabetes in summer 2013. He had informed the trustees that the school was not functioning properly; his concerns had included governors cutting costs to set up a £350,000 sports centre and women-only swimming pool (Pidd, 2013).

A subsequent Education Funding Agency internal audit report in September 2013, triggered by several whistle-blowers, identified nearly

£20,000 worth of irregular payments to suppliers. A number of governors were closely involved with the suppliers and one former governor had become the school's director of facilities. Overall, it was a damning report which revealed that trustees and governors were too heavily involved in running the school. The governors argued that they had to engage in running the school because the principal, deputy principal and business manager had all resigned. However, their resignations were tendered because the leaders felt they were not being allowed to lead and run the school correctly. Cutts-McKay provided copies of emails sent to the chair of governors setting out his concerns but they were ignored. In turn, the chair of trustees described him as 'evil' and of 'bullying' (Pidd, 2013).

The inspection report on Al-Madinah makes for chilling reading. The school was described as 'dysfunctional', 'in chaos' and not 'adequately monitored or supported' (Ofsted, 2013, pp. 1, 8). It was graded inadequate in all areas. Criticisms included staff being over-promoted into the wrong roles and a failure to appoint staff with the appropriate skills and qualifications. Governors had failed to ensure that children were safe, which led to the school being closed for a week as the single central register of staff was incomplete. Staff were working with children but no safeguarding checks had been recorded. Department for Education and Education Funding Agency officials had to undertake the necessary checks themselves to speed up reopening.

At the Ofsted inspection feedback meeting, the lead inspector told governors it was the worst school he had ever seen and they should be ashamed of themselves for allowing it to get into this position. It was an hour of unremitting negative feedback before the inspectors politely left with only ritual thanks for hospitality. The atmosphere was hostile, and it was left to me and my colleague from the Education Funding Agency to pick up the pieces with governors.

Shadow Secretary of State for Education Tristram Hunt described the free school programme as a 'dangerous free-for-all, an out-of-control ideological experiment that had closed a school, leaving 400 children losing an entire week of learning' (Watt and Pidd, 2013).

Following the Education Funding Agency and Ofsted reports, Al-Madinah was placed in triage with school improvement support coming from the Greenwood Academies Trust. Its CEO, Sir Barry Day, took over as chair of governors and spent two days a week in the school getting it back on track. The secondary department closed and it has run as a primary school since. By December 2014, with strong governance from Day, support from Greenwood and a new head, Al-Madinah was on the road to recovery. Ofsted reinspected and judged it to require improvement across the board (Ofsted, 2014b). Rebranded as Zaytouna Primary School, and run by the Zaytouna Education Trust, the school struggled to recruit sufficient pupil numbers and financial problems continued (Dickens, 2017).

In 2018, it joined the Transform Trust multi-academy trust. It remains an Islamic free school but is now anchored within a family of eighteen community and Church of England primary schools across Nottinghamshire and Derbyshire. Transform Trust states that its purpose is 'to be innovative and inclusive' and its values are decidedly mainstream and orthodox.[5] This is a long way from the troubles that caused educational notoriety in 2013 at Al-Madinah. It has been absorbed into a highly respected multi-academy trust with all the conventional checks and balances that this brings to the school's operation.

What actually happened behind the scenes in 2012 and 2013 has many similarities with Trojan Horse in Birmingham. Al-Madinah was properly established as a Muslim-ethos free school, but its trustees and governors took it down a road way outside of English education and equalities law. Its original policies, signed off by a Department for Education adviser, were liberal and progressive. There were few signs of the troubles ahead when the adviser visited during the first term. In spring 2013, the governors began to undermine and threaten the principal and his team. Tactics included abusive calls and anonymous messages aimed at frightening the principal. Governors became progressively more involved in day-to-day decision-making, which the staff commented on negatively in an internal survey. Governors ran the school themselves without an interim principal for a time during the summer term 2013, and introduced discrimination against girl pupils and women members of staff in the name of Islamic beliefs. Underneath this blatant abuse of a free school's funding agreement with the Department for Education, a host of irregular financial and human resources decisions were taken that smacked of nepotism, self-interest and a complete disregard for high-quality teaching and learning.

Because Al-Madinah was the first Muslim-ethos school within the flagship free schools programme, it was monitored closely. The default ideological position from the Department for Education was that free schools

---

5   See http://www.transformtrust.co.uk/about.

were given the benefit of the doubt and were assumed to be working well unless proven otherwise. The whistle-blowing in summer 2013 was a rude shock to the system.

References

Adams, Richard (2014) Ofsted Inspectors Make U-Turn on 'Trojan Horse' School, Leak Shows, *The Guardian* (30 May). Available at: https://www.theguardian.com/education/2014/may/30/ofsted-u-turn-trojan-horse-park-view-school-leak.

Bains, Inderdeep and Spencer, Ben (2013) Female Teachers at Islamic School 'Made to Sign Contract Agreeing to Wear Headscarf Even If They're NOT Muslim', *Daily Mail* (20 September). Available at: https://www.dailymail.co.uk/news/article-2426626/Female-teachers-Islamic-school-sign-contract-agreeing-wear-headscarf-theyre-NOT-Muslim.html.

BBC News (2015) 'Trojan Horse' School 'Renamed Easter Eggs So They Did Not Sound Christian' (8 December). Available at: https://www.bbc.co.uk/news/uk-england-birmingham-35044459.

Brighouse, Tim and Woods, David (1999) *How to Improve Your School.* Abingdon and New York: Routledge.

Brighouse, Tim and Woods, David (2008) *What Makes a Good School Now?* London: Network Continuum.

Brighouse, Tim and Woods, David (2013) *The A–Z of School Improvement: Principles and Practice.* London: Bloomsbury Education.

Clarke, Peter (2014) *Report into Allegations Concerning Birmingham Schools Arising from the 'Trojan Horse' Letter* (HC 576). Available at: https://assets.publishing.service.gov.uk/government/uploads/system/uploads/attachment_data/file/340526/HC_576_accessible_-.pdf.

Department for Education (DfE) (2014) *Promoting Fundamental British Values as Part of SMSC in Schools* (November). Available at: https://www.gov.uk/government/publications/promoting-fundamental-british-values-through-smsc.

Department for Education (DfE) (2020) Adderley Primary School: 2019 Performance Data. Available at: https://www.compare-school-performance.service.gov.uk/school/103159/adderley-primary-school/absence-and-pupil-population.

Department for Education (DfE) and Morgan, Nicky (2015) Oral Statement to Parliament. Birmingham Schools: Update from Nicky Morgan (29 January). Available at: https://www.gov.uk/government/speeches/update-on-birmingham-schools.

Diamond, Colin (2020) Compassion in the 'Second City': Made in Birmingham. In Maurice I. Coles with Bill Gent (eds), *Education for Survival: The Pedagogy of Compassion.* London: UCL IOE Press, pp. 123–134.

Dickens, John (2017) Al-Madinah Free School Rebrands, But Can't Shake Financial Troubles, *Schools Week* (24 June). Available at: https://schoolsweek.co.uk/al-madinah-free-school-rebrands-but-cant-shake-financial-troubles.

Education Funding Agency (2013) Review of Financial Management and Governance at Al-Madinah Education Trust (October). Available at: https://assets.publishing.service.gov.uk/government/uploads/system/uploads/attachment_data/file/279520/Financial_management_and_governance_review_Al-Madinah_Education_Trust.pdf.

Education Funding Agency (2014) Review of Park View Educational Trust (May). Available at: https://www.gov.uk/government/publications/review-of-park-view-educational-trust.

Elkes, Neil (2014) 'We're Sorry' Council Leader Admits Staff Ignored Trojan Horse Issue for 'Fear of Being Accused of Racism', *Birmingham Mail* (18 June). Available at: https://www.birminghammail.co.uk/news/midlands-news/birmingham-mail-trojan-horse-investigation-7456936.

Faux, Andrew (2017) Michael Gove's 'Brain Flip' Poisoned Schools Extremism Debate, *The Guardian* (4 July). Available at: https://www.theguardian.com/education/2017/jul/04/michael-gove-extremism-trojan-horse-schools.

Gabbatt, Adam (2010) Michael Gove Sets Out Coalition's Plan for Free Schools, *The Guardian* (18 June). Available at: https://www.theguardian.com/politics/2010/jun/18/michael-gove-coalition-plan-free-schools.

Gilligan, Andrew (2014) Trojan Horse: How We Revealed the Truth Behind the Plot, *The Telegraph* (15 June). Available at: https://www.telegraph.co.uk/education/educationnews/10899804/Trojan-Horse-how-we-revealed-the-truth-behind-the-plot.html.

Gove, Michael (2006) *Celsius 7/7: How the West's Policy of Appeasement Has Provoked Yet More Fundamentalist Terror*. London: Phoenix.

Hills, Suzannah and Osborne, Lucy (2013) 'Clothing Must Cover the ENTIRE Body': Revealed, the Strict Dress Code at Islamic School That Forces Women Teachers to Wear a Hijab Regardless of Religion, *Daily Mail* (24 September). Available at: https://www.dailymail.co.uk/news/article-2430475/Islamic-school-Derbys-dress-code-forces-female-teachers-wear-hijab-regardless-religion.html.

Holmwood, John and O'Toole, Theresa (2018) *Countering Extremism in British Schools: The Truth About the Birmingham Trojan Horse Affair*. Bristol: Policy Press.

Hughes, Stephen (2014) Reaction to Trojan Horse is Disproportionate, *Local Government Chronicle* (17 June). Available at: https://www.lgcplus.com/services/children/reaction-to-trojan-horse-is-disproportionate-17-06-2014.

Iqbal, Karamat (2013) *Dear Birmingham: A Conversation with My Hometown*. N.p.: Xlibris.

Kershaw, Ian (2014) Investigation Report: Trojan Horse Letter [Kershaw Report]. Available at: https://www.birmingham.gov.uk/downloads/file/1579/investigation_report_trojan_horse_letter_the_kershaw_report.

Kerslake, Bob (2014) *The Way Forward: An Independent Review of the Governance and Organisational Capabilities of Birmingham City Council* (December). Available at: https://www.gov.uk/government/publications/birmingham-city-councils-governance-and-organisational-capabilities-an-independent-review.

Kidson, Mark and Norris, Emma (2011) *Implementing the London Challenge Institute for Government*. Available at: https://www.instituteforgovernment.org.uk/sites/

default/files/publications/Implementing%20the%20London%20Challenge%20-%20 final_0.pdf.

Nash, John (2014) Golden Hillock School [letter to Tahir Alam] (9 June). Available at: https://assets.publishing.service.gov.uk/government/uploads/system/uploads/ attachment_data/file/318471/140609_Golden_Hillock.pdf.

Ofsted (2002) Inspection of Birmingham Local Authority (April). Available at: https:// files.ofsted.gov.uk/v1/file/50003646.

Ofsted (2004) Inspection Report: Adderley Primary School (13–16 September). Available at: https://files.ofsted.gov.uk/v1/file/796821.

Ofsted (2008a) Annual Performance Assessment of Services for Children and Young People in Birmingham City Council 2008 [letter to Tony Howell] (17 December). Available at: https://files.ofsted.gov.uk/v1/file/50003639.

Ofsted (2008b) Inspection Report: Adderley Primary School (4–5 March). Available at: https://files.ofsted.gov.uk/v1/file/878761.

Ofsted (2012) Inspection Report: Park View Business and Enterprise School (11–12 January). Available at: https://files.Ofsted.gov.uk/v1/file/1889019.

Ofsted (2013) School Report: Al-Madinah School (1–2 October). Available at: https:// files.ofsted.gov.uk/v1/file/2276225.

Ofsted (2014a) Birmingham City Council: Inspection of Services for Children in Need of Help and Protection, Children Looked After and Care Leavers and Review of the Effectiveness of the Local Safeguarding Children Board (23 May). Available at: https:// files.ofsted.gov.uk/v1/file/50004265.

Ofsted (2014b) School Report: Al-Madinah School (3–4 December). Available at: https://files.ofsted.gov.uk/v1/file/2448876.

Ofsted (2016) School Report: Adderley Primary School (13–14 December). Available at: https://files.ofsted.gov.uk/v1/file/2638239.

Ofsted (2020) Official Statistics: Main Findings: State-Funded Schools Inspections and Outcomes As At 31 March 2020. Available at: https://www.gov.uk/government/ statistics/state-funded-schools-inspections-and-outcomes-as-at-31-march-2020/ main-findings-state-funded-schools-inspections-and-outcomes-as-at-31-march-2020.

Oldham, Jeanette (2014) Trojan Horse Investigation: School Head Warned Over Signs of Extremism Four Years Ago, *Birmingham Mail* (31 May). Available at: https://www.birminghammail.co.uk/news/midlands-news/trojan-horse-exclusive-birmingham-school-7196892.

Pidd, Helen (2013) Al-Madinah School's Headteacher Admits He Was Whistleblower, *The Guardian* (22 October). Available at: https://www.theguardian.com/ education/2013/oct/22/al-madinah-headteacher-admits-whistleblower-cutts-mckayckay.

Sahlin, Mona (2010) Don't Trust the Conservative Education Policy – They Want to Implement Our Swedish Failures, *The Guardian* (2 May). Available at: https://www.theguardian.com/politics/2010/may/02/conservative-education-policy-swedish-failures.

Select Committee on Education and Skills (2002) *Second Report. Secondary Education: Visits to Birmingham and Auckland* (HC 486). Available at: https://publications. parliament.uk/pa/cm200203/cmselect/cmeduski/486/48603.htm#note7.

Shackle, Samira (2017) Trojan Horse: The Real Story Behind the Fake 'Islamic Plot' to Take Over Schools, *The Guardian* (1 September). Available at: https://www.theguardian.com/world/2017/sep/01/trojan-horse-the-real-story-behind-the-fake-islamic-plot-to-take-over-schools.

Smith, Mark K. (2014) The Impact of Austerity on Schools and Children's Education and Well-Being, *Encyclopedia of Pedagogy and Informal Education*. Available at: https://infed.org/mobi/the-impact-of-austerity-on-schools-and-childrens-education-and-well-being.

Taylor, Diane (2015) Trojan Horse Row: Governor Banned from Involvement with Schools, *The Guardian* (7 September). Available at: https://www.theguardian.com/education/2015/sep/07/trojan-horse-governor-banned-schools-birmingham.

Vasagar, Jeevan (2012) An Inspector Calls: The Day the Head of Ofsted Visited One School, *The Guardian* (27 March). Available at: https://www.theguardian.com/education/2012/mar/27/michael-wilshaw-ofsted-school-inspector.

Warsi, Sayeeda (2017) *The Enemy Within: A Tale of Muslim Britain*. London: Penguin Random House.

Watt, Nicholas and Pidd, Helen (2013) Al-Madinah Free Faith School Expected to be Closed by the Government, *The Guardian* (17 October). Available at: https://www.theguardian.com/education/2013/oct/17/al-madinah-free-school-faces-closure-government.

Chapter 2
Growing up in Birmingham: place and identity

Kamal Hanif

Introduction

A head once referred to the children in reception class as 'mutes' when I attended training on leading primary practice around 2011. Oblivious to how offensive this was, she believed that because they were of Asian background it was okay to call them this and went on to self-congratulate about what her school does with the poor mums.

I am not a mute, and neither are our children, parents or communities. Black Lives Matter has opened the door for debate, dialogue once more and it is for us to appreciate and accept each other's differences and celebrate them. Let it not be another fad.

Kamal Hanif

Kamal Hanif is Birmingham through and through. He lives close to the secondary school that he attended as a pupil and Waverley Education Foundation Trust which he formerly headed up as CEO. Having been awarded an OBE in 2012 for his services to education, his journey from schoolboy in Small Heath to becoming an international contributor on diversity and equalities (Ofsted, 2014d) appears seamless. Rising quickly through the ranks after qualifying as a teacher and being talent-spotted by an Ofsted inspector as headship material, Hanif appeared destined to succeed. With his family worshipping in the local mosques and shopping on the local high streets in Small Heath, it looks like a model journey that exemplifies much that is good about English pluralism.

Yet nothing was straightforward. In spite of working in a city known for its innovation and drive towards educational equality, Hanif continues to rail against institutional racism that lies deep. It first emerged when he was learning his trade as a young teacher and re-emerged grotesquely during Trojan Horse when his suitability to lead a school was questioned because he was a Muslim.

Hanif's professional journey has been dogged by racist attitudes from White colleagues and subversive behaviour from within his own community for taking a stand on issues such as lesbian, gay, bisexual and transgender (LGBT) rights. When I first met him in 2014, he wanted to reassure me that the anonymous allegations about the misuse of school funds for a personal holiday were groundless – and they were, of course, having been fully and openly investigated. By stepping outside the socially conservative norms of his home community he became a target. There was resentment at his success and the soaring performance of Waverley School. As a Muslim head teacher, he became the subject of both an Islamophobic witch-hunt from within his own school around the time of Trojan Horse and from the local Muslim community for being too progressive. Heads I win, tails you lose.

Hanif's chronicling of events during his career, including working at Park View, reveals how he had to pick his way through school factions, with White racists never far from the surface. He talks positively of head teacher Lindsey Clark's support for girls' education, a culturally inclusive curriculum and music education. He also recognises the damage done by a small group of governors at the time Park View became an academy and took on responsibility for Golden Hillock and Nansen schools, which then became the epicentre of Trojan Horse. Hanif was installed as a member at Park View when Tahir Alam resigned in July 2014 and worked with the new leadership to address the issues revealed in the Ofsted (2014b, 2014c) and Education Funding Agency (2014b) reports. Always loyal to the pupils and their families, he was part of the solution as a leader with unique education and community credentials.

Growing up in Small Heath, Hanif's affectionate description of the community resonates with the way Baroness Warsi (2017, p. xx–xxi) talks of her childhood in Savile Town, Dewsbury. Like many communities in Birmingham and West Yorkshire, it made the transition from predominantly White working class, through an era of diversity with many groups mixing well, to the South Asian Muslim-majority character and identity we see today.

Appointed as head teacher in 2005, Waverley was first judged outstanding under his leadership in 2010 (Ofsted, 2010). In 2012, it was again judged outstanding in all respects with this glowing endorsement of Hanif's personal impact over seven years of headship: 'The school's continuing success is largely due to the inspirational and committed leadership of the headteacher and his leadership team. A relentless drive for the very best in everything is the basis of every decision that is taken' (Ofsted, 2012, p. 6).

Ofsted's (2014d) monitoring inspection, part of the Trojan Horse round of inspections commissioned by the secretary of state, was similarly positive with leadership and management judged to be outstanding. The emphasis during this round of inspections was on the relationship between leadership and safeguarding. The following quotations are highly relevant in view of what happened subsequently:

Behaviour and safety of pupils:

'Students move around the site calmly and responsibly ... They show a very good awareness of the risks to their personal safety and well-being both in and beyond school ... Students are free to express their views and concerns and feel that there is always an adult to turn to, and help them.' (p. 2)

'Attendance has risen and is now around the national average ... staff are alert to the possibility of absences being associated with forced marriages or female genital mutilation and always act on concerns.' (p. 3)

'No student has been permanently excluded for the past three years.' (p. 3)

Quality of leadership in and management of the school:

'A strong culture of ensuring the very highest standard of safeguarding pervades the school.' (p. 3)

'Students' very mature and well-developed appreciation of issues relating to different sexualities is a positive reflection of the confident emphasis this is given in the curriculum. The school is a Stonewall champion school.' (p. 3)

In the midst of the Trojan Horse era, under Hanif's leadership, Waverley had become Birmingham's first Stonewall Gold champion school, which was anathema for some in the local community.[1] The campaign to discredit Hanif's regime post-dated the Trojan Horse entryism that Clarke (2014) and Kershaw (2014) describe in depth. From 2015 onwards, it was not possible for governors or trustees to target heads they disliked and attempt to pull them down using the playbook of disruptive tactics. Consequently, Hanif's detractors began to operate outside the school gates with a campaign to undermine his leadership and the flagship status of the school.

On many occasions as director of education for Birmingham City Council, I needed to reassure senior officials in Ofsted that they were being fed disinformation and there was no foundation to the allegations of weak leadership at Waverley. Eventually, given the high number of complaints – even though most of them were anonymous – Ofsted was obliged to inspect. And when word spread that inspectors were in school, the pupils were incited to misbehave and be rude to inspectors. The inevitable chaos led to a downgrading from outstanding to requires improvement (Ofsted, 2017).

The contrast with the 2014 report is stark. From 'calm and responsible' pupils in 2014, inspectors found disruption caused by 'poor behaviour' in 2017 (Ofsted, 2017, p. 1). Those pupils who were 'free to express their views and feel that there is always an adult to turn to' (Ofsted, 2014d, p. 2) had transformed into pupils who 'do not believe their opinions are valued sufficiently, or that their concerns will be treated sensitively enough' (Ofsted, 2017, p. 13). Early years provision remained outstanding but it was in the secondary phase of the school – where pupils had been encouraged to behave negatively by voices outside the school – that the damage was done. The decline in behavioural standards was attributed to the arrival and departure of two head teachers, which undoubtedly did introduce an unsettling element. But Hanif was a constant, and those attributes Ofsted purred about in 2012 and 2014 – which set the values, ethos and inclusive direction of the school – had not changed.

---

1   A Stonewall Gold school has been benchmarked to assess its inclusion of lesbian, gay, bisexual, transgender, queer and others (LGBTQ+) policies and practice. The award confirms that the school is leading the way in celebrating diversity and supporting LGBTQ+ children and young people to fulfil their potential. For more information see https://www.stonewall.org.uk/school-champions/ stonewall-school-champion-awards.

Similar events took place at the neighbouring Bordesley Green Girls' School. It too was downgraded from outstanding (Ofsted, 2014a) to requires improvement (Ofsted, 2018), as the inspectorate was bombarded with anonymous complaints about the head teacher and her regime. Judith Woodfield, like Hanif, had presented challenges to the local community with her uncompromising approach to safeguarding the pupils at the school. The glowing praise in the 2014 Ofsted report where the new head teacher's passion and 'rigorous analysis of student's progress', allied to 'outstanding' leadership of teaching (Ofsted, 2014a, p. 7), evaporated in the face of 'multiple serious safeguarding cases' (Ofsted, 2018, p. 3). The stellar behaviour of pupils observed by inspectors in 2014 had deteriorated by 2018 thanks to external players who sought to destabilise and discredit the head teacher and her senior team. Pupils were encouraged to misbehave in front of the Ofsted inspectors knowing that this would have a negative impact on the overall judgement on the school.

Events at Waverley, Bordesley Green and more recently the protests against the teaching of LGBT awareness to pupils at Anderton Park and Parkfield primary schools (Diamond, 2019b, 2019c) reveal that some members of the local community still consider it acceptable to undermine school leaders who refuse to conform with their view of what is acceptable for Muslim pupils.

For Hanif, the journey continues. The Black Lives Matter movement has provided fresh impetus to challenge institutional racism, which will exist until the balance of power is wrestled from those who promulgate a colour-blind meritocracy. English education policy is moored in a denial of racism, and there is little acknowledgment of those who would rewrite standard imperial history lest it pose an existential threat to their privilege (Olusoga, 2016).

Colin Diamond

Growing up in Birmingham: place and identity

Kamal Hanif

Small Heath – a diverse community

I was born, grew up and still live in Small Heath, an area in the east of Birmingham with high levels of deprivation, poverty and inequality.

Over the past fifty years, the local community has evolved due to migration, which has changed the identity of Small Heath like any inner-city community. Growing up in the 1970s, the area was diverse. My street had Pakistani, English, Irish, Caribbean, Jamaican and Indian families all living alongside each other, and that was my community.

Religious festivals were celebrated by all, weddings were attended by all and we all had a strong community bond. Mosques in those days initially started out in houses; there was one at the top of Charles Road at the corner of Coventry Road above the shoe shop, and one on Somerville Road.

The Small Heath carnival was an annual event which we all attended. Coventry Road, the main arterial route into the city, had many high street stores such as Boots and Woolworths, but as the 1980s saw the decline of the local BSA motorcycle factory, we witnessed the closure of many high street shops, which were soon to be replaced by independent retailers.

There were a few Asian clothes retailers, the main ones being a shop on the Coventry Road called Public Cloth Stores and one on Green Lane, which I used to go to with my mother, especially ahead of the Eid celebrations. We had the odd halal butchers shop, and a local cinema on Walford Road in Sparkhill that would show the latest Bollywood films (which is now incidentally a Hindu temple).

Police presence was limited in number, unlike what we see today, and even the relationship with the local bobbies was one of mutual respect rather than suspicion.

I also remember when the National Front marched through the area, and we would be told to stay in the house and not look out the window. This was my earliest exposure to prejudice and racism, perhaps not fully understanding what these things really meant, but knowing I had to be careful because of the colour of my skin. To 'stay safe' was something most young Asian and Black children were told.

At school there wasn't much focus on culture or understanding where students came from; my friends in primary school were of different nationalities and religions. But, over time, the area saw changes as more and more Asian families moved in and other communities moved out.

The mosque is a strong hub for most Muslim families, and it was the same in my household. As a young child my parents sent me and my siblings to a woman who lived across the road to learn to read the Qur'an. Mostly, we would be trying to avoid a beating for misbehaving or not doing our homework. All we were taught was a parrot-training form of education by reciting phonetically, without any understanding of the meaning of the Qur'an, but we learnt the verses (so that we could pray) and most notably our five daily prayers. Religious practice was very much to learn to read the Qur'an from start to finish and then start again. Completing the reading of the Qur'an was a milestone, like passing your GCSEs.

Whilst attending the local secondary, formerly Oldknow Junior School, I would attend madrasa at the mosque afterwards, where we were taught Urdu and the basic tenets of Islam. However, at Oldknow school I was involved in performing in school productions, which often resulted in me missing or being late for madrasa. The mosque was a hub and quite often split on national lines; my mosque was frequented by Pakistani Muslims from the Mirpur region of Kashmir. There was a strong identity around being Kashmiri and the dispute between Pakistan and India.

The mid-1980s – aspirations rising

In my second year at secondary school, I moved to Waverley School – a school of 300 or so students, where very little was offered in relation to the performing arts, which annoyed me. There was also no stability at the school; we went through a cycle of head teachers who came and went. A strict uniform policy was in place, which required girls to wear a skirt, although this was challenged to allow them to wear trousers. School management at the time didn't appear to be interested in looking at the needs and rights of their communities. I was amongst the last cohort to study O levels and CSEs; the year group below sat the new GCSE examinations. In my last two years at school there was a male staffroom and a female staffroom, and we were hit by teacher strikes. This was 1987.

I enjoyed science and performed well in my exams, which resulted in me getting good grades in an era when there were no league tables. I remember having to argue to take the O level in physics, as this appeared to be reserved for White students, despite the fact that there were only a few in my year group. As one White student never attended, I was allowed to take his place and sit the exam. I had to challenge the school on why I could not take this subject, despite it being one of my strongest; a good example of bias. At the time I wanted to go into medicine, but I was advised by the careers adviser to be more realistic and consider working in a local shop. Aspirations for students from my community were clearly quite low.

In the mid-1980s, Birmingham, like other provincial cities across the country, experienced racial tensions which resulted in riots. I vaguely remember driving through the area of Handsworth after the riots when we visited family friends in the area. During this period there was a lot of local activism on the issue of independence for Kashmir. I remember the local MP Roger Godsiff at meetings and how he raised the issue in parliament.

After I finished school, I went on to study at Matthew Boulton College, which was located on Pershore Road, but my friends all went to St Philip's RC Sixth Form College. This was a period when things started to change. Young Muslims of my generation were still balancing our cultural identity of being a Pakistani Muslim and our Britishness. There was greater diversification and cultural changes. We would see an explosion of the bhangra scene. With BBC Network East now broadcasting, I recall college students talking excitedly when it aired a daytime bhangra event at the Dome in the city centre. This would have been seen by the students' families, much to their dismay as it was a distraction from learning at school. We were also the first generation who aspired to go to university – we were a generation with many expectations.

During my childhood, religion was more about what we practised in our homes, with stories passed down by each generation, although we also learnt things at the mosque. There were no real sources of instruction or texts to go to for answers. I remember having an Urdu translation of the Qur'an from which my teacher would read. By the 1980s, I could receive and read a Qur'an that had been translated into English, which was a godsend. Religious knowledge became more accessible.

Student days and the impact of *The Satanic Verses*

I remember watching the influential Muslim missionary preacher, the South African Ahmed Deedat, leading debates at Birmingham Town Hall. Originally of Indian origin, the South African spoke of comparative religion and the place of Islam. An author of many books, he was a preacher with missionary zeal. In 1988, *The Satanic Verses* by Salman Rushdie was published, followed by the ensuing international media hype. The Rushdie Affair brought Muslim identity to our TV screens. Religious hate graffiti with derogatory comments on Islam soon appeared inside the lifts at college. It was the first time I had seen such written attacks on my religion and ethnicity.

The Rushdie Affair was a trigger, or the start, of what we now call Islamophobia. You had one community wanting to be heard and other communities intrigued about why Muslims in general could find a work of fiction so offensive to their religion, which precipitated demonstrations and the odd book-burning. This was followed by a fatwa against Salman Rushdie.[2] The controversy around *The Satanic Verses* uncovered a community who are part of the UK and hold a British identity, but who also identify themselves by their religion, country of origin and culture. Nevertheless, there were also good relationships at college between the different cultures, races and religions.

During the Rushdie Affair I was studying at university in Leicester, which was a very different environment to the one with which I was familiar. It was a city with a large Indian Gujarati population of Muslims and Hindus. I even shared a house with a Hindu and a Sikh. I remember being in the canteen queue in my first week and the topic of conversation being 'What

---

2   A fatwa is 'a ruling on a point of Islamic law given by a recognised authority' (https://www.lexico.com/definition/fatwa).

do you think about *The Satanic Verses*?' As a Muslim, you were almost expected to have a strong view on the matter. It was the first time I had heard derogatory terms from Sikhs and Hindus against Muslims, and I had to ask a friend on my course what they meant. This was not something I had experienced growing up in Birmingham.

My social circles were diverse. I also had White friends, and I quite often mixed with them on campus and beyond. Leicester was often cited as a model city of community cohesion; one such example was the city celebrating the largest Diwali festival outside of India. These moments shaped me and gave me a great appreciation of different cultures and religions, but it also afforded me the opportunity to learn about the differences between Muslims from different parts of the world and how they practise their religion. The city of Birmingham had not really celebrated its religious and cultural diversity in the same way as Leicester.

Into teaching – knowing your place in the staffroom

After university, I moved back to Birmingham to do my Postgraduate Certificate in Education, where I learnt about the challenges faced by young teachers from Black, Asian and minority ethnic (BAME) communities, as my course tutor was also of South Asian origin. We also had talks from a BAME lecturer which were inspirational in informing us about why teaching was essential; it was interesting to learn that he had moved to work in a university from the school sector as he felt that he had reached the ceiling of opportunities due to his BAME background. As an education student with a teaching background, I led the Equal Opportunities Society and did some work raising fellow students' consciousness about the issues of interdependence and diversity.

Birmingham was changing as a city. There were more purpose-built mosques, the Balti Triangle was thriving[3] and it was becoming more multicultural. My own local mosque, on Somerville Road, wanted to buy adjacent properties in order to expand and cater for the growing popula-

---

3   The Balti Triangle is an area of the city named after the number of restaurants serving curry using the balti method of cooking. The balti, a wok-style steel dish, was first used by Pakistani restaurateurs in the 1970s. Whilst there are still lots of curry houses in the area bounded by Ladypool Road, Stoney Lane and Stratford Road, few balti houses remain today, but the name has stuck.

tion. Mosque committees were developed and this often led to internal tensions over direction, control and power between committee members. It seemed to be a battle over status and hierarchy – some things never change.

My first teaching post was at Saltley School in 1993. By that time, one staffroom had been created by combining the male and female staffrooms. Although the school was progressive, I was one of the few BAME teachers and the only one from the local community. Despite the challenges, many in the community held the head teacher and deputies in high regard because they greeted them with 'Assalamu alaikum' ('I greet you in peace'). Using this salutation was not seen as an issue. Looking back, and having reflected on the continuing professional development courses I attended, female colleagues often spoke to me or sat next to me, but White male staff tended not to talk to anyone from a BAME background – especially if you were the only BAME person in the room. Sadly, this is still a common experience for many BAME staff in current times.

The head teacher at the school set up an equal opportunities committee. I recall that some colleagues wrote to ask if the school was operating a policy of not recruiting BAME teachers as only a few individuals had been appointed. Clearly, there were elements of prejudice and racism, which is still the case today. I see leaders in some schools wanting to do something to address the issues raised by Black Lives Matter. A number of steering groups have been established across the city, but there is still a lack of willpower and the can is kicked down the road. Leaders say, 'Let's send a BAME member of staff along to this working party,' not realising how condescending and actually racist this approach can be. In some circles and organisations where a lack of focus on recruiting and developing BAME teachers has been raised in front of me, I have been told: 'But our focus has been equality – we have done loads of work on gender representation and LGBT.' At which point I have to say, 'Stop diluting the focus on race and racism with other equality issues – they are two different things.'

Despite these obstacles, I was ambitious and wanted to progress. Once I was at an after-school social event with staff and remember some colleagues being very riled up because I was being considered for the 'second-in-department position' (often the first level of promotion for a young teacher) and they wanted to prevent it. Previously, I'd had no clue that this conspiracy was going on around me. I later found out from the head teacher that I was considered for the role but they were surprised how it had upset other staff. Another BAME teaching assistant had joined and I remember certain staff members telling her where she could and could not sit in the staffroom. I also recall hearing derogatory and prejudiced comments made about her community. A lot of work was being done on multiculturalism, but some racist views still remained underneath the surface and were rarely aired. Tensions often arose when students asked for somewhere to pray at lunchtimes during Ramadan.

Moving into school leadership against the odds

In 1996, I moved on to my first leadership role at Dame Elizabeth Cadbury, a school in which I excelled. I also joined the 11–19 committee of the Association for Science Education, which gave me great development opportunities. The appointment of a female head teacher caused shockwaves in the school as it was a small family organisation, with some staff who had been working there for years.

In the late 1990s, the issue of safeguarding and child protection started to become a bigger issue for schools. I remember delivering training and a few staff feeling very uncomfortable about discussing child sexual abuse. We now live in an era where safeguarding has become an important area within teaching. It shows how our views and the role of education has changed in such a short space of time.

During this period, I was told by my head teacher, Lesley Brooman, that Ofsted had commented on how they saw me as a future head teacher – something I wanted to achieve. My own head teacher's support and direction led me to follow a more departmental teaching and learning route rather than remaining in pastoral roles. In the school, with Lesley at the helm, there were no barriers for BAME leaders; before I moved to my next role she had appointed an Asian female deputy head teacher, who then went on to become a head teacher in another school. In the city of Birmingham, shifts were clearly starting to take place in education.

The impact of 9/11 and the rise of Islamophobia

In 2000, I moved to Harborne Hill School. It was a challenging school with an intake from the Handsworth and Aston areas, but it did great work developing diversity and inclusion. The school had a small but diverse staff; we were a strong united team. There was a family feel and colleagues looked out for each other.

It was the start of a new academic year, and I was in the staffroom working on my computer when a colleague came in and asked, 'Have you seen the news?' I hadn't. It was the breaking news of the 9/11 attack on the World Trade Center in New York. Overnight, the world had changed. In Small Heath, we heard of examples of Muslim women receiving hateful comments from travelling football fans about their religion, their hijab and the colour of their skin. Asian people started staying away from the area around St Andrews, the home ground of Birmingham City Football Club, if they were playing to avoid the racist taunts.

At work, I was shocked when a colleague asked me why a Muslim teacher could come into school dressed in a hijab; for them it was offensive. During my childhood, the hijab was a rare accessory amongst Muslim women; more typically they would wear the traditional salwar kameez with a matching scarf. The burka was a rarity. My first experience of seeing the burka was when I was 11 and family friends from the north of England came to visit us. At the start of the millennium, it was mostly younger Muslim women who wore the hijab and burka, which coincided with the increasing availability of Islamic literature. Post 9/11, more Muslim women began to wear the hijab, perhaps as a form of defiance against the intimidation they were facing. Islamic stores and Asian clothing stores started to sell the thobe (a long Muslim dress), again mostly worn by younger British-born Muslim men. The thobe is more associated with Arab attire but, amongst the younger generation, it seemed to be replacing the traditional male salwar kameez, which was perceived to be more cultural than the Islamic thobe. I would often change into my salwar kameez when I got home after work as I found it more comfortable.

It became the norm for Muslims – or anyone who was perceived to look like a Muslim – to be asked by non-Muslims, 'Are you practising?' 'Do you pray?' 'Do you use that mat thing?' It felt as if we were being judged on whether we were an extremist or not, and whether we could be trusted or not. I don't think people realised how offensive it could be to be subjected to these lines of questioning. Sometimes, I wondered if it was general ignorance or whether people just didn't take the time to find out the difference between Eid and Diwali, a Hindu festival. I have many Sikh and Hindu friends who would be shocked about how little wider British society knows about the major religious festivals.

With every terrorist attack, the Muslim community faced more scrutiny, even though we had nothing to do with it, in the same way that the wider White community wouldn't if a man committed a terrorist crime in the name of White supremacy. Since the 7/7 London bombings, if you are a Muslim, you are conscious not to carry a rucksack on the Tube. There was media demonisation and trolling on social media towards Muslims (and Hindus) every time a Muslim suspect was arrested.

Since the 1970s, there has been a journey from Islam being a family and home-based practice focused on learning the Qur'an and being able to say your prayers, to a society where we have seen a British-born Muslim generation looking to understand the teachings and interpretations of the Qur'an and Islam as a whole. When culture and religion became interlinked, we began to see British Muslim families creating their own form of British Islam.

As other newly arrived Muslim communities settled in Birmingham from 2002, mostly from Somalia, the Muslim community in Small Heath became more diverse, with each sub-community having their individual identity but united by religion.

Park View School

In the autumn of 2003, I started my new role as deputy head teacher at Park View School – the school that became the centre of the Trojan Horse affair. On the day of my interview, a member of staff came up to the candidates and handed us all a letter. I didn't read it, but some did, and they rescinded their applications. As I understand, the letter was offensive about the community and staff from ethnic minorities – and about Muslims in particular – stating that they were going to 'take over the school'. This resulted in a number of court hearings against the school. I could see the terrible toll it took on the head teacher, Lindsey Clark, who stood against racist behaviour.

As deputy head teacher of the school, I saw tensions starting to rise in Alum Rock against the Somali community. You would hear comments such as, 'They are taking over our businesses and shops' – a repeat of the old rhetoric that the local British Pakistani community had faced in the 1970s. Developing community cohesion became a priority at the school.

Lindsey had done her utmost to support the students, recognising their religion and culture and giving them a broad and rounded education. Having come from a senior role in a girls' school, she was a very strong advocate for girls' education. We developed a culturally inclusive curriculum which recognised excellence from all cultures. Lindsey was passionate about having a broad curriculum. She had appointed a new music teacher to work with the local authority music service to develop a programme that was more inclusive of wider musical and cultural influences. This initiative became extremely popular with the students; you could still see evidence of its impact in 2014 when I was asked to go in and help with the Trojan Horse issues. It was difficult to maintain a balance between conventional approaches to curriculum development in the arts and broadening them out to reflect Islamic musical and cultural traditions, but, most importantly, it was about bridging the gap between home and school.

Some Park View staff clearly held racist and bigoted views. I recall a member of staff talking within earshot of me about a social event for White colleagues and how she 'enjoyed being racist'. Later, the same individual brought a grievance through her union claiming that it was threatening for White women to have a Muslim deputy head teacher because of 9/11. She also questioned how I could be leading on literacy, despite having written several publications, because I had English as an additional language. She did not know that I grew up in a household with my brother and his English wife and that Urdu was not my strongest language. Tensions were evident amongst staff across the school. For example, colleagues in the English department would try to aggravate their co-workers in the maths department around the thorny issues of religion and racism. A White male teacher in the maths department was seen as a traitor for supporting his Muslim colleagues.

As Muslim staff at the school were experiencing racism, they felt they had to do more to have their religion, identity and culture respected by developing a stronger emphasis on cultural inclusion. The local authority was also doing work to address the underachievement of minority ethnic groups, and, with input from the national strategies (Strand, 2015), to reduce racial tensions and barriers. As a school, we were sharing our successes and good practice with the local authority Asian Heritage Achievement Group, and the school even presented ideas at a conference looking at the underachievement of Pakistani boys. But, despite all of this great work, it was clear that there was not a broad understanding across the city on how to develop inclusive pedagogy in our schools.

The fruits of our success were slowly coming together as the students began to become more aspirational and develop a sense of belonging. They understood that religion was more about guiding how they would live their lives, and therefore they could be both British and Muslim as British Muslims. They became more resilient. They respected others' cultures, ways of life and clothing. Friendship groups recognised that not everyone will wear the hijab or the thobe. We saw excellent results as girls started to perform better than boys in subjects and exams. We worked with young boys who were often under pressure to conform to 'street culture' or who would be bullied if they were performing well at school. We reaffirmed with them that it is healthy to aspire and to move into careers their parents would not have dreamed about.

Trojan Horse – the aftermath and recovery

What is not often talked about is the damage the Trojan Horse affair did to the local community. Lies and conspiracies set schools in the area back at least ten years because the destabilisation led to difficulties in recruiting staff and governors.

In 2014, I was a part of the Kershaw review group, whose findings differed from those reported by Secretary of State for Education Nicky Morgan to the House of Commons in July (DfE and Morgan, 2014). At this time, as a result of the anti-Muslim rhetoric whipped up by former Secretary of State for Education Michael Gove and the round of twenty-one Ofsted inspections, I faced considerable racist behaviour from some teaching union reps because of my submissions, and I did not receive responses to my letters of complaint to their executive officers. A systematic campaign to incite my staff to rebel and to remove me from my job took off, simply because I was Muslim and therefore I must be part of a clandestine conspiracy to turn my school into a Muslim enclave.

Local representation in the years preceding the Trojan Horse affair was an issue for school governors. As governing bodies changed and local community members fought for the rights of their students, there were often challenging debates about how poorly the predominantly British Pakistani students were doing at school. During my time at Park View, governance was fair, free, liberal and inclusive. Yet, still to this day, in other schools I often hear comments from school leaders on how if a BAME individual raises a valid point they are perceived as an extremist or troublemaker. School leaders need to engage with the community they serve, walk the streets around the school and engage in events with other local stakeholders, rather than just commute between school and home. This could make a huge difference.

The melting away of teachers and governors following Trojan Horse

Waverley was judged to be an outstanding school in 2014. However, I could not release the report because I was waiting for official confirmation. Initially, the press were reporting that the school had been judged as requires improvement. Michael Gove stood up in parliament and declared that only three schools in the round of twenty-one Trojan Horse inspections had received good or outstanding, and named them – all of which, coincidentally, had White leadership. I was told that Gove had based his speech on media reports rather than reading the actual Ofsted reports. As a Muslim head, I was blamed for not releasing the inspection outcome, despite acting with professionalism and integrity.

As a direct result of the Trojan Horse affair, certain community members became fearful of becoming school governors. This made the recruitment process difficult for our own governing body as some individuals felt that it could tarnish their own careers if they were associated with schools in the area.

The recruitment of staff became more difficult in all the local schools, and in particular schools situated in the high-percentage BAME areas of Birmingham. It reminded me of when I first became a head teacher: I was told that I might get more White males applying for roles if I took my name off the job advert. My response was, 'If my name puts them off, then are they the right people for our children?'

Trojan Horse had the same effect, with schools wary of appointing anyone with a Muslim-sounding name. Applicants were judged by their religion and their appearance. Labels were thrown around and people were pigeonholed. I was once referred to as a 'moderate' in an article because I was clean shaven, something at which I took personal offence. Who gets to decide what label I am, and what does being 'moderate' mean?

So much good work undone

The majority of governors in the Trojan Horse schools and in the east end of the city worked to secure changes which led to big improvements in student outcomes up to 2014. They networked and learnt from each other, shared best practice and wanted the voice of parents to be heard. Trojan Horse – by which I mean the actions of a small number of governors and the way things were inflamed by Michael Gove – had the opposite effect and caused unforeseen damage to the local schools and communities, which are still recovering.

A key focus of Ofsted's Inspection Framework (2019) was the curriculum and curriculum intent. This provided the opportunity to look once again at race, religion, gender, sexuality, disability, age, equality and excellence from the perspective of all communities and re-examine our own biases and prejudices. I am told constantly by students that the curriculum is not relevant to them because it doesn't include their stories and experiences. The teaching of fundamental British values has often been misconstrued and corrupted into teaching exclusively about Britain. As long as that continues, being of Birmingham, as opposed to being in Birmingham, will remain a problem.

References

Clarke, Peter (2014) *Report into Allegations Concerning Birmingham Schools Arising from the 'Trojan Horse' Letter* (HC 576). Available at: https://assets.publishing.service. gov.uk/government/uploads/system/uploads/attachment_data/file/340526/HC_576_ accessible_-.pdf.

Department for Education (DfE) and Morgan, Nicky (2014) Oral Statement by Nicky Morgan on the 'Trojan Horse' Letter (22 July). Available at: https://www.gov.uk/government/speeches/oral-statement-by-nicky-morgan-on-the-trojan-horse-letter.

Diamond, Colin (2019a) Parkfield School and No Outsiders: We Must Learn from Trojan Horse History in Birmingham, *Schools Week* (20 January). Available at: https://schoolsweek.co.uk/parkfield-school-and-no-outsiders-we-must-learn-from-trojan-horse-history-in-birmingham.

Diamond, Colin (2019b) Teaching About LGBT in English Schools: How the Arrival of Mandatory Relationships and Sex Education Has Been Used to Divide Schools and the Communities They Serve, *University of Birmingham* (11 April). Available at: https://https://www.birmingham.ac.uk/news/2019/teaching-about-lgbt-in-english-schools-how-the-arrival-of-mandatory-relationships-and-sex-education-has-been-used-to-divide-schools-and-the-communities-they-serve.

Diamond, Colin (2019c) There Is a Way Out of the Schools LGBT Protest Mess – But Ministers Need to Get Behind It, *The Guardian* (6 August). Available at: https://www.theguardian.com/education/2019/aug/06/way-out-of-schools-protest-mess-birmingham-trojan-horse.

Education Funding Agency (2014) Review of Park View Educational Trust (May). Available at: https://www.gov.uk/government/publications/review-of-park-view-educational-trust.

Kershaw, Ian (2014) *Investigation Report: Trojan Horse Letter* [Kershaw Report]. Available at: https://www.birmingham.gov.uk/downloads/file/1579/investigation_report_trojan_horse_letter_the_kershaw_report.

Ofsted (2010) Inspection Report: Waverley School (28–29 April). Available at: https://files.Ofsted.gov.uk/v1/file/947913.

Ofsted (2012) School Report: Waverley School (5–6 December). Available at: https://files.Ofsted.gov.uk/v1/file/2156923.

Ofsted (2014a) School Report: Bordesley Green Girls' School & Sixth Form (6–7 February). Available at: https://files.ofsted.gov.uk/v1/file/2341389.

Ofsted (2014b) School Report: Golden Hillock School – A Park View Academy (2–3 April). Available at: https://files.api.Ofsted.gov.uk/v1/file/2391869.

Ofsted (2014c) School Report: Nansen Primary School – A Park View Academy (2–3 April). Available at: https://files.Ofsted.gov.uk/v1/file/2391873.

Ofsted (2014d) No Formal Designation Monitoring Inspection of Waverley School [letter] (12 May). Available at: https://files.Ofsted.gov.uk/v1/file/2391813.

Ofsted (2017) School Report: Waverley School (28–29 November). Available at: https://files.ofsted.gov.uk/v1/file/2748325.

Ofsted (2018) School Report: Bordesley Green Girls' School & Sixth Form (22–23 May). Available at: https://files.ofsted.gov.uk/v1/file/50008739 .

Ofsted (2019) *Guidance Education Inspection Framework* (updated 23 July 2021). Available at: https://www.gov.uk/government/publications/education-inspection-framework/education-inspection-framework.

Olusoga, David (2016) *Black and British: A Forgotten History.* London: Pan Macmillan.

Rushdie, Salman (1988) *The Satanic Verses*. London: Random House.

Strand, Steve (2015) *Ethnicity, Deprivation and Educational Achievement At Age 16 in England: Trends Over Time* (June). Available at: https://assets.publishing.service. gov.uk/government/uploads/system/uploads/attachment_data/file/439867/RR439B-Ethnic_minorities_and_attainment_the_effects_of_poverty_annex.pdf.pdf.

Warsi, Sayeeda (2017) *The Enemy Within: A Tale of Muslim Britain*. London: Penguin Random House.

Chapter 3
Unrepresentative and ill-equipped education bureaucracy

Karamat Iqbal

Introduction

Mind the gap. Karamat Iqbal has been exposing the gap between policy, rhetoric and practice on the ground for many years. Sent to Birmingham aged 12 by his parents, straight from the home village in Azad Kashmir, he was brought up by his sister and encountered both freedom and trauma in his new city (Asian Youth Culture, 2021). He became attached to Birmingham in spite of a less than propitious entry to its education system in 1970 when he was racially bullied from day one at school. This affectionate, yet challenging relationship has been chronicled fully in *Dear Birmingham: A Conversation with My Hometown* (2013).

In his chapter, Iqbal has updated the status of the British Pakistani communities in Birmingham through the lenses of the disproportionate impact of COVID-19 and employment data from Birmingham City Council and the Birmingham Education Partnership (BEP). The theme of Pakistani boys' underachievement at school is a constant in his research. This narrative is informed by Iqbal's engagement with several generations of policy development aimed at improving the overall position of British Pakistani communities from the 1970s onwards at local and national level.

What went wrong? Why are the figures for Black, Asian and minority ethnic (BAME) school leaders, including those of British Pakistani heritage, in the city so stubbornly low? (See Chapter 16.) Why have the targets set by Birmingham City Council for the employment of British Pakistanis not been secured? What has prevented initiatives spawned by the National College for School Leadership and Birmingham City Council's education services from gaining more traction? And why have Pakistani boys made so little progress? It has not been for want of trying, with multiple attempts by the Birmingham Advisory and Support Service to promote, for example, an Asian Heritage achievement group, the regular sharing of school performance data and a conference organised to examine raising the achievement of Pakistani boys. All of this work petered out as a result of austerity-driven budget cuts introduced by the coalition government from 2010 onwards and government policy to reduce the role of local authorities, but there was no doubting the sense of purpose and mission.

To understand the lack of penetration, Iqbal has taken us into critical race theory, exploring David Gillborn's research, which unpacks the processes that have shaped and sustained racial inequalities (see, for example, Rollock and Gillborn, 2011). He also considers Kenneth Newton's interpretation of Max Weber's theory of bureaucracy, with its hierarchy of authority, salaried careers and specialised qualifications, all of which have ended up excluding non-White employees.

Current education policy is driven by raw meritocracy. It has an aversion to embracing the elements that are the pre-conditions for minority ethnic groups to thrive. Not the least of these is the promotion of curricula at every level of education to 'deliver a positive experience for students and staff of BAME heritage' (Miller and Callender, 2019, p. 288). Social mobility is locked in reverse gear (Major and Machin, 2020). Iqbal holds out hope for local education solutions. The most potent curriculum development is now found at school and multi-academy trust level, with nationally 80% of multi-academy trusts having a local footprint (DfE, 2014). As Thomas Perry reminds us (see Chapter 4), the headline data about performance and outcomes masks individual personal and school successes. Glass ceilings are being broken across the city through individual endeavour, as Iqbal's journey attests.

Colin Diamond

Unrepresentative and ill-equipped education bureaucracy[1]

Karamat Iqbal

Background

It was in January 1971, fifty years ago, that I took a ride on the number 8 bus from our house in Nechells to the immigrant reception centre. In those days, this was the norm in Birmingham: when an immigrant child arrived in the city, they would be sent to one of two such centres for their schooling. Although it was already known that speaking more than one language was a good thing, bilingualism did not appear to count if you were an immigrant, so no one cared (and this still seems to be the case) that I knew Pahari, Urdu and bits of Farsi and Arabic. After learning sufficient English, at the start of the following academic year I transferred to Nechells Secondary School on Eliott Street; the building is now used as a primary school.

Upon arrival at my new school, I was sent to my classroom. The teacher was not there at the time. My memory of that occasion is not a pleasant one. A very tall White boy picked me up, banged me against the wall and said: 'We don't want any more f****** P****!'[2] He then put me down and turned to the rest of the class for recognition. The White children cheered him. The Pakistani children just watched. After three years there, I left with a couple of good CSEs and began work as a clerk in industry. Thankfully, I was given day release to attend Sutton Coldfield College of further education. Later, when I was employed by the council as a youth and community worker at the Muntz Street community school, I attended Matthew Boulton College. Thanks to these two colleges and the adult education evening classes I attended, after six years I was able to get on to a teacher training course at Westhill College, which was later incorporated into the University of Birmingham.

---

1   This chapter is derived from Karamat Iqbal, *Dear Birmingham: A Conversation with My Hometown* (N.p.: Xlibris, 2013) – an affectionate and authentic account of the British Pakistani community in Birmingham.
2   I have detailed this incident and others in my book *A Biography of the Word 'Paki'* (2017). The writing was triggered by a racist incident I experienced at the hands of my adviser colleagues.

Upon completing my Bachelor of Education, I joined the Birmingham Multicultural Support Service, which placed me at Golden Hillock School. Later, I moved to Wolverhampton, first as an education officer at the Race Equality Council and then as a deputy director of the Equal Rights and Opportunities Management Unit at Bilston Community College. This was followed by a return to Birmingham as a schools adviser at the Advisory and Support Service. It was during this period that I began researching the educational underachievement of White working-class children in the city – still the largest underachieving group in England. This led to doctoral research into the education of Pakistani boys – the second largest underachieving group.

The broad exclusion of Pakistani-Birmingham from power and opportunities, in spite of many well-intended initiatives, is likely to be worse now than it was then. According to the Race Disparity Audit (2017), the Pakistani community continues to be the most disadvantaged when compared with other ethnic groups:

> 'Pakistani ... people were the most likely of all ethnic groups to live in the most deprived neighbourhoods.' (p. 28)

> 'People in the Pakistani ... [ethnic] group ... received the lowest average hourly pay.' (p. 29)

> 'People in the most deprived neighbourhoods tend to be disadvantaged across multiple aspects of life. Pakistani ... people were overrepresented in the most deprived neighbourhoods in England: 31% or around 343,000 of the Pakistani population ... lived in the most deprived 10% of neighbourhoods in England.' (p. 33)

> 'Pakistani ... workers were more likely than workers in other ethnic groups to be concentrated in the three lowest-skilled occupation groups.' (p. 26)

More recently, it has been reported that the Pakistani community work in high-proximity occupations with a very high potential of automation and have been hard hit by furloughs and layoffs because of COVID-19 (Allas et al., 2020).

My most recent book (Iqbal, 2019) is based on my doctoral research, undertaken in three local state secondary schools. This showed that the

Pakistani community had a respect for education,[3] and that teachers were highly revered, referred to as roohani (spiritual) parents. Equally, the community valued their religion which makes some demands on the schools (Iqbal, 2021). John Ray, who had spent many years as a community governor in local schools, including at Golden Hillock School where he was the chair of governors, said to me: 'The continuing underperformance and alienation of British Pakistani boys is a vital matter for our whole society, going much beyond education and in urgent need of remedy.'

As to education standards, the Annual Education Performance Report: 2019 Examinations and Assessments by Birmingham City Council (2020, p. 77) stated that in Progress 8, 'Pakistani pupils make the least progress'. In Attainment 8, 'Pakistani pupils are below the overall national average' (p. 79).

Representative education bureaucracy

It is well known that a workforce that is ethnically representative results in a better service for minorities, who benefit from 'discretionary efforts' which are a product of the workers' social background. According to a report commissioned by the National Audit Office (Sivadasan et al., 2004), there is a link between workforce representation, service delivery and knowledge of the customer population. When organisations incorporate workers with lived experience, it can lead to increased levels of trust between clients and service providers, an enhanced client-centred perspective and higher quality service provision. As they are able to draw on their own lived experience, the minority staff in a school provide a bridge between the minority children, parents and wider community and the mainly White 'commuter professionals', who are, according to the Swann Report (1985, p. 604), 'often living well away from the catchment areas of their schools'. The presence of own-race workers is especially appreciated by the economically disadvantaged sections of the community.

Minority educators also act as role models for the children they are teaching. Mayor of London Sadiq Khan, in his mayoral victory speech, said:

> It was my head teacher Naz Bokhari [the first Muslim head teacher], an outstanding teacher and a role model for me and

---

3 Education was seen as multidimensional: talim (knowledge), tarbiyat (character) and tahzib (cultured).

thousands of other children at Ernest Bevin College, who encouraged me to go to university and aim to put something back into society. He made me realise that skin colour and background should never be a barrier to fulfilling your potential. (Bokhari, 2020)

According to the National Governance Association: 'Having a diverse governing board provides a connectedness between the school and its community, and ensures all stakeholders feel valued. It can increase the confidence of the community in the school because those making decisions understand the lives, context and aspirations of the community it serves.'[4]

Another key anniversary in 2021 was the publication of the report of the Birmingham Stephen Lawrence Commission, *Challenges to the Future* (2001). This was the city's response to Stephen's murder in 1993; such was the positive commitment to race equality in those days. Published twenty years ago, the report raised several issues, some of which are still waiting to be addressed. For example, it set employment targets for the city council. The target for the Pakistani community (6.9%) had still not been achieved in 2020 when the community was 5.19% of the council workforce. For the commission, in addition to having an ethnically representative workforce in schools, it was important for fair representation on governing bodies.

A little-discussed issue with reference to governance is language, which still needs to be tackled. In a report by Cox (2001), attention was drawn to the exclusion from the governing bodies of individuals not fluent in English. They experienced an atmosphere that tended to favour educated professionals who had a better grasp of the jargon associated with the educational process. Cox also pointed out that some people from ethnic minorities felt they were not taken seriously because their limited English often meant they were unable to put their point across effectively in meetings. As a result, many attended meetings infrequently before drifting away.

The following response from one of my parent doctoral interviewees sums up the problem. He was quite well educated. He explained to me that he had participated on school governing bodies at his children's schools but found that the English language was a barrier:

---

4   See https://www.nga.org.uk/News/Campaigns/Everyone-on-Board-increasing-diversity-in-school-g.aspx.

I frequently felt unable to participate in meetings. I could understand what was going on, but it was hard to contribute to the
discussion. What might take someone with English half an hour
would take me forty-five minutes. It was hard to find the right
words to express myself. I could not speak fluently.

When a situation of un-representation exists, the message being com-
municated to the excluded community is: you are not welcome; you
have nothing worthwhile to say; we will decide for you. Meanwhile, the
(public) servant continues to become the master. In his book about dem-
ocratic processes and decision-making in Birmingham, Newton (1976)
used Weber's thinking to ask: who controls the bureaucratic machinery?
Is it the technical specialists, the head teachers or the ordinary members
of the community whose money is used to pay for the public servants?
Weber (1994, p. 292) spoke of the 'dictatorship of the official'. Is that
what we have in our schools, multi-academy trusts and elsewhere?

The comparison is between a governor who might have left school with
few or no qualifications, dealing with an education leader who earns
many times as much and who has numerous qualifications. What is more,
within our diverse context, it is often a White dictatorship and a White
commuter bureaucracy at that. Very rarely are school leaders from within
the communities whose lives are affected by the decisions being made or
resources being allocated. In an interview with me, Tim Boyes, chief executive officer of BEP, spoke of arrogant, narrow-minded 'technicians sitting
now in some head teacher seats who know how to get good results but
have got a very limited sociological understanding of their school and its
locality and its communities'.

Ethnic monitoring

Ethnic monitoring is essential for addressing inequalities in representation. Previously, the local authority was the go-to place for such data,
but their powers and resources have been stripped back as a result of
the impact of the Academies Act 2010 which has fragmented the English
education system. That damage was compounded by a decade of austerity. Now, schools and trusts must be approached individually, and the
outcome can be unpredictable. Not all of them gather the data, report
on it or use it for developing strategies to address race inequality. The

data categories can also vary, making it difficult to compare organisations. Some schools have a very high number of employees who do not give their ethnicity. Most schools don't appear to collect ethnicity data for governors. It is worth pointing out here that when categories such as 'Muslim', 'Asian', 'ethnic minority' or 'BAME' are used they can hide the particular exclusion of certain communities, such as the Pakistanis.

I contacted selected schools in the city for ethnicity data on pupils, employees and governors via the Freedom of Information Act route. Overall, the responses revealed that the percentage of Pakistani pupils far exceeded the percentage of Pakistani staff. The picture on governor representation was a mixed one: some schools did not provide any data and those that did provided the data under a mixed set of ethnic categories. This is a problem that will need to be addressed across the city.

I asked whether schools operated any kind of positive action programmes to address under-representation. Most did not respond to this question. Those that did said the following:

- We don't have any positive action programmes to address any under-representation.

- We recruit in compliance with the safer recruitment procedure which covers equality/diversity.

- We have not considered it necessary to undertake any positive action programmes due to strong BAME representation within the workforce and governing body.

- We are an equal opportunities employer and welcome applications from all. Staff appointments are made according to the most suitable candidate for the role.

One city

In November 1997, the then parliamentary under-secretary for school standards, Estelle Morris, said that it was 'absolutely right that ethnic-minority children should be taught by teachers from their own communities' (Ghouri, 1997), but she added that all children would benefit from a diverse teaching force. A similar point was made by the Department for

Education and Skills in a report on mainly White schools whose pupil populations were served by an almost entirely White teaching staff (Cline et al., 2002). In their sample of fourteen schools there were only three minority-ethnic teachers. During the research, head teachers and other staff had argued that 'there would be many advantages to their school in having teachers from a wider range of cultural backgrounds on the staff' (p. 135). There are a few schools in Birmingham with a mainly White pupil body, but, equally, there are White teachers who would benefit from operating in a more diverse workforce. Not only would it help to improve the education that pupils receive, it would also enable staff and parents to experience first-hand the contribution that minorities can make.

In schools where teachers and pupils are of the same ethnicity, the education can be narrow and the children's lives very parochial. Such schools can twin with other schools of a different ethnicity in order to broaden the knowledge-base of their children and employees.

One secondary school on the edge of the city has 85% White pupils, a similar percentage of White teachers and 100% White governors. Such schools would benefit from a city twinning programme, which brings together monocultural ethnic majority and monocultural ethnic minority schools, so their children, teachers, governors and the wider community can learn from each other. In discussing this issue with me, one senior Birmingham educationalist stated: 'If parental choice is a way of our children avoiding difference and staying with our own social groups, how can we justify this? If we care for the poor, then surely we need to engineer ways of guaranteeing schools that are mixed in terms of class as well as ethnicity.'

In 2010, community cohesion was deprioritised in schools and removed from Ofsted inspection criteria. In my view, these moves had profoundly negative consequences because schools in the city needed to create new links – for example, through twinning programmes, by prioritising learning heritage languages such as Urdu (not only in schools with large numbers of Pakistani pupils) and breaking down barriers by teaching the history of migration into the city.

Case study: Birmingham Education Partnership

In Birmingham City Council's (2016) report *Changing Times: The Future of Education in Birmingham*, we are reminded that Birmingham has a rich and diverse ethnic, religious and cultural make-up; it has 187 different ethnic groups. In 2013, the city had the highest number of pupils (40%) with English as an additional language in England. Muslims are the largest pupil religious group and Pakistanis are close to becoming the largest pupil ethnic group.

According to its articles of association, BEP was set up for the advancement of education for the public benefit. In the furtherance of its work, it 'shall at all times actively promote and take into consideration the principles of equality of opportunity' (BEP, 2014, p. 5, s. 3.4). BEP's core funding comes from Birmingham City Council. Its 2018 school improvement contract required it to adopt an equalities policy that would comply with its statutory obligations under the Equality Act 2010 – that is, not to discriminate directly or indirectly with respect to recruitment, training and promotion.

I am unashamedly a practitioner of the 1980s world of equality legislation and policies. I learnt that where there are no policies to transparently guide an organisation, it is left to chance, common sense and the prejudices of its officers. I have advised many an organisation that in order to demonstrate organisational principles to all major stakeholders, the requirement is to consistently adhere to adopted policies. However, these policies will only be consistently effective if they are reviewed and updated when applicable and all staff members are correctly trained (Devon Voluntary Action, 2014, p. 1).

Over the past few years, I have maintained contact with BEP, in order to gather data on the ethnic diversity of their board and employees and examine its policies on equality. Previously, BEP had informed me that they did not possess such policies (as they were not a public body). Through the city council, I have now been supplied with their equal opportunities and dignity at work policy, which was approved by the board in July 2020. BEP had 10% Pakistani employees. Previously, they had 10% minority presence on the board. With the departure of Mushtaq Ahmed Khan in 2019, the board became 100% White, as was the senior leadership team at the time. I am reminded of an article by Jane Haynes (2020) with the headline: ' "Everyone is White" – Call for More Diversity in Top

Team at Birmingham City Council'. Such situations have been described as 'hideously white' (Greg Dyke referring to the BBC, quoted in Hill, 2001) or as 'snowy peaks' (Vasista, 2010).

Jane Haynes' article had resulted from a Freedom of Information request by Atif Ali – a product of the best of our education establishments (Somerville primary and Small Heath secondary schools, Wolverhampton and Birmingham universities). It is encouraging to see the younger generation raising its voice on issues of under-representation. Atif said: 'It is crucial, now more than ever, that people who look like me are around the table when decisions are made, that ultimately affect us.' He goes on to recommend what should be done about it: 'For long-term, the council should look at creating job opportunities at the local authority for those from under-represented background[s] with a view to nurturing them into leadership positions and onto the council Management Team' (Haynes, 2020).

Unrepresentative (and ill-equipped?)

I have been reflecting on the implications of unrepresentative education bureaucracy through reading and discussion with colleagues who have greater expertise and knowledge of multicultural education. One, a leadership consultant, after having had a look at the BEP website with its many White faces, responded: 'Given the student demographic that BEP and its senior leadership team is supposedly there to serve ... one must ask whether the present composition of BEP has the cultural competence to address systemic racism.'

A culturally competent bureaucracy is one which has the knowledge, skills and values to work effectively with diverse populations and to adapt institutional policies and professional practices to meet their unique needs. Such competence results in an ability to understand, communicate with and effectively interact with people across cultures. Culture in our context is often intertwined with religion. I recall a conversation with a senior and respected Birmingham educationalist who later moved on to a regional role. She told me she preferred the good old days when religion was kept quiet and in the background instead of how it is nowadays – that is, present in the school and the public square, forever making demands for accommodation.

Here, it is worth referring to a report on the Trojan Horse affair made by Dr Mashuq Ally (who was assistant director of equalities, community safety and cohesion) and Wyn Williams (programme lead, education services) at Birmingham City Council. According to their findings, which resulted from meeting with Muslim community representatives, much of what had been criticised by Ofsted was 'simply the schools responding to meet the needs of local Muslims' (Ally and Williams, 2014, p. 4). They state that 'schools should reflect the Muslim communities in which they are situated' (p. 5) and express the belief that accommodation can be made for religious sensitivities on social issues within the mainstream state sector. Furthermore, they say that 'religious conservatism should not be confused with extremism' (p. 9). To do so, and to respond to religion competently, requires a level of religious literacy.

Those on the receiving end of inspections have pointed out that Ofsted inspectors did not have a clue what they were looking for or at when they inspected the twenty-one schools in spring 2014. They were found to have the most rudimentary of training and literacy in Islam and Muslims before going in and looking for manifestations of Islamic extremism. Furthermore, they 'had an agenda that calls into question Ofsted's claim to be objective and professional in its appraisal of standards in schools serving predominantly Muslim pupils' (Richmond, 2014).

Upon my invitation, Robin Richardson also commented on Birmingham's position in relation to race equality. A Brummie by birth, Robin was the first director of the World Studies Project (1973–1979). He then became an adviser for multicultural education in local government (1979–1985) and the chief inspector for education in a London borough for the next five years, before taking up the role of director of the Runnymede Trust. Robin observed that his own experience of Birmingham in the 1980s and 1990s was that it was a beacon for the rest of the country with respect to race equality in education. He therefore found the apparently substantial and abject retreat from its earlier commitment deeply saddening.

So, what does 'good' race equality policy and practice look? An excellent example of this was provided by the National College for School Leadership (Dimmock et al., 2005). The report was based on five 'good leaders' of multi-ethnic schools. These leaders demanded that the values of their staff cohere with principles of social justice and equality, and that staff demonstrate a willingness to understand the cultures and background of their pupils and school community. They also attempted to recruit and retain staff with similar cultural and ethnic backgrounds to those existing in the school community.

There is plenty of research about the benefits of having minority teachers in schools.[5] The opposite is the case when they are absent: there are no minority role models, the school is deprived of their particular cultural expertise and understanding of racism, and the bridge that such teachers provide between the school and the minority community is missing. There is also a lack of advocacy for minority pupils and a stereotype threat. More broadly, it becomes difficult for schools to provide a culturally responsive pedagogy and to fully understand the pools of knowledge and cultural capital of minority children.

In the early days of post-war migration, White-only decision-making bodies were to be expected, but surely this has to be different now. The post-colonialism work of the thought-leader Gayatri Spivak (1988) is very relevant to our situation. She posed the question: 'Can the subaltern speak?' and answered that he or she could not and had to depend upon Westerners; only they could fulfil this role. The subalterns could not represent themselves and must be spoken for. The same message is given to Asian, Black and other minorities when mainly (or wholly) White boardrooms meet to make important decisions, to distribute power and resources. It must be time for such 'white spaces' (Anderson, 2015) – settings in which White people are overwhelmingly present and ethnic minorities are typically absent, not expected or marginalised when present – to become diverse, including in the upper echelons of power.

Every now and then we are reminded of the brutality of racism. Most recently, this was with the tragic death of George Floyd – a reminder in case we had forgotten Stephen Lawrence. Many decent White people in positions of responsibility come out and say how terrible racism is and they want it to be over. They are then reminded that the necessary change is dependent upon them. Systemic, structural and institutional racism implicates them because they are the ones running the show. According to Barnardo's, 'Talking about white privilege means looking at how our own actions maintain and support racist systems and structures – regardless of intent, and that's going to be uncomfortable' (Barnardo's, 2020).

---

5   See, for example, Howard (2010); Basit and Santoro (2012); Roch and Pitts (2012); and Kohli and Pizarro (2016). For a full list see Iqbal (2019).

Allyship is about members of the majority and powerful White group supporting the cause of the marginalised group members (Terry, 2020). This can involve providing listening support and empathising, which can be relatively easy. It is what any good colleague would do. However, some of this behaviour can be 'performative allyship' (Morris, 2020) – that is, being seen to be doing so. Often, such allegiance is professed by the ally in the hope of avoiding potential scrutiny. What is actually required of an ally – which can be more difficult – is providing visible advocacy with the aim of challenging the organisation or system on behalf of oppressed individuals and groups. Also, if you are prepared to share your White space and give up some of your power and privilege, then do not expend your energy on admiring the problem. Instead, do something about it, however little.

It is important to make clear that my vision is one of multiracial diversity – White, Asian, Black and other minorities – all together as equal partners and in all situations. So, alongside White staff we have a Sikh head teacher in a mainly Kashmiri school, Caribbean teachers with Asian children, Muslim staff in mainly White schools. I believe strongly in the idea that 'we teach who we are'. In other words, our teachers come to the classroom not just with content from the national curriculum but also their personal selves, their family and community identities, their ethnic histories and much more besides. We owe it to our children, all of them, to give them an opportunity to access the full diversity of such knowledge.

David Gillborn (2008) has argued that unless a policy is consciously designed to challenge race inequalities, it is likely to reinforce those inequalities and perpetuate a White hegemony. A similar point was made by Kenneth Newton (1976) that a 'neutral' policy means that discriminatory practices are given free rein. The days of colour-blind education and teacher employment are surely over.

Paul Miller (2016, p. 13) has developed a typology of institutions which provides a useful starting point:

■ Engaged – BAME staff at all levels of the hierarchy, including (senior) leadership roles.

■ Experimenting – small number of BAME staff in posts and a smaller number of BAME staff in leadership roles.

- Initiated – minimal compliance with equality duties and BAME staff recruitment is restricted, with only a few BAME staff in posts but no BAME staff in leadership roles.

- Uninitiated – no framework or plan in place to meet the legal duty of the organisation and no BAME staff in post.

Which type of organisation is yours?

As to teacher recruitment, there continues to be wholesale under-representation of Pakistanis in schools, colleges and the city council.

Given the White dominance in our education system, is institutional racism still with us? Institutional racism was defined in the Macpherson Report (1999, p. 49) as:

> The collective failure of an organisation to provide an appropriate and professional service to people because of their colour, culture, or ethnic origin. It can be seen or detected in processes, attitudes and behaviour which amount to discrimination through unwitting prejudice, ignorance, thoughtlessness and racist stereotyping which disadvantage minority ethnic people.

A city- and system-wide strategy would be required to address this problem. We need to follow good advice and learn from the past. In 1987, Birmingham City Council adopted a positive action strategy to ensure that 20% of new employees were from ethnic minorities. I made a similar case for positive action for Pakistanis in *Dear Birmingham* to tackle the structural and institutional racism they have experienced, and I would recommend the same approach now to address the particular under-representation of the community in the education workforce. The focus needs to be at all levels: on entry into teaching and support functions, on development from support staff into teaching and on promotion into leadership.

Racial discrimination, including anxieties about encountering racism in schools, can have an impact on the retention of minority trainee teachers. Fear of prejudice and stereotyping from colleagues, pupils and parents can deter people from entering the profession. If we wish the situation to be different then we have to effect positive change. If nothing is done, my prediction is that the representation gap between the pupil population and teachers and governors will become even wider and there is likely to be a continued lack of Pakistani education leaders. A similar positive action strategy is needed for under-representation in governance where the under-representation of Pakistanis has been a long-standing problem.

There is plenty of advice available going back to the 1970s when equality commissions were set up. In the context of education, we can turn to bodies such as the former National College for School Leadership. It has advised that adverts, job descriptions and person specifications are worded positively to attract people from under-represented groups – for example, 'we would like to particularly attract people from BME backgrounds because we are currently under-represented at this level' (NCSL, 2008, p. 28).

The college pointed out that positive action is not about 'giving some people more favourable treatment':

> Positive action initiatives are designed to enable employers to encourage people from certain groups who are under-represented in the workplace to apply for jobs and promotions. Some people may perceive that they might not 'fit in' to some [white] organisations because of their lifestyle or background; their past experiences of some organisations may have led them to think they would not be welcome as an employee. (NCSL, 2008, p. 33)

It provided the following case study, which could be adapted by multi-academy trusts and school partnerships:

> In order to address the under-representation of BME teachers, a local authority established a coalition of eight schools. This helped to pool their resources. One of the initiatives the coalition developed was a positive action training scheme for aspiring BME teachers. Each school identified or created several trainee teaching positions and advertised these trainee positions in the local media, including the local BME media. ...
>
> The outcome: in the first year, 15 trainees were recruited and put onto appropriate training and professional development courses. In its second year the coalition is looking to appoint up to 25 trainees. (NCSL, 2008, p. 35)

I and other equality practitioners have advised against the use of the word-of-mouth recruitment method because it discriminates against ethnic minorities. Sadly, leaders continue to approach their friends about a job or a seat on the board. Maybe it would help to equalise the situation if the same method was used to recruit under-represented minorities. This has the support of the National Governance Association (2020); they call it the 'tap on the shoulder' method. When Estelle Morris was minister for school standards, schools were recommended to involve Community Learning Champions (DfEE, 1999) as a part of the 'community in the school, the school in the community' strategy. There are such people in most communities who could play a role in education governance.

As for Pakistani children, for many years we have seen their proportion in the city schools increase: from 16.7% (1995) to 18.9% (2005) and 24.5% (2011). We could have done better in raising their education standards and recruiting Pakistani teachers, especially in senior roles.

What of the future? What education standards do we wish to see, especially amongst our disadvantaged communities? Here it is worth quoting from the BEP Annual Report 2017/18 on the Raising Attainment of Disadvantaged Youngsters project. According to the rationale for the project, the attainment gap between disadvantaged young people and their non-disadvantaged peers widens from primary school into secondary and increases over time, through to university and beyond: 'When targets are set for students in Year 7, they are based on their attainment at KS2. However, if they have already underachieved at KS2 underachievement is perpetuated, which makes it increasingly difficult to close the gap; in fact the gap widens' (BEP, 2018, p. 6).

Conclusion

We learn from peace studies that conflict usually involves grievances that have festered for long periods. Then some (but not all) come to the surface. We only have to consider the social disturbances in 2011. The shooting of Mark Duggan by police in London was the trigger that brought numerous grievances to the surface across the country, including Birmingham. This also happened with the Trojan Horse affair. Its preconditions, according to Tim Boyes' 2010 presentation to the Department for Education, included school–community disconnect, weak school leadership and low standards. Later, he said that the affair had further damaged trust between schools and the communities they served (see Iqbal, 2019).

What preconditions are in place now? Minority communities, espe- cially the Pakistanis, continue to be excluded from the local education bureaucracy. The problem has been made worse by Trojan Horse, as a consequence of which many in the community do not wish to come forward for fear of being seen as troublemakers. The minority who are willing find the mainly White environment at meetings, especially at some multi-academy trust boards, hostile. They are treated with sus- picion, especially if they ask awkward questions about inequalities and educational standards. I have some personal experience of this.

How do those who are excluded and aggrieved feel? How let down are the parents of large numbers of children who leave school without the benchmark qualifications? How will such grievances be expressed, and what will be the trigger?

Sadly, we lost Maurice Irfan Coles recently. He had been a senior adviser for multicultural education in the Birmingham education department, when such posts existed. I refer here to two contributions from him. First, he pointed out that the Birmingham approach to education, which had a multicultural/anti-racist/equal opportunity perspective in all its schools, had three aims:

1   To be aware of and to counter racism.

2   To be aware of and to provide for the particular needs of pupils, having regard for their ethnic, cultural, historical, linguistic and religious backgrounds.

3   To prepare all pupils for life in our multicultural society. (Coles, 1997)

Second, in 2013, he brought together several education experts with long-standing experience of working in Birmingham. The list included Professor Mick Waters, Dr John Lloyd, Gilroy Brown, Nargis Rashid and the Reverend Jackie Hughes, diocesan director of education in Birmingham. Between them they agreed that:

> an education service must have an overarching teleological vision, a sense of what an educated person should look like after ... years of compulsory schooling. This vision must be translated into a series of clear and explicit values which underpin the notion of an educated person. These values in turn are predicated upon processes that demand that young people, their parents and their

communities must be at the heart of any educational service. (Coles, 2013)

In her opening speech at the National Association for Language Development in the Curriculum: Multilingual Britain conference in 2020, Victoria Murphy, the chair of the organisation, explained the current state of affairs in national education. She said that 'the multilingual and multicultural nature of English schools is frequently neglected from important government documents'.[6] She added that there is a very strong anti-multilingual, anti-multi-ethnic and anti-multicultural rhetoric in public discourse.

In spite of the hostile national context, education locally has the potential to become central to our city's future, through the values it imparts to the young people and the understanding and cohesion it generates amongst diverse communities.

References

Allas, Tera; Canal, Marc; Hunt, Vivian; and Olanrewaju, Tunde (2020) Problems Amid Progress: Improving Lives and Livelihoods for Ethnic Minorities in the United Kingdom, *McKinsey & Company* (15 October). Available at: https://www.mckinsey.com/industries/public-and-social-sector/our-insights/problems-amid-progress-improving-lives-and-livelihoods-for-ethnic-minorities-in-the-united-kingdom.

Ally, Mashuq and Williams, Wyn (2014) Trojan Horse Joint Scrutiny Board [presentation] (9 September). Available at: http://moseleyschoolparentscommunityassociation.yolasite.com/resources/Secular%20State%20School%20System%20-%20Mashuq%20Ally.pdf.

Anderson, Elijah (2015) The White Space, *Sociology of Race and Ethnicity,* 1(1): 10–21.

Asian Youth Culture (2021) 1970s–90s Oral Histories: Karamat Iqbal, *Asian Youth Culture.* Available at: https://asianyouthculture.co.uk/oral-histories/karamat-iqbal.

Barnardo's (2020) White Privilege – A Guide for Parents (30 October). Available at: https://www.barnardos.org.uk/blog/white-privilege-guide-for-parents.

Basit, Tehmina and Santoro, Ninetta (2012) Playing the Role of 'Cultural Expert': Teachers of Ethnic Difference in Britain and Australia, *Oxford Review of Education,* 37(1): 37–52.

Birmingham Education Partnership (BEP) (2014) Articles of Association. Adopted by Special Resolution on 27 November 2014. Available at: https://find-and-update.company-information.service.gov.uk/company/08945454/filing-history/QTNMTE1ORVhhZGIxemtjeA/document?format=pdf&download=0.

---

6   Karamat Iqbal (@ForwardPartners), Twitter post (21 November 2020, 12.30pm). Available at: https://twitter.com/forwardpartners/status/1330126390562344960?s=21.

Birmingham Education Partnership (BEP) (2018) *Annual Report 2017/18*. Available at: https://www.bep.education/wp-content/uploads/2018/06/BEP-ANNUAL-REPORT-2017-18-FINAL.pdf.

Berglund, Jenny (ed.) with Iqbal, Karamat (2018) *Creating Coherence in Education for British Muslim Pupils: European Perspectives on Islamic Education and Public Schooling* [ebook]. Sheffield: Equinox.

Birmingham City Council (2016) *Changing Times: The Future of Education in Birmingham* (September). Available at: https://www.birmingham.gov.uk/downloads/file/16860/ebd38_bcc_changing_times_report_sep_2016.

Birmingham City Council (2020) *Annual Education Performance Report: 2019 Examinations and Assessments* (March). Available at: https://www.birmingham.gov.uk/downloads/file/16429/annual_education_performance_report_2019.

Birmingham Stephen Lawrence Commission (2001) *Challenges for the Future – Race Equality in Birmingham: Report of the Inquiry Commission*. Birmingham: Birmingham City Council.

Bokhari, Harris (2020) Why It's Vital That the First BAME Heads Are Recognised, *TES* (9 October). Available at: https://www.tes.com/news/why-its-vital-first-bame-heads-are-recognised.

Cline, Tony; de Abreu, Guida; Fihosy, Cornelius; Gray, Hilary; Lambert, Hannah; and Neale, Jo (2002) *Minority Ethnic Pupils in Mainly White Schools*. London: Department for Education and Skills. Available at: https://dera.ioe.ac.uk/4601/1/RR365.pdf.

Coles, Maurice I. (1997) Race Equality and School Improvement: Some Aspects of the Birmingham Experience, *Multicultural Teaching*, 15(2): 12–14.

Coles, Maurice I. (2013) Reform of the National Curriculum in England: Consultation Response (22 April).

Cox, G. (2001) *The Causes of Minority Ethnic Underrepresentation As School Governors in East Birmingham*. Birmingham: East Birmingham Plus Parents Association.

Department for Education (DfE) (2014) *Transparency Data: Open Academies, Free Schools, Studio Schools and UTCs in Development*. Available at: https://www.gov.uk/government/publications/open-academies-and-academy-projects-in-development.

Department for Education and Employment (DfEE) (1999) *Schools Plus: Building Learning Communities. Improving the Educational Chances of Children and Young People from Disadvantaged Areas*. Available at: https://dera.ioe.ac.uk/5589/7/building%20learning%20communities_Redacted.pdf.

Devon Voluntary Action (2014) Policies Your Organisation Should Have: A Guide for Community and Voluntary Organisations. Available at: http://www.devonva.org/UserFiles/File/We_Want_Help/Info_and_Guidance/Policies_Full_Guide.pdf.

Dimmock, Clive; Stevenson, Howard; Bignold, Brenda; and Shah, Saeeda (2005) *Effective Leadership in Multi-Ethnic Schools: School Community Perspectives and Their Leadership Implications. Project Report*. Nottingham: National College of School Leadership.

Ghouri, Nadine (1997) Wanted: The Best Minority Teachers, *Times Educational Supplement* (7 November).

Gillborn, David (2008) *Racism and Education Coincidence or Conspiracy?* Abingdon and New York: Routledge.

Haynes, Jane (2020) 'Everyone is White' – Call for More Diversity in Top Team at Birmingham City Council, *Birmingham Mail* (11 June). Available at: https://www.birminghammail.co.uk/news/midlands-news/everyone-white-call-more-diversity-18389143.

Hill, Amelia (2001) Dyke: BBC is Hideously White, *The Observer* (7 January). Available at: https://www.theguardian.com/media/2001/jan/07/uknews.theobserver1.

Howard, Jocelyn (2010) The Value of Ethnic Diversity in the Teaching Profession: A New Zealand Case Study, *International Journal of Education*, 2(1): 1–22.

Iqbal, Karamat (2013) *Dear Birmingham: A Conversation with My Hometown*. N.p.: Xlibris.

Iqbal, Karamat (2019) *British Pakistani Boys, Education and the Role of Religion: In the Land of the Trojan Horse*. Abingdon and New York: Routledge.

Iqbal, Karamat (2021). My Religion is Important in My Life, *Prism Journal*, 3(2): 80–83. Available at: https://openjournals.ljmu.ac.uk/index.php/prism/article/view/432/377.

Kohli, Rita and Pizarro, Marcos (2016) Fighting to Educate Our Own: Teachers of Color, Relational Accountability, and the Struggle for Social Justice, *Equity & Excellence in Education*, 49(1): 72–84.

Macpherson, William (1999) *The Stephen Lawrence Inquiry*. Available at: https://assets.publishing.service.gov.uk/government/uploads/system/uploads/attachment_data/file/277111/4262.pdf.

Major, Lee Elliot and Machin, Stephen (2020) *What Do We Know and What Should We Do About Social Mobility?* London: SAGE Publications.

Miller, Paul (2016) 'White Sanction', Institutional, Group and Individual Interaction in the Promotion and Progression of Black and Minority Ethnic Academics and Teachers in England, *Power and Education*, 8(3): 205–221.

Miller, Paul and Callender, Christine (2019) Concluding Remarks. Agenda-Setting Research: Theory, Practice. In Paul Miller and Christine Callender (eds), *Race, Education and Educational Leadership in England: An Integrated Analysis*. London: Bloomsbury, pp. 287–290.

Morris, Carmen (2020) Performative Allyship: What Are the Signs and Why Leaders Get Exposed, *Forbes* (26 November). Available at: https://www.forbes.com/sites/carmenmorris/2020/11/26/performative-allyship-what-are-the-signs-and-why-leaders-get-exposed/?sh=5637eb0e22ec.

National College for School Leadership (NCSL) (2008) *A Guide to Achieving Equality and Diversity in School and Children's Centre Leadership*, compiled Lutfur Ali. Available at: https://dera.ioe.ac.uk/2058/1/download%3fid=17099&filename=achieving-equality-and-diversity.pdf.

National Governance Association (2020) *The Right People Around the Table: A Guide to Recruiting and Retaining School Governors and Trustees*, 3rd edn. Available at: https://www.nga.org.uk/Knowledge-Centre/

Governance-structure-roles-and-responsibilities/Roles-and-responsibilities/
Composition/The-right-people-around-the-table-a-guide-to-recru.aspx [members-only content].

Newton, Kenneth (1976) *Second City Politics*. London: Clarendon Press.

Race Disparity Audit (2017) *Summary Findings from the Ethnicity Facts and Figures Website* (October, rev. March 2018). London: Cabinet Office. Available at: https://assets.publishing.service.gov.uk/government/uploads/system/uploads/attachment_data/file/686071/Revised_RDA_report_March_2018.pdf.

Richmond, Robin (2014) Ofsted Credibility at Stake Over 'Trojan Horse' Schools Inquiry, *The Guardian* (3 June). Available at: https://www.theguardian.com/education/2014/jun/03/ofsted-credibility-at-stake-trojan-horse.

Roch, Christine and Pitts, David (2012) Differing Effects of Representative Bureaucracy in Charter Schools and Traditional Public Schools, *American Review of Public Administration*, 42(3): 282–302.

Rollock, Nicola and Gillborn, David (2011) Critical Race Theory (CRT), *British Educational Research Association* online resource. Available at: https://www.bera.ac.uk/publication/critical-race-theory-crt.

Sivadasan, Suja; Shergold, Miriam; Law, Sally A.; Kahan, James P.; and Thompson, Robert (2004) *Delivering Public Services to a Diverse Society*. London: HMSO.

Spivak, Gayatri C. (1988) *Can the Subaltern Speak?* Basingstoke: Macmillan.

Swann, Michael (1985) *Education for All: Report of the Committee of Enquiry into the Education of Children from Ethnic Minority Groups* [Swann Report]. Available at: http://www.educationengland.org.uk/documents/swann/swann1985.html.

Tackey, Nii Djan; Casebourne, Jo; Aston, Jane; Ritchie, Helen; Sinclair, Alice; Tyers, Claire et al. (2006) *Barriers to Employment for Pakistanis and Bangladeshis in Britain and Constraints*. Department for Work and Pensions Research Report No. 360. Available at: https://webarchive.nationalarchives.gov.uk/ukgwa/20130125093835/http://research.dwp.gov.uk/asd/asd5/report_abstracts/rr_abstracts/rra_360.asp.

Terry, Paul (2020) Allyship, Antiracism and the Strength of Weak Ties: A Barber, a Professor and an Entrepreneur Walk into a Room, *American Journal of Health Promotion*, 35(2): 157–162. Available at: https://doi.org/10.1177/0890117120982201.

Vasista, Veena (2010) *'Snowy Peaks': Ethnic Diversity at the Top*. London: Runnymede. Available at: http://www.runnymedetrust.org/uploads/publications/pdfs/SnowyPeaks-2010.pdf.

Weber, Max (1994) *Weber: Political Writings (Cambridge Texts in the History of Political Thought)*, ed. Peter Lassman and Ronald Speirs. Cambridge: Cambridge University Press.

Chapter 4

The educational achievement of Birmingham's children, 2002–2018

Thomas Perry

Introduction

For many years there had been concerns about the educational performance of Muslim pupils in Birmingham's schools. Karamat Iqbal
(2013) devoted a chapter in his book *Dear Birmingham* to educational
failure, backed up by the poor outcomes for Pakistani and Bangladeshi
pupils attaining good GCSEs between 2006 and 2011. The largest group
of Muslim pupils came from the British Pakistani community. Many
approaches were taken by Birmingham City Council to tackle chronically
low educational progress and outcomes, both directly by working with
schools and indirectly through race equality and community cohesion initiatives (Coles, 2008).

In 2007, the Muslim Council of Britain launched its publication, *Towards
Greater Understanding: Meeting the Needs of Muslim Pupils in State
Schools*. At the time, Tahir Alam was chair of its education committee and
Birmingham's voice was rightly heard at the table as it had 'the world's
biggest expatriate Kashmiri population' (Muslim Council of Britain, 2007,
p. 13). Sir Tim Brighouse, by that time chief adviser for London schools,
attended the launch. In 2008, Maurice Irfan Coles, a former staff inspector specialising in anti-racism for Birmingham City Council, published his
Every Muslim Child Matters with the aim of mapping the issues encountered by young Muslims against the new Every Child Matters landscape.

So, what was happening to this generation of predominantly British
Pakistani children at school? How were they faring compared with other
groups in the city and set against the national picture in England? Were
the authors of *Towards Greater Understanding* correct in their view that
improving the education and opportunities for Muslim pupils was linked
with 'a belief that the children can only be served by Muslim leaders
and teachers' (Clarke, 2014, p. 123) and an approach that is driven by
Muslim rather than ethnic identity? We know that in Birmingham these

perspectives were a key ingredient in the simmering dissatisfaction with educational outcomes that warped into Trojan Horse behaviours, with ultimately negative consequences.

Perry's chapter provides a unique perspective. He has analysed National Pupil Database (NPD) data from the Department for Education across the years 2002–2018, so we have a longitudinal picture of pupil performance from those who started Key Stage 1 in 2002 through to those who were in Key Stage 5 in 2018 – the Trojan Horse years. The NPD data is analysed through the lenses of the school population's ethnicity, gender and socio-economic composition.

We can see that the biggest single influence on academic progress is socio-economic status. In plain English, those pupils who come from low-income households are more likely to attain poorly, with the largest impact evident at Key Stage 1, which lessens by Key Stage 4. Schools are making that difference. The picture in relation to ethnicity is more complicated as there is significant variation between groups. Figure 4.5 is key to our understanding: the Pakistani pupils, overwhelmingly the focus of Trojan activities, start from a low baseline and gradually improve through the key stages, although slipping back slightly in Key Stage 5.

The Birmingham data broadly matches the national picture and verifies the longstanding concerns about this large cohort in the city and elsewhere in England. The contrast with other South Asian groups is powerful, with Bangladeshi pupils making strong progress from a low baseline and Indian pupils displaying strong performance across the key stages. Most worryingly, Black Caribbean pupils start behind and stay behind in this cohort, and this must be of concern for education leaders and policy-makers.

When ethnicity, gender and socio-economic status are combined, we can conclude that boys from disadvantaged households, regardless of ethnicity, are most likely to have poor outcomes. These boys come from all ethnicities and faith communities and constitute many amongst the 'forgotten third' (EPI, 2019) – those pupils who do not achieve standard passes at English and maths. Their characteristics include social disadvantage, English as an additional language, special educational needs and ethnicity. Looking deeper, there is a broad range of variables underpinning GCSE performance including household income, family composition, parental employment status, engagement and background.

To unleash the potential of boys and girls from such backgrounds requires a multifaceted approach that includes policy areas beyond the remit of the education sector. We know that family influence far outweighs that of schools in determining social mobility. The 'dark age' of declining absolute social mobility since 2008, with less economic growth and more societal inequality, has made it an uphill struggle (Major and Machin, 2020).

As Perry points out, we must remember that the biggest differences in performance are found within rather than between groups, and 'There are plentiful stories of both success and underachievement in every single community and social group.' The education leadership journeys captured in Part II of the book illustrate how schools can defy gravity with their outcomes – none more so than those in the Star Academies trust led by Sir Mufti Hamid Patel. For our purposes here, a community-serving, outward-looking educational philosophy allied to rigorous teaching and learning shows exactly what can be achieved with the predominantly Muslim pupils who attend these schools.

Colin Diamond

The educational achievement of Birmingham's children, 2002–2018

Thomas Perry

Understanding context through data

Birmingham is a shining example of a vibrant, multicultural city. Children growing up in Birmingham encounter and mix within and across diverse communities. We have known for some time that educational outcomes are significantly patterned by socio-economic, community and pupil characteristics. These shape rather than determine opportunities and educational careers for children and young people. Nonetheless, decades of research have documented enduring and significant relationships between pupils' demographic and socio-economic characteristics and educational outcomes (Mortimore et al., 1994; Perry, 2016; Leckie and Goldstein, 2019).

Our accountability system is still yet to acknowledge what educators have always known and the data clearly shows that the individual and social experiences, contexts and circumstances of children and young people matter. There is a world beyond the school gates, which impacts on pupils' outcomes, influences the school culture and, arguably, should be reflected in the curriculum and ethos of schools. This is not to say that schools cannot challenge as well as stretch the educational boundaries of their communities, but simply that the key to understanding schools is to see that they are situated in a context. Or, to coin a phrase, no school is an island, entire of itself (Falk, 2018). Neither is a multi-academy trust a self-sufficient archipelago or peninsula – if that is not stretching the metaphor too far.

The importance of context – and the challenge and support in both directions which characterises a healthy school–community relationship – is examined throughout this book. The contribution of this chapter is to offer a 'helicopter view' of academic attainment by ethnicity and other pupil characteristics. It presents data on how the associations between them have changed through the last decade across the city of Birmingham as compared to the national picture.

I present analysis of the National Pupil Database for eight consecutive school cohorts of pupils, with data spanning sixteen years and containing the educational records of over four million children and young people. These data allow us to examine annual cross-sections, but also to follow entire cohorts across their education careers and examine whether these have any tendency to play out differently according to their personal and background characteristics. The latest research along these lines is from Parsons and Thompson (2017) on which this analysis aims to build.

Before proceeding, I must provide not one but two important 'health warnings'. The first concerns what can be concluded from population statistics. Readers may well be aware of the so-called ecological fallacy. This is where one erroneously infers something about individuals from the average characteristics of their group or context. In this case, assuming that average educational outcomes for populations and sub-populations tell us something about any individual. In fact, what the data unequivocally show is that most of the variation we see is within rather than across groups. There are plentiful stories of both success and underachievement in every single community and social group. Throughout this chapter, I will be carefully choosing my language to stress that the results are a big but crude picture of averages and their relative contours. These might lead us to larger structural, systematic questions, but they will tell us very little about individuals.

The second important health warning concerns the distinction between description and explanation. Drawing causal conclusions from correlational data is famously fraught and ill-advised. These data provide far more questions than answers. The appropriate response to seeing that one particular group has higher or lower performance is to ask why. This chapter has neither the space nor the data to explore the myriad and complex causal factors that underlie the patterns in the data that can be observed, and I advise against seeing these data as evidence towards any particular or preferred explanation.

With that said, I hold that the following big picture provided by the data is informative. It helps us to see the overall patterns of education in Birmingham and how they are changing, reminds us that school context matters and identifies starting points for further investigation.

Methods and data

Numerous years of research methods training compel me to provide a short section describing the data and methods employed for this analysis, and several technical notes about how the data were wrangled into a state fit for presentation. If you are eager to get to the results, and would prefer to avoid this detail, feel free to skip to the next section.

The data come from the National Pupil Database coupled with the annual school census, which provide data for pupil demographic characteristics and academic results which can be linked across pupils' school careers. Table 4.1 gives an overview of the cohorts for which key stage (KS) performance data were available and the years in which the cohorts reached their end-of-key-stage assessments.

Table 4.1. Data available by cohort and year of key stage examination

Cohort	KS1	KS2	KS3	KS4	KS5
C1	2002	2006	2009	2011	2013
C2	2003	2007	2010	2012	2014
C3	2004	2008	2011	2013	2015
C4	2005	2009	2012	2014	2016
C5	2006	2010	2013	2015	2017
C6	2007	2011	–	2016	2018
C7	2008	2012	–	2017	–
C8	2009	2013	–	2018	–

Table 4.2 details the performance measures available for these cohorts at each of the key stages. There have been some changes in the measures across this period, particularly at Key Stage 2, where we have moved from examination-based scores to teacher assessment in science (C5 onwards) and in English (C8). I used teacher assessments where tests were not available. For Key Stage 1 and 2 English measures I used either the official measure or took the average of both reading and writing scores, as available. The English Baccalaureate (EBacc) measures have remained

fairly consistent, notwithstanding the shift from the Best 8 measure to Attainment 8 (from C6) and changes in the underlying score tariffs and changing list of approved qualifications within and across the periods these measures were used.

Table 4.2. Attainment measures available by cohort

Cohort	KS1	KS2	KS3	KS4	KS5
C1	Maths	Maths (fg)	Maths (ta)	Best 8 score[*]	Total Key Stage 5 point score
C2	Science	English (fg)	English (ta)	EBacc Maths	
C3	Reading	Science (fg)	Science (ta)	EBacc English	
	Writing				
C4				EBacc Science	
C5		Maths (fg)		EBacc Humanities	
		English (fg)			
		Science (ta)		EBacc Languages	
C6				Attainment 8	
C7				EBacc Maths	
C8		Maths (fg)		EBacc English	
		Reading (fg)		EBacc Science	
		English (ta)		EBacc Humanities	
		Science (ta)		EBacc Languages	
fg = fine-graded, ta = teacher assessed					
[*] Overall score across the best eight GCSE/equivalent examinations, including an English and maths score bonus.					

The approach taken to making comparisons across all data, in line with Parsons and Thompson (2017) and elsewhere, was to standardise all attainment results within each cohort for each key stage, putting them on a scale with mean zero and standard deviation of 1. This created measures which were approximately normally distributed, centred on zero and spanned approximately three points above and below. The standardised scale used is illustrated in Figure 4.1.

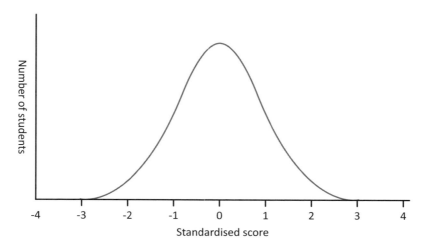

Figure 4.1. Standardised scores

Putting these different measures on a common scale disguises some of the variation in score distribution, granularity, recording and quality of the data. It is likely therefore that some of the observed movement in the outcome data is a result of measurement error and assessment changes rather than genuine changes in absolute or relative performance. The other issue encountered is that extracts in the National Pupil Database contain a considerable amount of missing data (Gorard, 2010). Here, the free school meals (FSM) status and ethnicity codes were missing in many cases. I report the number of observations for each analysis. The population figures are in line with those provided in the national statistics (DfE, 2018); however, I cannot rule out the possibility that these missing data will have influenced the results.

Finally, there was the issue that the data extracts included all exam entries in any given calendar year. As a result, there were numerous instances, particularly at Key Stage 4, of pupils appearing across several records. The focus here, however, was on the performance of cohorts rather than all pupils taking an examination at a given key stage in a given calendar year, so the analysis focused in on just pupils' results from the identified cohorts in their key stage examination years. In most instances, the school year group of pupils was recorded, and in the remaining cases, pupil birth months and years were used to identify specific cohorts for analysis and identify the record containing their overall key stage results.

Birmingham's ethnic and socio-economic composition

Our starting point is to look at the make-up of the Birmingham school population compared to the national population for the cohorts in focus (see Table 4.1). Table 4.3 provides an overview of ethnicity, gender, English language status and FSM status (a measure of disadvantage) for eight focus cohorts who started reception from the 2001/2002 to the 2009/2010 academic years. These figures show higher than national average rates of disadvantage (as measured by FSM status), the above average proportion of pupils with English as an additional language (EAL), and the ethnic diversity of the city and its sizable groups of pupils with Asian ethnic backgrounds relative to England overall, notably of Pakistani heritage.

Table 4.3. Population descriptive statistics (all cohorts): Birmingham and national

	All other areas of England		Birmingham	
Ethnic group	n	%	n	%
Asian – Bangladeshi	37,492	1.6%	2,733	5.5%
Asian – Indian	73,996	3.2%	3,450	6.9%
Asian – Other	44,457	1.9%	707	1.4%
Asian – Pakistani	80,125	3.5%	10,948	21.9%
Black – African	82,712	3.6%	1,770	3.5%
Black – Caribbean	28,905	1.2%	2,183	4.4%
Black – Other	14,882	0.6%	464	0.9%
Chinese	12,474	0.5%	174	0.3%
Mixed – Other	39,263	1.7%	1,229	2.5%
Mixed – White and Asian	24,133	1.0%	667	1.3%

	All other areas of England		Birmingham	
Ethnic group	n	%	n	%
Mixed – White and Black African	11,920	0.5%	149	0.3%
Mixed – White and Black Caribbean	27,311	1.2%	1,518	3.0%
White – British	1,647,175	71.2%	20,592	41.2%
White – Irish	8,913	0.4%	446	0.9%
White – Irish/ Gypsy/Roma Traveller	3,306	0.1%	13	0.0%
White – Other	107,132	4.6%	725	1.5%
Other ethnic group	38,621	1.7%	1,205	2.4%
Information not obtained/ refused	31,862	1.4%	957	1.9%
Other characteristics	n	%	n	%
Free school meals status	367,855	15.1%	17,087	30.7%
English as an additional language	507,806	14.6%	24,609	32.0%
Female	2,082,305	50.2%	43,047	50.0%

Source: ONS.
Complete cases by variable: ethnicity data (n = 2,364,609),
FSM (n = 2,487,074), EAL (n = 3,552,961), gender (n = 4,237,244).

Birmingham attainment relative to national attainment

The first set of results compare Birmingham's performance to national levels. The first five charts in Figure 4.2, reading top left to bottom right, show the gap in performance between the eight focus Birmingham cohorts and the national results, cohort by cohort. The final graph shows the average total gap at each key stage for all cohorts. Note that due to a change in national assessment policy, Key Stage 3 data were only available for the first five cohorts; therefore, the Key Stage 3 average figure excludes later cohorts.

Taken together, these results suggest that there was a moderate gap at Key Stage 1 for all cohorts which closed by Key Stage 4 for later cohorts (3–8) and even earlier, at Key Stage 2, for the final cohorts (6–8). There appears to have been some improvement in relative scores at both Key Stage 2 (2006–2013) and Key Stage 4 (2011–2014) over their respective periods, with the latter plateauing from 2014. Overall, these results suggest that Birmingham pupils tend to perform below national averages, but that this is not immutable and shifts with changes in assessment design, population characteristics and schooling quality.

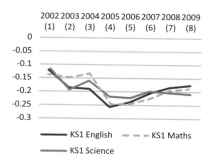

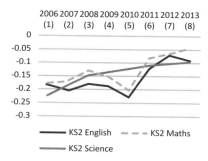

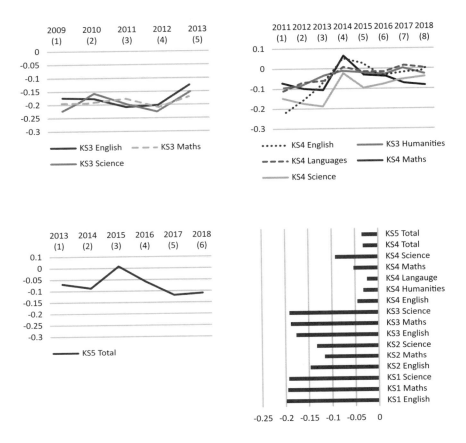

Figure 4.2. Birmingham to national performance gap by cohort (1–8),
Key Stage (1–5) and subject area
KS1 (n = 3,536,549), KS2 (n = 3,499,525), KS3 (n = 2,023,256),
KS4 (n = 3,801,215), KS5 (n = 2,261,577)
Source: ONS.

Birmingham and national attainment
by pupil characteristics

The next set of results examine how pupil background characteristics are related to educational performance and whether these associations differ for Birmingham and the rest of the country. Figures 4.3 and 4.4 show that, compared to all other pupils in these cohorts, there is a large performance gap between pupils on FSM and a smaller gap for pupils with EAL and for boys. The EAL gap is clearly narrowing as pupils progress across the key stages. Putting this in the wider context, the most recent national data show that EAL pupils who joined the English system in Key Stage 1 are outperforming pupils with English as their first language both in attainment and progress terms (Allen-Kinross, 2019; Leckie and Goldstein, 2019; DfE, 2020). There is a smaller but still apparent narrowing of the FSM gap through the key stages, for the country in general and particularly for Birmingham children. Finally, it can be seen that the gap for males is more patterned by subjects, with boys performing worse in Key Stage 1 and Key Stage 2 English, but slightly better or roughly in line with girls in maths across the key stages.

There are several areas in which Birmingham and national results differ: first, the large EAL bonus for Key Stage 4 (EBacc) languages evident nationally is very small in Birmingham; second, the FSM gap is slightly smaller at Key Stage 2 and Key Stage 4 in Birmingham, despite being larger at Key Stage 1; third, boys in Key Stage 1 and Key Stage 2 in Birmingham are considerably behind their national counterparts, with a gap still evident but narrower at Key Stage 4.

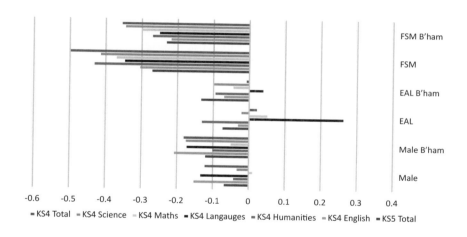

Figure 4.3. Birmingham and national attainment by pupil characteristics, Key Stage 4
Source: ONS.

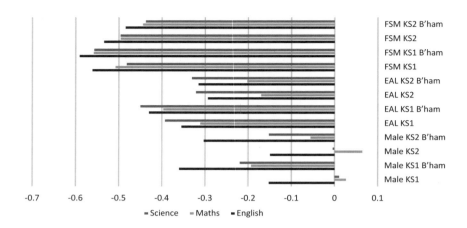

Figure 4.4. Birmingham and national attainment by pupil characteristics, Key Stage 1–2
Source: ONS.

Academic attainment by ethnicity in Birmingham

The next set of results, shown in Figure 4.5, examine patterns of average performance across the key stages for the largest six ethnic groups in Birmingham (see Table 4.3) and whether these differ between Birmingham pupils and pupils nationally.

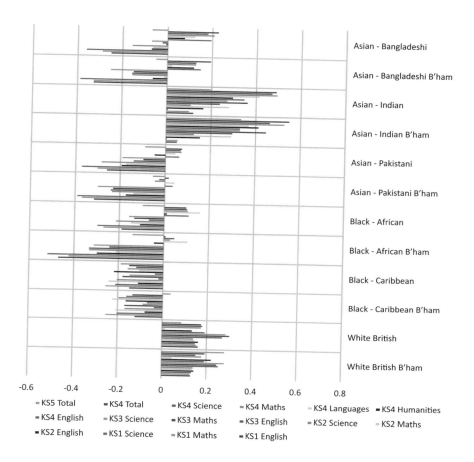

Figure 4.5. Birmingham and national attainment by pupil characteristics, Key Stage 1-5
Source: ONS.

What is perhaps striking about these results is the extent to which there are distinct 'profiles' of average performance across the key stages by group, and that these profiles are so similar between Birmingham pupils and pupils nationally. The clearest difference with the national picture for Birmingham pupils is for Black African pupils in Birmingham, who — whilst they share a similar profile shape – are around 0.1–0.2 below Black African pupils elsewhere throughout their school careers. When this average result was broken down by cohort (data tables not shown), it was clear that this gap was more pronounced in earlier cohorts (1–4) but is still evident in later ones, with the magnitude of the gap decreasing over time. Whilst clearly there is more to do to close the gap, this direction of travel does provide some consolation for the concerning overall average, and encouragement that the gap can be closed.

It is noticeable that across ethnic groups, the profiles differ in their shape. Some groups (White British and Black Caribbean) have a largely consistent difference through the key stages. For pupils of Bangladeshi, Indian, Pakistani and Black African backgrounds – with the exception of Key Stage 5 – there is a relative improvement in position across the key stages, consistent with the previous results of Parsons and Thompson (2017). Key Stage 5 seems to be a stage where the closing and reversing of gaps seen across earlier key stages is not apparent, and the success at Key Stage 4 has not translated into comparable relative results at Key Stage 5.

As discussed in the introduction, this data analysis is not designed to comment on the underlying causes of these differences. What is clear is that there are appreciable differences in educational performance by ethnic group across the course of pupils' school careers, that for some groups these differences change and in many cases reverse as pupils get older, and that there is a clear similarity in the profile of differences for pupils in Birmingham and nationally.

Academic attainment during and around Trojan Horse

This final section of results delves into the overall figures by ethnicity and gender provided above (i.e. as averages across all cohorts) for selected ethnic groups. This book has a focus on the Trojan Horse scandal in Birmingham; as a result, this analysis looks at the difference between performance in Birmingham and nationally for pupils recorded as Bangladeshi and Pakistani ethnicity. The (standardised) score differences reported in Table 4.4 are differences between the ethnicity-gender groups' average performance and that of the corresponding ethnicity-gender group in the national data, so are designed to highlight any discrepancies between Birmingham results and results elsewhere, rather than describe absolute levels of performance.

Table 4.4. Difference between Birmingham and national, Key Stage 1-3

Key Stage 1 – Difference between Birmingham and national

Group		2002 (1)	2003 (2)	2004 (3)	2005 (4)	2006 (5)	2007 (6)	2008 (7)	2009 (8)
Bangladeshi Female	English	-0.18	-0.11	**-0.25**	-0.10	-0.12	-0.07	-0.13	-0.14
	Maths	-0.13	-0.08	-0.11	0.16	-0.10	-0.01	-0.11	-0.16
	Science	**-0.31**	-0.16	-0.14	0.00	-0.09	-0.09	-0.07	-0.07
Bangladeshi Male	English	-0.09	0.06	0.01	**-0.20**	-0.13	-0.01	-0.05	0.06
	Maths	0.00	0.18	0.09	-0.08	-0.08	-0.06	-0.06	0.10
	Science	-0.12	**0.21**	0.12	-0.01	0.01	0.12	-0.04	0.09
Pakistani Female	English	0.06	-0.01	-0.07	-0.14	-0.08	-0.13	-0.05	-0.02
	Maths	0.03	0.00	-0.06	-0.08	-0.06	-0.17	-0.04	-0.01
	Science	0.13	0.04	-0.06	0.04	-0.04	-0.04	-0.01	0.02
Pakistani Male	English	**0.22**	-0.19	-0.06	-0.17	-0.05	-0.01	-0.08	-0.04
	Maths	0.09	**-0.20**	0.01	-0.15	-0.06	-0.02	-0.07	-0.06
	Science	**0.25**	-0.13	-0.01	-0.12	0.09	0.01	-0.06	-0.05

Key Stage 2 – Difference between Birmingham and national

		2006 (1)	2007 (2)	2008 (3)	2009 (4)	2010 (5)	2011 (6)	2012 (7)	2013 (8)
Bangladeshi Female	English	-0.03	0.02	-0.24	0.03	-0.08	-0.03	-0.01	-0.04
	Maths	0.05	0.01	-0.20	0.08	-0.05	0.09	0.06	-0.07
	Science	-0.11	-0.11	-0.23	0.10	-0.01	0.02	-0.05	-0.06
Bangladeshi Male	English	0.08	0.08	-0.01	-0.01	-0.32	0.01	0.09	0.14
	Maths	0.01	0.14	0.06	0.04	-0.11	0.14	0.14	0.21
	Science	-0.02	0.00	0.04	0.06	-0.02	0.06	-0.01	0.14
Pakistani Female	English	0.06	0.02	-0.09	-0.08	-0.06	-0.11	0.07	0.06
	Maths	0.06	0.02	-0.02	-0.02	-0.02	-0.04	0.08	0.08
	Science	0.09	0.08	0.05	-0.04	0.02	-0.05	0.07	0.08
Pakistani Male	English	0.20	-0.06	-0.09	-0.03	-0.09	0.00	0.09	0.06
	Maths	0.24	-0.05	0.05	0.06	0.00	0.08	0.05	0.08
	Science	0.24	-0.08	0.00	0.00	0.10	0.03	0.00	0.10

Key Stage 3 – Difference between Birmingham and national

		2009 (1)	2010 (2)	2011 (3)	2012 (4)	2013 (5)
Bangladeshi Female	English	**-0.40**	-0.12	**-0.22**	-0.01	-0.16
	Maths	-0.13	-0.05	**-0.31**	0.01	-0.14
	Science	**-0.45**	-0.05	**-0.45**	-0.05	-0.13
Bangladeshi Male	English	-0.18	-0.10	**-0.26**	-0.02	**-0.21**
	Maths	-0.01	-0.04	-0.17	-0.18	-0.15
	Science	**-0.24**	-0.06	**-0.32**	-0.06	-0.13
Pakistani Female	English	0.02	-0.02	**-0.22**	-0.13	-0.12
	Maths	-0.04	-0.07	-0.16	-0.16	-0.18
	Science	0.06	0.06	-0.19	-0.18	-0.18
Pakistani Male	English	0.05	**-0.36**	-0.19	-0.16	-0.03
	Maths	0.16	**-0.33**	-0.11	-0.11	-0.07
	Science	0.09	-0.11	-0.16	-0.18	-0.10

Source: ONS.

Looking at differences by ethnicity, gender and cohort between Birmingham and the rest of the country, it was clear that most of the differences were relatively small (i.e. under 0.1 or less). Moreover, given the level of variation and lack of measurement precision when examining groups of this size, differences of this magnitude are likely to be no more than statistical noise or measurement error. Even for small to moderate differences (i.e. about 0.1–0.3), caution is needed given the level of variation and lack of measurement precision when examining groups of this size. In Tables 4.4 and 4.5, I have emboldened all figures of an absolute magnitude greater than 0.2.

In general, the results show that differences in performance by gender, ethnicity and cohort between Birmingham pupils and pupils nationally were highly similar with some statistical spikes – mostly, but not all, in the negative direction. There appear to be both positive and negative spikes for Bangladeshi and Pakistani ethnicity pupils in cohorts 1 to 5 in the early key stages (Key Stage 1 and 2) but these are not consistent, and there were examples in other groups, such as for White British males in 2010 (not shown), so occasional positive or negative results are not unusual.

The largest differences were negative Key Stage 3 spikes in 2009 and 2011 (but not 2010) for Bangladeshi girls and, to a lesser extent, boys; for Pakistani boys in 2010; and a negative spike for Bangladeshi girls in Key Stage 4 English, maths and science in 2011. Although, as noted above, given the level of variation in the data and methodological limitations, these differences should be treated with caution, both in terms of whether they represent genuine 'shocks' in performance and why they might have occurred, if so.

Table 4.5. Key Stage 4 – Difference between Birmingham and national

		2011 (1)	2012 (2)	2013 (3)	2014 (4)	2015 (5)	2016 (6)	2017 (7)	2018 (8)
Bangladeshi Female	English	**-0.48**	-0.17	-0.11	0.18	-0.09	-0.04	0.00	-0.08
	Humanities	-0.01	-0.02	0.14	0.05	-0.08	0.09	0.09	0.05
	Languages	-0.03	0.05	-0.09	0.16	-0.14	-0.11	**-0.22**	**-0.21**
	Maths	**-0.23**	0.00	-0.11	0.09	-0.01	-0.08	-0.12	**-0.20**
	Science	**-0.49**	-0.16	-0.19	0.08	0.01	-0.04	0.01	-0.13
	Total	-0.05	0.05	-0.07	0.15	-0.03	-0.07	-0.05	-0.12
Bangladeshi Male	English	-0.13	-0.16	-0.04	0.05	-0.15	-0.01	-0.04	0.05
	Humanities	0.11	0.00	-0.02	0.06	0.02	-0.17	0.06	0.07
	Languages	0.08	-0.08	-0.07	-0.04	0.07	-0.14	-0.14	-0.13
	Maths	-0.05	-0.07	-0.04	0.03	-0.07	-0.02	-0.08	-0.04
	Science	-0.08	-0.04	**-0.29**	0.04	-0.19	0.10	0.04	0.02
	Total	-0.09	-0.04	-0.02	0.00	-0.12	-0.01	-0.02	0.00

		2011 (1)	2012 (2)	2013 (3)	2014 (4)	2015 (5)	2016 (6)	2017 (7)	2018 (8)
Pakistani Female	English	-0.10	0.01	-0.06	0.03	-0.01	-0.11	-0.02	-0.04
	Humanities	0.11	0.21	0.00	0.12	0.07	-0.02	0.10	0.01
	Languages	0.02	0.11	-0.05	0.07	0.15	0.03	-0.02	-0.12
	Maths	0.00	-0.07	-0.14	0.00	-0.03	-0.09	-0.12	-0.18
	Science	-0.16	-0.07	-0.10	0.02	-0.07	-0.16	-0.09	-0.11
	Total	0.10	0.08	-0.04	0.04	0.00	-0.11	-0.08	-0.11
Pakistani Male	English	0.01	-0.17	-0.30	-0.03	0.08	-0.02	-0.01	-0.01
	Humanities	-0.04	-0.11	0.02	0.12	0.12	0.08	0.05	-0.02
	Languages	0.18	0.15	0.07	**0.21**	0.11	0.04	-0.02	-0.15
	Maths	0.05	**-0.25**	-0.10	0.04	0.04	-0.01	-0.13	-0.17
	Science	0.00	-0.04	-0.22	-0.09	-0.14	-0.03	-0.07	-0.12
	Total	0.07	-0.27	-0.10	0.03	0.09	0.00	-0.07	-0.11

Source: ONS.

Conclusion

This chapter closes where it started: by discussing the value and importance of context. Analysing educational data by subgroups invariably reveals large variation within and across groups and highlights the dangers of looking at averages rather than variation. Our national school performance measures still do not take into account context in any form, thereby providing misleading measures of school effectiveness for parents, the inspectorate and educators. We continue, knowingly, to publish measures that are advantageous to selective schools and schools with a high proportion of pupils with EAL, and disadvantageous to schools with a disproportionate number of pupils on FSMs and pupils of particular ethnicities (Perry, 2016, p. 1059; 2019; Leckie and Goldstein, 2019).

The other point to return to is the limitations in these data. These were initially framed as a health warning for the results to come. In this reprise, however, I would like to emphasise their value as a starting point for future enquiry. The results presented in this chapter raise as many questions about what is driving them. Why does good progress from Key Stages 1–4 tail off at Key Stage 5? Why are Black African pupils in Birmingham behind their peers elsewhere, and why has this gap narrowed? What lies behind the lack in Birmingham of the EAL language bonus at Key Stage 4 (EBacc) seen elsewhere? What are the determinants of the low relative performance of Black Caribbean pupils, and what can be done about it? These are all questions which researchers and school leaders should take seriously and pursue. The overall lesson of the data for educators, researchers and policy-makers is clear: the individual and social experiences, contexts and circumstances of children and young people matter.

Leadership takeaways

- There is an enduring and significant relationship between pupils' demographic and socio-economic characteristics and educational outcomes. However, most of the variation in outcomes is within schools and within groups; the headline data tell us very little about individual pupils.

- School leaders can, however, use data to identify higher and lower performing pupil groups and use this information as a starting point for targeting support and school improvement.

- Comparing Birmingham pupils to pupils nationally, these results suggest that Birmingham pupils tend to perform below national averages, but that this is not immutable and shifts with changes in assessment design, population characteristics and schooling quality.

- There are remarkable similarities in the average performance of different ethnic groups for Birmingham and nationally, suggesting that systematic, structural and community (dis)advantages linked to ethnicity are present.

- Performance profiles by ethnicity over the course of cohorts' school careers varies. Some groups have a largely consistent relative level through the key stages. For some, there is a relative improvement in position across the key stages. Key Stage 5 seems to be a stage where the closing and reversing of gaps seen across earlier key stages is not apparent, and the success at Key Stage 4 does not always translate into comparable relative results at Key Stage 5 for some groups.

- The national and school-level data pose many important questions for school leaders about differential performance and educational inequalities by ethnicity, gender, English language status and socio-economic status. School leaders are well placed to identify and work to tackle these inequalities (although, this does not – in this author's view – release government and community from their responsibility to address social problems, nor excuse the accountability system's wilful blindness to school context and (dis) advantage.

Acknowledgements

I would like to thank the Department for Education and the Office for National Statistics (ONS) for providing access to the National Pupil Database data which has made this research possible. Please note that this work contains statistical data from ONS which is Crown copyright. The use of the ONS statistical data in this work does not imply the endorsement of the ONS in relation to the interpretation or analysis of the statistical data. This work uses research datasets which may not exactly reproduce national statistics aggregates.

References

Allen-Kinross, Pippa (2019) EAL Pupils Outperform Native Speakers If They Join Schools Early, *Schools Week* (17 June). Available at: https://schoolsweek.co.uk/eal-pupils-outperform-native-speakers-if-they-join-schools-early.

Clarke, Peter (2014) *Report into Allegations Concerning Birmingham Schools Arising from the 'Trojan Horse' Letter* (HC 576). Available at: https://assets.publishing.service.gov.uk/government/uploads/system/uploads/attachment_data/file/340526/HC_576_accessible_-.pdf.

Coles, Maurice I. (2008) *Every Muslim Child Matters: Practical Guidance for Schools and Children's Services*. Stoke-on-Trent: Trentham Books.

Department for Education (DfE) (2018) Schools, Pupils and Their Characteristics: January 2018. Available at: https://www.gov.uk/government/statistics/schools-pupils-and-their-characteristics-january-2018.

Department for Education (DfE) (2020) *English Proficiency of Pupils with English as an Additional Language: Ad-Hoc Notice* (February). Available at: https://assets.publishing.service.gov.uk/government/uploads/system/uploads/attachment_data/file/868209/English_proficiency_of_EAL_pupils.pdf.

Education Policy Institute (EPI) (2019) T*he Forgotten Third: A Rapid Review of the Evidence*. Available at: https://www.ascl.org.uk/ASCL/media/ASCL/Our%20view/Campaigns/EPI-report-The-Forgotten-Third-A-rapid-review-of-the-evidence.pdf.

Falk, Alastair (2018) No School is an Island, *TES Magazine* (27 July). Available at: https://www.tes.com/magazine/article/no-school-island.

Gorard, Stephen (2010) Serious Doubts About School Effectiveness, *British Educational Research Journal*, 36(5): 745–766. DOI: 10.1080/01411920903144251.

Iqbal, Karamat (2013) *Dear Birmingham: A Conversation with My Hometown*. N.p.: Xlibris.

Leckie, George and Goldstein, Harvey (2019) The Importance of Adjusting for Pupil Background in School Value-Added Models: A Study of Progress 8 and School Accountability in England, *British Educational Research Journal*, 45(3): 518–537. DOI: 10.1002/berj.3511.

Major, Lee Elliot, and Machin, Stephen (2020) *What Do We Know and What Should We Do About Social Mobility?* London: SAGE Publications.

Mortimore, Peter; Sammons, Pam; and Thomas, Sally (1994) School Effectiveness and Value Added Measures, *Assessment in Education: Principles, Policy & Practice*, 1(3): 315–332. DOI: 10.1080/0969594940010307.

Muslim Council of Britain (2007) *Towards Greater Understanding: Meeting the Needs of Muslim Pupils in State Schools. Information and Guidance for Schools*.

Available at: http://www.muslimparents.org.uk/app/download/5777027680/
MCBSchoolGuidance.pdf.

Parsons, Carl and Thompson, Trevor (2017) Ethnicity, Disadvantage and Other
Variables in the Analysis of Birmingham Longitudinal School Attainment Datasets,
Educational Review, 69(5): 577–599. DOI: 10.1080/00131911.2017.1281227.

Perry, Thomas (2016) English Value-Added Measures: Examining the Limitations
of School Performance Measurement, *British Educational Research Journal*, 42(6):
1056–1080. DOI: 10.1002/berj.3247.

Perry, Thomas (2019) 'Phantom' Compositional Effects in English School Value-Added
Measures: The Consequences of Random Baseline Measurement Error, *Research
Papers in Education*, 34(2): 239–262. DOI: 10.1080/02671522.2018.1424926.

Chapter 5
Learning for governance from Trojan Horse

Emma Knights

Introduction

You could feel the oxygen being sucked out of the room. The clerk had warned me just before the governing board meeting started that there would be 'Trojan behaviour'. And so it came to pass. One trustee began by questioning the minutes of the meeting three months ago; the substance was trivia designed to bring the meeting to a halt before it had got going, much to the exasperation of the chair and other trustees. Why? The sense of 'here we go again' was pervasive. It was 2015, when the trustees of this multi-academy trust had been replaced and a new board was in place, yet the undercurrent had not gone away. I was working for the Department for Education and overrode the issue in short order. We moved on and business commenced.

This cameo illustrates what had happened at many governing body meetings in the decade preceding 2014. What began as constructive questioning of school performance had been twisted into a narrative designed to undermine head teachers. The attritional tactics paid off, and in the worst-case scenarios head teachers were forced to quit their posts.

On the face of it, what was not to like? Governors were recruited from the local British Pakistani community and, in some cases, had attended the school themselves as pupils. Chronic underachievement and low aspiration had dogged their own school days, so it was to be applauded that they had returned as adult citizens to challenge poor performance and get schools to raise their game. It wasn't easy penetrating the largely White, professional domain of school governance, as Karamat Iqbal points out in Chapter 3 on lack of representation. For those governors with English as an additional language, that brought its own challenges. For those with no professional foothold, they experienced imposter syndrome.

As a governor trainer for Birmingham City Council, Tahir Alam recognised the potential that governing bodies had to influence the direction of a school, and he is praised in the Trojan Horse letter. The author, or authors, of the letter certainly knew the power that governing bodies had to lobby for an Islamist agenda, even though their outlandish prose conjured up images of the satirical film Four Lions rather than describe the day-to-day voluntary work of school governors.[1] Whoever wrote the letter understood that certain governors had undermined school leaders for their own cause over many years in Birmingham and had offered to share tactics with those seeking to destabilise schools in Bradford. The Kershaw Report (2014, p. 7) lists fourteen state schools in Birmingham where the investigators focused and finds that ten of them had governors installed to 'encourage Islamic ideals', with a further four schools where there was a possibility that this had occurred.

Knights had a ringside seat with the National Governance Association's (NGA) offices a stone's throw away from the Council House in Birmingham. Her advice was sought early in the Trojan Horse saga as school governance was at the fulcrum of events. Elements of entryism, manipulation, nepotism and poor regulation (at local authority and Education Funding Agency levels) were identified by both Clarke and Kershaw's investigation teams. Knights (2014) produced one of the best contemporary accounts that helped to explain Trojan Horse, and has continued to lobby for a greater focus on governance as the counterweight to over-focusing on school leadership.

The Trojan Horse behaviours identified in the Kershaw Report (2014, p. 6) had gathered momentum long before the coalition government was elected in 2010 and were deeply embedded in Birmingham's state-maintained schools. As one head teacher put it to me, the Academies Act 2010 enabled some academy trustees and governors not just to 'run with the ball but steal it', leading to damaging consequences at Park View Educational Trust and Oldknow Junior School. However, it would be wrong to analyse events purely through a Trojan Horse lens. There were other examples of poor governance in the city when the history of convertor academies – Baverstock, Calthorpe, James Brindley and Perry Beeches – is examined.[2] As Knights states regularly when addressing audiences on the critical nature of governance, 'organisations with strong governance

---

1   *Four Lions*, dir. Chris Morris (Film4 Productions, 2010).
2   See the end-of-chapter references for the key Ofsted reports.

do not fail' – and in all cases here, governors had not ensured there was sufficient objective scrutiny of the actions of the academies' leaders.

The architects of academy policy had assumed that it would be easy to transplant local education authority schools from maintained to academy status, with greater freedom and independence conferred en route. Whilst, as David Carter and Laura McInerney (2020) state correctly, most academies don't fail, there are many examples of car crashes along the way. Schools were allowed to convert to academy status on thin evidence and imploded soon afterwards, with many subsequently needing re-brokerage into a multi-academy trust. Others were left behind as 'orphan schools' that no multi-academy trust wanted because they were too difficult or too expensive to improve, and a crop of scandals emerged from the academy sector (as documented by Pat Thomson (2020) and Warwick Mansell at Education Uncovered[3]).

Academy governance is complex because it has welded together aspects of charity law, company law and education law in a uniquely English way (Paxton-Doggett, 2016). Academy trustee powers are considerably greater than their governor counterparts in maintained schools. At the same time, governance remains an unremunerated, voluntary task undertaken by an estimated 250,000 governors and trustees in England according to the annual NGA surveys (Garrington et al., 2020). When I worked at the Department for Education, there was an assumption by schools ministers like Lord Agnew and Lord Nash that academy governance would be populated by people with similar professional backgrounds to themselves as high-powered financiers. The reality is very different – and this has to be a good thing. We would not wish to see school governance divorced from its local origins; the voices of parents, community representatives, democratically elected politicians and staff must be heard.

Current English school governance embraces several different models, including individual local authority-maintained schools with less than 100 pupils through to large multi-academy trusts with over seventy academies. However, the characteristics of successful school governance in all schools are founded in collective governor behaviour, which sets the strategic direction, holds leaders to account and ensures the best use of

---

3   See https://www.educationuncovered.co.uk.

resources – all informed by Nolan's (1995) Seven Principles of Public Life, as encapsulated beautifully in the following graphic from the NGA:

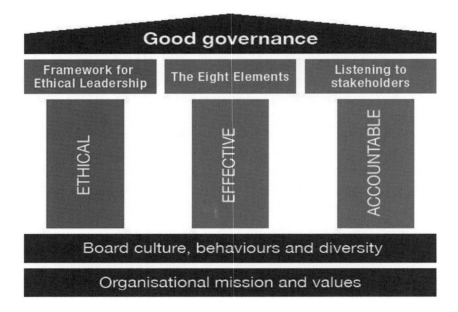

The following chapter demonstrates what happens when governance is allowed to spiral out of control in the pursuit of individual agendas and selfish aims.

Colin Diamond

Learning for governance from Trojan Horse

Emma Knights

The national spotlight falls on Birmingham's schools

When press stories began to surface in February 2014 about a possible Trojan Horse plot in Birmingham, some commentators thought the NGA might have inside information; after all, the schools being named were about five miles from our office in central Birmingham, which is round a few corners from Birmingham City Council House in Victoria Square. I did know the council's very new chief executive, Mark Rogers, who had just arrived from Solihull. He had served as president of SOLACE (then the Society of Local Authority Chief Executives and Senior Managers), and in that capacity had approached us to work on clerking governing body meetings. Together, we launched a campaign called Clerking Matters, which still aims to raise the profile of clerking and develop governance professionals within schools and trusts, although we haven't yet achieved a career pathway. But that is a different story — a longer and a less dramatic one.

NGA is a national charity supporting, developing and representing governors, trustees and clerks in state schools across England. I think it is healthy for a national organisation to be outside the Westminster bubble, but we have no more locus in Birmingham schools than in Cornwall or Cumbria. Almost two-thirds of schools and academy trusts now buy our membership packages or e-learning subscriptions, but no more than in Birmingham or the West Midlands than anywhere else. Although, once we were alerted to Trojan Horse, the proximity possibly added a further intensity and kinship. NGA is proud of its Birmingham roots and, of course, we want to understand the city in which we are based and where many of our staff live and serve as school governors. Countless journalists, reviewers and inspectors descended on schools in Birmingham; even from my helicopter view, I could see it was a deeply upsetting and unnerving experience for the pupils and families caught up in the situation.

But, unlike most contributors to this book, my role was much more peripheral and not as personal. I had no skin in the game. However, it was absolutely clear that as soon as the Trojan Horse allegations raised their head, there were issues of governance. NGA needed to understand what had happened, and what was still happening, in order to help prevent the same mistakes from transpiring again.

The whole crisis centred on who had the power and control in schools. The facts were so disputed, and emotions ran so high, that it was so easy to lose sight of this central issue. The Trojan Horse letter described a five-stage process to remove head teachers and gain control of some Birmingham schools (see Chapter 1).

I was pleased to be approached by the city council in April to join its arm's-length review group, chaired by West Midlands director for preventing violence to vulnerable people, Stephen Rimmer. It included government officials, local councillors, community leaders, religious leaders and MPs. All the heavy lifting in terms of the city council investigation was being done by Ian Kershaw and his fairly small team, which had to include legal expertise and take large amounts of evidence from witnesses. The review group met several times over the summer term to act as a critical friend to Kershaw's work and once to read the final report. I was impressed by the knowledgeable contributions, coming at such a sensitive situation from a range of perspectives. In particular, the commitment and support from other faiths, and the way they were working together in the city, gave some hope, whilst at the same time I was conscious of my own very limited understanding of the communities concerned.

There was an absolute political imperative for the investigations to report by the end of the summer term of 2014; politicians didn't want families to leave for the school holidays without knowing the outcomes, and a parliamentary recess was nearing. This led to immense pressure to complete both reviews. An extraordinary amount was carried out and considered in a short period compared with most legal processes and inquiries. The timetable and media intensity meant members of the group had very little time to scrutinise the final investigation report.

During this time, there was also a change of secretary of state for education, with Nicky Morgan replacing Michael Gove in a cabinet reshuffle just days before she had to decide what to do with the investigation report her predecessor had commissioned from Peter Clarke, the former head of the Metropolitan police's counter-terrorism division. Gove has considerable interest in the topic: in 2006 he had written a book called *Celsius 7/7: How the West's Policy of Appeasement Has Provoked Yet More Fundamentalist Terror*, with one chapter named 'The Trojan Horse'. The book itself had been controversial and provoked polarising reactions. Whilst still at the Department for Education, Gove had a very public falling out with Theresa May, then home secretary; he criticised her handling of counter-terrorism and she accused his department of failing to act when concerns about the Birmingham schools were brought to its attention in 2010. According to news reports, after an investigation into the row by Cabinet Secretary Sir Jeremy Heywood, Gove had to apologise to Prime Minister David Cameron for quarrelling with a cabinet colleague via the press (BBC, 2014).

Ofsted was also very active, inspecting twenty-one schools in the area and writing to Gove on 9 June 2014, setting out its findings. These included revelations that in some of the schools governors had exerted 'inappropriate influence on policy and the day-to-day running' and 'use[d] their powers to change the school in line with governors' personal views' (Ofsted, 2014a, p. 2). Overall, Ofsted did not cover itself in glory. It had failed to spot warning signs two years earlier when it awarded an outstanding judgement to Park View, which was described by Clarke (2014, p. 14) as 'the incubator for much of what has happened and the attitudes and behaviours that have driven it'.

This was personally embarrassing for the chief inspector, Sir Michael Wilshaw, as he had visited the school and met the chair of governors, Tahir Alam, who was subsequently revealed in the Clarke report to be at the centre of the controversy. Wilshaw was quoted in the press as saying: 'Park View is doing fantastically. Walking around the school and talking to children, they all appreciate being here. The students are so ambitious for themselves and that is so heartening' (Keogh, 2012). More broadly, Sir Michael has stated that 'You can sense a good school as soon as you walk in, as soon as you walk through the door, you sense what the school is about. The first half an hour tells you what the school is like' (Elgot, 2014). Furthermore, 'there's no reason why they shouldn't [do well] if they've got the right culture, the right leadership, good teaching, good systems' (Vasagar, 2012).

Poor governance exposed

Both investigators – Clarke and Kershaw – interviewed a wide range of witnesses and collected thousands of pages of evidence. The many different stories all added up to a similar picture. Kershaw (2014, p. 9) 'identified serious governance issues that exist in a small number of schools in East Birmingham as a result of, at best, poor skills, and at worst, serious malpractice by members of certain governing bodies'. What began as a desire amongst that small group to lead change in school leadership in order to improve education for Muslim communities in failing schools was reported to have involved 'an improper manipulation of school governance': 'These individuals have sought to intervene in the delivery of education, but by using inappropriate methods' (p. 4).

Clarke (2014, p. 90) concluded: 'I have seen no evidence to suggest that there is a problem with governance generally; however, there appears to be a problem with certain governors in some Birmingham schools.' He added: 'I would not want to generalise about the governance of academies but this enquiry has highlighted that there are potentially serious problems in some academies' (p. 87).

The investigations by the Education Funding Agency into Oldknow Academy Trust (EFA, 2014a) and Park View Educational Trust (EFA, 2014b) also revealed serious issues with governance – for example, lines of responsibility had been blurred by the involvement of governors in the day-to-day management of the schools.

Issues identified around governance included:

- Governors not understanding the respective roles and responsibilities of governors and those employed to operate schools.

- The effective takeover of the governing body by like-minded people.

- Nepotism in appointments to the governing body: no evidence that governors had been chosen based on their skills and experience, and/or governors not appointed in accordance with the academy's articles of association.

- Individuals associated with each other holding teaching posts or being members of the governing body (or both) at a small number of local schools.

- Rapid advancement of new or inexperienced governors to the role of chair.

- Governors using their position to advance a particular agenda: 'I have noted already that some governors and newly appointed senior staff have implemented conservative Islamic practices into schools' (Clarke, 2014, p. 40).

- A strategy of harassment to oust the head teacher.

- Interference by the governing body in the curriculum and the day-to-day running of the school.

- A pattern of disruptive behaviour by governors: 'This includes inappropriate, unprofessional and disruptive behaviour during meetings and in carrying out their duties' (Kershaw, 2014, p. 9).

- Action by governors to defeat proposals from head teachers at governing body meetings through organised filibuster or by leaving meetings prior to voting, rendering meetings inquorate.

- Governing bodies did not see themselves as the guardians of good behaviour or ensure their members acted in line with the Nolan principles.

- A breakdown in trust between governors and staff, including senior staff; many members of staff and some head teachers were frightened of expressing views contrary to those promoted by governors.

- Some weaknesses in the financial management and oversight of some schools.

- Due to weaknesses in the systems and the poor oversight of school governance, these behaviours had been allowed to happen unchecked.

Some commentators attempted to frame this solely as a failure of academy oversight. However, this argument did not bear any scrutiny. Both maintained schools and academy trusts were involved, and neither the local authority nor the Department for Education had understood the situation prevailing in this handful of schools.

Governance advice from NGA in 2014

The Department for Education accepted all Clarke's recommendations, but given that the failure of governance was at the centre of Trojan Horse, the recommendations struck me as fairly minimal. Those recommendations were filed in the House of Commons Library, and that is how it felt: filed under TH. When you consider the urgency and intensity of the debate between March and July 2014, very little action was taken nationally in the following months on the governance issues revealed. As with all other parts of the schools sector, there was an emphasis on governing boards receiving training on British values and Prevent rather than getting their house in order on the basics of good housekeeping. What had been billed as a major crisis appeared to be dialled down by the new Department for Education leadership.

There followed some minor amendments to the Department for Education's *Governance Handbook* (2020), but given how much effort was being put into countering extremism, it surprised me that so little was produced or said by the department. It was almost as though this is for 'people like them' (those troublesome inner-city communities in East Birmingham) and not for the rest of us. The wider lessons applicable to the practice of governance were not much discussed and barely even shared. NGA therefore stepped into the breach and produced a substantial guidance note (NGA, 2014) over the summer holidays which covered in some detail the top ten lessons, which we identified at the time as the following:

1. Principles of public life

The best guarantee for ensuring Trojan Horse-type situations do not occur is for all those who participate in governance to act ethically according to the seven principles of public life, often known as the Nolan principles: integrity, selflessness, objectivity, accountability, openness, honesty and leadership (Committee on Standards in Public Life, 1995).

The governing board has the corporate responsibility for setting high standards of behaviour. Every governing board should have a code of conduct. Most boards have had a code for many years. Three quarters (75%) of respondents to NGA's Annual Governance Survey in 2021 had signed a code of conduct, 16% had not (Henson et al., 2021, p. 12).

2. Conflicts of interests

Using governing positions to advance other agendas was at the heart of the planned Trojan Horse takeovers. Schools have never been as alert to potential conflicts of interest as they need to be. Declaring an interest is not the end of the matter; it is the beginning of a conversation about how that interest is to be mitigated. So often, 'leaving the room' for the relevant discussion is seen as sufficient mitigation, but the Trojan Horse case makes it clear that the influence of powerful people extends far further than being present at a meeting. Individuals do not need to be at a meeting for their will to prevail when others are engaged in doing their bidding.

3. Diversity and avoiding groupthink

One of the main lessons is the need to avoid small groups of people (cliques) obtaining undue influence on the governing board. A diverse board will be stronger and healthier with a wider range of ideas, knowledge and experiences, and it will make better decisions in the interests of the pupils. In that guidance note, we foreshadowed the work which has become not only the Everyone on Board recruitment campaign, but also influenced NGA's more extensive diversity, equality and inclusion work.[4]

4. Appointment and reappointment to the board

Getting the right people round the table has always been another of NGA's eight elements of effective governance, and at the time in 2014 NGA was developing more detailed guidance for governing boards on recruitment. This would include the expectation that volunteers are interviewed before appointment to ensure they have skills or experience to fit with the needs of the governing board.

---

4   See https://www.nga.org.uk/News/Campaigns/Everyone-on-Board-increasing-diversity-in-school-g.aspx.

5. Staying strategic

A strong theme in all the investigations was that some governors and trustees had become involved in operational matters – the day-to-day running of certain schools. Volunteers do, on occasion, struggle to understand where the line is between the strategic and the operational, although there is so much guidance and support on this topic that it should not be difficult to resolve. However, the situations described were not just a blurring of the boundaries, but regular transgressions into the role of school leaders.

Habits can be built up over time which can then be difficult to question. For example, in one report on Oldknow Academy Trust it states: 'the Chair is in the academy on Friday afternoons; he also visits the academy unannounced throughout the week' (EFA, 2014a, p. 4).

6. Reflecting the community and listening to parents

Both Clarke and Kershaw concluded that parents in East Birmingham had not called for the conservative religious ethos demanded by some of the activist governors. For example:

> while the majority of parents welcome the good academic results that some of these schools produce, they are not demanding that their children adhere to conservative religious behaviour at school. On the contrary, I received evidence that it is a minority of parents who want this to happen. I have been told by many witnesses, however, that most parents do not have the confidence to argue against the articulate and forceful people who seek their imposition, for fear of being branded as disloyal to their faith or their community. (Clarke, 2014, p. 95)

A governing board should ensure that it listens to the range of views within the parent body and community, rather than pay undue attention to a vociferous minority. As with much in governance, this is much easier said than done. It is fundamentally important that governing boards have an understanding of the community or communities from which the pupils are drawn. One of the three pillars of good governance is accountable governance. At the same time, it is important not to forget that in culturally homogeneous communities, schools are often the only places where children can learn about other faiths, cultures and ways of living.

7. Broad and balanced curriculum

It is entirely within the governing board's remit to concern itself with the offer to pupils; more than that, it is the board's duty to ensure that the curriculum is broad and balanced and provides for the spiritual, moral, social and cultural development of its pupils. However, the curtailing of the curriculum was identified as one way in which governors and trustees attempted to further their own particular agenda. The use of assemblies was another area of concern. A few subjects were removed from the timetable and there were some constraints on the resources that teachers were allowed to use.

Clarke (2014) concluded that governors had overstepped their responsibilities by restricting schemes of work and insisting on an Islamic approach to such subjects as personal, social, health and economic education, science, religious education, and relationships and sex education. He reported that 'conservative Islamic practices' had been introduced into some schools, 'so that children are not allowed to hear musical instruments and are not allowed to sing'. Changes had also been made to the art curriculum so that pupils 'may see and draw only designs but not full faces or images considered immodest' (Clarke, 2014, p. 40). There was also some evidence of moves to restrict the curriculum options of girls.

8. Relationships with head teachers and leadership development

Within the published reports, there was much description of dysfunctional relationships between governing boards and head teachers, such as 'overly challenging and sometimes aggressive in the management of head teachers' (Kershaw, 2014, p. 4) and 'inappropriate demands on head teachers by repeatedly requesting information' (Kershaw, 2014, p. 4). Sir Michael Wilshaw (2014) noted that 'the leaders have struggled to resist attempts by governing bodies to use their powers to change the school in line with governors' personal views'. One of the unreasonable requests quoted was to ask a head teacher to justify every decision he had made, which resulted in him having to write a 300-page document in response.

9. Human resources

The investigations identified a wide range of irregularities in employment practice, particularly in recruitment for senior posts, including failing to advertise, nepotism and irregular remuneration. At NGA, we were already encouraging governing boards to ensure that a member of staff has a human resources (HR) function, alongside the requisite HR skills and knowledge, and that a member of the board itself also comes from an HR background. Unlawful and unethical practice is less likely to be successful when others are confident and experienced on a topic.

10. Safety of pupils

The reports emphasised the governing board's role in ensuring the safety of pupils, and raised the issue of Disclosure and Barring Service checks and governors' knowledge of safer recruitment procedures. In some schools, leaders and governors had not adequately addressed the risks specific to their community. In particular, they had not focused on how children might be vulnerable to extremist influences, female genital mutilation or forced marriage.

2015 onwards – locally and nationally

I did a few media interviews in the year that followed, and one studio programme late in the evening about the whole affair which involved a range of national and local voices. Some parents from some school communities strenuously rejected the inquiry findings: they thought Clarke and Kershaw had got it wrong. They believed the Trojan Horse letter was a hoax (this was never proved one way or the other), so there were suggestions that the investigations were therefore null and void. However, it appeared to me that the findings were being interpreted via a particular lens. A strong view was expressed locally that the letter and the reports misrepresented their community: there was no evidence of widespread plotting and the reports made it clear that the players involved were fairly small in number and moved between schools.

No longer fuelled by national politics, the media circus moved on swiftly and the episode soon left the public eye. After the press feeding frenzy, local communities were left to pick up the pieces with new head teachers and new academy trusts.

Nicky Morgan reported to parliament in January 2015 that she had 'increased my department's capacity and expertise in counter-extremism

– dramatically expanding the Due Diligence and Counter Extremism Group in the DfE and placing it under the leadership of a full-time director' (DfE and Morgan, 2015). We had a number of telephone meetings with the counter-extremism unit, but disappointingly they produced little of relevance to governance. I remember one eye-opening conversation when worries had been reported to us from a local source about an individual standing for election to a governing board in a different town, and the Department for Education was unable to suggest anything at all that should or could be done. Despite all the rhetoric about ensuring that unsuitable people did not serve on governing boards, progress had not been made to first base.

Birmingham's Trojan Horse review group was meant to come back together a year later, but didn't. However, the programme of work undertaken by Birmingham City Council (which had been found not to have dealt well with allegations from head teachers) was significant and held to account, particularly by Sir Mike Tomlinson, who was appointed by the secretary of state to be education commissioner for Birmingham. There were a number of recommendations for the council to improve its support and monitoring of governing boards. For example, Birmingham City Council completely overhauled its process for proposing and reappointing local authority nominated governors to maintained schools. The implementation of stronger, more 'fit for purpose' governance policies in the local authority maintained schools generated a considerable amount of work in Birmingham. I am aware from their national network that many other local authorities followed suit.

In January 2015, the Wormald review on warnings received by the Department for Education prior to the Trojan Horse affair was published. It largely gave the department a clean bill of health, although it found that 'the Department has lacked inquisitiveness on this issue' (Wormald, 2015, p. 12). The report did not seem to have the rigour of an external investigation.

Without a doubt, fundamental British values were the biggest legacy over the next year or two, and the subject of many governors' training events and conferences. Ofsted school inspectors would ask about the topic for some time after, but there was nothing substantive on how to govern without exerting too much influence or stepping on management's toes. To my knowledge, Ofsted did not ask anything about ensuring correct employment practice, even though in his letter to the secretary of state, the chief inspector had identified 'manipulating staff appointments' as one of the three ways in which governing boards had sought to 'impose and promote a narrow faith-based ideology in what are non-faith schools' (Wilshaw, 2014).

There is also the wider question of the purpose of school inspection and whether – even now, with all this intelligence and hindsight – an Ofsted inspection under the current framework would uncover these issues of undue influence and interference from governors. Clarke (2014, p. 88) reported: 'I have been told that issues at some of these schools might have been detected earlier had the Ofsted inspection framework been more sensitive to changes in governance and its impact on the character of the school.' The new inspection framework introduced in September 2019 did not improve this,[5] and, arguably, removing the requirement for a specific finding on governance has actually exacerbated the problem (Henson and Sharma, 2020).

In its report, the House of Commons Education Committee (2015, p. 16, citing Adams, 2014) also picked up on Ofsted's role:

> In a letter to the Guardian just before the publication of the Ofsted reports, Sir Tim Brighouse and a group of other leading educationalists and Muslim leaders argued that:
>
>> It is beyond belief that schools which were judged less than a year ago to be outstanding are now widely reported as 'inadequate', despite having the same curriculum, the same students, the same leadership team and the same governing body.

The committee went on to conclude: 'The Trojan Horse affair … is less about extremism than about governance and the ability of local and central agencies to respond to whistle-blowers and challenges posed by individual schools' (p. 29).

---

5   See https://www.gov.uk/government/publications/education-inspection-framework/education-inspection-framework.

Reflections six years on

What has been learnt about governance from Trojan Horse

Given the intensity of the work at the time – the political imperative and the media noise was huge – it is surprising how little the lessons from Trojan Horse have permeated official guidance. The Department for Education has since downgraded the role of its counter-extremism work which now has a very low profile. Given that all the formal inquiries agreed on the centrality of governance, it is odd that their impact on the governance community has been negligible.

The *Governance Handbook* (DfE, 2020, p. 26) still includes in its questions to ask: 'How is the school ensuring that it keeps pupils safe from, and building their resilience to, the risks of extremism and radicalisation? What arrangements are in place to ensure that staff understand and are implementing the Prevent duty?' Although for a few years questions relating to fundamental British values were covered in Ofsted inspections, more recently it has not been a frequent topic of conversation between inspectors and governing boards. Curriculum is now at the heart of the Ofsted framework, but it is not discussed very much through the lens of fundamental British values.

The Department for Education is now much more careful in terms of the conflicts of interest rules for academy trusts, with the Education and Skills Funding Agency taking the lead (EFSA, 2020). However, you could be excused for thinking potential conflicts are only commercial and always about financial gain. Not all interests are about money. In Trojan Horse, the interest being advanced was a version of Islamic belief. There are also conflicts of loyalty which are often overlooked until it is too late. Getting friends and relations involved in governance or as employees was at the heart of the Trojan Horse takeovers, and also feature in many cases of fraud.

The change of mindset in Birmingham City Council should have resulted in head teachers voicing such complaints about their governing boards being more supported, and much effort was made to do so. However, only a couple of years ago, I was saddened to find an experienced executive head teacher of an academy trust still feeling isolated in the light of the community's religious agitation. This made it clear to me that the culture of fear amongst school professionals recorded in the Trojan Horse investigations had not disappeared entirely and that particular head teachers' requests for support were still going unheard.

Ethical leadership

The Nolan principles existed in 2014, as did governing board codes of conduct. These documents in themselves do not protect against unethical behaviour; they can even be referred to as a defence. However, there has been a real movement over the past four years to promote ethical decision-making, which has very much been education sector led. The Association of School and College Leaders set up an Ethical Leadership Commission, built on the Nolan principles, to develop the Framework for Ethical Leadership in Education which was published in January 2019 (ASCL, 2019). NGA coordinated a two-year pathfinder programme involving over 300 schools and trusts across England which reported in January 2021 on the range of ways in which the framework has been used (Sharma, 2021).

Board behaviours, dynamics and culture

What makes the difference to board practice is the way in which the people round the table embrace principles, standards and codes, and are committed to upholding them, not treating them as a tick-box exercise. This means being willing to challenge when others may be falling below them. Being prepared to have courageous conversations has always been one of NGA's eight elements of effective governance; however, challenging the behaviour of another member of the board is not something every governor or trustee is happy doing. For example, over the years, we have noticed that individuals not only find it very hard to assess the significance of their own conflicts, but also each other's when they are face to face. As well as considering their own behaviour, board members must be willing to signal when another's behaviour is inappropriate or competing interests become too much to mitigate. Done well, this requires conduct and judgement in line with the Framework for Ethical Leadership.

The culture of the governing board is in great part set and developed by the chair, and supported by vice-chairs and committee chairs. It can be difficult to describe, but fairly easy to identify when observing a board meeting. The 'way we do things round here' will be apparent to the astute newcomer. In the last six years, NGA, along with others in the sector, has been putting far more emphasis on the need to ensure a healthy culture.

There are still some boards where control is being exercised by a small number of people, rather than each member of the board weighing the information and situation equally. Although board members are equals in theory, the dynamics may produce something very different in practice. The chair needs to ensure that all members of the board contribute and be alert to cliques beginning to form. This problem is far more difficult to tackle if it is the chair who is inculcating this way of doing business.

The NGA suggests six years as the maximum length of service on a single board for a chair (on our own board of trustees this has been set at three). This is not just about avoiding these extreme and unusual manipulations, but to ensure that relationships do not becomes cosy and complacent. The chair and vice-chairs need to plan succession and actively recruit strong new members who will bring fresh perspectives.

Whistle-blowing

A healthy culture allows and enables whistle-blowing. Dealing with it – whether as the whistle-blower or as the recipient of information – has always been very tricky. This topic was raised in the Trojan Horse investigations and in the subsequent House of Commons Education Committee report (2015). It should have been further discussed by the Department for Education and deserves more airtime across the education sector in its aftermath. Whistle-blowing never quite reaches the top of anyone's agenda; although I wrote a piece for Protect in 2018 (Knights, 2018), it needs an update already!

Appointment, reappointment and removal

Over the past six years, a change in recruitment practices to boards has been pushed by the NGA with the support of the Department for Education. It has accrued a fair amount of success. Interviewing governors and trustees was largely unheard of in 2014 and has since become standard practice for many governing boards, although not universally so. In 2017, the Department for Education changed its guidance to include reference to interviewing volunteers, and this remains in place (DfE, 2020). Some boards are still wary of recruiting people they do not know, but this is now a minority view as the importance of diversity becomes more widely appreciated.

Some of the central players in the Trojan Horse schools had been governors for many years, conferring upon them disproportionate influence. In many other sectors there are limits for terms of office; the NGA promotes eight years as a maximum on the same board. This is not a popular suggestion amongst many long-serving governors and trustees who are, understandably, hugely committed to a particular school or trust. The Department for Education's *Governance Handbook* now states, and has done for a few editions:

> With effective succession planning in place, it can be beneficial for strong chairs to move on to another school or academy trust after a reasonable time (e.g. two terms of office). This can help to share expertise across the system and prevent boards stagnating or individuals gaining too much power and influence solely through their length of service. (DfE, 2020, pp. 45–46)

But the advice is largely ignored, and I have yet to hear the case made by anyone other than the NGA.

The risks posed by long service are compounded by automatic reappointment at the end of the first four-year term, which is common practice. There should be a review of a board member's contribution before reappointment for a second term. Although many local authorities now take reappointment seriously, their nominations account for a small proportion of those serving in maintained schools and are very rare in academy trusts.

It is important to ensure that a governing board is made up of a combination of new and experienced members, which involves timely discussion and proactive management. It is a case of balance and looking at those governing as a team with a collective set of diverse skills and knowledge, including of the community. Despite skills audits having been carried out for years and the NGA producing material on the topic, succession planning of boards in the school sector is still not embedded.

It is important that the net for potential volunteers is cast as wide as possible, whilst also acknowledging, as Clarke (2014, p. 93) did, that 'it is important to encourage the public spiritedness of local people to serve as governors'. Indeed, it is interest in the local community that drives much volunteering. As part of NGA's Everyone on Board work, we have been encouraging Black, Asian and minority ethnic volunteers, but the legacy of Trojan Horse lives on, with Muslim people in Birmingham still asking us whether they are welcome on governing boards.

There has been extension to the powers to remove governors in maintained schools, and members in academy trusts can remove trustees. However, this is rightly only used in extreme circumstances. It would be invidious to remove the person who asks awkward questions. Much was made centrally of the ability to remove governors and trustees advancing extremist agendas, but in practice only Tahir Alam – identified at the centre of the Trojan Horse affair – was barred from governance roles in maintained schools and academies (DfE, 2015).

Governing in more than two schools or trusts

Given that the recommendation for governors not to be on the board of more than two schools or trusts was accepted by the secretary of state, the case for it has never truly been made by the Department for Education. The reasoning behind the recommendation – to prevent individuals gaining an inappropriate amount of power and influence – has never been fully explained. Instead, it is downplayed as a pragmatic question about time: 'It is likely that only in exceptional circumstances will an individual have the capacity to serve effectively on more than two boards – but this is rightly a matter for the board or other appointing body to decide' (DfE, 2020, p. 41). Neither Clarke nor Kershaw recommended that decisions on who should serve should be left to the governing board.

The recruitment of volunteers is relentless, and there are times when making more use of those committed people who are prepared to govern in an additional school or trust is easier than finding and inducting someone new. Furthermore, successful chairs are sometimes transferred to other struggling trusts by the Department for Education with positive outcomes, and similarly in maintained schools by local authorities. Whilst this may be a useful approach for the second trust, there should be transparency to the process and the risks. I have recently suggested to the department that they could now use Get Information About Schools to examine the extent of this issue, and have an, albeit belated, open conversation.[6]

---

6   See https://www.get-information-schools.service.gov.uk.

Developing governance knowledge

A study by Judge and Kashefpakde (2019) looking at the progress made in school governance over the last decade highlighted that, by and large, governing boards were more likely now to invest in their own training and development. Although not universal, there is a general understanding that this voluntary role requires both induction and continuing professional development. However, in his report, Kershaw (2014) identified a lack of training uptake in both of these areas as a problem, citing evidence of lack of skills and knowledge in financial and strategic oversight, risk management and employment practice, which left governing boards unable to fulfil their legal obligations. This situation is by no means uncommon. It tends to be the most insular governing boards who miss out on training and networking.

The Department for Education has been investing in governance leadership development for a number of years, although the programme ended in March 2021. However, the department's support for governance has always fallen short of what was suggested by Sir Michael Wilshaw, who wanted mandatory induction training. This call has been supported by the NGA and almost all the respondents to our annual governance surveys (Garrington et al., 2020). Clarke also asked the Department for Education to consider the benefits of an accreditation scheme for governor training providers, but I am unaware of this ever having been properly considered.

There is also the issue of the governance knowledge of school leaders, which is not always as secure as it should be. Many head teachers are appointed with very little understanding of the role and/or of the relationships involved. This is a constant topic of conversation within the NGA and for those devising leadership qualifications, including the Department for Education's own national professional qualifications (NPQs). I have been assured that it will be taken seriously by the recently announced providers of the revised NPQs.

Collective acts of worship

Acts of worship were a feature of the Trojan Horse affair, but this topic has been buried. Every school in England is legally required to provide a collective act of daily worship for every pupil, although in practice many ignore it. According to the Education Reform Act 1988 this should be 'wholly or mainly of a broadly Christian character',[7] unless permission is granted to change this if the school has a clearly defined non-Christian religious community. For many years, the NGA has argued that collective worship – as opposed to school assemblies – is inappropriate unless schools have a religious foundation. Despite polling that shows the majority of parents also support NGA's stance, we have found that neither the government nor other players in the system are brave enough to engage in this discussion. Clarke (2014, p. 48) concluded that he found activity which 'appears to be a deliberate attempt to convert secular state schools into exclusive faith schools in all but name', but this related issue of inappropriate evangelising in non-faith state schools does not get spoken about by the powers that be.

Conclusion

To this day, we don't know who wrote the Trojan Horse letter or why, and the subsequent investigations showed that related activities happened in only a small number of schools. However, the letter does outline a possible route to obtaining power.

Could it happen again? Secretary of State Nicky Morgan said she wanted 'to ensure that our system of standards and accountability for all schools should better withstand the threats of extremism of all kinds' (DfE and Morgan, 2014). In Birmingham, the transformation programme at the city council was much more profound than anything that happened nationally. Park View Educational Trust has transformed its governance, and its successor, CORE Education Trust, won an Outstanding Governance Award from the NGA in 2017. We continue to work with them.

I am not convinced that enough has been done to counter extremism on a national scale. Despite Clarke's recommendations being accepted by the Department for Education, Trojan Horse has ended up being treated as an issue for some East Birmingham communities and their schools, as can be seen in the 2015 parliamentary statement (DfE and Morgan, 2015). The incident centred around the influence and power that a network of individuals were able to seize by diverting processes for their own ends.

---

7   See https://www.legislation.gov.uk/ukpga/1988/40/section/7/enacted.

Can this risk ever be entirely eliminated? Possibly not, but much more could have been done to highlight and reduce it.

The corrections taken across the school system to eliminate – or, more realistically, tighten – the route taken by these individuals in East Birmingham have been minor. Arguably, it is just as possible now as it was in 2014 for individuals to gain influence in a governing body and remove head teachers who are not supportive of their agenda. Local authorities should be more aware in 2022 of the need to avoid an 'intolerant and aggressive Islamic ethos' (Clarke, 2014, p. 95), but other intolerant approaches may not be so noticeable from outside the institution, especially in the early days.

Instead, the system relies on good people taking up positions of power and influence in schools and trusts, people who are vigilant to any such behaviour and who would call it out in a timely and authoritative fashion. To do so, they need to understand their communities in a granular and thoughtful way, seeking stakeholders' voices but being fully alert to who is speaking for whom and without fear of challenging. They need to be willing and able to have courageous conversations. This is not work that will ever come to an end: the NGA continues to support boards with the demanding role of ensuring that stakeholders are engaged. We have declared it to be the fourth core function of governing boards, but it would be useful if the Department for Education and the inspectorate emphasised its importance too.

One legacy of the COVID-19 lockdowns has been the strengthened relationships between many schools and their communities, and this more widespread mutual understanding should help to protect against small groups gaining control. The governing board's role in setting the values, ethos and culture is absolutely central to a school system in which everyone flourishes.

References

Adams, Richard (2014) Education Experts Voice Fury Over Ofsted's 'Trojan Horse' Schools Inquiry, *The Guardian* (3 June). Available at: https://www.theguardian.com/education/2014/jun/03/education-experts-ofsted-trojan-horse-birmingham-schools.

Association of School and College Leaders (ASCL) (2019) *Navigating the Educational Moral Maze: The Final Report of the Ethical Leadership Commission*. Available at: https://www.ascl.org.uk/ASCL/media/ASCL/Our%20view/Campaigns/Navigating-the-educational-moral-maze.pdf.

BBC News (2014) Michael Gove Apologises Over 'Trojan Horse' Row with Theresa May (8 June). Available at: https://www.bbc.co.uk/news/uk-politics-27750921.

Carter, David and McInerney, Laura (2020) *Leading Academy Trusts: Why Some Fail, But Most Don't*. Woodbridge: John Catt Educational.

Clarke, Peter (2014) *Report into Allegations Concerning Birmingham Schools Arising from the 'Trojan Horse' Letter* (HC 576). Available at: https://assets.publishing.service. gov.uk/government/uploads/system/uploads/attachment_data/file/340526/HC_576_ accessible_-.pdf.

Committee on Standards in Public Life (1995) *Guidance: The Seven Principles of Public Life* (31 May). Available at: https://www.gov.uk/government/publications/ the-7-principles-of-public-life/the-7-principles-of-public-life--2.

Department for Education (DfE) (2015) Regulation of School Managers and Governors: Prohibition Direction [for Tahir Alam]. Available at: https://www.gov.uk/government/ publications/direction-tahir-alam-barred-from-managing-independent-schools.

Department for Education (DfE) (2020) *Governance Handbook: Academy Trusts and Maintained Schools* (October). Available at: https://assets.publishing.service.gov.uk/ government/uploads/system/uploads/attachment_data/file/925104/Governance_ Handbook_FINAL.pdf.

Department for Education (DfE) and Morgan, Nicky (2014) Oral Statement by Nicky Morgan on the 'Trojan Horse' Letter (22 July). Available at: https://www.gov.uk/ government/speeches/oral-statement-by-nicky-morgan-on-the-trojan-horse-letter.

Department for Education (DfE) and Morgan, Nicky (2015) Oral Statement to Parliament. Birmingham Schools: Update from Nicky Morgan (29 January). Available at: https://www.gov.uk/government/speeches/update-on-birmingham-schools.

Education and Skills Funding Agency (EFSA) (2020) *Academies Financial Handbook 2020: For Academy Members, Trustees, Accounting Officers, Chief Financial Officers and Auditors* (June). Available at: https://assets.publishing.service.gov.uk/ media/5f4754ac8fa8f5362e74ba76/Academies_Financial_Handbook_2020.pdf.

Education Funding Agency (EFA) (2014a) Review of Oldknow Academy Trust (May). Available at: https://assets.publishing.service.gov.uk/government/uploads/system/ uploads/attachment_data/file/318401/Review_of_Oldknow_Academy_Trust.pdf.

Education Funding Agency (EFA) (2014b) Review of Park View Educational Trust (May). Available at: https://assets.publishing.service.gov.uk/government/uploads/system/ uploads/attachment_data/file/318392/Review_of_Park_View_Educational_Trust.pdf.

Elgot, Jessica (2014) Ofsted Boss Sir Michael Wilshaw Gave Wild Praise to 'Trojan Horse' Park View School in 2012, *Huffington Post UK* (9 June). Available at: https:// www.huffingtonpost.co.uk/2014/06/09/michael-wilshaw-trojan-ho_n_5472783.html.

Gove, Michael (2006) *Celsius 7/7: How the West's Policy of Appeasement Has Provoked Yet More Fundamentalist Terror*. London: Phoenix.

Henson, Sam and Sharma, Nina (2020) *A View from the Board: Ofsted's New Education Inspection Framework*. Birmingham: National Governance Association. Available at: https://www.nga.org.uk/getattachment/News/NGA-News/March-2020/ Governance-not-consistently-recognised-in-new-Ofst/NGA-View-from-the-Board- (Ofsted)-Report-(WEB)-Stg2B.pdf?lang=en-GB.

Henson, Sam; Sharma, Nina; and Tate, Megan (2021) *School and Trust Governance in 2021: Governance Volunteers and Board Practice*. Birmingham: National Governance Association. Available at: https://www.nga.org.uk/Knowledge-Centre/research/Annual-school-governance-survey/School-governance-in-2021.aspx.

House of Commons Education Committee (2015) *Extremism in Schools: The Trojan Horse Affair. Seventh Report of Session 2014–15* (HC 473). Available at: https://dera.ioe.ac.uk/22429/1/9780215084200.pdf.

Judge, Dominic and Kashefpakde, Elnaz (2019) *Governing Our Schools 10 Years On: What Has Changed in School and Trust Governance?* London: Education and Employers. Available at: https://www.educationandemployers.org/wp-content/uploads/2019/10/Governing-our-schools-10-years-on-FINAL-WEB-2.pdf.

Keogh, Kat (2012) Ofsted Head Visits 'Outstanding' Alum Rock School, *Birmingham Mail* (24 March). Available at: https://www.birminghammail.co.uk/news/local-news/ofsted-head-visits-outstanding-alum-181734.

Kershaw, Ian (2014) *Investigation Report: Trojan Horse Letter* [Kershaw Report]. Available at: https://www.birmingham.gov.uk/downloads/file/1579/investigation_report_trojan_horse_letter_the_kershaw_report.

Knights, Emma (2014) Lessons from the Trojan Horse, *SecEd* (4 September). Available at: https://www.sec-ed.co.uk/best-practice/lessons-from-the-trojan-horse.

Knights, Emma (2018) Whistleblowing in Schools by Emma Knights, Chief Executive, National Governance Association, Protect (14 November). Available at: https://protect-advice.org.uk/whistleblowing-in-schools-by-emma-knights-chief-executive-national-governance-association.

National Governance Association (NGA) (2014) NGA Termly Bulletin Autumn 2014.

Nolan, Michael (1995) *Standards in Public Life: First Report of the Committee on Standards in Public Life. Volume 1: Report* (Cm 2850-1). Available at: https://assets.publishing.service.gov.uk/government/uploads/system/uploads/attachment_data/file/336919/1stInquiryReport.pdf.

Ofsted (2014a) Advice Notes on Academies and Maintained Schools in Birmingham. Advice Notes from Sir Michael Wilshaw HMCI to the Secretary of State for Education on School Inspections in Birmingham (9 June, updated 8 July 2016) Available at: https://www.gov.uk/government/publications/advice-note-on-academies-and-maintained-schools-in-birmingham.

Ofsted (2014b) School Report: The Baverstock Academy (24–25 September). Available at: https://files.ofsted.gov.uk/v1/file/2431489.

Ofsted (2015) School Report: James Brindley School (13–14 January). Available at: https://files.ofsted.gov.uk/v1/file/2457433.

Ofsted (2016a) School Report: Calthorpe Academy (27–28 April). Available at: https://files.ofsted.gov.uk/v1/file/2580119.

Ofsted (2016b) School Report: Perry Beeches the Academy (21–22 September). Available at: https://files.ofsted.gov.uk/v1/file/2614025.

Paxton-Doggett, Katie (2016) *How to Run an Academy School: The Essential Guide for Trustees, School Leaders and Company Secretaries*, 2nd edn. London: ICSA Publishing.

Sharma, Nina (2021) *Paving the Way for Ethical Leadership in Education: Pathfinder Schools and Trusts*. Birmingham: National Governance Association. Available at: https://www.nga.org.uk/getmedia/b66f7207-0d86-484f-9589-80b5090ce9e6/Ethical-Leadership-Report-2021.pdf.

Thomson, Pat (2020) *School Scandals: Blowing the Whistle on the Corruption of Our Education System*. Bristol: Policy Press.

Vasagar, Jeevan (2012) An Inspector Calls: The Day the Head of Ofsted Visited One School, *The Guardian* (27 March). Available at: https://www.theguardian.com/education/2012/mar/27/michael-wilshaw-ofsted-school-inspector.

Wilshaw, Michael (2014) 'Trojan Horse' Schools: Sir Michael Wilshaw's Letter to Michael Gove, *The Guardian* (9 June). Available at: https://www.theguardian.com/education/2014/jun/09/trojan-horse-schools-wilshaw-ofsted-gove.

Wormald, Chris (2015) *Review into Possible Warnings to DfE Relating to Extremism in Birmingham Schools*. Report by the Permanent Secretary at the DfE (January). Available at: https://assets.publishing.service.gov.uk/government/uploads/system/uploads/attachment_data/file/396211/Review_into_possible_warnings_to_DfE_relating_to_extremism_in_Birmingham_schools.pdf.

Part II

We Educate Birmingham Children

Case Studies in Urban School Improvement

Chapter 6

The pedagogy of equality: the role of the UNICEF Rights Respecting Schools Award in making schools safer and more inclusive

Azita Zohhadi

Introduction

Nelson Mandela Primary School sits just off Ladypool Road in what non-Brummies call the Balti Triangle. Visitors come to savour the Pakistani-Western fusion cuisine and check out the fashion shops. These Tripadvisor-savvy tourists have little idea of what happens in the local community in the back streets where they park, and perceptions are often shaped by negative, ill-informed media coverage with a constant tinge of Islamophobia (see Chapters 2 and 3). Beyond the chicken tikka masala homage and salwar kameez window shopping on the main road is a community where, culturally, teachers are seen as 'spiritual parents' (Iqbal, 2013, p. 21) and schools recognised as having the power to transform children's lives.

Azita Zohhadi's leadership journey at Nelson Mandela started and finished with the school retaining its outstanding Ofsted badge (Ofsted, 2000). Strong academic performance is captured by Department for Education data (DfE, 2021). It portrays a school with 84.5% pupils whose first language is not English, 40.3% eligible for free school meals and 18.5% with special educational needs support. Pupils exceeded the average English school performance in reading, writing and maths handsomely for the three years before COVID-19 brought testing to a halt in 2020. But none of the above is what defines Zohhadi's leadership and how she talks about her school. These results are the outcome of a leadership journey informed by vision and values, driven by reaching out into the community and beyond and inspired by Nelson Mandela's own wisdom and humanity.

It is far removed from the narrow role for schools with 'expert' managerial leaders that has been supported by government policy since 2010 (Lynch et al., 2012). That sterile road has resulted in a generation of school leaders inducted into Gove's 2010 neoliberal version of education who, until the pandemic arrived, had little sense of the need to build relationships beyond the school gates (Harris and Jones, 2020). However, Zohhadi's journey is not unique, and there are many other primary schools in Birmingham steered by heads with a similar philosophy. They are in it for the long haul and are unimpressed by the range of central government initiatives that have poured into the city since 2010.

Sustainable school improvement doesn't happen because leaders follow trends in pedagogy or behaviour control, claiming to be blessed by their selection of 'evidence-based data'. (See, for example, Nick Gibb's extraordinarily selective speech to the Freedom and Autonomy for Schools National Association (DfE and Gibb, 2017), in which he cherry-picks 'evidence' from bloggers.) The Nelson Mandela journey under Zohhadi's leadership exemplifies how strong inner-city primary schools can flourish sustainably without being conscripts to Gove's and Gibb's gladiators. Oh, and just one permanent exclusion in eleven years from this calm and happy school.

From 2009 to 2020, Zohhadi led Nelson Mandela through episodes including the Sparkbrook locality being identified as a 'terrorist hotspot' (Stuart, 2017), Trojan Horse, Brexit and the arrival of mandatory health, relationships and sex education (RSE) in primary schools, which all inspired fear and anxiety in her predominantly (97%) Muslim school. She experienced challenges from parents, governors and councillors who questioned her leadership. She could easily have been unseated, as a number of heads in the city were, by the intimidatory tactics. She overcame each episode in turn because she had based her leadership on a vision with identity at its heart. Her own childhood, of dual-heritage Yorkshire and Iranian cultures, deeply influenced the leader she became. She recognised that parents needed their local school to represent a safe haven for their culture, whilst simultaneously anchoring its work in the universal values of the United Nations Children's Fund (UNICEF) Rights Respecting Schools Award (RRSA).[1]

---

1   See https://www.unicef.org.uk/rights-respecting-schools.

The school she had inherited was inward-looking. The new head teacher was expected to lead from the classroom with a full-time teaching time-table. Over a decade, Zohhadi transformed Nelson Mandela into a school characterised by the quest for initiatives that would enrich the curriculum and take the children way beyond their local neighbourhood experiences. The Royal Shakespeare Company's First Encounters with Shakespeare productions of Julius Caesar, The Merchant of Venice and Twelfth Night held the community spellbound.[2] The children participated in Echo Eternal, an arts, media and civic engagement project delivered in schools for children of all ages that uses the testimony of British survivors of the Holocaust.[3] The school worked with artists to make a permanent artwork and a film, plus they curated a day at the Echo Eternal exhibition held at the Library of Birmingham (Echo Eternal, 2019). The children's 'Angel Echo' took up a short residency in Birmingham's St Philip's Cathedral in 2019 and in Coventry Cathedral in 2020. The defining moment was captured when Nelson Mandela pupils were filmed talking eloquently about the importance of the UN Convention on the Rights of the Child for their own lives in a celebration at Birmingham Repertory Theatre in 2017 (Birmingham City Council, 2018).

When English government consultation on the introduction of mandatory health and RSE lessons in 2018 led to major disruption outside two Birmingham primary schools (Diamond, 2019a, 2019b), which resonated of Trojan Horse tactics, Zohhadi was able to build on the strength of her community relations and avoid such conflicts. Her inclusive style of consultation with the school's families headed off potential trouble. Similarly, when engagement with pupils on their out-of-school learning at madrasa resulted in a spate of referrals to children's social care and resentment from parents – as it was perceived to be interference in how the community dealt with things – those tense encounters were cushioned by the presence of mature, open-door community relationships.

The Nelson Mandela journey is different from the others described in this section of the book because Zohhadi didn't lead a school out of special measures in the wake of the Trojan Horse round of inspections in 2014. She was able to support Nansen Primary School in its recovery from those events because Nelson Mandela was a strong, high-performing school with deep and healthy community roots. Fullan (2005) observes

---

2   See, for example, https://www.rsc.org.uk/first-encounters-julius-caesar.
3   See https://echoeternal.uk/participants/artists.

that sustainable school leadership is centred on engagement with deep human values. This perspective was amplified by Hargreaves and Fink (2006), who set out a seven-principle model for sustainable leadership. Those qualities are breadth, depth, endurance, diversity, justice, resourcefulness and conservation, and they can be seen in abundance in the leadership model at Nelson Mandela.

Zohhadi's analysis of her leadership journey is characteristically humble and modest. Her leadership is anchored in recognition of her own imperfections (Munby, 2019) and the need to reach out and learn from others. She questioned herself along the way and knew that authentic leadership at Nelson Mandela required more than the 'expert' and 'technical' repertoire that is lauded by the vanguards of managerialism (Lock, 2020). Such approaches are devoid of commitment to the community and don't recognise the place of schools within education systems (Waters, 2020, cited in Coles, 2020). Fortunately, the prevailing winds of current English government education policy are not seen as helpful by many primary heads like Zohhadi, and they have not been persuaded to abandon their values.

Colin Diamond

The pedagogy of equality: the role of the UNICEF Rights Respecting Schools Award in making schools safer and more inclusive

Azita Zohhadi

There can be no greater gift than that of giving one's time and energy to help others without expecting anything in return. (Mandela, 2004)

Self-evaluation, review, audit, report, assessment, scrutiny, policy, league tables, inspections, benchmarking: all words familiar to anyone working in education where we are, rightly so, held accountable for impact and value for money. This public accountability system drives leaders to focus on how to achieve the highest academic outcomes and how systems, processes and use of finances move the school towards this end point. We might ask, what is wrong with that? We can easily get carried along by the wave, safely travelling in the same direction without needing to pause for thought and ask: where am I going? Do I still want to go there? How do I change direction? I find it fascinating that we are so thoroughly led by academic outcomes that it feels instinctive. Why wouldn't we want our children to be fully competent in the core subjects? We would be doing them a disservice to ignore the end-of-key-stage statutory tests and exams which point us firmly in that direction of travel.

The school's vision can get hijacked and end up being on the crest of the wave rather than in the undercurrent. Vision should be everything. Vision is where the school's hand is played; you place your cards firmly on the table for all the world to see. No poker face here, no hidden curriculum, no secret agenda. This is what we believe and who we are. When you arrive at a new school there are usually four vision scenarios: (a) there is one and it is what excited you about the school; (b) there is one but it doesn't align with your vision; (c) there is one, and it will suffice, so you can tick it off your list of priorities; or (d) there isn't one. Unfortunately, in some schools, the vision is simply an add-on, something for the website checklist, the sign outside school welcoming you in, the statement on the letterhead. I have yet to work in a school where the vision was my magnet. I have worked in a school where the vision did not exist: Fulham Primary School had a sunflower as a logo but its significance was long forgotten. I never knew why, despite trying to find out. I didn't change it as it seemed wrong to do so; it was part of the school's story and needed to remain. It pleases me to see that, thirteen years on from my headship there, the sunflower still remains.

Vision and leadership are a recognised partnership, but I would strongly advocate adding heart to this relationship. A school's vision needs to be a shared vision, and that means it cannot be the head teacher's alone. This does not, however, diminish the important role the head teacher has in developing, driving and promoting it. The head teacher must believe in it, breathe it and live it. For this, we must look within to find our passion, drive and ambition for our children and our staff. We then take our vision and shape it around the needs and context of our school community. What do we need to reflect in our vision to build on our foundations? Are there any existing barriers we need to remove which might be hindering or blocking this possibility? Then, of course, we need to implement it. In a successful school, each individual will be carrying the school's heart – sometimes beating quietly and unnoticed, whilst on other occasions pounding forcefully to remind and re-energise.

Nature, nurture and leadership

It is not possible to tell my leadership story at Nelson Mandela Primary School, and the importance of our vision of 'an inclusive school: putting your child at the heart of learning',[4] without going back further. Our vision is about equality, identity and inclusion. It goes deeper than simply furthering the children's academic outcomes: we also aim to develop compassionate, rights-respecting global citizens. Our vision is rooted in developing teams and partnerships beyond the school gates, and giving a voice to those who have yet to find it or find themselves surrounded by others who fail to hear them. Why am I so passionate about our vision? Who and what has shaped and influenced me to become the leader I am today? My leadership journey began long before I contemplated becoming a teacher. I must, therefore, take us back to when I was 9 years old,

---

4   See https://www.nelsonmandelaschool.co.uk.

when I recorded in my exercise book that when I grew up I wanted to be an air hostess, an actress or a teacher. I would like to think that it was the travel that put air hostess on the list, but no, it was more shallow than that: it was the glamorous lifestyle portrayed in the adverts.

I grew up in London with my Yorkshire-born mother, older brother and younger sister. My father lived in Iran. Amidst this backdrop, my mother set the scene for my vision of education and what I strive for as an educator. She ensured that her children's Persian heritage was very much part of our lives: our home was adorned with Persian textiles, rugs and ornaments, not forgetting the tastes and smells of Persian cookery.

Weekends with my mum were spent exploring the abundance of free activities that London had to offer – museums, art galleries, open-air theatre, parks, river walks and, of course, adventure playgrounds, where children were allowed to climb to great heights, swing on ropes and play with muddy old tyres, seemingly without a care in the world. A particular favourite visit of mine was Speakers' Corner in Hyde Park – the oldest free speech platform in the world. This was an opportunity to watch democracy in action, a place to watch as well as listen: animated faces, lots of gestures and movement all confined to the top of a soapbox. Everyone united by the fact they had something they wanted others to hear. It was exhilarating.

Every school holiday, our nuclear family became an extended family. Off we went to King's Cross station to begin our journey to Scarborough, each of us carrying our own suitcase of belongings when we were old enough to do so. We were already learning to take responsibility and develop our independence. Our voyage took us away from London both in terms of distance and landscape. In Scarborough, we had even more family love wrapped around us, as well as a myriad of contrasting places and experiences to absorb.

I use the verb 'absorb' deliberately, as it relates directly to my educational vision. I have learnt from experience that children need to be immersed in learning; it needs to penetrate into their bones. This is my definition of greater depth. It is important for educators to guide children to make links and connections, but it is equally important to allow them to forge their own. The contribution of the experiences I had outside of school on my learning, values, character and resilience is immeasurable. At Nelson Mandela, we strive to provide an accessible, diverse and enriching curriculum which extends beyond the school day. Family learning activities are

We Educate Birmingham Children
Case Studies in Urban School Improvement

central to this, thanks to the determination my mother had for learning to be a shared family experience.

Some of my childhood was overshadowed by the turbulence my father faced from living in Iran. The Iranian Revolution in 1979 led to the over-throw of the Shah and the replacement of his government with an Islamic republic. The Shah's regime had been considered by many as corrupt and as the puppet of non-Muslim Western power (namely the USA and UK). Communication with my father became difficult as we had heard that letters coming from the UK were being opened, and anyone writing anything that might be regarded as pushing Western views could lead to significant repercussions for the recipient. I don't know whether or not there was any truth in this, but the result was that communicating with my father was not as plentiful or free flowing as it deserved to be.

By 1980, Iran was at war with Iraq, and my father planned to return to England. A change in legislation introduced by Margaret Thatcher resulted in my father being unable to return to the UK, despite his green card granting him an indefinite stay. Any excitement I had for having a female prime minister disappeared. After a harrowing journey, my father arrived as an asylum seeker in the Netherlands where he lived in a refugee camp and asylum seeker home for many months. The Netherlands offered my father hope and eventually a place called home. He remembers vividly the people at the camp who supported him with acts of kindness, as well as interest in and time for him as a person.

Hopefully, I have captured the essence of my formative years and why working in primary education has been a natural vocation for me and has enabled me to impact on the development of others.

The power of words and actions

Learning, whether intentional or not, has a profound impact on who we are. We learn from the difficulties and challenges we face, as well as the positives. We need to remember the power of our words and actions. In my first week of secondary school, a teacher made a 'humorous' remark about me which resulted in much laughter from the class. However, I felt belittled. I can honestly say that from that moment on my love of school diminished. I still feel uncomfortable just thinking about it. A wrong word or look can have a devastating and long-lasting impression. I keep this thought close to me. At Nelson Mandela Primary School, we want our learners to feel confident about taking risks and making mistakes. We want them to know we are not judging them. Most of all, we want them to know they are valued.

I remember those words spoken to me as a child that knocked my confidence and those that built me up. I hated letting anyone down, so when I was criticised in front of my class for my poor handwriting, I retreated to my bedroom for hours each evening desperately trying to improve it. This was not to please my teacher but because I felt inadequate. A teacher's words should never make a child feel inadequate. If my teacher had created an environment where improvement was sought through encouragement, her words might not have been so hurtful. I can also recall those occasions when a teacher's words or actions gave me encouragement and a thirst for learning. My teacher recognised something in me that I had not known myself. I remember being selected to represent our school in a competition and I was made the team captain. I don't know why I was picked – I wasn't the brightest or most confident in my class – but I am sure that single action planted a seed in my mind that I could lead.

Before my headship at Nelson Mandela, I worked at Fulham Primary School in London. I started working there in 2002 in my first and only role as a deputy head. Four years later I became the head teacher. My mother worked as a teacher in the same local authority, Hammersmith and Fulham. When I got the job she expressed her concern as the school had a reputation of being a tough place to work. It was tough, but it was also an incredible school with a vast array of languages and cultures. Mobility was high and class cohorts rarely remained the same beyond a month. We had many families fleeing conflict as well as many children traumatised by life itself. Every class had high numbers of families actively involved with social services; over 70% of children were entitled to free school meals.

In challenging times you need to find strength. We found our strength in teamwork and laughter. Every day we were faced with the enormous responsibility of not only educating our children, but also rescuing many of them from the tragic circumstances they faced in their daily lives and giving them that sense of belonging and worth which had long been lost.

Shortly after becoming the head teacher we were due an Ofsted inspection. The local authority conducted their pre-inspection audit. They came in with a predetermined outcome. I was told in no uncertain terms that with our Key Stage 2 outcomes lower than the national level, the highest grade we could possibly expect from an inspection was satisfactory. My attempts to put forward a counterargument fell on deaf ears. Ofsted arrived two weeks later. In fact, we were graded good with some outstanding features – in spite of our Key Stage 2 outcomes (Ofsted, 2006). I remember the feedback well; the local authority adviser, rather than being happy, had a face like thunder. Clearly, Ofsted had seen many good things about the school and looked beyond just the Key State 2 results: they inspected our school with an open mind.

The lead inspector commended my 'excellent' self-evaluation framework for its detail, ambition and honesty. Racial harmony, safeguarding and commitment to equal opportunities were also deemed outstanding. That filled me with immense warmth. These aspects meant so much to me and my colleagues. The inspection team clearly saw Fulham Primary School's heart and recognised the value of our impact within the context of the barriers and challenges we had overcome. Progress and individual achievement were evident and our own data were not ignored. Our data analysis and monitoring systems were praised for being individualised: any cohort or subject analysis could be rendered out of date before it was published due to the high mobility. A sudden influx and exit of children following a bulk rehousing could turn a high-achieving cohort into a low one, and vice versa.

My years at Fulham Primary School were happy times. We all worked tirelessly together – staff, parents and community – to provide an enriched education as well as comfort and optimism for our children. Every interaction with the children and their families was built upon this ambition: we can overcome our circumstances and achieve beyond what we and others believe to be unachievable.

Taking on the leadership of an outstanding school

In 2009, the advert for head teacher at Nelson Mandela Primary School in Birmingham jumped out at me from the pages of the *TES*. I am sure that it had something to do with its namesake.

The school had recently received its third consecutive outstanding judgement. Ofsted instils a range of emotional responses in the teaching profession, but my experience at Fulham Primary School gave me the confidence to apply for the position. I felt that my success there legitimised my application. However, there was something that raised doubts in my mind. The governors were seeking to appoint a head teacher with a full-time class-based teaching role to follow in the footsteps of the outgoing head, who had been in post since the school opened in 1987.

Whilst applauding the head teacher for her approach (it had clearly brought the school much success), I knew that I wanted to lead from outside the classroom. Not wishing to waste anyone's time, I made my position clear towards the end of my application. (I was hoping they would be sufficiently interested in me before they read it.) The likelihood of getting shortlisted was poor; however, I felt compelled to try. The risk paid off, and so began my leadership journey with the city of Birmingham and Nelson Mandela Primary School. Being a head teacher is a privileged position, but being the head teacher of a school named after Nelson Mandela added another level of responsibility. I had a huge obligation to keep his achievements and subsequent legacy alive. Nelson Mandela Primary School must, above all else, strive for equality and compassion.

My handover meeting with the outgoing head teacher was arranged for the summer holidays. However, the meeting didn't happen, so my handover was quite literally a handover. I was greeted by the deputy head teacher holding an envelope containing a bunch of unlabelled keys. I was informed that the training days had been organised and I had been left a slot at the start. All the signs were there if I'd looked. This was a school that did things their way. Not wanting to tread on toes or dismiss the efforts made in preparing for the training days, I gratefully accepted my allocation.

The initial address from a new head teacher should leave staff feeling inspired and confident. How was I going to do that in such a brief slot when there was so much that I wanted to say? I chose to focus on one key message: that I considered my role to include supporting them as much as the children. I remember it well; in fact, I have played it back many times. The soundtrack stopped, the camera panned and everyone was stuck in a freeze-frame of horror. I had clearly said something seriously wrong.

Had I come across as uncaring by not focusing my role fully on the children? After that clanger, I was grateful to sit back and observe the rest of the day's training, although I spent the majority of the time wondering if I was in a checkmate position. Over the years, I heard from staff on more than one occasion that they remembered it well too, but not for the reasons I thought. They had been surprised at how high I had put them on my priority list. The school's budget had zero allocation for staff development. What did take place happened within the walls of the school, with very few people coming in or going out. The pupil outcomes were high, so why did they need to go elsewhere? Expectations of staff and children were clear and everyone within the school followed procedures precisely.

This approach will only work if the leader of the school has credibility. My predecessor did – the class-based head teacher was an inspirational teacher – and teaching across the school was strong. Some people find procedures and rules comforting, but not all; for some it can stifle and hinder growth. I also saw early on that there were colleagues with the potential to become leaders at the school whose leadership seed either hadn't been planted or, if it had, it wasn't getting the nutrients required. It was important for me to grow my staff and for them to grow others. Now, leaders at Nelson Mandela nurture and develop staff not only in our school but in schools across Birmingham and beyond. When someone moves on, they leave behind a team of staff that they have grown, ready to branch out to the next level.

From rote learning to problem-solving in class

So, let's return to my first meeting with the staff: room for improvement. Next, my first meeting with a parent: room for improvement. I managed to disappoint without even opening my mouth. A parent, who lived opposite the school, came bursting into my office to meet the new head teacher: 'Oh dear, you're not a Pakistani,' he gasped, before spinning around and leaving as quickly as he had entered! This event did not anger me; in fact, I found it quite endearing. Mr Hussain was proud and protective of his heritage. There wasn't a lot I could do about my background, so instead I embraced his disappointment and reflected. A significant proportion of Nelson Mandela Primary School's community identify as Pakistani. He wanted someone from his community to lead the school his children attended. He believed that in order to educate meaningfully you had to understand the community – and for him that meant being from the community.

I can understand Mr Hussain's viewpoint. I remember the news headlines when a new CEO was appointed in a school who had never worked in a school previously. A debate ensued: can someone lead a school with a deep enough understanding of the role if they haven't been a teacher? I believe that, as long as the CEO values the input of teachers and considers the impact of their decisions on staff, they can. We might never fully understand others, but we can, and should, take the time to learn about others – their cultures, contexts and experiences – and stand together side by side. I have not grown up in a Persian household, and I am ashamed that I cannot converse with my relatives in Farsi, but I still have a bond that goes beyond blood thanks to my mum taking the time to impart her understanding and love of Persian culture. What I took away from this meeting was the importance of identity. What Mr Hussain didn't know was that I valued diversity and relished the opportunity to learn and embrace my new school community. I was not going to sideline his or anyone else's identity.

I had a lot to think about, and I hadn't yet met the children. So, how did that go? I don't recall a specific moment but I can remember how it felt. The school was clearly a happy place. The children were well mannered, hardworking and somewhat serious. They walked around silently in lines – boy, girl, boy, girl. When I went into the playground to talk to them, they all looked at me oddly as they uttered their replies. I thought it might have been my London accent. It wasn't. As I walked through the school, I saw children and staff with their heads down and working intensely. It felt orderly and controlled.

A class lining up ready for assembly was like a military operation, as the children formed into their alternating boy–girl lines. I asked them to mix up and was again met with a long stare. 'Are we allowed?' a child asked his teacher. This might seem like a minor matter, but it wasn't for me. This issue resulted in quite a discussion at a senior leadership team (SLT) meeting. One senior leader commented, 'We always do it like that,' and had never questioned it. Another was adamant that the mixed pairs needed to continue as it ensured the children remained silent because the boys would not want to talk to the girls, and vice versa. They couldn't see how this was wrong on so many levels. What messages were we giving our children? Were we really setting the expectation that boys and girls don't get on?

I changed this policy; how could I not? However, there was a rumbling fear, which can take hold when a new person takes on the headship of an outstanding school with successfully established procedures. One change could be the trigger that causes everything to unravel. There were many more 'We always do it like that' conversations to follow. Some procedures have continued – I am not one to introduce change for the sake of it – but some have not. I have seen too many schools overwhelmed by new changes and initiatives they cannot keep up with.

At Nelson Mandela Primary School, the teaching of maths left me perplexed. Outcomes were high across the school but I was not inspired by the teaching. Please note, the teaching not the teachers. Each year group had a set of maths folders, one for each week. Inside each folder there was a photocopied test and, Monday to Thursday, every child in the school from reception to Year 6 had lessons based on the test paper, which was completed on the Friday.

At the end of each term all the children sat the same four tests – addition, subtraction, division and multiplication – with each line of questions getting increasingly difficult. The children in reception were given the same test as Year 6; the idea being that they would progress as far as they could. There was no consideration as to how this might make the child faced with endless questions they could not solve feel, or the child in Year 6 who had been getting 100% for years. This was the maths syllabus and planning for the year.

The children in reception were able to complete bus stop division, but the core understanding wasn't there. Fortunately, I did not need to convince the maths lead when I suggested the subject needed a major overhaul. Nelson Mandela needed to find a new way to do maths. Over the next few years we had more children achieving higher standards than ever before. Results did not drop, and we now had children who were able to problem-solve.

Navigating community tensions

I touched briefly on the importance of identity following my meeting with Mr Hussain; it cannot be underestimated. When I worked at Fulham, with our high pupil mobility, we made it our top priority. We all need to be valued and recognised for what we can contribute. A child who had been in the school for one week was as important to our school identity as a child who had been in the school for much longer. Identity is as much about the individual as it is about the group. It is much more than a uniform or a logo.

Nelson Mandela is a non-uniform school. In the application pack, it stated that the introduction of a school uniform would be led by the new head teacher. Previously, I had always been an advocate for a uniform (ah, so that is why I wanted to be an air hostess!), but after a short while at Nelson Mandela I had a change of heart. The school was a sea of bright colours and the children's characters were reflected in their clothing. Assemblies were a sight to behold. Pupils would come into school dressed in their special-occasion regalia, including sequins, ties and dicky bows!

In my twelve years of headship, the request to introduce a uniform came up on only a handful of occasions, usually following parent surveys. These parents believed that a uniform promoted identity, conformity and respectful behaviour. But behaviour at Nelson Mandela Primary School was not an issue, and neither was school identity. The children were united behind Nelson Mandela, proud of who they were and united in upholding his values. He was close by at all times: if ever there was an issue that needed further exploration, we would look to Mandela to help us with his words and actions. We didn't shy away from the fact that he wasn't perfect and that his methods of bringing about change were sometimes violent. In a 1979 letter to his then wife, Winnie, Mandela reflected on the contradictions in people's lives and what it is to be human: 'In real life we deal, not with gods, but with ordinary humans like ourselves: men and women who are full of contradictions, who are stable and fickle, strong and weak, famous and infamous, people in whose bloodstream the muckworm battles daily with potent pesticides' (Mandela, 2010, p. 234).

At Nelson Mandela Primary School, we learn the values of determination and self-belief. We look to Mandela for moral strength and guidance when faced with adversity. We had fully embedded Mandela's values, so we did not need a sudden injection of fundamental British values into our inclusive curriculum when we were required to do so as part of our Prevent duty. It was already there in abundance. This is not a criticism of the intentions of Prevent, but a realisation that how it is implemented can undermine the integrity of the intentions.

Safeguarding children is of paramount importance; it is probably what keeps most head teachers awake at night. A significant amount of my time at Fulham Primary School was spent managing safeguarding concerns and attending meetings with social services. We had a huge team of staff doing likewise. When I got to Nelson Mandela, I was surprised how few children were considered at risk or vulnerable due to safeguarding concerns. There was very little documentation to indicate that anyone had involvement from social services, and I didn't receive any invites to meetings with social workers.

When the time came for me to make my first referral to social services, I was called out of assembly the next day to meet with the parent at the centre of the referral. I stepped into my office only to be confronted by several angry parents. They were reprimanding me for taking matters into my own hands without calling upon them to deal with the matter. The matter was that a child had disclosed physical abuse. I explained the school's procedure, only to hear the all-too-common refrain: 'That's how we do it here.' A key aspect of Ofsted's framework used to require schools to evidence how they had listened to parental views; I wonder if this resulted in leaders making decisions based on feeing obliged to follow parents' views even when it didn't feel like the right thing to do.

Despite the uncomfortable confrontation, and thanks to the assistant head teacher who stood by my side, I did not waver. Safeguarding must trump parental views. You never get immune to the sadness you feel when a disclosure is made, but I also feel reassured that each disclosure is a sign that we have created an environment where children trust us to make things better for them. It is an unusual thing to be proud of, but I feel a sense of pride knowing that Nelson Mandela now has a list of children who are known to or currently being supported by social services. We have an even longer list of children whose concerns have been identified quickly, and early intervention has proved successful without needing the helping hand of social services.

During a few short years, Sparkbrook's fame for the Balti Triangle was being replaced rapidly as a terrorist hotspot. In 2010, the Project Champion initiative caused significant upset in Sparkbrook following the overnight appearance of surveillance cameras in mainly Muslim areas. There had been a lack of consultation and transparency with residents over the involvement of the counter-terrorism unit with the scheme, which aimed to monitor communities at risk of extremism. A report commissioned by the Henry Jackson Society into Islamist terrorism in Britain identified seventeen people from Sparkbrook and the surrounding area who were jailed for terror-related offences (Stuart, 2017). This was picked up in an article published in the Daily Mail (Bracchi, 2017), which stated: 'The back-to-back terraces of Sparkbrook, and similar neighbourhoods around the country, have often been cited as examples of multiculturalism. In truth, they have become segregated ghettos with high rates of crime and unemployment, where few British-origin households remain.' Imagine what reports and articles like this do to your sense of identity and sense of belonging.

I could not ignore the fact that Nelson Mandela Primary School is situated in Sparkbrook, and nor did I want to. One morning, soon after my arrival, a child and his mother arrived at the school distraught. Their home had been raided the previous night and he hadn't been able to do his homework. If he hadn't had homework to complete, we might never have known about this distressing situation. In February 2010, his father was convicted for publishing and distributing extremist texts.

Schools must not wrap children in cotton wool in our quest to protect them from the outside world. We need to create space and opportunity for them to discuss issues safely, to have the vocabulary to express opinions respectfully, and to acquire the knowledge and skills to keep themselves safe. We need to be prepared for what might be waiting in the shadows, sometimes revealing itself slowly and sometimes thrusting upon us in a blinding light. Trojan Horse (in 2014) and the Brexit referendum result (in 2016) erupted from the shadows and had a significant impact on the community at Nelson Mandela. A vast dark cloud hung above us, and it was my priority to do all I could to shift it. I knew that there would be no overnight thunderstorm to clear the air, but over the coming months and years we saw fragments of daylight, and over time I was sure we would have glorious sunshine.

Nelson Mandela Primary School has a 97% Muslim community. I could feel the pain and fear of the children and their families when Muslims were in the news yet again because of a terrorist attack, whether or not it was linked to Birmingham. On many mornings, I was approached at the school gates by parents wanting to talk about terrorism and their distress and anger at being portrayed as a threat to the fabric of Britain. These were families who had grown up in Britain, many of whom had attended Nelson Mandela. Parents and children expressed their feelings of isolation; they didn't know where they belonged anymore. There was an increase in the number of mothers wearing the hijab and niqab, proudly holding on to the visible signs of their faith and identity. A nearby school had several incidents involving girls bullying their peers for not wearing a headscarf. The wearing of the hijab even found its way into Ofsted inspector lines of enquiry for a short while (Adams, 2017, 2018).

Following requests from parents wanting to know what they could do to protect their families in the wake of terrorist events, we invited our local counter-terrorism liaison officer to one of our regular coffee mornings with parents. Attendance was higher than usual. Many desperately wanted to show us that they were not a threat, and that they too were afraid of terrorism and wanted to protect their children. Thankfully, parents also saw the school as a safe place to talk openly about sensitive topics, share concerns and work together to find solutions. Parents wanted to contribute and make a difference. Some went on to become community advocates for a local initiative called Our Families, Our Future, working with a local counter-terrorist police officer, whilst others worked with other networks to become Positive Parenting leads, physical and mental health champions and campaigners against female genital mutilation (FGM).

In my many years of teaching in deprived inner-city communities, I have embraced the contributions of parents. An overwhelming majority of families have a determined ambition for their children to have the opportunities they didn't. Education and educators are valued. All too often, I hear about the problem of 'difficult to engage' families and that they are the reason for poor outcomes. We must remind ourselves that these families hold the key to unlocking their child; they have an essential role to play and much to contribute. Working in partnership with families is an essential part of our role, difficult or not. I was quoted in *The Guardian*

(Beckles, 2007) on my clear commitment to equality of opportunity: 'If we can't work with the child's family, we are only working with half a child.' At Nelson Mandela, our vision talks directly to our families – our vision is about their child and we share their learning journey.

When I was asked to support Nansen Primary School in 2014, it was in special measures. Trojan Horse was a raw scar on the school community. Staff and families were entangled in a climate of mistrust and fear. I sensed early on how much the families valued education. Yes, they were angry – but with themselves as much as with the new leadership. They were also in shock and disbelief. How could the school they chose be failing their children? They looked at the data we showed them sceptically – surely, there was a hidden agenda? They wondered what we weren't showing them. I remember the turning point well: I presented our forty-page post-Ofsted plan in a meeting with Adrian Packer (CEO) and Pat Smart (trustee). You could almost feel the anxiety, guilt and anger lift. This document is what they needed to see; it showed them that we cared about their children and that we wanted them to join us on our robust route forward.

Challenges from a vocal minority of parents

Since 9/11 there has been a disproportionate interest in Muslims by the British media and a rise in the number of documentaries and reality TV shows. BBC Two's *Muslims Like Us* (2016) was advertised as an all-Muslim *Big Brother*. The programme was criticised for including an associate of the radical preacher Anjem Choudary. Fatima Salaria, a BBC senior commissioning officer, stated that it would have been 'totally irresponsible' not to include someone expressing radical views when 'we hear this idea that Muslims need to do more to challenge those voices in the community, and here you see that for real' (Addley, 2016). In the first episode there is a heated discussion about who best represents true Islam. One housemate is heavily criticised and insulted for being worse than a non-believer for having a liberal Western lifestyle. This touched a nerve with me that I hadn't known existed. Did any of our families have a negative opinion of me for being the offspring of a Muslim father who chose to marry a Roman Catholic? I had a strong relationship with our families, but it hadn't always been that way.

Muslims Like Us transported me back to 2010 and the start of my second year at Nelson Mandela Primary School. The deputy head teacher (who proudly talked about being described as a 'Rottweiler') had just retired. Rather than talk to me, she decided to wait until the summer holidays to raise a concern directly with the chair of governors about a changing room being turned into an office space. As the head teacher I had no private space of my own and I was unable to talk to anyone privately. The chair contacted me wanting an explanation. Why hadn't they been consulted? I had not consulted the governors about putting a desk and chair in a space that not only did not require any alterations but, in my opinion, was unsuitable as a changing room. When school resumed and I showed her the 'changing room', she was shocked that the space was in fact a large walk-in cupboard and not large enough for fifteen children to get changed in.

This incident marked the end of my first trouble-free year. What followed was a rather unpleasant year of animosity towards me from a handful of vociferous mothers and a father who was a parent governor. Nelson Mandela had an unwritten open-door policy. I have always welcomed families into school, but nothing could have prepared me for the literal interpretation of 'open door' at Nelson Mandela. Half an hour before the start and end of the school day, the doors would be opened wide (the building faced directly on to a public road) and families came in and filled the corridors. Lessons were disturbed, no one could get easily from one end of the school to the other and it was extremely difficult to know who was in the building. It relied on the receptionist knowing everyone personally. This was a serious safeguarding concern. In my first year, the site manager, SLT and library manager had to patrol the corridors and support the receptionist.

In September 2010, I changed the entrance (originally a temporary measure). Families now walked through the park at the back of the school where they were greeted by a member of the SLT. Anyone using the front entrance was unable to gain access to the children without signing in securely. The traffic congestion inside and outside school stopped overnight. Petitions were drawn up to complain about the changed entrance procedures. Why was I locking out the community? It was a difficult time; I was regarded by the five vociferous parents as an outsider who had something to hide. Throughout this time, parents could still come into school, but in order to do so they would either have to sign in or be welcomed by a class teacher – someone who knew them. (Each class-room has a door opening out on to the playground.)

One morning, a parent and a local community resident alerted me to the fact that there had been a meeting and that negative things had been said about me. On 14 December 2010, the Sparkbrook Ward Committee held a meeting with two local councillors in attendance, one of whom was the chair. I later obtained a copy of the public minutes from the council's website and was dismayed by what I read. The meeting occurred before the Trojan Horse letter was made public, but it shared a lot of similarities. Nelson Mandela Primary School didn't receive a Trojan Horse letter; however, had it done so, the content of this meeting would have come to mind immediately.

The inaccuracies and tone of the minutes were disturbing. The chair referred to meetings he had held with me when, in fact, I had never met the man. The minutes stated: 'A member of the public, who was also a School Governor, commented that he felt the Head Teacher was discon-nected from the community and that the Head Teacher did not listen to her Governors' (Birmingham City Council, 2010, p. 627). He stated that decisions were taken at the school without the involvement of the gover-nors, including turning a changing room into an office. A member of the public commented that parents needed to become more assertive and more knowledgeable. He added that he felt head teachers were 'running amok' in inner-city schools (p. 627). Another member of the public stated that 'his former Governing Body had been instrumental in removing a Head Teacher' (p. 627). Finally, councillor Salma Yaqoob[5] commented that 'there appeared to be a pattern developing across local schools and referred to issues in Anderton Park, Moseley and Ladypool Road Schools. She suggested that members of the community should share their expe-riences and commented that the Governors of these schools had powers and should be the decision makers at the Schools' (p. 627).

The negativity came from a small number of parents, and yet it upset and concerned me deeply. What was being said about me was unjustified. As a leader, it is really important to acknowledge how people are feeling and give them the opportunity to be heard. So, I asked staff to share their views and I held an open meeting (with translators) so that our parents had the time and space to talk. I listened and the assistant head teacher

---

5   A Birmingham politician who went on to become leader and vice-chair of the Respect Party. She was the Respect member for Sparkbrook from 2006 to 2011.

visibly made notes of everything that was raised using an overhead projector. All questions, views and concerns were discussed by the governing body. The tense atmosphere soon dissipated. We had created our own Speakers' Corner. Parents who felt unable to talk publicly came up to me to quietly express their gratitude that I was putting safety first.

The school's governing body discussed at length the contents of the minutes, they read the views of staff (who were fully in support of the changes) and challenged me robustly. My decision to continue to use the safer park entrance was agreed unanimously. The parent governor who had been negative towards me did not attend the meeting (or, indeed, any another governing body meeting) and eventually relocated. Fortunately, I had a governing body who realised early on that I had an extremely open and honest approach to leadership and valued the engagement of the community. The conflict over the new entrance occupied much of my time and was the lowest point of my career. Thankfully, I had the strength and resolve to pursue the changes so that the health and safety of our school community were not compromised.

Even though I knew this was all in the past and that relationships with our school community were strong, listening to the vitriol from one of the housemates on *Muslims Like Us* brought back feelings of vulnerability. The programme became a topic of conversation amongst school staff who, on the whole, felt that it was light-hearted. It continued to perturb me that there was a need for such a programme. Surely, we didn't need reality TV to demonstrate that Muslims are not all the same, that they come in all shapes and sizes, with a range of views and opinions, that they disagree and argue too? Are people in England really that ignorant?

Reality TV programmes are not scripted. Furthermore, people might not behave normally in a situation where they are surrounded by cameras; some might 'act up'. It is also possible for the context of comments to get lost in the editing process. A programme that legitimately sets out to explore issues can inadvertently cause division and build a climate of mistrust. When our beliefs and identity are threatened, our instincts can provoke us to defend. In the period leading up to the Brexit referendum, for example, we saw campaigns built on the notion that British identity was being threatened. During this time, Europe was facing the biggest refugee crisis since the Second World War. Britain's opposition to accepting refugees was one of the most vocal. The UK had some of the lowest numbers of asylum applications compared to mainland Europe.

Unsurprisingly, political parties like UKIP used the crisis to boost the Leave campaign, which blurred the distinction between European citizens (freedom of movement) and asylum seekers and refugees. On 23 June 2016, 51.9% of UK voters cast their preference to leave the European Union. Numerous surveys and opinion polls have asked Britons why they voted the way they did in the EU referendum. The two main reasons people voted Leave were 'immigration' and 'sovereignty'.[6]

During a class discussion the day after the Brexit vote, it was abundantly clear that the children were worried. Some believed they would need to leave their home and return to their family's country of origin. One child was extremely anxious and close to tears. His family couldn't afford plane tickets, so they wouldn't be able to leave. What would happen to them? Would they have to go to a camp or even to prison? These were real fears from children. Education cannot afford to ignore the emotional impact of events like Brexit on pupils. Is reaching national expectations a priority for you if you don't matter? We all need to belong, to have a sense of purpose and to believe that we have a future. All of these issues make a real difference to your outcomes: academic, social and emotional.

The UNICEF Rights Respecting Schools Award

In the period leading up to the European Union referendum, I attended a head teacher's briefing and heard Razia Butt, Birmingham City Council's schools resilience adviser, talking animatedly about UNICEF's RRSA. This was a eureka moment for me. I didn't know about RRSA; however, I was familiar with the United Nations Convention on the Rights of the Child (UNCRC). I had bought copies of UNICEF's (2000) book *For Every Child* for each class when I was working at Fulham. I was compelled by Razia's vision for all schools in the city to become Rights Respecting Schools. This was such a positive direction for Birmingham's schools. It was about children, it was about empowerment and it was about adults protecting children's rights. I believed that this initiative would hold Nelson Mandela Primary School's vision together and take it further than I had ever imagined. A Rights Respecting School is a community where children's rights are learnt, taught, practised, respected, protected and promoted. The award is not just about what children do, but also about what adults

---

6   See https://ukandeu.ac.uk/partner-reports/peoples-stated-reasons-for-voting-leave-or-remain.

do and how the charter of children's rights is embedded across all aspects of the school.

The articles in the UNCRC became our common language and we learnt together. Whilst each article is equally important, we soon discovered that different articles struck different chords. Our children were taking in their new knowledge and relating it to their own lives. One child expressed how article 16 (every child has the right to privacy) meant a lot to him as he was from a large family and never had his own space. Just knowing about this article gave him the confidence to discuss it at home. His family had never considered privacy issues before and together they found a solution. Our children's de-compartmentalised lives became joined up through the UNCRC. The articles apply to all children, at all times and in all places. The children were realising for themselves that it is not acceptable to be hurt or made to feel uncomfortable by any adult anywhere. They now had the knowledge to challenge situations they had previously tolerated. There were occasions when the children made disclosures after their friends had reminded them of their right to be protected from violence, neglect and abuse (article 19).

Rochelle Jeffery, the assistant head teacher for pupil voice and personal, social, health and economic education (PSHE), led us on our journey to becoming a Rights Respecting School. Rochelle is a perfectionist, and in the quest to get things right would try to do everything herself. Gaining the RRSA gave Rochelle the opportunity to flourish too as a leader. She realised that you have to let go of the reins and give others responsibility so they can learn to stand on their own two feet. She also gained the experience of working more closely with age groups outside of her comfort zone. Through the RRSA, our school was able to take pupil voice to another level.

Being a Rights Respecting School is not about fundraising; it is about empowering the children to campaign and raise awareness. It is about becoming active citizens locally as well as globally. It is about being outspoken and curious. In December 2017, the pupils chose, without adult prompting, to do something for the refugees living in Birmingham. The fact that they sympathised with the plight of refugees touched me. They wrote to Razia Butt stating: 'We would like to meet refugee children because we want them to know about their rights and help them get the most from them.' The children wanted to 'help them to feel less alone and more involved in our community'.

Razia was someone they knew and admired. She had been a member of Nelson Mandela Primary School's *Question Time* panel during Parliament Week. She was the person they called upon to help them with their cause. Within weeks, I found myself at Edgbaston Community Centre with our Rights Rangers meeting refugee children and their families. Our children gave a presentation about the UNCRC and gave the children their own summary copies. The children talked together and made friendship bracelets. The memory of watching them skipping happily together on a small patch of concrete will stay with me always. The children felt freedom. I discussed this experience with my local head teacher colleagues and we committed to opening our schools to refugee children in the afternoons on a rota basis, offering a range of activities so they would have the opportunity to meet, play and learn alongside other children. Sadly, this didn't happen as there were too many barriers beyond our control.

In June 2017, the school community achieved RRSA Level One (Silver). The assessment report for the reward stated: 'The ethos promotes children's developing sense of social justice and equity; everyone, especially the children, frequently talked about equality and inclusion; "Because everyone here is equal and everyone respects our rights, and the teachers too" … Senior leaders explained that equality and diversity work has been strengthened by the CRC, which "legitimises conversations" and that staff feel more confident to talk about sensitive issues' (UNICEF UK, 2017, p. 2).

I was happy to see how the UNCRC had impacted on our staff too. They felt confident about tackling difficult issues and not shying away from them. I came into education to support children on their journey of discovery and understanding. Children need to develop resilience so they can stand up for what is right and challenge what is wrong. They also need to be exposed to the horrors of life as well as its wonders. School is a safe and reassuring environment in which to do this.

The power of connection: Echo Eternal

In September 2018, Nelson Mandela Primary School joined thirteen other Birmingham schools in Echo Eternal, CORE Education Trust's commemorative arts, media and civic engagement project inspired by Holocaust survivor testimony. This was a natural next step for our school to complement and extend our RRSA work. Our children had a strong understanding about the importance of freedom of expression and the freedom to practise your religion (article 14).

When I was 11 years of age, I watched a documentary film called *Kitty: Return to Auschwitz* (Morley, 1979) with my mother in our front room. I remember it as if it were yesterday. It followed the moving journey of Holocaust survivor Kitty Hart returning to Auschwitz thirty-three years after being imprisoned there as a 16-year-old. This was my first introduction to the Holocaust. Kitty told her story and that of others in the camp with intensity. I had an emotional connection with someone I hadn't met. The power of her words connected me with the past.

Decades on, I can still recall her words and retrace her steps without having watched the programme again. The connection had a deep and lasting impact. Six million people is such a large number. How can we really comprehend it? How can we get beyond the number? Each murdered Jew was meant to be just a number, not a person with their own identity. Kitty stopped the numbers being just numbers. I don't remember learning about the Holocaust at secondary school. Would I have known about it if my mum had turned off the television because she thought I was too young or she wasn't interested? If I was growing up now, would I have watched the film or would I have been too busy filling my time on social media? If ... If... If ... There are some subjects that we cannot leave to chance.

For the children at Nelson Mandela, Echo Eternal was going to be their personal introduction to the Holocaust, their connection with those they do not know and their opportunity to shape their future responsibilities. The solemn testimony of Kurt Taussig, our Holocaust survivor, was going to stop the numbers being just numbers. Echo Eternal built upon our vision and values of respect, tolerance, understanding, equality, hope, aspiration, compassion, responsibility, love and determination. It furthered our children's understanding of faith, identity, discrimination and racism. It also gave them a strong sense of moral purpose and civic responsibility, empowering them to actively shape the world they live in.

Kurt became a refugee overnight; his life was changed in an instant. Every child at Nelson Mandela engaged with Kurt's testimony, guided expertly by Echo Eternal's staff in an age-appropriate way, and responded creatively to ensure that his words would speak eternally. Some children and parents also worked with Alistair Lambert, a sculptor I met whilst at Fulham, to make Echo Angel. Echo Angel was a sculpture made from nails, each one representing a 'lost soul' from the Holocaust. Kurt's story of loss and hope was captured eternally in a poignant yet resonant work of art, keeping his story alive for generations to come.

There are no limits to what can be achieved when we remove barriers. Having high aspirations and expectations are essential components of success. Children can engage with challenging topics when they are introduced thoughtfully. We must not underestimate them. A member of the public wrote in the visitor book placed at the Echo Eternal exhibition at the Library of Birmingham on the day a group of Nelson Mandela pupils curated the exhibition: 'The explanation given to me by a number of children proved beyond any doubt that producing the works of art has enabled them to understand the enormity of the Holocaust and how important it is that everyone remembers and understands what happened.'

In January 2019, Nelson Mandela Primary School was awarded RRSA Gold. The accreditation report (UNICEF UK, 2019) demonstrates how much heart remains in our school vision and how we work together to achieve it:

> Particular strengths of the school include ... A very strong focus on Article 19 in its widest sense including understanding of FGM, radicalisation and knife crime. (p. 1)

> There is widespread commitment across the school to the view that if children's holistic wellbeing is not supported, they will not flourish as learners. Consequently, there are strong and well-established systems to promote their physical, mental and emotional health. (p. 4)

> The culture of the school is highly inclusive and there is a conscious promotion of diversity and difference being promoted, valued and celebrated. One of the adults in the focus group commented that 'There is a strong sense of identity ... not having a uniform doesn't stop us from being a strongly cohesive community.' (p. 5)

The UNCRC led to an increase in child safeguarding disclosures which were passed to the council's designated officer, particularly referrals linked to incidents occurring in out-of-school settings. Many children were attending classes in madrasas to learn about Islamic culture and the Qur'an after school and at weekends. These disclosures rarely led to prosecution because all too often the children would retract their statements the next day. Birmingham City Council didn't just leave RRSA at the door of the school. Issues like these were identified and acted upon, resulting in system change.

Razia Butt invited me to join her steering group exploring some of the challenges and issues facing children in out-of-school settings in our local area. We looked at the government's call for evidence on out-of-school education settings (DfE, 2018) through the lens of the UNCRC. Some children were attending lessons in unsafe buildings. Sadly, there were examples of children being physically sanctioned for poor rote learning or behaviour, usually linked to having a special educational need. Some parents sent their children to out-of-school providers based on the affordability of the provision, not the quality. For some families, the out-of-school provision was linked to their faith and their desire to give their children strong religious foundations.

This resulted in some children attending overcrowded classes delivered by teachers with little experience of managing children with complex needs or delivering engaging lessons, which resulted in some poor and unsafe attempts at behaviour management. The parents were stuck between a rock and a hard place. They desperately wanted their children to have religious instruction but they could not afford to shop around. It wasn't something I had considered before; naively, I had assumed the provision was free. Unfortunately, poverty resulted in some cases where safeguarding was compromised, and in many cases families were unaware of this.

Razia led on the development of a pilot to ensure that out-of-school settings are a safe place for children in Birmingham to attend without the risk of harmful practices, including unsafe premises, unsuitable staff, inappropriate forms of punishment and discipline, and exposure to harmful extremist views. This wasn't rooted in reprimand but built around a climate of support, learning through the sharing of best practice and training.

Consulting on the new relationships, sex and health education proposals

In 2019, statutory guidance was published in England on relationships, sex and health education (DfE, 2019). This included a requirement in primary schools to teach about different families, including lesbian, gay, bisexual and transgender (LGBT). Thirty years previously, section 28 of the Local Government Act 1988 stated that a local authority 'shall not intentionally promote homosexuality' or 'promote the teaching in any maintained school of the acceptability of homosexuality as a pretended family relationship.'[7] (It was repealed in Scotland in 2000 and in England and Wales in 2003.) The statutory guidance also states that the religious background of pupils must be taken into consideration and that the core topics covered need to be 'appropriately handled': 'Schools must ensure they comply with the relevant provisions of the Equality Act 2010, under which religion or belief are amongst the protected characteristics … In particular, schools with a religious character may teach the distinctive faith perspective on relationships' (DfE, 2019, p. 12).

The language anticipated discord. The statutory guidance was published following a period of consultation which suggested that it was generally welcome, with the exception of LGBT education in primary schools. I was surprised that the Department for Education needed to remind schools to consider their communities and the Equality Act. Unfortunately, the flexibility given to schools at a local level resulted in some head teachers and schools being thrown into chaos and conflict almost overnight. A couple of Birmingham schools, which had been proud of their positive relationships with their families, found themselves in a divided community and at the centre of a media frenzy.

Rumours and fake news fuelled anger and confusion. Some parents genuinely thought that schools were teaching children as young as 5 how to have gay sex. Photocopied letters for schools were being circulated along with copies of leaflets advertising public meetings. I received a handful of letters from parents worried about the new framework, and I also had some really interesting conversations with parents at the school gate. I explained that we would not need to make any changes to our existing curriculum, but we would, of course, consult with parents.

---

7   See https://www.legislation.gov.uk/ukpga/1988/9/section/28/enacted.

Our consultation started with a series of presentations held at different times and days of the week, which were widely advertised with regular text reminders. In addition, all of the documentation was made available on our website. I attended all the meetings but did not lead them. It was important that we implemented the requirements and processes of the RSE guidance. We did not want to treat it like a unique or controversial subject, so we delivered it in the same way we would with any other curriculum change. We showed how our existing PSHE and diversity curriculum, RRSA work and behaviour policy covered all aspects of the new guidelines. We explained how this aligned fully with our school vision by continuing to give our children the skills and attitudes needed to make our world a happy, peaceful and tolerant place to live. We would continue to build emotional literacy and the children's understanding of themselves as part of a community, with the rights and responsibilities that brings. Parents were encouraged to join our steering group to finalise the draft curriculum.

I believe that the role our parents have – working in partnership with us on fulfilling our vision and our Rights Respecting Schools journey – provided a strong foundation for the implementation of our RSE policy. Parents and children recognised the importance of children's rights, and that they have a right to their own opinions and beliefs, but of equal importance is our responsibility to treat others with different opinions and beliefs respectfully. Families were invited to meetings to discuss the new RSE requirements and we actively sought parental involvement in the development of our policy and curriculum.

Although the meetings were well attended, there were also many empty chairs because several parents had already discussed their concerns with a member of the SLT at the school gates prior to the formal meeting. Those in attendance listened, asked questions and shared opinions. We addressed the rumours in the media and community openly by showing clearly what we were proposing to teach and what we were not. We shared the vocabulary and age-appropriate definitions we would use, we explained that our focus would be on healthy relationships not sexual relationships, and we clarified that we would not be teaching children about changing their gender but that we would teach about gender stereotypes and the importance of not being limited by them.

We also disclosed the full range of carefully selected books we would use to support our work. All of these had already been shared with each year group during our diversity workshops in the previous year. Some of our books were recommended by No Outsiders,[8] including the locally controversial but true story about penguins, *And Tango Makes Three* (Richardson and Parnell, 2005). We explained that the book wouldn't be used as a teaching point about same-sex relationships (both parent penguins are male), but we would not ignore it. Instead, we would focus on the importance of love and caring for each other. Our book collection and diversity curriculum incorporated all protected characteristics and showed how they were all equally important. The feedback was positive. Parents could see that we were being sensitive to their religious views, but they were also made aware that within their community there were other parents who felt strongly that their children needed to know that not all families are the same and that they should be tolerant of difference.

Everyone who wanted to join the steering group did so. We made some changes as result of the concerns raised. We moved some Year 1 lessons to Year 2, and we agreed that although boys and girls in Year 6 would have their lessons together, some sessions would be split into same-sex groups, although the coverage would remain the same. Personally, I would have preferred to keep the sessions mixed, with an opportunity for the children to have separate Q&As, because separating the children turns puberty and bodily changes into something they shouldn't talk about together. This was an example where the views of parents and some staff were prioritised over my own.

Postscript

When I joined Nelson Mandela Primary School in 2009, the school could have continued on its wave, going in the same direction and doing things the way it had always done with high academic outcomes. Instead, it changed direction and will carry on doing so. The school continues to thrive because it has strong partnerships and collaborations with everyone working together with a common purpose: ensuring that children are at the heart.

---

8   See https://no-outsiders.com.

The Headteachers' Standards (DfE, 2020) might give other schools the momentum to turn the tide. The standards do not refer to high academic outcomes; instead they point head teachers in the direction of creating 'a culture where pupils experience a positive and enriching school life' and to 'uphold ambitious educational standards which prepare pupils from all backgrounds for their next phase of education and life'. The word 'academic' does not feature; in fact, we need to 'ensure a broad, structured and coherent curriculum entitlement'. This offers an opportunity to turn the tide towards an education focused on health, character, values and creativity, alongside academic achievement.

I left my role as the head teacher of Nelson Mandela on 31 October 2020. Here is an extract from my last letter to the school community:

> Together we have achieved so much, and everyone has played their part. As parents you chose Nelson Mandela School to be by your side bringing up your child. We work together to provide an education that is much more than subject teaching. We have worked hard to develop the whole child – their academic, social, emotional, spiritual, physical and mental health. I was so proud when we achieved the highest Right Respecting School Award. It showed just how much we are following in the footsteps of our dear Nelson Mandela. We strive to uphold the values of respect, equality, compassion and love in all that we do. Our children have shown us that they can bring about change and improve the lives of others. They really are responsible global citizens. One day, our children will be our future leaders, scientists, healthcare professionals, artists, engineers, actors, designers, lawyers, parents, teachers, managers, authors, human rights activists, politicians ... I feel a sense of comfort in the knowledge that they are already actively campaigning to improve the lives of others and they continue to stand up for the rights of others.

Leadership takeaways

- Take the time to reflect on your education vision. Leadership does not require you to be someone else; make how you lead reflect your values and strive to inject it with heart.

- Our inboxes get bombarded by information on continuing professional development, awards and Kitemarks. Ask yourself: do they help me to achieve or enhance my school's vision?

- Community, community, community.

- Don't judge a school by its Ofsted grade. An 'outstanding' school still has to grow and improve, and 'special measures' and 'requires improvement' schools have a lot to give others.

- Conformity and working in unity does not necessarily indicate strong teamwork.

- Find that leadership seed in others and give it the conditions to germinate and grow and learn from mistakes.

- Always remember the power of your words and actions.

- Don't define or limit yourself or others by their background or circumstance.

- Parental views must not trump safeguarding.

- Don't ignore the richness and diversity of culture when teaching fundamental British values.

- Deliver a curriculum and provide an ethos that values more than academic outcomes.

- Take the time to think about the wave you are riding.

References

Adams, Richard (2017) Inspectors to Question Primary School Girls Who Wear Hijab, *The Guardian* (19 November). Available at: https://www.theguardian.com/education/2017/nov/19/school-inspectors-to-question-primary-school-girls-who-wear-hijab.

Adams, Richard (2018) Senior Ofsted Official Backs Headteacher Over Hijab Ban for Under Eights, *The Guardian* (1 February). Available at: https://www.theguardian.com/education/2018/feb/01/ofsted-chief-backs-headteacher-over-hijab-ban-for-under-eights.

Addley, Esther (2016) BBC Defends Extremist's Presence on Muslim Reality Show, *The Guardian* (9 December). Available at: https://www.theguardian.com/media/2016/dec/09/bbc-defends-extremists-presence-on-muslim-reality-show.

Beckles, Jennifer (2007) Ofsted Faces Special Measures on Equality, *The Guardian* (3 November). Available at: https://www.theguardian.com/education/2007/nov/13/schools.ofsted.

Birmingham City Council (2010) Sparkbrook Ward Committee Meeting Minutes (14 December).

Birmingham City Council (2018) Children's Rights Celebrated Across Birmingham Schools (13 July). Available at: https://www.birmingham.gov.uk/news/article/295/childrens_rights_celebrated_across_birmingham_schools.

Bracchi, Paul (2017) So How DID Birmingham Become the Jihadi Capital of Britain? 'Connection' of London Terror Attacker to Britain's Second City is More Than Just a Coincidence, *Daily Mail* (23 March). Available at: https://www.dailymail.co.uk/news/article-4344300/How-DID-Birmingham-jihadi-capital-Britain.html.

Coles, Maurice I. with Gent, Bill (eds) (2020) *Education for Survival: The Pedagogy of Compassion*. London: UCL IOE Press.

Department for Education (DfE) (2018) *Out-of-School Education Settings: Report on the Call for Evidence Conducted November 2015 to January 2016* (April). Available at: https://assets.publishing.service.gov.uk/government/uploads/system/uploads/attachment_data/file/698250/Out-of-school_education_settings-Report_on_the_call_for-evidence.pdf.

Department for Education (DfE) (2019) *Relationships Education, Relationships and Sex Education (RSE) and Health Education: Statutory Guidance for Governing Bodies, Proprietors, Head Teachers, Principals, Senior Leadership Teams, Teachers*. Available at: https://assets.publishing.service.gov.uk/government/uploads/system/uploads/attachment_data/file/1019542/Relationships_Education__Relationships_and_Sex_Education__RSE__and_Health_Education.pdf.

Department for Education (DfE) (2020) *Guidance: Headteachers' Standards 2020* (updated 13 October). Available at: https://www.gov.uk/government/publications/national-standards-of-excellence-for-headteachers/headteachers-standards-2020.

Department for Education (DfE) (2021) Get Information About Schools: Nelson Mandela School. Available at: https://www.get-information-schools.service.gov.uk/Establishments/Establishment/Details/103384#school-dashboard.

Department for Education (DfE) and Gibb, Nick (2017) The Power of Greater Freedom and Autonomy for Schools. Speech to the Freedom and Autonomy for Schools National Association Autumn Conference (2 November). Available at: https://www.gov.uk/government/speeches/nick-gibb-the-power-of-greater-freedom-and-autonomy-for-schools.

Diamond, Colin (2019a) Parkfield School and No Outsiders: We Must Learn from Trojan Horse History in Birmingham, *Schools Week* (20 January). Available at: https://schoolsweek.co.uk/parkfield-school-and-no-outsiders-we-must-learn-from-trojan-horse-history-in-birmingham.

Diamond, Colin (2019b) There is a Way Out of the Schools LGBT Protest Mess – But Ministers Need to Get Behind It, *The Guardian* (6 August). Available at: https://www.theguardian.com/education/2019/aug/06/way-out-of-schools-protest-mess-birmingham-trojan-horse.

Echo Eternal (2019) Echo #12 '10 Thousand Souls' [video] (19 October). Available at: https://www.youtube.com/watch?v=1KzaDON3PKc&feature=youtu.be.

Fullan, Michael (2005). *Leadership and Sustainability: System Thinkers in Action.* Thousand Oaks, CA: Corwin Press.

Hargreaves, Andy and Fink, Dean (2006) *Sustainable Leadership.* San Francisco, CA: Jossey-Bass.

Harris, Alma and Jones, Michelle (2020) COVID 19: School Leadership in Disruptive Times, *School Leadership & Management*, 40(4): 243–247. Available at: https://www.tandfonline.com/doi/ref/10.1080/13632434.2020.1811479.

Iqbal, Karamat (2013) *Dear Birmingham: A Conversation with My Hometown.* N.p.: Xlibris.

Lock, Stuart (ed.) (2020) *The researchED Guide to Leadership: An Evidence-Informed Guide for Teachers.* Woodbridge: John Catt Educational.

Lynch, Kathleen; Grummell, Bernie; and Devine, Dympna (2012) *New Managerialism in Education: Commercialization, Carelessness and Gender.* Basingstoke: Palgrave Macmillan.

Mandela, Nelson (2004) Address by Nelson Mandela at the Acknowledgement Ceremony of FCB Harlow Butler, Johannesburg (27 February). Available at: http://www.mandela.gov.za/mandela_speeches/2004/040227_butler.htm.

Mandela, Nelson (2010) *Conversations with Myself.* London: Pan Macmillan.

Morley, Peter (dir.) (1979) *Kitty: Return to Auschwitz* [film]. Yorkshire Television. Available at: https://www.youtube.com/watch?v=QIbIn18ND6I.

Munby, Steve (2019) *Imperfect Leadership: A Book for Leaders Who Know They Don't Know It All.* Carmarthen: Crown House Publishing.

Ofsted (2000) Inspection Report: Nelson Mandela Community School (8–9 May). Available at: https://files.ofsted.gov.uk/v1/file/764223.

Ofsted (2006) Inspection Report: Fulham Primary School (2–3 November). Available at: https://files.ofsted.gov.uk/v1/file/828435.

Richardson, Justin and Parnell, Peter (2005) *And Tango Makes Three.* London: Simon & Schuster.

Stuart, Hannah (2017) *Islamist Terrorism: Analysis of Offences and Attacks in the UK (1998–2015).* London: Henry Jackson Society. Available at: https://henryjacksonsociety.org/wp-content/uploads/2017/03/Islamist-Terrorism-preview-1.pdf.

United Nations Children's Fund (UNICEF) (1989) *The United Nations Convention on the Rights of the Child.* Available at: https://downloads.unicef.org.uk/wp-content/uploads/2016/08/unicef-convention-rights-child-uncrc.pdf.

United Nations Children's Fund (UNICEF) (2000) *For Every Child.* London: Hutchinson.

United Nations Children's Fund (UNICEF) UK (2017) Rights Respecting Schools Award. Assessment Report: Level One, Nelson Mandela Primary School (14 June).

United Nations Children's Fund (UNICEF) UK (2019) Rights Respecting Schools Award. Accreditation Report: Gold, Nelson Mandela School (25 January).

Waters, Mick (2020) Towards a Compassionate School System. In Maurice I. Coles with Bill Gent (eds), *Education for Survival: The Pedagogy of Compassion*. London: UCL IOE Press, pp. 27–43.

Chapter 7

One love: the creation of the CORE MAT

Adrian Packer

Introduction

I first met Adrian Packer in 2011 when he arrived at Goodison Park for an interview as principal of the new Everton Free School. He was the outsider hailing from the Medway towns rather than Merseyside and needed to keep his football loyalties a secret in the Everton boardroom.[1] He was given twenty minutes to deliver his PowerPoint presentation, and by the time he had finished the job was his. He electrified the room by synthesising his life experiences with his career to date and explaining how that had prepared him to lead Everton's new school.

Years working at the BRIT School, steeped in performing arts and media education, and then setting up Birmingham Ormiston Academy to bring the model to the West Midlands, had prepared Packer well for a high-profile role with Everton Football Club. Everton was the first premiership football club to apply to open a free school. This wasn't a routine mainstream school. In line with the mission of Everton in the Community (one of the UK's top sporting charities), Everton Free School would offer alternative provision to pupils who had been excluded from schools across Merseyside. In other words, Everton was putting its reputation on the line by opening its doors to 100 children with difficult educational histories – all wearing club-branded uniform.

The school opened in 2012 and was judged good with outstanding leadership and management by Ofsted (2014a). Packer had translated the vision into reality, establishing a school packed with innovative features and operating in the full media glare that surrounds everything the big football clubs do on Merseyside. His leadership credentials were orthodox in some senses, having designed and opened schools in urban England, but decidedly different with his roots in the theatre and his drive to seek high-level partnerships between education and sports and arts organisations.

---

1   He is a Liverpool FC supporter – not something that would have gone down particularly well at Goodison.

By 2014, Packer had taken on the role of CEO at Park View Educational Trust and executive principal at Park View School. The head of Ofsted, Sir Michael Wilshaw, did not 'get' this initially when he visited Park View. He thought that the recovery journey should be led in a military style (channelling his own tenure at Mossbourne Academy – see, for example, Kulz, 2017). How wrong he was. The last thing Park View needed was a top-down autocratic leadership model that would have suppressed all of the tensions and problems that emerged in September 2014. The school needed a leader who would listen and learn from all stakeholders, rather than implementing a drop-down formula for improvement.

Park View attracted attention like no other school caught up in Trojan Horse. It was at the centre of the media attention and the focus of the combined forces of the Department for Education (with its Education Funding Agency, education advisers and regional school commissioner officials) and Ofsted. This was because Tahir Alam was a 'central figure' (Clarke, 2014, p. 50) and key to understanding the Trojan narrative. His involvement with Park View went back to his own schooldays and ended when he resigned from being a member of Park View Educational Trust in July 2014. His influence on the school, including its transition to multi-academy trust status, and many other schools in the city is well documented. His impact on the policies, curriculum and staffing appointments at Park View was profound. He then sought to proselytise this model to other schools via his extensive networks in the city.

All new headship posts present challenges. Park View was off the scale because the staff body was riven, whistle-blowers were working alongside those faithful to the Park View model, and the future of the school was uncertain after plummeting from outstanding to requiring special measures. Senior leaders had been suspended and there was a leadership vacuum across the trust's three schools. The incoming trustees appointed Packer to lead the recovery journey knowing that whoever took on the job would be under intense scrutiny.

Perhaps the hardest legacy to deal with was Park View's strong performance at GCSE. Packer describes how the culture he inherited was based on a 'tough love' model predicated on command and control in the classrooms, with the inevitable displacement into the corridors. It was also predicated on a narrow vision of what education was required for 'these pupils', so the arts and sports were relegated in favour of a narrow curriculum. It took Packer some time to deconstruct and understand what was happening at Park View, whilst simultaneously re-brokering Golden Hillock School to Ark and reviving Nansen Primary School. Redefining and reinventing Park View as Rockwood Academy within the CORE Education Trust is a brilliant illustration of how success can be built on both community roots and external partnerships. It gives the lie to the notion that a 'tough love' (i.e. firm, traditional teaching and behaviour policies to match) approach is necessary for the Alum Rock community or any other inner-city community, regardless of ethnicity. His story complements the rich, three-dimensional understanding of leading urban schools in what are often called 'working class' communities (see Gilbert, 2018).

Packer describes how he needed to suppress his natural tendencies to look outwards beyond the school in the early days of leading Park View because privacy was at a premium and the first stage of the recovery journey required an internally focused approach. The world's media had been on the doorstep when Tahir Alam resigned in July 2014. No cameras were required to get the school functioning well again.

However, once the basics were in place and a new direction of travel had emerged, it was driven by the most creative of partnerships. This started with engagement with the Lawn Tennis Association, which saw Rockwood pupils spectating at Wimbledon and playing tennis with John Bercow, the speaker of the House of Commons – a far cry from petty disputes about whether female pupils should be involved in inter-school competitions because of alleged concerns from male members of staff wishing to protect their modesty. The Royal Birmingham Conservatoire began to engage with Rockwood and brought musical enrichment to the school. The finest manifestation is the award-winning Echo Eternal, a commemorative arts, media and civic engagement project inspired by the testimony of British survivors of the Holocaust and survivors of the 1994 genocide in Rwanda.[2] Echo Eternal brings together school pupils of all ages in a multi-media, multi-subject curriculum project that has culminated in an exhibition in the Library of Birmingham and performances at Birmingham Town Hall. The experiences, learning expeditions and performances for all those involved take children and staff way beyond their home communities.

Packer's chapter is central to this book because it synthesises themes and lessons learnt en route about how to turn schools to face the world and

---

2   See https://echoeternal.uk/participants/artists.

prepare their pupils not for a jingoistic version of fundamental British values but to become successful, globally compassionate citizens.

Colin Diamond

One love: the creation of the CORE MAT

Adrian Packer

'I chose to stay away from this circus,' was the unexpected boast from a Birmingham Education Partnership official during my first meeting with him nearly three years after I came to serve the communities of Park View, Nansen and Golden Hillock. These had been the Park View Educational Trust (PVET) schools in the eye of the Trojan Horse storm in September 2014. What I understood him to mean was that, from the outside looking in, he had formed a view that the whole affair had been something of a freak show. He had indeed kept a distance during the tough times, and I wondered why he had suddenly turned up to 'reflect on our achievements' with me. Ofsted had just left town giving us a clean bill of health, so I concluded that he, like so many others who followed soon after, was suddenly curious to see what all the fuss had been about now that the battle zone had been sufficiently de-risked. Far from feeling flattered by this sudden swell of attention, the parallels with where our story began were unsettling.

Earlier in 2012, the Edu-crowd would regularly flock to Park View School to learn from those 'outstanding' leaders who had given the community a school to be proud of – one bragging exceptional academic outcomes in so-called 'challenging circumstances'. By 2014, the boasting had inevitably become muted in the wake of one of the biggest school controversies ever seen in this country. In happier times, the strong consensus view from a proud team of staff had been that 'these children' in 'this community' responded best to a particular kind of education that had been pioneered in Birmingham's Alum Rock. Now, in the aftermath of the school's darkest hour, there still remained a confused and confusing sense of loyalty to this ideal, a treasured homemade recipe of success, despite the fact that the glory days had been so short-lived and the whole PVET plan had turned to dust.

The silent grief that now echoed through the once vibrant corridors was palpable and painful. In my aim to lift the mood during my first few days as the bouncy, new executive head teacher, I asked for access to the Park View loudspeaker system to play some music at home time. I recalled that the whole-school tannoy had been referred to in the Clarke report (2014,

p. 42) as part of a contentious call-to-prayer system. At the end of my first week, I decided to blast out Bob Marley's 'One Love'. This was to be the first of a playlist of music from different times and from various parts of the world to be played every home time in an attempt to recalibrate the mood that had been in steady decline for months. I admit that the inaugural track was a personal favourite, but I thought it was a particularly apt choice for a school community that once celebrated as one but now grieved in silos. It played out to giggles from children and frowns from adults. In the senior leadership team meeting the following Monday, it was put to me that I had been recklessly provocative and that I did not understand 'this community'. I was, it seemed, immediately at odds with the particular kind of education that worked for 'these children'.

I turned to a senior colleague who had very quickly and generously become my go-to cultural sense-check confidante. He explained that he had found the music difficult to accept on a personal level, but he encouraged me to continue to do what I felt was right because he trusted my judgement in doing what I believed to be in the school's best interests, and that second-guessing what the community might or might not say would be a distraction from the main business of looking after the children. He suggested toning it down, perhaps playing something once a week rather than daily. So, the music played on and I never once received a complaint about this from anyone in the community. I received plenty of complaints about many other matters, but never the music.

The reaction from the majority of senior leaders about 'One Love' brought the reality of the task ahead of me into sharp focus. I realised that it would be a strategic disaster to implement too much of a 'brave new world' style of leadership in these fragile, early days. Instead, I understood the need to deconstruct the component parts of the kind of education I had inherited in order to begin the process of rebuilding the whole thing again from scratch. Furthermore, I would have to do this in full view of plenty of people waiting for me to trip up. My first two weeks under this new, uncomfortable spotlight were broadly made up of attuning myself to an unsettled and volatile political landscape; inheriting the role of commissioning officer over a dozen staff investigations following two high-profile and contentious inquiries; confronting reporters at the school gates demanding statements and interviews; attempting to understand the nuances of some deep-rooted staff tensions and the inevitable factions that followed; composing a post-Ofsted action plan in response to three of the most damning inspection reports of all time;

absorbing the concerns of understandably angry and frustrated parents; negotiating peace deals with local politicians; and, to top it all off, accommodating my first unannounced Ofsted monitoring inspection led by the then Her Majesty's Chief Inspector Sir Michael Wilshaw (Ofsted, 2014b).

And then there were the children who deserved better and wondered how they had ended up in this mess. My first student meeting at Park View was sobering. 'They talk about us a lot. Why don't they try to talk with us?' was how they answered my question about the effects of the barrage of recent negative media coverage. I immediately called a filmmaker friend and asked him to make an in-house documentary from a student perspective. I saw an urgent need to control our own narrative and to amplify the students' voices by capturing their thoughts and feelings about these events on their terms. This became an important theme of the approach I went on to promote: to turn adversity on its head and take our lead from those most adversely affected – the children.

Despite the early day Trojan Horse madness back in 2014, it was to be these lucid and eloquent student voices that inspired my resolve and guided me to stay focused on the business of promoting a 'carry on carrying on' approach, to negate the drama, calm the atmosphere and always think of the students' best interests when making the tough decisions. Above all, I wanted to keep us all out of the headlines. This was an unnatural impulse for me. After my short-lived career as an attention-seeking theatre performer, I worked for the high-profile BRIT School and then for Everton Football Club as founding principal of the new Everton Free School. In all those previous existences, I had proactively sought out opportunities to make the headlines. No, I had to learn to bite my tongue, and instead focus on making small and quiet inroads amidst the blur of all the noise around us.

That noise was complex and difficult to manage. Intelligent adults had become embroiled in a free speech free-for-all – the equivalent of children talking over each other, getting louder and louder until they are enveloped in their own incoherence. Everyone had a view about who was or was not to blame, what did or did not actually happen. Conspiracy theories were wild and wacky; a culture of fear and suspicion prevailed. It is not surprising that another of my early duties was to refer dozens of staff towards emergency therapeutic interventions with many of them suffering from post-traumatic stress.

Challenging the culture at Park View

I soon came to embrace the mantra that in order to properly understand chaos one must put oneself at the centre of it. In my case, the understanding came through my eventual realisation that the hitherto PVET ethos held on to so dearly by pretty much everyone left standing related to the premise that 'these children' – who were from predominantly conservative Muslim families and from areas of so-called deprivation – responded best to a 'tough love' kind of education. This invariably meant being confronted and shouted at when they stepped out of line. What I recall most vividly was the extraordinary number of children in corridors facing walls. Compliance had been the name of the game for some time. It had been justified because it was all part of the bigger plan, which was emblazoned across the school minibus: 'Park View: breaking the links between demographic, deprivation and destiny', or something very similar. It may as well have said: 'Poor children on board'.

As someone who grew up in an area comparable to Alum Rock, albeit in another part of the country, I thought this was a condescending sentiment, but I was pleased to meet and work closely with the leaders who had promoted this view because I was struck by their noble intentions to do the right thing. They were motivated by social justice, to even the playing field and to improve life chances for children from disadvantaged minority groups. However, some of the most enthusiastic supporters of this approach tended to talk about the children in a way that made the whole set-up feel like a laboratory experiment. This is where I drew the line. In contrast, there were quieter, more authentic role models, staff I immediately felt an affinity with and, crucially, who were once one of 'these children' from the local area, from similar family and cultural backgrounds. My bond with them became important to me and steered my understanding of the local context.

Ultimately, I had new ideas for PVET because I saw the so-called 'challenging circumstances' differently and not as anything to do with social or economic deprivation. The school had boasted exceptional academic outcomes for some years. It is certainly true that GCSE results had been above national averages, but at what cost? The focus on GCSE outcomes (including a particularly heavy emphasis on BTECs when they were the equivalent of multiple GCSEs) had been intense because the school's headline results had become the ultimate and unapologetic indicator of success. But the majority of children I met when I arrived were, by any measure, culturally introspective and therefore impoverished; no amount of GCSEs would prepare them for life beyond school. My view of the challenging circumstances was therefore that children were being deprived of a fully rounded education as a result of the emphasis on academic outcomes, which apparently came about because of a 'social deprivation' label being thrust upon them whether they liked it or not.

I resolved to shift the focus to look beyond GCSE results, but not at the expense of high standards and high aspirations. I also continued to encourage a positive emphasis on faith and provide safe opportunities for students to express themselves on their terms. This was difficult to support because we had been hit hard by falling staff capacity levels. When PVET collapsed, a huge void in leadership opened up. This created the conditions for subsequent complex subplots to evolve; staff became caught up in cultural crossfire, misguided and muddled alliances formed, and many, disillusioned by the whole affair, made the ultimate choice to walk away from it all. Results inevitably suffered. Our institutional self-esteem was at rock bottom, so it would take more than some aspirational rhetoric from me or anyone else to shift the dial. We needed action and some quick-win, tangible results, and it was never going to be a one-person job. We needed a team, but that would be much easier said than done.

PVET faced a profound image problem, particularly at Park View. For example, the school had been supported generously for many years by a well-known bank. The Trojan Horse label would certainly have been an uncomfortable one for them, given that their brand features, yes, a horse. Of course, it was merely a coincidence that, by the time I arrived, this relationship had been reconsidered and was now no more, but it was a sign of what was to come. Our brand had become toxic. Our children reported going to events and being met by students from other schools whispering to each other and glaring with disgust, as though the freak show had come to town. We heard reports that our students felt that putting Park View on their CVs would do nothing but harm their future plans.

The brand damage, and the inevitable capacity depletion, was most felt at Park View, but it had implications across all three schools for which I was responsible. They had all been affected by, at worst, a combination of suspensions, walk-outs and long-term sickness absences and, at best, those who had just about held on to the end of the previous academic year but handed in letters of resignations on the first day back in September 2014.

My first staff address at Park View was surreal. I had driven down from Liverpool where I had said my farewells to an incredibly loyal team at Everton Free School. The mood there had been somewhat subdued, but I knew this would be nothing compared to what I was about to experience. I was mindful of my role as chief mood-maker and I knew it would be a tough opener. I was nervous, and I wondered if any attempts to lighten the mood would be misplaced. I feared hostility, suspicion and resentment. I was right on all counts; it was to be a bad start. The abiding image is one of a sea of tightly folded arms, frowning faces and more head shaking than I could ever have imagined.

However, there was one pleasant surprise after that first meeting. A group of about eight members of staff stayed behind to personally welcome me with a warm handshake and words of encouragement. What happened next was extraordinary: almost every single one of them was subsequently suspended. Teachers hitherto referred to by letter (Teacher A, Teacher B, etc.) in the Clarke (2014) report now had actual names, as one by one they were identified and one by one they were added to the ever-growing list of casualties.

I understood that the investigations (into double figures) of suspended staff needed to be concluded quickly, and with great care and diligence. Frustratingly, our investigations became muddled in the public perception with those conducted by the National College for Teaching and Leadership, which ultimately collapsed because of the way evidence was handled. Our enquiries and subsequent hearings were, in contrast, exemplary and concluded in a timely manner. Even the prime minister at the time, David Cameron, got this wrong. In a visit to Birmingham, he was asked by the press about Trojan Horse and said he wanted to send out a strong message that the investigations needed to be concluded quickly. He thought he was putting pressure on us. In fact, he was referring to his own government agency, yet he and pretty much everyone else did not understand the difference. These misunderstandings did us no favours.

It was undoubtedly during the investigation process that I encountered the most varied range of 'truths'. It was always a challenge to work out who or what to trust. The answer, it turned out, came from my own accidental provocation – from the message of 'One Love'. I came to realise that the one thing everyone I met during the early days generally always agreed on was that there was a need to move on. I recognised that we could only ever do that as a single cohesive unit, so mistrust had to be removed as a barrier to this aspiration. It was healthy, of course, that we might all have come from different backgrounds and even have different motivations, but I resolved that, whether an individual deserved or demanded my attention, if they were committed to moving on then I would reach out to them with an inviting hand.

A partnership vision for CORE

As our numbers grew and we made our first small but progressive steps, an unofficial strapline emerged that we were 'fuelled by humility'. We became determined to shift the emphasis away from the blur of noise towards the clarity of purpose. My job was to lead that single community of people who simply wanted to join in with an agenda that focused on children and halt the advance of any more adult point-scoring. It became an exhausting but exhilarating endeavour and yielded some immediately rewarding outcomes. With a small but motivated task force now mobilised, I was rejuvenated and felt more strategically focused.

We developed a two-pronged approach to an emergency rescue-style school improvement strategy. Firstly, and perhaps most obviously, was the need to present a well-coordinated counter-narrative. This would involve more than a mere rebrand. My aim was to create a reimagined PVET by turning the headlines upside down. For example, when the news stories started to break in 2014, there was one that included a particularly negative report about tennis and gender segregation at Park View (Authi, 2015). I sought out the head of education at the Lawn Tennis Association (LTA) whom I had worked with before and respected very much. I pointed out to him how few minority groups I had noticed in the crowd at a recent Davis Cup tie held in the UK. I saw an opportunity for us to become part of a solution to his problem rather than him solving our problem. We quickly crafted a fantastically exciting partnership arrangement, which included large quantities of sponsored equipment, tickets for the students to go to Wimbledon and the World Final at the O2 in London, coaching for the girls from Judy Murray at Edgbaston and playing tennis with MPs, including John Bercow, the speaker of the House of Commons. It was (and still is) a win-win relationship.

Secondly, we would make lots of new friends. Inspired by the LTA model, we focused on sport, arts and cultural organisations as well as local businesses. The benefits of this strategy would be twofold: it gave us much more capacity to offer what is now commonly referred to as cultural capital for our students, and it improved our image by association (the latter was, of course, compatible with the first part of our strategy to reimagine ourselves). In persuading new partners to sign up, we found inspiration from the rather unlikely source of Bob Geldof. I had recalled how Geldof reported how he assembled the Band Aid contributors in the 1980s. He had told Bono (or someone like him) that he had got Boy George (or someone like him) on board, he had told Boy George he had got Sting (or someone like him) on board and so he continued, making different pop stars feel compelled to sign up because others already had (even though maybe they hadn't quite yet confirmed!). We did something similar, starting with the strength of the LTA brand. We ended up with a list of more than a dozen new prestigious and supportive partners within a matter of weeks. My address book helped because of longstanding links with the creative industries.

We got some impressive early traction through these partnerships, and as we started to feel better about ourselves, we began turning some very small corners very slowly. Then the Department for Education, which was lurking around every one of those corners, pounced. They asked me to explore new sponsorship options for Park View and Nansen (we had already agreed to re-broker Golden Hillock to Ark). Initially, we approached about a dozen potential sponsors – some local, some national. However, where we had managed to get plenty of partners on board, we were less successful in convincing a new sponsor to step forward. The risk was too great, and there were no obvious signs of Ofsted green shoots despite our optimism that there soon would be. The solution transpired very naturally: we would have to do it ourselves. This provided an important moment in time for us to regroup and ask ourselves who we were, what we wanted to achieve, how to make that happen and, perhaps above all, why *we* should be the ones taking the risk in the first place.

I convened a workshop to address these questions and to flesh out the details of what our reimagining could do to give 'these children' their schools back to them. They had never done anything wrong, so we had to get it entirely right this time round. The workshop lasted a whole day and was led by one of our trustees, Ammo Talwar, who went on to become our chair. He had stood shoulder to shoulder with me since day one. I respected his opinion a great deal, not least because he had previously made it abundantly clear what kind of leader I had to be if he and other local activists were to support me. It was sobering as he explained very straightforwardly that I had to be a 'stayer'. I had to commit to finish my teaching leadership career with this trust and these schools. If I had thoughts of flying in, fixing it and flying out again, in order to have something impressive on my CV, I was the wrong man for the job. I knew from an early stage that this was going to be more than a career move; it was going to be a lifestyle choice.

We were joined in the workshop by one of the three original new trustees brought in by the Department for Education, Pat Smart – a very successful and driven primary head teacher; by our chair at the time, Waheed Saleem, a brilliantly attuned political type with strong links locally; and, finally, sitting quietly at the end of the table, the real secret of our success and a Trojan Horse survivor, Joanne Tyler. Joanne's key attribute was that she understood the whole affair from a 360-degree perspective. She knew Trojan Horse had never been a simple 'them and us' clash of ideologies. She was and remains incredibly balanced, having both whistle-blown against some of the previous leadership regimes and given support in evidence for others. This reimagining process for her was therapeutic. She had stood on the front line with great courage and was doing much more than just standing still. She was a tower of strength – driven, pragmatic and sensitive.

Joanne and I had inevitably become kindred spirits, but there were some important and useful differences between us. Fondly referred to as the 'Dream Crusher', Joanne finds creative chat tiresome. She sat patiently in the workshop which had been full of such chat. At the end of the morning session, I realised she had not said anything. Knowing she was likely to provide the ultimate distillation of thinking and a much-needed focus, I asked if she had anything to add. She had been scribbling notes on her pad and told us that buried beneath all the chat, five words featured repeatedly – collaboration, opportunity, respect, excellence and equality.

Collaboration had been at the forefront of our thinking. We were absolutely committed to an outward-facing approach because the schools had imploded. The early partnership strategy had been very successful in lifting the mood and improving the day-to-day experiences for students and staff. We were passionate about broadening horizons and allowing our students to be defined by these new experiences, not merely by GCSE results and certainly not by Trojan Horse.

Our discussions about *opportunity* had related to the deprivation narrative. We wanted opportunities for children that were not about breaking conceptual links between deprivation and destiny, but instead about making practical links for every child. This would involve promoting a sense of pride about where they and their families are from, but to be equally open-minded about what is possible in life and where this could lead them in the future. We would do this by showing children what it looks like out there, not talking about it theoretically. We wanted good governance to be a driver of the opportunity agenda, creating a structure where local governance would be charged with focusing on our most vulnerable and disadvantaged children.

Respect came from our collective understanding that the trust and its schools had lost their self-respect and that the infighting was a symptom of this. We wanted a respect agenda which guaranteed that our students would feel safe and happy – no more staring at walls in corridors. We also wanted to create a culture of respect for the business of educating children. Professional standards had eroded with basic errors becoming commonplace. At its worst, this put children at risk. Safeguarding records were a mess and reporting was haphazard and confusing. The quality of teaching was also suffering because staff motivation levels were low. Children were bored; generally compliant but not at all stimulated. They deserved much better.

Excellence had to be front and centre of everything we did. If we were going to reset the bar, we knew we had to set it high. We also understood the need to create high expectations because standards were plummeting before our eyes. We also needed to attract the best staff. It is perverse that schools in a privileged context generally attract excellent teachers. We wanted to overcome this challenge by communicating with passion and energy that working in our schools would be a privilege with great rewards.

The fifth word was *equality*, which we agreed would run through all our endeavours. We were therefore left with, as Joanne pointed out, five words that would give us our new identity. We were to become CORE Education Trust, fuelled by humility as we served the needs of children who deserved better. These five values were, in fact, more about what we valued rather than values per se. We would do everything through the lens of these values. With the new trust established, our next task was to go back to the children and ask them if they wanted to rename Park View. They did. We came up with some names (my suggestion was Ebadi Academy after Iranian Nobel Prize winner Shirin Ebadi), but it was one of the students who reminded us about the importance of being proud of where we are from. They combined the Rock of Alum Rock and the Wood of Washwood Heath to make Rock Wood Academy. We made it one word and had a mass vote of the students, staff and families. Rockwood was a clear winner; Ebadi came last!

It would be just twelve months later when CORE Education Trust faced its first big test. Our schools would be inspected by Ofsted at the end of their monitoring inspection cycle. We didn't have long to prove that delivering a CORE Education would be successful, but we got quite an endorsement from those inspections (Ofsted 2016a, b). What was most rewarding was the heavy emphasis of praise on the trust's role in the rehabilitation of the schools. We didn't let it go to our heads. We knew that we were never going to solve everything for everyone, and that some of what we had achieved was about that moment in time and could not be replicated in the future. However, what we did manage to achieve in those 2016 inspections was a validation in a kind of education that wasn't conceptual but was about genuinely meeting a local need in very practical terms. It was based on a day-to-day application of giving the children in our schools what they deserved – that is, the very best educational opportunities and experiences, not simply because of where they are from but because of the possibilities of where they might go next.

New challenges were then presented to us. Following the successes of the 2016 inspections, we promised not to put ourselves through anything similar ever again. We were exhausted. However, once we had caught our breath and found a new rhythm, we realised that what we had done was exactly what we should keep on doing: going where others dare not. So, when the opportunity to step forward came again, we relished it. We were soon asked to consider taking on four more schools from another trust that had been embroiled in controversy following a financial irregularity scandal. The pattern of failure was unnervingly similar to PVET, but this time we had those five magic words that would steer us into our next chapter with confidence, resilience and determination at our core. The circus was back in town, and we were more ready than ever to roll up (roll up) our sleeves and go again.

Leadership takeaways

- **On leading through crisis:** Be the best you, not the second-best someone else, but always choose your words carefully and avoid confusing authenticity with raw emotion. Composed eloquence is one of your best friends when you find yourself at the centre of chaos, and sometimes no words at all can be the best option.

- **On trusting new colleagues:** Accept that there are always different versions of historical events in a school; make up your own mind about how to interpret these events – but take your time to hear as many versions as possible before you do. Building trust is central to any leadership team, but always keep in mind that self-interest can present itself in many mysterious ways, so treat over-friendly colleagues with caution!

- **On slogans:** Keep it simple. Avoid over-intellectualising what you are trying to achieve, even if what you are trying to achieve is underpinned by something conceptually intellectual.

- **On partnerships:** Look beyond your immediate context. You can never do everything you want to do alone, so take pride in your address book and use it wisely. Go way beyond your local community.

- **On getting results:** Insist that 'results' and 'context' are inextricably linked. What you set out to achieve for the children in your care should be based on *their* context, not *your* agenda.

- **On values:** Believe in them, embody them, exemplify them and always make your decisions inspired by them.

References

Authi, Jasbir (2015) Park View Banned Girls from Mixed Sports Because It Made 'Male Staff Uncomfortable', Hearing Told, *Birmingham Mail* (26 October). Available at: https://www.birminghammail.co.uk/news/midlands-news/park-view-banned-girls-mixed-10334889.

Clarke, Peter (2014) *Report into Allegations Concerning Birmingham Schools Arising from the 'Trojan Horse' Letter* (HC 576). Available at: https://assets.publishing.service.gov.uk/government/uploads/system/uploads/attachment_data/file/340526/HC_576_accessible_-.pdf.

Gilbert, Ian (ed.) (2018) *The Working Class: Poverty, Education and Alternative voices.* Carmarthen: Crown House Publishing.

Kulz, Christy (2017) Heroic Heads, Mobility Mythologies and the Power of Ambiguity, *British Journal of Sociology of Education*, 38(2): 85–104, Available at: https://doi.org/1 0.1080/01425692.2015.1044071.

Ofsted (2014a) School Report: Everton Free School (14–15 May). Available at: https:// files.ofsted.gov.uk/v1/file/2410306.

Ofsted (2014b) Special Measures Monitoring Inspection of Park View School the Academy of Mathematics and Science (11 September). Available at: https://files. ofsted.gov.uk/v1/file/2424809.

Ofsted (2016a) School Report: Nansen Primary School (8–9 March). Available at: https://files.ofsted.gov.uk/v1/file/2561760.

Ofsted (2016b) School Report: Rockwood Academy (16–17 March). Available at: https://files.ofsted.gov.uk/v1/file/2561768.

Chapter 8

I went to Highfield Junior and Infant School as a kid

Sajid Gulzar

Introduction

Few school leaders have the opportunity to turn around the primary school that they attended as a child. To do so in the context of Trojan Horse is unique. Sajid Gulzar grew up in the middle of Alum Rock, very close to Park View School. He worked in a number of primary schools in East Birmingham, serving his apprenticeship in the years when Trojan-type activities were underway, and was then asked to sponsor Highfield Primary School as CEO of the Prince Albert Community Trust (PACT). As he observes in this chapter, no two school improvement journeys are the same – and, in the context of the community confusion following the 2014 round of Ofsted inspections, his analysis and understanding of the situation brings an invaluable perspective.

In summary, by 2014 Highfield was a dysfunctional school where governance and leadership had been poor for many years. It had never been viewed as a good school by Ofsted. Surrounded by primary schools with better reputations in the community, Highfield became more vulnerable following the Ofsted inspection in 2014 as it had 25% pupil turnover (Ofsted, 2014d). Those leaving the school were doing relatively well and were being replaced by children who had been out of school for a long time and/or recently arrived in the country. The Kershaw Report (2014) identified that Highfield had been targeted as a poor-performing school where governors had been installed to encourage Islamic ideals. Had this made any difference in practice? Not according to Gulzar. The Highfield school improvement journey has many distinctive elements, but this was no Adderley scenario with years of tedious disruption and serial changes of head teacher. And the parents wanted that hitherto elusive 'decent education' with no hints of extremism or separatism in the air.

PACT was formed in 2015 based on the mothership, Prince Albert Junior and Infant School, which had long provided exceptional education for its pupils and families in Aston. A few hundred metres from Villa Park, the home of Aston Villa Football Club, this quintessentially inner-city school in its Victorian buildings had served many different communities over the years. Its most famous former pupil is Ozzy Osbourne and there are regular pilgrimages of Black Sabbath fans to see his alma mater. Heavy metal music took its inspiration from the hard, percussive noises found in Birmingham's forges and factories. But by the second decade of the twenty-first century in England's post-industrial second city, new communities were playing very different music. Prince Albert had, like many Birmingham primary schools, adapted to serve a pupil cohort from predominantly Asian and British-Asian families.

My first visit in June 2015 (during the Ozzy Osbourne tourist season) was exciting. Here was a primary school definitely not obsessed with standard assessment tests (SATs) results. Instead, it was focused on extending its early years and foundation stage organisation of learning and pedagogy upwards into Key Stage 2 because it was working so well for the pupils. The jagged cut-off point between reception and Key Stage 1 had been removed successfully, and now it was time to explore how to continue a rich early years model further up the year groups. That took professional confidence and courage.

It was a natural choice for Birmingham City Council to ask Prince Albert to work with its neighbouring Heathfield Primary School based on such a strong track record, and a brilliant choice for the Department for Education to ask the newly formed PACT to sponsor Highfield in the wake of the Trojan Horse inspections and the findings of Clarke and Kershaw.

Gulzar's description of that journey – from headship of a single primary school to being the CEO of a five primary school multi-academy trust, with the new Prince Albert High School opening in 2021 – has many learning points. At times, capacity was stretched to the limit, if not overstretched. Results dipped in 2016 at the high-flying Prince Albert Primary School, which led to Gulzar questioning his decisions and offering to tender his resignation. Fortunately, it was not accepted and PACT has gone from strength to strength. The trust had been able to draw on deep resources from both its teaching and administrative staff. The principle of installing home-grown top-notch classroom practitioners as heads of school worked well. This was possible because PACT had invested in its own continuing professional development (CPD) programmes, with a custom-designed post to lead CPD in the senior leadership team. Many of the features of

Gulzar's transition from head teacher to CEO are described in Carter and McInerney (2020, ch. 2).

The skill set is built on strong moral purpose, which is why Gulzar felt compelled to take on Highfield. The first dimension – one that he lectures master's students on at the University of Birmingham's Education Leadership Academy – is understanding change. So often underestimated by school leaders (at individual institution or systems level), a deep working knowledge of the dynamics of change management is critical.

Being able to move from the dance floor to the balcony and back down again is another key attribute. Gulzar describes it in Trekkie language (we all have our secrets!) and refers to the importance of visible leadership in PACT's DNA when building trust in the schools it has taken into its family. Equally, he acknowledges that the CEO role involves reading the dance floor from above, exactly as described by Heifetz and Linsky (2002, pp. 53–54): 'The only way you can gain both a clearer view of reality and some perspective on the bigger picture is by distancing yourself from the fray.' But if you want to affect what is happening, you must return to the dance floor: 'So you need to be both among the dancers and up on the balcony. That's where the magic is, going back and forth between the two, using one to leverage the other.'

I have seen excellent head teachers lose touch with what is happening on the ground/dance floor when they become CEOs. They feel they have moved on, so they delegate those vital forays along the corridors and into classrooms and staffrooms. Leading school improvement at scale does require adjustments and a fundamental rethink of the role, as Carter and McInerney (2020) set out, but this should not be at the expense of keeping your feet firmly on the ground.

Why was it a brilliant choice to ask PACT to sponsor Highfield (or, to use the language always used inside PACT, 'to join the family')? Because in the wake of Trojan Horse there was significant damage to the professional development and profile of Black, Asian and minority ethnic leaders, particularly Muslim leaders (as Rosemary Campbell-Stevens describes in Chapter 15). As a result of the media coverage of Trojan Horse – largely arising out of its portrayal as being inextricably linked to extremism – trust was at a premium, and many Muslim leaders and governors questioned whether they were wanted in Birmingham's schools. Gulzar and his team provided an unequivocal 'yes' to such questions and demonstrated that many of the solutions to the schools found wanting as a result of Trojan

Horse could be found within the community; a community whose name was frequently evoked by Tahir Alam as wanting a conservative education fit for Muslim children. What the community told Gulzar in 2015 was that they wanted a 'decent education'. By 2019, Ofsted gave their official stamp of approval and for the first time since Gulzar was a pupil in those classrooms, Highfield was officially a good school (Ofsted, 2019).

Colin Diamond

I went to Highfield Junior and Infant School as a kid

Sajid Gulzar

The challenges of taking on a 'Trojan Horse' school in special measures

School improvement in a school deemed to be failing is, in many ways, a strange process. With the lens of hindsight, the thing that is most obvious is that no two schools are the same. You can learn as much about a school as it is possible to learn from the incumbent leaders, the Department for Education, the parents, the local authority and so on. However, none of this will give you a sufficiently accurate picture of the status quo to understand what is really going on. Even extensive press coverage doesn't inform fully. Real awareness involves time spent inside the school with the children, staff and parents. This is the only way to understand the beating heart of the school – its maladies and foibles – and therefore to understand exactly what the school needs in order to improve effectively and sustainably. No two schools are the same and no failing school is 'easy' to turn around. However, there are degrees of hard and tough and complicated.

Highfield Junior and Infant School has always held a special place in my heart. It is where my schooling began, in September 1978 at the age of 4. In the 2000s I worked in a school just up the road from Highfield. I still lived in the area and would often walk to work, which took me past my old school on a fairly regular basis. I am youngest of five children, a second-generation immigrant and the first in my family to attend university – a familiar enough story. What is unusual is my return to lead the school thirty years after leaving as a pupil.

My Trojan Horse journey began before Highfield was placed in special measures. In early 2013, Prince Albert Primary School started supporting Heathfield Primary School. I was in the fourth year of my first headship when I was asked if there was capacity to support a 'vulnerable' school. I was in complete agreement with the local authority's judgement that the school was certain to be placed in special measures if inspected. A year on and both Heathfield and my own school, Prince Albert, were in a good place. Prince Albert was an exceptional school and Heathfield was entering a period of stability during which meaningful and long-lasting school improvement was well on its way. Heathfield was inspected in November 2013 and graded as requires improvement (Ofsted, 2013), with the recognition that the school was clearly moving in the right direction.

In April 2014, Heathfield was inspected again as part of the raft of Trojan Horse inspections taking place in twenty-one inner-city Birmingham schools (Ofsted, 2014b); I am still in the dark as to why Heathfield was inspected. (Heathfield was re-inspected in November 2014 (Ofsted, 2014d) – that is three inspections in the space of fifty weeks.) However, what I am clear about is that the Trojan Horse inspection almost knocked two schools – one exceptionally good (Prince Albert) and one improving (Heathfield) – off course for good. The section 8 'no formal designation' safeguarding inspection of April 2014 is probably best described as brutal. This is not perhaps the place to go into too much detail, but the inspectors paid mere lip service to the quality of education and effectiveness of safeguarding. The thrust of the inspection seemed to be to find evidence of an insidious and corrupt extremist underbelly to feed the moral panic in the media. The team chose a focus so narrow as to render the process almost meaningless in terms of the actual point of inspection.

Having experienced a Trojan Horse inspection first hand at Heathfield, it was unclear what we would find at Highfield. It was a time of rumour, claim and counter-claim. Anything from a takeover of schools by extremists to a gross overreaction from the authorities was being mooted as the 'truth'. What my team and I found was a school community in disarray. Every parent I spoke to wanted the same thing. They may have articulated their wishes in different ways but there was a general consensus: a decent education for our children. If there were extremist elements amongst the parent body, four years on they are yet to surface. Understandably, the parents were upset and exasperated by both the quality of education their children were receiving and the damaged reputation of the school.

Inside the school, we found a lack of trust amongst staff, particularly for the senior leadership team (not necessarily individual senior leaders). Expectations were not just unclear; in fact, there was a great deal of confusion. Conspicuous by its absence was any kind of extremist or separatist agenda. The governing body had been disbanded by 2014, but the press was awash with stories of an extremist influence within the community at certain schools in the city, including Highfield. I am yet to see this influence beyond the odd parent with slightly strange ideas about the role of school in promoting their religion, which is no different to any other school I have worked in since I qualified as a teacher.

The delicate balancing act of extending capacity in a very strong school across to one that was improving but still vulnerable and another that was failing, was exceptionally difficult to achieve. The risk of taking on Highfield at the time we did was immense, and it was not a risk that I fully appreciated at the time. My former deputy head teacher, now deputy CEO, certainly did; she cautioned me but ultimately supported me. Our recently formed trust board also expressed concerns but were won over by the moral argument. The deputy CEO was and still is largely the intellectual and strategic force behind the internal leadership development infrastructure that enabled us to mitigate that risk. Personally, the pull of Highfield was very strong. Ultimately, it was the moral argument that decided the situation. For me it was quite simple: this was my old primary school in the neighbourhood where my parents still live. The school that gave me the educational foundations that were the first steps on the path I now tread. A school that was failing over 800 children, their parents and staff. A school that had never been judged good by Ofsted and was poorly regarded by the community it served.

Building capacity at PACT

By 2015, our central support team was already well developed, which was unusual for a trust consisting of only two schools. I was very fortunate to be working with a group of non-teaching professionals who were able to have an immediate impact at another school. Not only was this within their own area of expertise, but they were also able to work as a team and support one another. In practical terms, this led to the implementation of effective systems for safeguarding, pastoral support, finance, human resources, administration, IT and all things relating to the site and buildings. It wasn't exactly an act of genius to allow a group of people who were experts in their field to work on a specific area of school improvement, having first identified exactly what needed to be done. I really worry when I come across head teachers and CEOs who feel they need to be an authority on every area of the business, from curriculum to human resources and so on. I have always found that surrounding yourself with very able people with a real depth of knowledge in a particular field is the surest route to the improvement and success of a school. The genius again though was my deputy CEO, who had also insisted that non-teaching senior leaders benefit from leadership development in the same way as teaching and learning colleagues.

By January 2016, all except one of the previous leadership team had either retired or moved on from Highfield. Approximately half of the teachers for the school's twenty-eight classes were temporary staff from agencies. There was a combination of very short-term to long-term supply teachers, with some classes seeing several different faces during the course of a single week. During that academic year, the children in these classes saw well over 100 teachers. In Year 6, all four classes were staffed by supply teachers.

Understandably, perhaps, pupil behaviour was exceptionally challenging. Disorder was commonplace, low-level disruption was the norm in most classrooms and fights during lessons were not unusual. In my first week as head teacher, I carried out over a dozen fixed-term exclusions for physical or extreme verbal abuse of an adult. At Highfield, the parents who shouted the loudest and showed the most aggression often got their way. Staff were routinely undermined and spoken to aggressively or disrespectfully. The overwhelming majority of parents wanted the same things that we wanted for the children: a good education in a safe, happy and welcoming environment in a school where they felt valued and supported when they needed it. Many parents had already or were attempting to vote with their feet, so many of our pupils were on the waiting lists of better schools in the area. The children who had left or were leaving tended to be the ones who were succeeding educationally. They were being replaced by a combination of new arrivals to the country or children who had spent a significant period of time out of school. In one twelve-month period we lost almost 200 pupils.

The previous regime had left behind a culture that was toxic and characterised by suspicion and mistrust. Clearly, the staff were feeling vulnerable and unsettled. In the wake of several teachers leaving, others were seriously considering their options. Staff described a school that provided little meaningful direction, development or support. Any of the systems that may exist in a regular, healthy school were conspicuous by their absence, including those for child protection and safeguarding in general. Other challenges included buildings that were in a very poor state of repair, very high pupil mobility and the school's very poor reputation locally.

The leadership capacity we had established was fully stretched during the first year or so. For the start of the 2015/2016 academic year, we had moved some teachers across from Prince Albert to Heathfield to strengthen the teaching. All the Prince Albert teachers were replaced by newly qualified teachers, in the knowledge that we had an exceptionally robust support and development programme for early career teachers, along with plenty of capacity to deliver it. What we had not planned for or anticipated at that point was the scale of what was going to face us at Highfield, nor the maternity leave of two senior leaders from Prince Albert. In the absence of an incumbent leadership team at Highfield, I took with me two assistant head teachers from the lead school. Both had started their teaching careers at Prince Albert and had been teaching for a couple of years by the time I began my headship there. This would be the first real stress test of the internal leadership programmes that had been the brainchild of my deputy head teacher and had been developed with the knowledge and insight of leadership coaches from the world of business. The intention of the programmes was to spot talent and create bespoke pathways to develop leadership skills, attributes and aptitudes, all underpinned by the culture and the ethos of the school.

Initially, the two assistant heads focused solely on improving teachers and teaching. My main focus was to begin to gain the trust and confidence of the parents and the community, and to work with the central support team to implement systems, structures and policies that would enable the school to function. During the first few weeks and months, simple and essential systems and structures were introduced in order that the school could begin to function as a healthy organisation. At the very start, though, what was needed was absolute clarity of purpose, well-defined expectations and consistency of message. This was the beginning of a change in culture that was necessary to enable school improvement to take place. It was the beginning of trust. The majority of staff were shell-shocked from their experiences over the previous two years or so. There was a sense of fragility about the school, particularly when it came to staff confidence and their belief that things could improve.

The importance of visible leadership

The key to gaining confidence, building trust and creating a culture in which the school could begin to improve was to ensure that leaders were visible and available. The only senior leader remaining from the previous team was the deputy head teacher. She had worked at the school for over thirty years; in fact, she was there during my time as a pupil. She was universally respected by staff, pupils and parents alike, and it was abundantly clear that she was very much part of the solution for the future prosperity of the school. She became an essential bridge between the old and the new. Before she eventually retired, she was able to help us in gaining the trust of the staff and parents.

As senior leaders, we focused on relationships. At all of our schools you will find a number of senior leaders out on the playground at the start and end of the day. All of our head teachers see time spent in the playground as essential to parental engagement and trust, and Highfield was no different. As a senior team, we made sure that there was an open-door policy for staff – and for those who didn't come to us, we went to them. We were able to convince staff that all monitoring was for the purpose of their development and to ensure that we were able to provide additional support where it was needed the most.

A big bump in the road

By the end of the academic year, after two terms of running Highfield, all three schools were feeling the strain. Key Stage 2 outcomes in 2016 were disastrous, expectedly so at Highfield but not at the lead school. There were a number of mitigating circumstances: a significant change in the testing regime, disruption (both planned and unplanned) at senior leadership level and so on. At the time, getting involved with Highfield felt like a mistake: had we bitten off more than we could chew? We had prided ourselves on a 'no surprises' culture where we were able to predict outcomes with a relative degree of certainty based on how well teachers and leaders knew the quality of provision and their depth of knowledge of the pupils and their individual circumstances. Sitting in an office with my senior team – consisting of the deputy CEO, heads of school and deputies – it felt almost like a bereavement. It was one of the lowest points for me as a senior leader and for us as a team.

After the initial shock, I did two things. The first was to sit with the person I trust the most in education – Phillipa Sherlock-Lewis, my deputy CEO – to reflect on and analyse what had happened. Could we pinpoint a specific decision, course of action, particular circumstances, a timeline or poor decision-making? The second was to see the chair and vice-chair of the trust and offer my resignation (which was declined by the trustees). That may sound a tad dramatic (the resignation that is) but I felt it was necessary. I have always tried to lead ethically and morally, and at the time I felt as if I had misled the board. I had assured them of the academic success of our established schools and that simply had not happened. In looking for answers to what had happened, in trying to understand, I reflected on my own leadership. Had I become complacent? Had I become too distant from the schools since starting to lead Highfield? The other reason for offering to resign was that I needed to know if I had the full, unequivocal backing of the board, and the only way to establish that was to give them the choice of accepting my resignation. It is important to note that resigning was the last thing I wanted to do. I felt I had a moral obligation to identify and fix the problems that had got us to this place.

A point to note here, and one that I think many heads who become CEOs will understand, is that it is a difficult transition. There is no blueprint; every trust is different. A couple of years ago, I ran a session for executive heads and CEOs for the Schools, Students and Teachers Network's executive headship programme. I spoke about my personal experience of going from the leadership of a school to the leadership of a multi-academy trust which includes that school. It is not easy to let go of a school you have led successfully, where you have built healthy and productive relationships with the entire school community, and where you are trusted. It is especially difficult to let go when you are still ultimately responsible for that school and where you are taking away the very things that made it successful in order to support a failing school. Being a lifelong Trekkie (more *Next Generation* than the original series), I finally understood Captain Picard's reluctance to leave the bridge and move upstairs. I had taken the decision to fade into the background in order to give the head teacher and the leadership team of Prince Albert school the time and space to establish themselves without the looming presence of the previous head teacher complicating and confusing matters. Had I stepped too far back?

Was I too entrenched in the school in special measures to fully appreciate the challenges elsewhere?

The deputy CEO and I adopted the principles of 'black box thinking' (Syed, 2015), and we looked in detail at every aspect of the situation across all three schools. We examined and reviewed the reading curriculum, not only in Year 6 but across every year group. We looked at leadership support for teachers and its effectiveness, including the quality and content of CPD programmes. Heads and deputies went out to schools with similar challenges and operating in similar circumstances which had been successful in navigating the changes to emphasis of SATs, reading in particular. All of this happened before the end of the academic year. They also produced a very clear and robust plan for improving outcomes from 2017. This included fundamental changes to the reading curriculum from early years through to Year 6, as this was the area in which we had seen the steepest decline. The idea that united us all during this period was: we never wanted to feel like we did in July 2016 again. Ever. This was underpinned by the fact that we saw this as a failure of leadership, not of the teachers. The teachers were therefore onside from the very beginning in terms of the changes that were made, which was coupled with clear direction and high-quality CPD.

With the exception of 2016 (retrospectively) and 2017, we have never been a school or trust that has been overly concerned with SATs results. In the first two or three years of my headship, the Key Stage 2 outcomes were not earth-shattering at the start. Our focus was on getting it right in the early years foundation stage and Key Stage 1. Better outcomes followed eventually, and we were absolutely fine with that because we knew the fundamentals were strong. In fact, at the very start of the Ofsted inspection at Prince Albert (February 2015), the lead inspector questioned our self-evaluation grading of outstanding as she felt that the RAISEonline analysis of pupil outcomes over the previous three years showed a school that required improvement. However, the inspectors found that the school was clearly outstanding in every inspection category. This level of focus on Key Stage 2 outcomes therefore was unusual for us. The changes bore fruit very quickly, with a significant upturn in outcomes that has largely been maintained.

By the start of 2017, a year on from going in as executive head, Highfield was relatively calm – relative to what we had found a year before, that is. Control had been achieved through establishing very clear expectations for staff, children and parents. We were by and large all working towards the same aim. Progress was slow and tentative, but it was steady. The two assistant head teachers who had joined me from Prince Albert were now head and deputy, and were supported by a leadership team made up of colleagues appointed largely from within the trust. Whilst I was operationally involved at Highfield, my deputy CEO made sure that the central team developed and continued to establish effective systems and structures to ensure that risks to the trust were minimised and the possibility of future growth was strengthened, as well as ensuring that the improvement or stability of the existing schools was maintained. The overwhelming majority of the permanent staff we inherited remained at the school, reaping the benefits of the development on offer.

Highfield school was eventually inspected by Ofsted in January 2019 and graded good for the first time. By then, it had enjoyed a period of stability in terms of leadership and staffing in general. The behaviour of the children was unrecognisable compared to early 2016, and despite the odd 'Highfield' day (which, incidentally, still happens from time to time), the children were happy, learning and beginning to thrive. At the time of writing, several of the original Highfield staff have been promoted within the trust. Elsewhere, Heathfield had been inspected in 2018 and been judged good, and we had taken on Birchfield (another inner-city Birmingham school) after it had been placed in special measures in June 2017. In November 2019, we began working with Banners Gate Primary School soon after it was placed in special measures. The school officially joined the trust on 1 December 2019 as Sutton Park Primary.

All of the learning from the first two ventures has ensured that the overall level of risk to the trust has been better managed each time we have taken on a failing school. However, there is no doubt that each time we do this the existing schools are weakened for a period. The capacity utilised in those early months and up to the first two years is significant.

Trojan Horse issues as a distraction from poor school performance

Ultimately, certainly for us, Trojan Horse was a bit of a red herring. The issues at Highfield were simply down to poor leadership over a sustained period of time. The school was systematically dysfunctional, and despite the efforts of many dedicated and hardworking staff it was spiralling out of control. The culture was wrong and there was an absence of structure and expectation. However, to be fair to Highfield, this has been the case to a lesser or greater degree at each of the schools we have supported and then taken on. Surprisingly, what we have learnt from leading failing schools is that improving the quality of the education is perhaps the most straightforward of tasks. Where it gets niggly, knotted and difficult is aspects such as human resources, contracts and finances. Staffing structures at such schools are rarely fit for purpose (or never, in my experience). Due diligence is therefore essential, as is the process of ensuring that each department is working effectively.

At both Birchfield and Banners Gate, we restructured the workforce before conversion. This is a painful and taxing experience for any staff team, whether or not they are directly affected. I deliberately led on the restructure myself to ensure that the leadership teams leading the schools did not become the subject of people's ire. As logical and as reasonable as it may be to make staff redundant for the greater good, the impact on individual lives is huge. It is people's ability to pay their bills and provide for their families. Quite understandably, it is a time when they are emotional and even angry, and this anger and frustration is often aimed at those who are seen as responsible. I figured that the last thing school leaders needed was division in their schools. Some discord is inevitable, but once the restructure is complete, then the healing process can begin, in the absence of the individual who initiated it. School leaders can be the ones to establish unity and a shared direction of travel.

In terms of improving the quality of education, a simple approach has worked time and again. Each time we have taken on a school, we have appointed a head of school from within the trust. Typically, this has been a colleague who had been a teacher at Prince Albert school. Two of them started at the lead school as newly qualified teachers. They had a track record of outstanding classroom practice and of improving teaching across the primary age group. They are highly professional, efficient and resilient but, perhaps most importantly, they are steeped in the values and the culture of the trust. They have been subject to several internal leadership development programmes, which have included coaching by an external (to the trust) coach. They are excellent at building and maintaining relationships and really see the value in community engagement.

At the point when they are appointed to the head of school role, their experience is such that they might not be considered for a similar post elsewhere (four of our heads of school were promoted from assistant headship without serving as deputy heads for any significant period of time, if at all). What we are convinced about every time, though, is their ability to develop teachers and therefore teaching. They have a depth of understanding of all of the elements needed to improve the quality of education and they are exceptionally child and family focused. Their mission is helped immeasurably by having an outstanding central support team which allows them to focus fully on their core purpose. Each of the heads of school is mentored either by myself or the deputy CEO.

The importance of investment in CPD

A real long-term focus on staff development has enabled us to grow relatively sustainably during the first few years of the life of the trust. With each new school we are able to apply more of what we have learnt to mitigate that risk. The moral purpose to improve education for children who have been failed is as strong as ever; however, it is tempered and balanced by experience and learning from the past.

I often think back to Prince Albert school between 2012 and 2014. It remains the best school I have ever had the privilege to work in, and I haven't seen many (if any) schools as consistently good from nursery through to Year 6. The school was full of exceptional teachers with bags of buy-in performing at the top of their game. All of that was compromised for the greater good. Many of those teachers are now senior leaders who have turned around, or are in the process of turning around, failing schools. They know in their bones what exceptional learning and teaching looks and feels like. The aim now is for all five of our schools to provide an exceptional education for our pupils.

Leadership takeaways

- Keep your moral purpose at the centre of everything you do. It will help you to navigate through the stormiest of seas. It is invaluable when faced with making difficult decisions.

- Culture is everything – it is the thing that will get you through the most challenging of times.

- There is no such thing as a quick fix in relation to a failing school. Plan and act for the long term.

- Long-term sustainable school improvement is always contingent upon a team rather than the ego of one 'super' head.

- Know what you are good at and trust others in their fields of expertise.

- There will be many setbacks on the journey of improving a failing school – expect them, embrace them and learn from them.

- Your staff are your greatest asset; invest in their development. This will always bear fruit.

- A good mentor is essential, both as a critical friend and for validation.

References

Carter, David and McInerney, Laura (2020) *Leading Academy Trusts: Why Some Fail, But Most Don't*. Woodbridge: John Catt Educational.

Heifetz, Ronald and Linsky, Marty (2002) *Leadership on the Line: Staying Alive Through the Dangers of Leading*. Boston, MA: Harvard Business Review Press.

Kershaw, Ian (2014) *Investigation Report: Trojan Horse Letter* [Kershaw Report]. Available at: https://www.birmingham.gov.uk/downloads/file/1579/investigation_report_trojan_horse_letter_the_kershaw_report.

Ofsted (2013) School Report: Heathfield Primary School (28–29 November). Available at: https://files.ofsted.gov.uk/v1/file/2303709.

Ofsted (2014a) Monitoring Inspection Visit to Heathfield Primary School (25 February). Available at: https://files.ofsted.gov.uk/v1/file/2343429.

Ofsted (2014b) No Formal Designation Monitoring Inspection of Heathfield Primary School (30 April –1 May). Available at: https://files.ofsted.gov.uk/v1/file/2391805.

Ofsted (2014c) School Report: Heathfield Primary School (18–19 November). Available at: https://files.ofsted.gov.uk/v1/file/2440262.

Ofsted (2014d) No Formal Designation Monitoring Inspection of Highfield Junior and Infant School (2–3 April). Available at: https://files.api.ofsted.gov.uk/v1/file/2391853.

Ofsted (2015) School Report: Prince Albert Junior and Infant School (4–5 February). Available at: https://files.ofsted.gov.uk/v1/file/2467065.

Ofsted (2018) School Report: Heathfield Primary School (12–13 June). Available at: https://files.ofsted.gov.uk/v1/file/50004640.

Ofsted (2019) School Report: Highfield Junior and Infant School (16–17 January). Available at: https://files.ofsted.gov.uk/v1/file/50058680.

Syed, Matthew (2015) *Black Box Thinking: The Surprising Truth About Success*. London: John Murray.

Chapter 9

We are family: creating social capital in Hodge Hill

Bev Mabey

Introduction

'Balwant Bains will soon be sacked and we will move in,' bragged the author(s) of the Trojan Horse letter. It was sent to the leader of Birmingham City Council in November 2013. How extraordinary that the prophecy proved to be correct as Bains actually signed a compromise agreement with the council in January 2014 and departed from his post as head teacher of Saltley School. Peter Clarke's (2014) report contains a full chapter on events at Saltley because, for him, it illustrated many of the themes that emerged during his investigations, culminating in the departure of the head teacher.

Bains was appointed as head teacher in September 2012. Saltley School was graded good by Ofsted in May 2013; the school's 2013 GCSE results were the best in its history. Yet, in spite of these obvious positive indicators, Bains was harassed and undermined by his governors. The classic Trojan Horse playbook was rolled out with the aim of ousting the head teacher: the undermining of an Ofsted inspection, the governing body taken over by like-minded individuals and the reinforcement of Muslim identity to the exclusion of others (Clarke, 2014). There is no comfort in digging out this information from the Clarke report, but it is a salutary reminder of events, even as some observers still maintain that the Trojan Horse letter was a hoax. The incidents outlined above prove otherwise.

Saltley School was just a short distance from Washwood Heath Technology College. When Saltley was judged to require special measures (Ofsted, 2014b), the obvious choice for a sponsor was on the doorstep. Bev Mabey had taken over as head teacher of Washwood Heath in 2005 when it was one of the lowest-performing schools in England. By 2012, it was in the top 13% for progress and value added.

Mabey was the longest-serving secondary head in Birmingham and chaired the Secondary Headteachers' Forum for many years. She dealt with low-level Trojan-style disruption to the governance of her school early in her tenure. It is significant that her first 'takeaway' points (at the end of this chapter) refer to the need for strong governance and securing the right balance between community representation and skill sets. Too often, as a result of Trojan Horse entryism, the emphasis had been on the former at the expense of the latter (Kershaw, 2014). She also emphasises the need for clear lines of accountability between governors and leaders, which can become blurred, as both the Clarke and Kershaw reports testify.

By the time Ofsted arrived at Washwood Heath in April 2014, during the Trojan Horse inspection round, her leadership was praised: 'She sets high standards and powerfully promotes equality of opportunity' (Ofsted 2014a, p. 3). The hallmark of her leadership lay in strong relationships with community groups and local agencies for which she was 'well respected' (p. 3). These relationships, combined with rigorous approaches to contentious issues like religious extremism and handling the Prevent agenda, meant that she was well-placed to convert Washwood Heath to academy status and take on the ailing Saltley School.

According to the Washwood Heath Multi-Academy Trust Strategic Plan (2021–2024), the multi-academy trust now consists of seven schools – a mixture of primary and secondary, all in areas of high deprivation. When Mabey talks to students at the University of Birmingham about her leadership journey, she is characteristically direct. PowerPoint slides focus on the seven Nolan principles (Nolan, 1995), a necessary reminder of the principles in public life which underpin her leadership values and act as a map for all aspects of leadership and governance. She knows her schools well and uses the sigmoid curve, a popular management tool that helps organisations to understand their improvement journeys, to plot their progress. She simplifies what is inevitably a complex, non-linear journey for schools, which is a characteristic of the best leaders. And she fully understands that deep, sustainable change cannot be rushed: it takes time to build and embed for the long term. Her language is clear and shorn of any management speak or leadership jargon. She stresses the importance of collaboration and distributed leadership, using phrases like: 'Players don't win trophies, teams win trophies,'[1] and the quotation

---

1   This line is often attributed to José Mourinho.

that always stays with students about self-awareness and the affective mode: 'They may forget what you said – but they will never forget how you made them feel' (Carl W. Buehner, quoted in Evans, 1971, p. 244).

Washwood Heath Multi-Academy Trust has grown deep roots, which means that it is not easily destabilised and is an integral part of the local community. The annual Grand Iftar celebration brings together the family of schools, all the partner agencies, faith group representatives and local hero guest speakers who inspire the current generation of pupils. The young people play musical instruments, dance and sing – a powerful statement that the arts are part of the DNA in this trust. As the power and influence of local authorities over civic education have waned, trusts like Washwood Heath have filled the void at a community level by creating social capital that can be found, literally, street by street and family by family.

Colin Diamond

We are family: creating social capital in Hodge Hill

Bev Mabey

Digging deep relations in the community

If you google 'Saltley Academy' today, the only mention of Trojan Horse is in the headline of a newspaper article about the television programme *The Great British School Swap* (Paxton, 2019). The article outlines the contrast in public perception between the academy as shown in the programme (and as shown by being willing to be part of the programme) and a school embroiled in a scandal. The roots of that journey, however, go back many years before the scandal emerged and reveal the importance of building on solid ground in terms of community relationships, vision, strategy and governance. It is strong relationships that are the driver of this journey.

In 2005, the first community operational advisory group met. This was a model for bringing together schools, the police and the community in a shared effort to address local issues and build community strength and resilience. It was later replicated across the city as the way to bring people together and break down barriers to cooperation. The involvement of leaders from Washwood Heath helped in the formation of key relationships with community representatives, with three members of the group subsequently becoming governors of the then Washwood Heath Technology College (soon to become Washwood Heath Academy). The importance of having members of the community with shared values – who could be a conduit of views to and from the wider populace – was essential in building a governing body which formed and supported an agenda of school improvement. Alongside these colleagues, a broad, knowledgeable and committed team of governors was established, the core of which now form the board of Washwood Heath Multi-Academy Trust.

At these early stages, there were tangible benefits from having a working relationship with the police, such as school-based police officers. Having an officer on-site who was able to engage with the students, get to know them, earn their trust, undertake preventative work with vulnerable individuals and share important information was a fantastic resource. The austerity measures introduced by the coalition government led to the demise of this service; we are only just beginning to see the cost of this as a society. The loss of a relationship between students and officers is not just a missing strategy. It has also created a vacuum which, for some, is filled with distrust and disrespect.

However, the working relationships with police (and other partners) continue. The Mentors in Violence Prevention scheme, which develops students' leadership skills through working with their peers to identify and respond to potential incidents of violence, is supported by both the police and the prison service. Work at this time also led to the creation of school–police panels which, to this day, help the two services to support one another effectively and dramatically reduce recidivism rates. Latterly, the development of the police cadets also contributes to strengthening police, school, families and community relationships.

Washwood Heath Academy ahead of the curve with its RSE policy

The strength of governorship enabled the leadership of what became Washwood Heath Academy to develop a clear ethos for school improvement, very much including the spiritual, moral, social and cultural (SMSC) development of students. An example of this was the implementation of the relationships and sex education policy (RSE) (DfE, 2019). The relevant subcommittee did contain a minority of governors who wished to, at best, water down our teaching about homosexual relationships. There is no doubt that, during discussions, the clarity of the statutory guidance aided us in being able to adopt this policy. In more recent times, we have seen what can happen on these issues when politicians behave like children hiding behind the sofa during *Doctor Who*. A full curriculum was in place at Washwood Heath, with no question mark over music, drama or multi-faith religious education. Music, in particular, has gone on to be an area of outstanding strength across all of the schools in the trust, which celebrate every significant celebration, including Diwali, Christmas and Eid, to mention a few.

Under the leadership of then deputy head teacher, Pete Weir, the RSE policy and work on British values and cultural enrichment was well established when the Trojan Horse letter emerged and the scandal broke. By geographical necessity, Washwood Heath Academy received a two-day visit from Ofsted based around the theme of what was beginning to be referred to as 'British values' (Ofsted, 2014a). On the initial tour of the school, we met a man with a gun in the corridor. It was a pre-planned day in which the normal timetable was suspended. Year 9 had been researching individual soldiers who had died on the first day of the Battle of the Somme, and the man with the gun (clearly a fake weapon) was a history teacher dressed as a Tommy.

As part of our commemorations of the centenary of the start of the First World War, all of Year 9 were working on model gravestones, on which they wrote the name and details of the individual they had researched. Alongside some creative academic study and the construction of a trench, by the end of the day, approximately 13,000 'gravestones' in the shape of dominoes were created and set up for a moving, silent ceremony in which the dominoes fell. The 'gravestones' were then transferred to Birmingham Repertory Theatre, where they were used onstage as part of a new play about the start of the war.

This was the first major project in an ongoing relationship between Washwood Heath Multi-Academy Trust and the theatre group Stan's Cafe (pronounced 'caff'),[2] who had worked with many schools in the days of Creative Partnership funding (which, by 2014, seemed like a half-dreamt-of world from an alternative universe). As a school, we believed in, and were prepared to invest in, projects to enrich the curriculum for both students and staff alike. Stan's Cafe would play a major part in a later chapter of the story.

The lasting memory of that extraordinary day was a meeting between the personal, social, health and economic education coordinator and one of the inspectors. During the meeting, the coordinator went through the resources used in our RSE programme for learning about lesbian, gay and bisexual relationships.[3] The resources stridently ensured that students were able to discuss and explore the issues fully and articulate a range of views, whilst also being very clear about prevailing attitudes in

---

2   See http://www.stanscafe.co.uk/education-and-training.html.
3   The term LGB is authentic to the timeframe; subsequent reforms have altered this phrase to include transgender (LGBT) and queer and others (LGBTQ+).

wider society. The inspector was convinced. Indeed, she gave the impression that she had not seen such clarity and unambiguousness in an RSE approach before.

Saltley's broad and balanced curriculum

With Washwood Heath's credentials in the promotion of SMSC, safeguarding and the wider curriculum securely reaffirmed by the inspection, the decision for Washwood Heath Multi-Academy Trust to become the sponsor of choice to support Saltley School seems, in retrospect, a natural one, with Pete Weir becoming the acting and later permanent head teacher. The writers are not in a position to comment on what had occurred to plunge a previously securely good school into special measures, but there was no permanent head teacher and an interim executive board was in place. What can be said, however, was that the stereotype that emerged of the 'Trojan Horse school' as the scandal raged in the media was not met by the reality at Saltley.

Firstly, the curriculum was full. Admittedly, the arts were not a strength, but all three main art subjects (music, drama and art) were offered, and the school was starting the process of building a specialist arts block, which opened in September 2015. Multi-faith religious education and citizenship were studied to GCSE by all, although the profile of the latter needed to be raised in the eyes of the students. There was a well-planned RSE programme, but opting out was by reply slip and too easy. A change whereby parents wishing to withdraw their child met with the head teacher to discuss their concerns soon reduced this to single figures.

However, staffing had been affected at a senior level in English and maths as a result of the issues at Saltley, and staff were divided over the causes of those issues. For many, this represented a divide between Muslim and non-Muslim staff. A process of emotional healing took place during a significant part of the first year from September 2014, alongside the creation of an exciting, engaging and challenging vision for learning, which had exploring British values at its heart.

For the most part, many colleagues were simply in shock that their lovely school had collapsed so horribly. Step one was to reassure them that, whilst academisation was coming, the name 'Saltley' would continue. In an approach inspired by the methods of Archbishop Desmond Tutu (if that doesn't sound too grandiose), the plan was simply to let people talk about their views and how things could move forward, without the fear of any divisiveness from the past being used against them. Some used the opportunity to speak in confidence about how they felt about the previous year, some tearfully; others preferred to talk about the future. Either way, it demonstrated that there were no 'goodies' and 'baddies' here, but simply a school that needed direction to heal and improve the provision for the young people. Neither could wait, so the plan was to do both at the same time.

Along with a number of projects and pieces of developmental work which brought people together, there were two areas for the whole-school community where the ethos we were developing could be set out – one planned and the other reactive. Firstly, at Christmas, we held a forty-five-minute assembly for the whole school, which meant that it was delivered three times. Student leaders explained the meaning and messages of Christmas (explicitly for Christians, for Muslims and for all) and lit an Advent wreath; students and staff sung Christmas songs (both sacred and secular); and staff performed a pantomime. This followed on from a reflection on places in the world that were troubled.

This pattern has been retained ever since, along with its key feature: in the middle of the programme two community leaders from Birmingham, one Muslim and one Christian, talk about their work together, to model for the school community how people of different faiths can reach out to each other and build harmony. The Reverend Canon Martin Stephenson, vicar of St Peter's Church, Hall Green, and Shahin Ashraf MBE, then of the Muslim Women's Network and soon to be a member of the school's local governing body, presented on 'Families Together' – a series of joint Christian–Muslim events held at St Peter's. They both described the importance of Christmas to them. They also read versions of the birth of Jesus from the Qur'an and the Bible; Shahin read from Luke and Martin read the translation from the Qur'an. Martin later wrote in a church newsletter that the assembly covered the full extent of Christmas: the story and what it means to people, reflection on the needs of others and our response, and an opportunity to celebrate together and have fun.

The second whole-school event was driven by the events of February 2015, when three schoolgirls from London hit the headlines when they left their families to travel to Syria and the Islamic State group. Firstly, an assembly, the slides from which were shared by schools within the city, who explored what they had done and why. We went on to explain some of the reasons why Islamic scholars believe that Islamic State are in fact anti-Islamic. (The content was read and supported by Muslim senior middle leaders prior to the assembly.) We then reaffirmed our safeguarding procedures and explained how we, as a school, were going to explore British values. The assembly coincided with St David's Day; the main event would reach its climax on St George's Day.

The origins of the project lay with Stan's Cafe, who had brought together a small group of head teachers at Billesley Primary School, hosted by the executive principal, Johanne Clifton. James Yarker, Stan's Cafe's artistic director, wanted to deepen the work with this cluster of like-minded schools, to work on the issues we felt needed to be addressed and that would benefit from being tackled creatively. British values was the topic we selected. We needed an activity that would model the style of learning we were nurturing within the academy. This would involve at least one year group but impact on all, unite and raise the spirits of the whole-school community, and explore the concept of British values meaningfully and with academic rigour. James went away and then returned with a proposal.

The result was St George's Steps. On either side of Easter, Year 7 worked with local artists on designing, making and setting online, tablet-friendly activities relating to an in-school art installation. Around the school, a number of laminated footprints and imagery appeared. Visitors were encouraged to plant their feet on the footprints and try to work out the story behind the scene, which included the Magna Carta, the Gunpowder Plot, the death of suffragette Emily Davison, the mass trespass of Kinder Scout, the Second World War, a village cricket match, the visit of the Queen to Birmingham in 2012, and St George and the Dragon. The latter was a montage of words (racism, homophobia, fear and so on). The results can still be seen on Stan's Cafe's website.[4] The students' pride and ability in showing the many visitors, young and old, around the installations was palpable. However, the key was the learning. This was most evident in the Emily Davison section: genuine shock amongst the students at how recent 'votes for all' has been; fascination with Davison's motivation and intentions; and, most powerfully, the student-set online question: 'Who upheld British values at this time and what were they?'

4   See http://www.stanscafe.co.uk/project-stgeorges-steps.html.

Engagement with UNICEF's Rights Respecting Schools Award

Media interest – in stark contrast to that of the previous year – closed the opening chapter of the story of Saltley Academy (McKinney, 2012). It was officially less than two months old, but it was ready to move onwards and upwards. We needed a new vehicle to embed the meaning of that one project permanently into the life-blood of the academy. The answer was the United Nations Children's Fund Rights Respecting Schools Award (RRSA). Saltley was superbly led to what is now known as Silver by the then deputy head teacher, Astrid Edwards, who has since supported many schools in this process, and then by a senior middle leader to Gold.

The framework of the RRSA meant that the language of rights entered every aspect of academy life: from each policy to the objectives of individual lessons across the curriculum, and from conversations about behaviour to activities on enrichment days. The focus on RRSA in assemblies framed every message the students received in this context. The formation of multi-vehicle partnerships, support for charities and greater awareness of the rights of others not only drove the continued development of the academy ethos, but also convinced the student body of the role of citizenship as a central part of their education, both in the holistic sense and in raising their aspirations in and estimations of the timetabled subject.

The commitment to RRSA is enshrined in the Saltley Pledge, which all students, staff and governors sign annually. The pledge and the signatures are displayed in the main entrance. It states:

> Saltley Academy is founded on the principle of all respecting the dignity and rights of each and every individual. Respectful relationships are at the core of this learning community, which will enable our young people to respect all whom they meet and to understand and develop the skills they need to embrace the responsibilities of being an outstanding learner and an active, contributing and content citizen.

This underlying principle has now spread across all the academies within the trust, providing us with the foundation on which we will continue to build and develop long into the future.

Leadership takeaways

■ The governing body is representative of the school and community it serves. However, the skill set of the members must cover all bases.

■ The terms of reference for the governing body must be well defined with clear lines of reporting and accountability. The governors must understand their role and their relationship with the leadership of the school.

■ The school's mission and values must underpin every aspect of school life. As a leader, walk the talk of your ethos and culture and ensure that all stakeholders do the same.

■ Make sure your curriculum is broad and balanced and includes the arts and music.

■ Take the time to find out about your local audience and understand the community's dynamics, pressures and priorities.

■ Develop strong and meaningful relationships with your local multi-agency neighbourhood teams. Ensure they are visible and have a role to play in your school community.

References

Clarke, Peter (2014) *Report into Allegations Concerning Birmingham Schools Arising from the 'Trojan Horse' Letter* (HC 576). Available at: https://assets.publishing.service.gov.uk/government/uploads/system/uploads/attachment_data/file/340526/HC_576_accessible_-.pdf.

Department for Education (DfE) (2019) *Relationships Education, Relationships and Sex Education (RSE) and Health Education: Statutory Guidance for Governing Bodies, Proprietors, Head Teachers, Principals, Senior Leadership Teams, Teachers*. Available at: https://assets.publishing.service.gov.uk/government/uploads/system/uploads/attachment_data/file/1019542/Relationships_Education__Relationships_and_Sex_Education__RSE__and_Health_Education.pdf.

Evans, Richard L. (1971) *Richard Evans' Quote Book*. Salt Lake City, UT: Publishers Press.

Fuller, Martin (dir.) (2019) *The Great British School Swap* [TV mini-series]. Channel 4. Available at: https://www.channel4.com/programmes/the-great-british-school-swap/on-demand/67350-001.

Kershaw, Ian (2014) *Investigation Report: Trojan Horse Letter* [Kershaw Report]. Available at: https://www.birmingham.gov.uk/downloads/file/1579/investigation_report_trojan_horse_letter_the_kershaw_report.

McKinney, Emma (2012) Trojan Horse One Year On: Saltley School at Centre of Scandal Becomes an Academy, *Birmingham Mail* (21 April). Available at: https://www.birminghammail.co.uk/news/midlands-news/trojan-horse-one-year-on-9081759.

Nolan, Michael (1995) *Standards in Public Life: First Report of the Committee on Standards in Public Life. Volume 1: Report* (Cm 2850-1). Available at: https://assets.publishing.service.gov.uk/government/uploads/system/uploads/attachment_data/file/336919/1stInquiryReport.pdf.

Ofsted (2014a) No Formal Designation Monitoring Inspection of Washwood Heath Academy (12 May). Available at: https://files.ofsted.gov.uk/v1/file/2391809.

Ofsted (2014b) School Report: Saltley School and Specialist Science College (9–10 April). Available at: https://files.api.ofsted.gov.uk/v1/file/2391825.

Paxton, Charlotte (2019) From Trojan Horse Scandal to Great British School Swap – Fall and Rise of Saltley Academy, *Birmingham Mail* (28 April). Available at: https://www.birminghammail.co.uk/news/midlands-news/trojan-horse-scandal-great-british-16178742.

Washwood Heath Multi Academy Trust (2021) Strategic Plan 2021–2024. Available at: https://washwoodheath.s3.amazonaws.com/uploads/document/Washwood-Heath-MAT-Strategic-Plan-2021-24.pdf?t=1626690858.

Chapter 10
It takes a whole community to bring up a child

From Golden Hillock to Ark Boulton: a case study in transformative leadership

Herminder Channa

Introduction

When Herminder Channa became principal of Ark Boulton Academy, she took on a school where pupil, parent and staff confidence was extremely low. The first time she took me on a tour of the school in 2015 the atmosphere was tense. Most classes did not have permanent teachers, with 65% of the staff on supply. It had not yet found its direction of travel.

When I visited in 2018, it felt transformed with a full complement of permanent staff, no exclusions and no former pupils who were not in education, employment or training (NEET) over the previous two years. The entrance had been moved to face the community on Golden Hillock Road and the whole frontage had been transformed with its new bright blue livery. The tired old staffroom now closely resembled a Google or Apple-style chill-out space where colleagues could relax and recharge. Serious lesson prep was done elsewhere in a new dedicated room. The school exuded confidence – so much so that I wanted to share how rapidly it had improved from the difficult days of 2014. Senior Department for Education officials and Birmingham City Council's chief executive visited and were impressed. The school they saw bore no resemblance to how it had become known nationally as part of Park View Educational Trust.

Channa worked hard to build community trust. She brought her experience from Nishkam High School, a highly successful Sikh-ethos free school in Birmingham which opened in 2012 and secured outstanding grades across the board in its first Ofsted inspection (2014b). In short, she knew what good looked like – a prerequisite for leaders who turn around schools. The first question to ask colleagues when embarking on such a journey is always: do you know what good looks like? Without forming a collective view of what good is, there is no improvement map.

Nishkam had opened on time in its temporary premises because the local Sikh community had worked over the summer to transform a warehouse into a school.[1] Channa brought that spirit to the mainly Muslim community of Sparkbrook. She convened a group to paint the front of Ark Boulton over the summer holidays. People noticed, joined in and brought trays of tea, samosas and cakes for the workers. She clearly cared about the community and they started to care for her.

This was a far cry from the events that preceded the Ark academy chain taking on the former Golden Hillock School. The substantive head teacher had left under a compromise agreement which had been 'aggressively pursued' (Clarke, 2014, p. 79) by the chair of governors following one bad set of examination results. The school had become a member of Park View Educational Trust in October 2013 and was subsequently judged to require special measures when inspected (Ofsted, 2014a). The pupils were reported to be 'courteous and respectful' (Ofsted, 2014a, p. 1) and keen to learn, but everything else about the school was deemed dysfunctional and the pupils unsafe. The sex and relationships curriculum (part of personal, social, health and economic education) had been reduced to a narrow, restricted version which ignored, for example, the risks for young women in society.

At the heart of this improvement journey is the character education curriculum based on the work of the Jubilee Centre for Character and Virtues at the University of Birmingham.[2] The centre was established in 2012 and works to understand, research and promote character education virtues in the contexts of family, school and society (Iyer et al., 2020). It has influenced curriculum development in partner schools which have established a high level of engagement with the centre's work. This includes whole-school policies and day-to-day and extracurricular activities. Pupil numbers continued to grow in 2020 as the COVID-19 pandemic increased the quest for a more values-based model of education, with a total of over 2,000 studying with the centre. The eight case-study schools analysed in *Windows Into Schools: Celebrating Character* (Thompson et al.,

---

1   See https://youtu.be/bL6bwGThiKc.
2   See https://www.jubileecentre.ac.uk/355/about.

2020) all prioritise character education and provide rich examples of how this approach can add value to school identity, purpose and direction.

Looking out beyond the local community is also a feature of this improvement journey. Channa comments on how little these young people knew of their own city and had rarely, if ever, visited its central attractions. Aspiration to do well at school was confined to looking for success in examinations, and not linked to how pupils could contribute to and benefit their community.

The new Ark Boulton vision started with role modelling at home for younger siblings and moved outwards towards engaging in civic arts projects. In contrast, the orthodox formulae for school improvement, hemmed in and informed by the Department for Education and Ofsted, narrow norms and take no significant account of wider personal growth or enrichment. For Channa, whilst the basics had to be in place, validating that sense of pupils' belonging was the bedrock of improvement.

Colin Diamond

Chapter 10

It takes a whole community to bring up a child

From Golden Hillock to Ark Boulton: a case study in transformative leadership

Herminder Channa

Why had things gone so wrong?

A decade of underachievement, re-brokerage to a second academy chain, high levels of supply staff and judged as an inadequate academy by Ofsted – twice. It was no surprise that parents and carers who trusted the education of their sons and daughters to their Golden Hillock School, as well as educationalists and operational staff who worked at the school, were left feeling hurt, angry and confused about the decline of their school. A generation of young people had had their life chances and opportunities limited. Ark Boulton Academy came into being in September 2015 as a result.

The questions most on my mind during the summer of 2015 were 'How?' and 'Why?' How had this school, which was at the heart of its community, declined in this way? Why were parents so angry? Why was there a falling roll? Why were a settled teaching staff choosing to leave? High levels of dysfunctionality and confusion had taken over.

During that summer, I wanted to meet with as many parents, pupils and teachers as possible to understand their views and perspectives of the school. That was my starting point. Ark Boulton did not just have to address the current poor educational provision and staffing crisis; there was a bigger challenge, which was how to win back the trust of parents and teacher communities. I knew that if the academy and community were going to make progress, then as leaders we needed to acknowledge and confront the challenges of the past, understand more deeply the cultural barriers faced by communities, whilst also building trust and creating a shared vision that all stakeholders could believe in. Forgiveness and compassion were at the forefront of my mind as we developed the vision. Why? I understood that unless the community was able to do both, only then could the school move forward.

In numerous meetings and one-to-one discussions, I absorbed anger and acknowledged what had gone wrong without criticism of the previous leadership team. I was saddened by what I heard. One mother said to me, 'I don't want my daughter to turn out like me.' Parents had lost confidence in the education system. Teachers had experienced too much change and unpredictability: a new academy name, another new principal, a new uniform and an increasing number of supply teachers because recruitment was proving difficult due to reputational damage. For Year 11 pupils, it was their fourth principal, third uniform change and third logo change!

What became clear was that I was surrounded by adults who cared, parents who wanted an excellent educational provision for their children and young people who wanted to learn. A real sense of community and warmth came through. I understood why the hurt and mistrust was so deep-seated. Over 90% of pupils who attended the school lived no further than five to fifteen minutes walking distance. Parents – mothers in particular – watched through their front-room windows as their children crossed the road. Parents and carers huddled together outside the school gates for conversation and interaction. The school was welcoming, the pupils felt safe and everyone was friendly.

Conversations with pupils were always going to be the most insightful. I started with the obvious ones about the school: what are your favourite lessons, and why? What do you want to do/become in the future? What has been your most memorable school trip/visit? Have you visited the new Birmingham library? Have you attended the Symphony Hall? I spoke with numerous pupils (and I consulted many, so the following statement is in no way generalised) who had not heard about the new flagship library which had opened towards the end of 2013. Nor did they know about the Symphony Hall.

There was no lack of enthusiasm from pupils but, more worryingly, there was a lack of ambition and knowledge about their surroundings, the facilities that were available to them, the plays and shows to which they had access and what was on offer for the next stage in their education. Pupils did not connect with being part of a local, national or international community in which they had a place. It was apparent that this was a community that defended its school, but they had been let down by the oversight system over several years.

I was even more convinced that the phrase 'Trojan Horse' was being used as a convenient explanation for underachievement in schools and all that was going wrong in the city. For some, it provided a simplistic justification for a well-established narrative. The 'some' were not yet prepared to acknowledge that there had been a failure in the oversight system over many years. Young people from some communities were not receiving the same standards of education as others in the city, teachers were not being developed and school leaders had not been provided with the correct support in a timely fashion.

My takeaway from all the interactions I had was that our vision must incorporate both the strength of support from the community and the challenge to improve outcomes. It needed to connect communities to their city, it must ensure the future of a generation of young people who are prepared and equipped to give back to their community, and it must leave the academy in a stronger place for the next generation to follow.

My visioning activities helped me to understand that the pupils needed to believe they were part of something bigger and had an understanding of their moral and social responsibilities. They needed to realise that their action (or inaction) had a direct positive (or negative) impact on the society in which they lived. For academy staff, it was crucial to provide stability and create a culture where they felt they were able to make a difference beyond academic standards. In practice, it was an opportunity to create a real climate of service within the community – supporting those who are less fortunate and developing an understanding of current challenges which need to be overcome one action at a time.

All pupils who attend Ark Boulton Academy will go on to university or leave equipped to pursue a high-quality apprenticeship or career of their choice, so they are able to look after their parents, become role models for younger siblings and upskill their community.

It takes a whole community to raise a child

The clear vision was received well by all. However, I was fully aware that although parents felt optimistic, they were also cautious and distrustful of the new leadership. Teachers were hopeful of change but also pessimistic as they had heard it all before. Pupils took the arrival of yet another principal and academy rebrand in their stride. They were neither excited nor hopeful of change. This thinking was common amongst the older children. One pupil said to me, 'Miss, it would be good if you stayed – you will calm everything down.' Calmness – a strength I am aware I have – was very much required. The hard work was about to start.

In a school where so much needed to be done, I adopted the phrase 'less is more'. I had decided that as a staff we would focus on three priorities and deliver on those first. As a leadership team, it was therefore crucial that we identified the correct priorities. In the first year, these were solely aimed at securing and establishing culture and ethos at all levels. It would have been tempting to have more priorities with an overt focus on, for example, learning outcomes or behaviour. This is where my calmness came into play: having broad shoulders, encapsulating the big three priorities and anchoring the vision on which we were going to deliver.

As the principal, it was for me to guide, to reassure, to be visible and to be approachable. I was adamant that anything that did not fall into the priorities we had set were not going to be discussed. As a result, I was fully aware that some things would not be completed to a high standard. But that was okay, initially, and I made sure my staff knew why at every opportunity.

In the summer of 2016, I decided that we would paint everything blue, including the school fence on to Golden Hillock Road. Some staff referred to me being 'obsessed', as they could not easily see which priority this addressed. The colour blue has the properties of calming the mind and aiding concentration. This was needed if we were going to secure the right culture in the academy. Staff who were sceptical soon came around, as one of the first thing visitors commented on was the calmness. It was now in the walls! In August, when I came in to check how the paintwork was progressing, parents from nearby houses came and offered us food and smiles. One parent commented 'Wow! Our street looks so bright and big.' Another said, 'Don't leave our children.' It is a remark that will stay with me.

There is always going to be tension between school improvement, the rate at which it happens and, most notably, how we develop, retain and support colleagues at the start of a difficult journey. As leaders – privileged to be able to lead educational establishments wherever they are in their journey – it is important to understand that journey, temper any urges to criticise the outgoing leadership, and embrace the responsibility and urgency to put things right.

The strength that comes from being part of a multi-academy trust meant that the academy was very quickly able to provide training for staff, implement tested curriculum models, set up accurate data systems, introduce robust testing materials and provide a network of peers across eighteen secondary academies, which could offer support and experiences via learning communities, phone, email and video link. The impact of the trust, and the speed by which systems and processes were rolled out, embedded, used and applied consistently by academy staff had to be seen to be believed. By the time of our first monitoring inspection in December 2015, many staff who completed the Ofsted questionnaire reported 'that they know what the academy is trying to achieve and that they are proud to be a member of the academy' (Ofsted, 2015, p. 3).

The transformation can only be described as a well-choreographed sequence of intentional and purposeful events. All those involved had clarity about their role and responsibilities, and had been given the tools and confidence to execute them with intentionality and purpose. The academy was getting stronger, outcomes were improving rapidly, first-choice applications had tripled and the school was fully staffed. By 2017, Ark Boulton was out of special measures and judged to be good in every category.

At Ark Boulton, we use the phrase 'increasing our standard level of performance'. Each term, we revisit and practise the strategies in our toolkits to become the best versions of ourselves. Yes, some strategies and routines took longer to perfect than others, but as leaders we knew what needed to be practised. It was the senior leadership team who planned and delivered the strategies until we all got it right.

Character education and the virtues

Trust was now building, with all stakeholders and teachers becoming more confident in their classroom craft, but this was only half the job done. To see our academy vision in action, we launched the Ark Boulton character development curriculum in September 2016. This is now the foundation that allows us to deliver on our vision. We supported our teachers to develop their skills beyond teaching and learning; as leaders, it was our responsibility to create the conditions which allowed our staff to role model and practise the virtues we wanted to see in our pupils. Teachers at Ark Boulton care with compassion, listen with love and help with humility. These actions are now visible in our pupils too.

In 2018, Ark Boulton achieved the Values-based Education (VbE) Staff Quality Mark for underpinning universal positive human values, such as respect, integrity, honesty and compassion within the curriculum and academy life.[3] The academy went on to host the third annual VbE conference in October 2019; VbE is committed to academic excellence in union with the enhancement of moral, emotional and spiritual sensibilities.

Further endorsement of our character development curriculum was seen in April 2019 when the academy was awarded the Leading Aspect Award for leading practice in the virtues strand of our curriculum. The award recognises and celebrates leading educational practice and is awarded to schools that are judged to offer cutting-edge delivery of an aspect of teaching and learning.[4]

At Ark Boulton we firmly believe and celebrate the importance of shared identity, which is rooted in the ethos of our virtues. Our character development curriculum is a thread running throughout all aspects of school life, from morning arrival to the academy, movement around and into lessons, monitoring and assessment, through to exposition speeches. The school day has been created around this focus on character, which gives integrity and gravitas to personal and social development within the school curriculum.

I have been asked many times to share 'How did I do it?' or 'How did Boulton improve?' These questions always have two answers: the technical (which is process focused) and the authentic (which is made up of four key parts).

---

3   See https://valuesbasededucation.com.
4   See http://www.leadingaspectaward.org.uk.

The technical answer is easy to explain. You put together an improvement plan, train teachers, organise meetings, hold parents' evenings, monitor the impact and repeat. It is an approach that will suit a certain type of leader. However, the authentic answer characterised my approach.

Firstly, my connection to the why and purpose of wanting to take on this school was profoundly deep. I was able to identify with the community. Parents, just like mine, wanted nothing more than the best education for their children. They valued it. I had complete clarity once I had met with the community; the vision of 'It takes a whole community to raise a child' was the right one. I was lucky enough to grow up in this type of environment. I had always wanted to lead a school alongside a community, and this was going to be possible at Ark Boulton. I also knew that the role needed me to commit to seeing through a whole cohort; sustainable, embedded school improvement takes time. It is more than just a quick win in the August results. It is the foundation to a self-improving school community which pushes itself to do better year on year.

Secondly, I am consciously aware of my strengths and weaknesses. For leaders, this is a must! These traits will guide our behaviours, language and how we engage with those in our schools. Asking if you are not sure, accepting that mistakes may have been made and saying sorry is what makes us human. Being confident in decision-making is equally important. For me, those decisions will always be informed by research for which evidence of impact is significant. This is an important principle. As leaders, it is our responsibility to be forward-thinking and up to date with the latest research, so we can plan effectively and support colleagues with workload, so they are able to focus on their well-being. Learning together and leading with humility are a great combination when they are in balance. Leaders have a responsibility to continually develop and role model the behaviours we wish to see.

Thirdly is the importance of building relationships and connectedness. Things happen for a reason; I am sure of it. Yes, we are individuals with our own free will and responsiblity for our own judgements, but we are also part of something bigger. This feeling of connectedness implies certain responsibilities, such as looking after one another and ensuring that we develop those around us. Staff employed at Ark Boulton – beyond the basics of human resources, safer recruitment processes and simply answering the questions presented – are there for a reason. As leaders, we must look deeply into every appointment we make and make sure we know how we will develop our colleagues to be the best versions of themselves. We must take the time to talk and get to know them. To paraphrase Carl Buehner (Evans, 1971, p. 244), people will forget what you said, but how you make an individual feel will stay with them indefinitely.

Finally, leaders need to have a caring personality and be able to challenge directly. In the summer of 2017, I was given the book *Radical Candor: Be a Kickass Boss Without Losing Your Humanity* by Kim Scott (2017) by my regional director. Initially, I thought of it as simply another leadership book; I never imagined it was going to have such a profound influence on my leadership behaviours and practice moving forward.

The book showed for me the way in which some of the conversations in the early years of my leadership put me very firmly into the quadrant of 'ruinous empathy' – for example: 'too nice', avoids issues, positive change cannot happen (Scott, 2017, p. 40) – and this was not okay! Facing up to my tendency to sugar-coat problems and not bring them to people's attention, and, worse still, not developing someone I had the privilege to lead, was not easy.

Having clarity about what great leadership behaviours look like is just as important as the mission we set for our schools. Mission and leadership are not separate entities; they are intertwined and interconnected. Without an intentional and continuous focus on developing new leaders, a school is unable to continue improving its community for the generations that follow once the current leader moves on.

What legacy am I going to leave behind?

One of the toughest issues we face as leaders is our legacy. It should consist of a public promise that we will and should be judged on. I am responsible for creating the conditions that will allow educationalists to shape the minds and attitudes of the next generation. Young people whose characters are strong and resilient. Young people who are humble, compassionate and know they have a responsibility to give back, upskill and leave their communities in a stronger place. For me, leadership is rooted in the understanding that we are here to serve selflessly, without reward or recognition. We must ask ourselves continuously what we are leaving behind for future generations, and what we are able to do for them now. Whatever we do, we do so knowing that it may not benefit us in our lifetime, but it will benefit those in twenty-five or fifty years' time.

Leadership takeaways

- **Look to the future.** Educationalists carry a great responsibility to ensure that future generations thrive, that we communicate frequently with the parents who entrust us with their children's future, that we treat pupils, parents and staff with love and care, and that the teams we are privileged to lead develop into the best versions of themselves.

- **Leadership is about enabling colleagues to become the best versions of themselves.** Our children deserve our very best. That means the adults around them have to be capable of doing the best they can, in every interaction, every day. As leaders, it is our job to make sure that happens.

- **Radical candour is a powerful tool.** As leaders, one of the most important roles we play is establishing the conditions for colleagues to develop into high performers in their areas of expertise. Equally important is how we respond with radical candour and respect towards those colleagues who do not meet our expectations. Building capacity and expertise is essential for establishing a culture of continued self-improvement. This approach is the foundation and bedrock of Ark Boulton Academy's improvement journey.

- The first question I ask myself is: is this colleague unaware, unable or unwilling? These three categories offer a simple checklist. By having candid conversations in a timely manner, we can unpick the roots of any problems with colleagues, and by using Scott's radical candour model, we can put in place the right training and/or support, so they are able to become their best professional selves.

  - This means that if a colleague is *unaware*, I must take responsibility for that. I need to communicate (and, at times, over-communicate) my expectations more clearly. As leaders, we need to be brave and humble.

◼ If a colleague is *unable*, that is a joint task. Then, it is my responsibility to provide training to enable them to develop the skills or capacity so they can become experts in their area.

◼ When a colleague knows what is expected, has demonstrated the ability to carry out the task but chooses not to, then they move into the *unwilling* category. As leaders, we must try to identify the cause of the unwillingness, but the reality is that if they opt not to perform the task you need them to do at the level you need them to do it, that is not okay. At best, you may provide the right support to enable capacity and expertise to continue developing in a vibrant and self-improving way. At worst, you may provide the right support but the disconnect from the school vision and mission is too great, and we will wish our colleague all the best. Either way, the next steps are clear.

References

Clarke, Peter (2014) *Report into Allegations Concerning Birmingham Schools Arising from the 'Trojan Horse' Letter* (HC 576). Available at: https://assets.publishing.service. gov.uk/government/uploads/system/uploads/attachment_data/file/340526/HC_576_ accessible_-.pdf.

Evans, Richard L. (1971) *Richard Evans' Quote Book*. Salt Lake City, UT: Publishers Press.

Iyer, Padmini; Albakri, Muslihah; and Smith, Neil (2020) *The Influence of the Jubilee Centre for Character and Virtues in Character Education in Schools*. Birmingham: Jubilee Centre for Character and Virtues. Available at: https://www.jubileecentre. ac.uk/userfiles/jubileecentre/pdf/news/JCCV_Character_Education_Survey_Report. pdf.

Ofsted (2014a) School Report: Golden Hillock School – A Park View Academy (2–3 April). Available at: https://files.api.ofsted.gov.uk/v1/file/2391869.

Ofsted (2014b) School Report: Nishkam High School (30 April–1 May). Available at: https://files.ofsted.gov.uk/v1/file/2396941.

Ofsted (2017) School Report: Ark Boulton Academy (3–4 May). Available at: https:// files.ofsted.gov.uk/v1/file/2691609.

Scott, Kim (2017) *Radical Candor: Be a Kick-Ass Boss Without Losing Your Humanity*. New York: St Martin's Press.

Thompson, Aidan; Fullard, Michael; and Edwards, Danielle (2020) *Windows Into Schools: Celebrating Character*. Birmingham: Jubilee Centre for Character and Virtues. Available at: https://www.jubileecentre.ac.uk/userfiles/jubileecentre/pdf/ Research%20Reports/Windows-into-Schools-Celebrating-Character.pdf.

Chapter 11

Healing wounds, building trust and bridging communities: Birmingham's post-Trojan Horse challenge

Sir Mufti Hamid Patel

Introduction

Sir Mufti Hamid Patel is rightly proud of everything that Star has achieved since its creation in 2011. He has demonstrated a Midas touch educationally, with some extraordinary achievements along the way, including the top-performing schools in England (Tauheedul Islam Girls' High School and Sixth Form College). He is an educational polymath who makes contributions at a national level in diverse fields, including teacher training, leadership and community cohesion. His influence on education policy continues to grow.

At a time when many argue that the role of schools is too narrow and the curriculum not future facing (Huynh, 2019), Patel has found the 'gaps in the hedge' (Brighouse, 2015, cited in Theobald, 2018) and his academies exemplify all that is good about creating social capital whilst simultaneously conjuring academic excellence. His chapter unpacks the key ingredients to this success and offers a way forward underpinned by a decade of solid evidence.

It came as no surprise to learn that Star Academies had been named as a UK Business Hero by the British Chambers of Commerce in November 2020, in recognition of the campaigns they had led to support their school communities during COVID-19 (Nadeem, 2020). At a national level, Star had spearheaded projects aimed at helping schools to minimise the impact of closure for most pupils and supporting parents who had suddenly become their children's teachers. The StarLine initiative reached over one million parents and carers in the lockdown of spring and summer 2020, whilst the Reopening Schools Toolkit gained wide support from the sector for its practical advice. Within its family of schools, eight of which are in Birmingham, it established Star Family Hubs to provide food, toiletries and personal protective equipment within the communi-ties they serve.

Birmingham has benefited enormously from the arrival of the Tauheedul Education Trust (now rebranded as Star Academies) in 2014, which estab-lished two free schools. Both Eden Boys' School and the Olive School are highly successful, having secured outstanding judgements across the board from Ofsted at their first shot (Ofsted, 2018, 2019). Patel skilfully positioned the new free schools in a city that has long-established gram-mar schools with high social currency. The King Edward grammar schools are perceived to be the acme of the education system by many parents and competition to secure a place for children is high. A large private tutoring industry for the 11-plus examination thrives in Birmingham. As Patel observes in this chapter: 'Star's curriculum is unashamedly aca-demic. In a city where prestigious grammar schools thrive, we strive to provide our pupils with the qualifications that will equip them to compete on the world stage. The progress made by pupils at Eden Boys' School, Birmingham places the school in the top 1% nationally. The school also has the highest attendance in the country.'

Since opening the first two free schools, Star has been fully involved in the re-floating of Small Heath secondary school. For many years a flag-ship school, having been rated outstanding three times since opening in 2002, Small Heath tumbled into special measures in January 2015.[1] Large-scale complex education re-engineering has taken place with a minimum of background noise from these school communities, which is remarka-ble given the legacy of mistrust post-Trojan Horse. This is the hallmark of Patel's leadership and the culture he has created at Star. Heifetz and Linsky (2002, p. 108) refer to this approach as 'controlling the heat'. The skilled leader knows exactly how to raise or lower the temperature when leading change. For example, Patel never shirks from uncomfortable facts about a school's performance, but this is tempered by his calm, empa-thetic understanding of the situation.

Patel listened carefully to governors from Muslim communities in Birmingham who were alienated by Trojan Horse and felt their motives for engagement with schools were being questioned. The model of gov-ernance he outlines is thorough and designed to ensure that governors are well prepared to offer active, informed governance. Multiple checks

---

1   See https://reports.ofsted.gov.uk/provider/23/103548.

and balances exist to ensure there could never be any question of governors' probity, which is necessary for everyone's security in the wake of Trojan Horse. Careful consideration is given to engaging with governors from local communities who may feel nervous about contributing to the debate about how schools are operating. Governors are required to engage on performance and culture, which are intertwined at all Star schools. This approach ensures there is a balance between academic ambition and community contribution.

Eden Boys' School exemplifies how it is possible to secure the highest academic outcomes, whilst the pupils continuously engage in the community. Its Twitter feed enables followers to join its community activities in real time. Serving hot meals, helping rough sleepers and raising funds to help the disadvantaged occur regularly and are a defining feature of this outward-looking school.

Patel is invariably modest about his leadership of Star. He is softly spoken and self-effacing; a calm voice in the midst of turbulent waters. Star's thirty schools serve communities in disadvantaged areas from Morecambe to Hackney. This chapter offers a deep insight into his own values and vision which truly transform young peoples' lives and enrich the communities where they live.

Colin Diamond

Healing wounds, building trust and bridging communities: Birmingham's post-Trojan Horse challenge

Sir Mufti Hamid Patel

The national response to the Trojan Horse allegations may not have rooted out extremism in Birmingham's schools, but it shone an uncomfortable spotlight on the city and illuminated weaknesses in leadership and governance. The episode exacerbated a culture of division, a polarisation between 'us' and 'them' and deepened a sense of disempowerment that was already festering in some areas.

For people who felt disengaged from mainstream institutions, the fear and suspicion that accompanied the events of spring 2014 set them further adrift. Some sections of the population felt that Islamophobia was tacitly embedded in city life, evidenced by the growth of far-right organisations, tensions associated with the Prevent agenda and the perception that stop-and-search powers were being implemented in a way that was inherently racist. As communities increasingly felt they had no safe space in which to express their faith, their insularity grew and the chasm between ethnic groups widened.

As the UK's second largest city, Birmingham has extremes of both affluence and poverty: 41% of its neighbourhoods are amongst the 10% most deprived nationally – a picture that is worsening (Department for Communities and Local Government, 2015, p. 10). As is the case in other large, diverse conurbations, different localities in Birmingham are home to communities with their own cultural identities. Around 22% of Birmingham's 1.2 million population identifies as Muslim (Birmingham City Council, 2013, p. 18). The South Asian communities that comprise much of the Muslim population live in the most deprived wards of the city, in places where segregation is most apparent, where housing is most likely to be of poor quality and where employment is often low status. Small Heath, Sparkhill, Alum Rock and Bordesley Green are amongst the most disadvantaged. Historically, schools in these areas have been the most challenging and with the poorest performance, although some had begun to turn their fortunes around prior to the Trojan Horse debacle.

Birmingham is also acknowledged as being Europe's youngest city, with 46% of the population aged under 30 (Harris, 2019, p. 30). Municipal government was born in Birmingham under Joseph Chamberlain and the city council is one of the largest in Europe. However, representation of the youth voice in decision-making has been limited until recently and comparatively few young people have benefited from involvement in community leadership. Initiatives such as the Birmingham Aspiring Youth Council (with its tagline 'Generating change for a changing generation') and the UK Youth Parliament are now effecting positive change by giving young people a voice.

Overlaying the Trojan filter on this picture of disadvantage and disempowerment inevitably compounded problems.

Education and innovation have always been valued in Birmingham. The city has a long history of creativity and transformation, manifested in its reputation as the eighteenth-century manufacturing powerhouse of the world and its more recent profile as a centre of medical excellence. State education was pioneered in Birmingham in the 1850s. Two British prime ministers, Stanley Baldwin and Neville Chamberlain, studied metallurgy at Mason Science College, the forerunner of the University of Birmingham. The city is home to Britain's largest public lending library and has an international profile for arts and music. Developments continue at pace: HS2 and the 2022 Commonwealth Games will bring further opportunities for employment and regeneration. Birmingham is an aspirational city of opportunities.

The challenge for the city in the aftermath of Trojan Horse is how to heal wounds, build self-esteem and establish connections between fragmented communities, so that everyone can contribute to and benefit from the next phase in the city's transformation.

The key aspects of Star Academies' work in developing outstanding schools relate to establishing values, developing governance, restoring community cohesion and inspiring a culture of academic excellence. These features underpin highly effective schools anywhere. In the post-Trojan Horse Birmingham context, they have particular contextual resonance. Not only do schools need to strengthen bonds with their own neighbourhoods, but they must also reach out to build bridges between communities.

Repairing fractures by focusing on values

Realising opportunities and ambitions for prosperity depends upon supporting and involving all sections of the city's population (including those that are Muslim), capitalising on people's skills and talents, and rekindling their belief and pride in their city. Providing a first-class education is at the root of this necessary metamorphosis.

Star's involvement in Birmingham began with the opening of two free schools – Eden Boys' School (for boys aged 11–16) in 2015 and the Olive School (for girls and boys aged 4–11) in 2016. Because the city's population is young, school place provision is an ongoing priority and we were able to contribute to meeting the demand for places. Our aim was to establish dynamic schools providing a knowledge-rich curriculum and underpinned by a vibrant faith dimension. We wanted to build schools epitomising our core Star values – service, teamwork, ambition and respect. Living by these values required our schools to be outward-looking and aspirational. We wanted our pupils to be sustained by their faith and proud to share their talents. Above all, we wanted our schools to begin to heal rifts and build shared understanding.

Both of these faith-free schools were judged to be outstanding by Ofsted at their first inspections (Ofsted, 2018, 2019), testimony to the relentless hard work of staff and pupils who began in temporary buildings and eventually moved to state-of-the-art new premises. Opening as a new school on a temporary site presents problems but also opportunities as it demands the first focus to be the establishment of routines and expectations that underpin high-quality education. These ways of working can then be transferred into the new accommodation. The curriculum and relationships, rather than the bricks and mortar, become the beacon of hope for the future. In Asian communities, teachers are revered, trusted and respected. Our schools are harnessing these positive qualities to mend a society broken in the Trojan aftermath.

The success of the trust's first two free schools in the city inspired confidence for the growth of our regional hub, which now includes a further two free schools, created from Al-Hijrah, and two further non-faith spon-sored academies. We have also established a West Midlands arm of the outstanding Star Teachers school-centred initial teacher training pro-gramme in the city.

Developing a new model of governance

People with whom we worked in Birmingham told us that shortcomings in governance in some schools resulted from a lack of systematic over-sight and direction over time, creating a vacuum in which poor practice developed.

A decade prior to the Trojan Horse affair, there had been a drive to recruit school governors in the city who were reflective of the communities they served. This initiative was initially successful, and the local author-ity was heralded as being pioneering and progressive for its inclusivity. Appointed governors were understandably unhappy with the standards in low-performing city schools and wanted the best for their pupils; how-ever, they were sometimes ill-equipped to affect change because they had not received the training and support to enable them to hold school leaders to account.

A policy imperative for schools to reflect the cultural needs of the commu-nity was interpreted differently in various contexts. This was unsurprising because there was, according to some leaders, a lack of guidance on what was and was not permitted. Without an agreed framework in which to operate, governors worked in ways they had defined for themselves. Some governors, with a strong interest in education, took positions on multiple governing bodies. We have not seen any evidence to suggest that this was a systematic strategy to assume control of schools, but rather a reflection that there were insufficient candidates putting them-selves forward to become governors. Consequently, when gaps opened up, they were filled by existing governors from other schools.

Staff and parents told us that some longstanding governors gravitated into cliques, which created unhelpful groupthink and led to invidious comparisons being made between head teachers. Where governors had relatives employed in schools, their roles became obfuscated and nepo-tism was able to occur. As the distinction between strategic leadership

and operational management became muddied, some governors reportedly became embroiled in organisational matters. Whilst most governors
were well-intentioned, not all were skilled or experienced in working
with school leaders and holding them to account. Some school leaders
noticed that governors met outside and inside schools, merging into a
homogeneous group that was perceived as a bullying force. Equally, some
governors were unable to handle the pressures exerted by small factions
within the community who had particularly strong views about schools'
curriculum content and modus operandi. Where there was lack of guidance around faith and cultural expectations, it was possible for practices
to develop that could be perceived as being at odds with life in a pluralistic society founded on liberal values.

Like other strong multi-academy trusts, Star has the infrastructure to
develop effective governance because we have the capacity to provide
training and back-up support. Governors hold schools accountable for
performance and culture. All schools have a trained safeguarding governor whose role includes checking that the Prevent agenda is properly
implemented. Each of our faith schools has a designated governor who
ensures that pupils' faith and character education is delivered in accordance with the trust's principles. Through our policy framework, we have
brought transparency and given parents a channel through which they
can raise complaints and concerns. Standard items on meeting agendas
include the register of pecuniary interests, and a comprehensive code of
conduct for governors is revisited annually. The performance management of head teachers is carried out in accordance with a central set of
criteria focused on securing improvement within the context of national
drivers and policy initiatives. Minutes are scrutinised and a representative of the CEO attends each termly meeting. These checks and balances
both support and safeguard governors; transparency and accountability
are crucial. The strategic oversight of the work of the local governing
body means that the trust moves forward as a family of schools aligned
to the core values.

It remains important that local governing bodies include representation
from their communities. Training programmes to boost the confidence
and skills of governors are a prerequisite of strong leadership. Governors
also need support in ascertaining the views of parents and communicating schools' developments to them. In the aftermath of Trojan Horse,
finding willing and capable volunteers remains difficult. We know that
many skilled people are reluctant to put themselves forward for office

in case their motives are called into question. Some are unhappy that the role of governor is different within an academy than in a maintained school, as they believe that the power to influence strategy is weakened. Our executive meets with governors to hear their views and find the best ways forward.

Work remains to be done to reassure people about the role they can play in securing a world-class education for their children. Our schools are reaching out to potential governors through informal means, such as holding coffee mornings for parents, so they can meet in a relaxed forum. Parent councils have become an established part of school life, as have pupil councils. Everyone's voice matters, and these channels enable all voices to be heard.

Creating religious literacy

Throughout the period of prolonged restrictions during the COVID-19 pandemic, communities of all faiths have found ways of uniting to reaffirm their bonds and beliefs. Worship via online platforms does not give the same feeling of togetherness that gathering in a space dedicated to prayer and reflection provides, but it is a powerful acknowledgement that people need to feel connected to those who have similar values and goes some way to filling a void. In Star schools, any pupil who is self-isolating joins assembly online precisely to reaffirm their sense of being an important member of the school community. Assemblies include an element of worship.

Collective worship has been a mainstay of British education for many years and remains crucially important in all schools, irrespective of which faith is at their foundation or whether they are secular in nature. Giving young people opportunities to explore the healing that faith brings is an important part of our work. In an increasingly diverse and insular society, the time has come to reopen the national debate on the place, priority and relevance of collective worship, reflecting its value to the mental health and well-being of our pupils.

Regardless of which faith individuals subscribe to, they need to have a space to express themselves in their own society without fear of ridicule or rejection. The Trojan Horse saga left some young people feeling isolated and confused about their own identities because they perceived their faith as being under attack.

Star Academies has grown into a mixed multi-academy trust, including schools that have a faith designation and schools that were formerly community schools maintained by local authorities. Some of these schools serve a predominantly White population, located in northern coastal towns where social and economic problems are endemic and educational outcomes typically low.

Our faith schools are united by the 4Cs framework (character, creativity, community, curriculum). Within this programme, schools invite pupils to engage in spiritual reflection through reading and discussing broad religious messages. These are chosen as illustrations of how life can be lived well and they are a central part of our schools' personal development offer. The programme is mirrored in our non-faith schools through the Rising Stars programme, whereby pupils are introduced to the inspirational words of notable thinkers and taught how to explore and apply these as templates for their own lives. Our young people hold wide-ranging beliefs and we want them to feel confident and informed to express what it means to be atheist, agnostic or humanist or to subscribe to any world religion. For those that have not decided which belief system they feel comfortable with, we offer a safe space to explore personal identity. It is only by developing the language of reflection and enquiry that we gain mutual understanding.

Maintaining dialogue to espouse fundamental British values is crucial in effective schools. These conversations are not only with pupils, but also with their parents and community members. Without these open discussions, young people's lives can be pulled in conflicting directions. Faith is not a binary issue; values have to be lived and experienced. This is a complex picture that has too often been reduced to parsimonious sound bites by the mass media. Without openness, tolerance and understanding, suspicion will continue to hinder development.

Star's inclusive approach does not denigrate the Islamic faith; quite the reverse. Our faith schools provide opportunities for prayer and reflection but no pupil is compelled to pray. It is important that pupils grow spiritually and intellectually, explore their own cultural identity and celebrate who they are. This is not about proselytising but about understanding the role of belief in society. Religious literacy is a feature of reflective organisations which understand their own beliefs and are receptive to learning about others.

Building bridges by establishing beacons of community cohesion

Trojan Horse intensified the feeling amongst some Muslims that there was no safe space in which to have a voice. Many felt that expressing their faith openly would give rise to establishment suspicion. Crossing the divide between 'us' and 'them' was crucial to the creation of a sense of belonging required to enable civic leadership to flourish. Outstanding schools consolidate bonds within their own communities and reach out to build bridges with people who may have different beliefs and cultural heritage. Social capital is strong when these bridges are firmly cemented.

When community cohesion was inspected and judged as a specific aspect of schools' work, school leaders focused upon it explicitly in their self-evaluation and improvement planning. Spiritual, moral, social and cultural education is still an integral part of Ofsted's inspection handbook, but schools' contribution to community cohesion has not been overtly inspected since 2010. It is possible that hardworking leaders with multiple priorities lost some focus on this aspect of their schools' work. Fragmentation tends to occur when schools are not operating as the glue in their communities.

At Star, we are clear that schools are educational organisations that have to operate as vital organs of their local and wider communities. Schools must reach out rather than turning in on themselves. We promote twinning initiatives, inter-faith events and a rich programme of activities focused on encouraging pupils of all faiths and none to share their experiences and learn from one another as the bedrock of community cohesion.

We see the legacy of Trojan Horse persisting in the current equalities debate which has been manifested visibly in Birmingham. Trust is priceless; it binds communities and enables sensible debate and the building of social capital. Without this trust, people can adopt confrontational standpoints as they are fearful that aspects of their faith or beliefs are being eroded. Creating harmony from discord is only done through discussion and through a willingness by all parties to listen to each other's viewpoints. Schools must always be safe places to discuss ideas, including those related to faith.

Finding the right programmes to use as vehicles for pupils' personal development is a key aspect of many outstanding schools' work. Pursuing the United Nations Children's Fund Rights Respecting Schools Award, for example, provides a great opportunity to review and embed values, link rights with responsibilities and instil in young people a sense of what it means to be an active citizen.

At Star, we have developed the R-18 Leadership Framework for pupils from reception year to sixth form to develop their skills as civic leaders, performers and philanthropists. Pupils in our primary schools – Olive, Birmingham and Olive, Small Heath – are used to taking on leadership roles in lessons as well as through the established school council structure. They are taught from a young age how to initiate change through the proper channels, such as by inviting civic guests into school to explore local issues with them. Our pupils pursue Star Diplomas, coveted awards that are made on the basis of various criteria, including the number of hours they spend supporting their community through volunteering their time and talents. Our schools work in partnership with the police, mayors, British Army and a wide range of universities and businesses. We engage in Prevent-inspired programmes, recognising that extremism takes many forms and that strategies to tackle it are part of the toolkit our children need to equip them for life.

Personal, social and health education has the same prominence as core subjects in our curriculum. The stresses of COVID-19 have exacerbated the poor mental health suffered by many young people. They need to know that we care deeply for them, that their views matter and that their best days are still to come.

Ensuring academic excellence to support social integration and mobility

Improving examination results is key to securing social mobility. The link between poor academic outcomes and poor quality of life has been forged through generations: Birmingham's fortunes may have been secured during the Industrial Revolution, but literacy levels and life expectancy amongst factory workers were correspondingly appalling. Our technologically advanced society offers little chance of emergence from the poverty trap for pupils who have not secured basic passes in English and mathematics; consequently, schools in disadvantaged areas must continually redouble their efforts to provide young people with a brighter future.

Star's curriculum is unashamedly academic. In a city where prestigious grammar schools thrive, we strive to provide our pupils with the qualifications that will equip them to compete on the world stage. The progress made by pupils at Eden Boys' School, Birmingham places the school in the top 1% nationally. The school also has the highest attendance in the country. This success is the result of well-designed policies, consistently implemented, and a 'tough love' culture in which everyone is valued and nobody is left behind. The school operates a food bank, raises thousands of pounds for local charities and provides a vibrant programme of extra-curricular opportunities.

The same expectations have transformed Small Heath Leadership Academy. When the school joined Star it was broken and chaotic. Fighting on corridors was not uncommon, staff strikes had resulted in lost learning and the school had plummeted from its outstanding Ofsted grading to the nadir of special measures within a matter of months. It is now a calm, optimistic place with a rapidly improving academic profile and much to celebrate.

The renaissance of Small Heath is the result of committed leadership, clear processes and an unswerving belief that only the best is good enough for the young people it serves. A 'wishing tree' in the school's foyer is a powerful symbol of the school's values. Pupils add their thoughts to its branches – poignant leaves of hope that show their capacity to make a difference. Transformed behaviour at the school has been characterised by pupils moving through various stages of compliance (following rules mechanically, conforming to avoid getting into trouble, avoiding upsetting authority) to now seeking to be the best version of themselves. This shift in culture reflects improved self-esteem and mirrors the mood that is emerging in the wider community. Parents trust the school: our goals are congruent and our relationships are strong.

All Star schools have pupil councils. Senior representatives from these councils meet as a trust-wide council on a termly basis to provide their views on how their schools can be improved. They are thoughtful, articulate young people who embody Star's mission to 'Nurture today's young people, inspire tomorrow's leaders'. They effect the policies we develop as a trust. Their voices are heard.

Delivering a knowledge-rich curriculum

Effective teaching of a carefully sequenced, knowledge-rich curriculum is key to any school's effectiveness. Birmingham City Council's curriculum statement (2019) aims to guarantee the future of the city's children and chimes with the mission across our schools. Academic success is not about the arid memorising of information, but rather the genuine acquisition of core knowledge, skills and experiences referred to in the current Ofsted (2021) framework as 'cultural capital'. We are committed to equipping our young people with the vocabulary of success. Our schools focus explicitly on the teaching of linguistic structures that enable our pupils to express their opinions with confidence. The corollary to this is that they learn how to actively engage with other people and listen critically to different viewpoints.

We teach pupils about diversity. It is only by learning about the complexity and variety of people's lives and contexts that children grow into reflective citizens.

At Star, we have five leadership foundations through which we aspire to create future leaders. We intend for all our pupils to have opportunities beyond their timetabled lessons to engage in sports, arts, creative activities, social enterprise and opportunities linked to their career aspirations. This programme ranges from an exciting menu of sports activities through to digital programming and extensive charitable work. Some of our schools run well-supported Scout groups or Combined Cadet Forces. Whatever provision they make, it is designed to encourage pupils to develop their skills and interests, whilst having fun and establishing friendships that will sustain them through whatever challenges they may face.

Our aim is to give all our pupils the best possible start in life so they can pursue the most fulfilling careers. Social integration comes from attending good universities or engaging in prestigious vocational training. This vision is redemptive for our communities.

The Trojan Horse affair was undoubtedly a bleak episode in Birmingham's life, but the city is strong and forward-looking. Hope for the future is epitomised in its iconic buildings and vibrant enterprise, and most significantly in the energy and optimism of its young people.

Leadership takeaways

- Establish a set of strong core values to which the entire school community can subscribe.

- Make your values explicit and embed them in all aspects of the school's work.

- Maintain a culture of positive vigilance to ensure the school is safe at all times.

- Develop a framework of policies and procedures to underpin transparent governance.

- Take time to listen to the views of parents and community members. Understand their viewpoints.

- Recognise and value faith as an integral part of many people's lives.

- Understand why people feel bruised and be part of their healing solution.

- Seek, value and act upon feedback.

- Empower young people by giving them a great education, so they are equipped to make the best choices about their futures.

- Encourage pupils to be the best versions of themselves – day in, day out.

- Nurture self-esteem and a sense of personal identity amongst your school community.

- Bind and bridge communities so that schools contribute to and benefit from their city's vibrant infrastructure.

References

Birmingham City Council (2013) *2011 Census: Birmingham Population and Migration Topic Report* (October). Available at: https://www.birmingham.gov.uk/downloads/file/4564/2011_census_birmingham_population_and_migration_reportpdf.

Birmingham City Council (2019) Birmingham Curriculum Statement. Available at: https://www.birmingham.gov.uk/downloads/download/452/birmingham_curriculum_statement.

Brighouse, Tim (2015) Seizing the Agenda: 'Finding the Gaps in the Hedge' [video]. Speech at Whole Education sixth annual conference, 2 December. Available at: https://www.youtube.com/watch?v=lGUV5-NG8V8.

Department for Communities and Local Government (2015) *The English Indices of Deprivation 2015.* Available at: https://assets.publishing.service.gov.uk/government/uploads/system/uploads/attachment_data/file/465791/English_Indices_of_Deprivation_2015_-_Statistical_Release.pdf.

Harris, Catherine (2019) The Birmingham Economic Review 2018: People – Population and Employment, *University of Birmingham: City REDI* [blog]. Available at: https://blog.bham.ac.uk/cityredi/the-birmingham-economic-review-2018-people-population-and-employment/#:~:text=to%20be%20entrepreneurial.-,Birmingham%20is%20the%20youngest%20major%20city%20in%20Europe%2C%20with%20under,all%20the%20English%20core%20cities.

Heifetz, Ronald and Linsky, Marty (2002) *Leadership on the Line: Staying Alive Through the Dangers of Change*. Boston, MA: Harvard Business Review Press.

Huynh, Edison (ed.) (2019) *The Future of Education: Views from the Classroom*. London: Institute for Public Policy Research. Available at: https://www.ippr.org/files/2019-09/views-from-the-classroom-sept19.pdf.

Nadeem, Alima (2020) Star Academies Named UK Business Hero After Projects During Pandemic, *Lancashire Telegraph* (11 November). Available at: https://www.lancashiretelegraph.co.uk/news/18862066.star-academies-named-uk-business-hero-projects-pandemic.

Ofsted (2018) School Report: Eden Boys' School, Birmingham (22–23 May). Available at: https://files.ofsted.gov.uk/v1/file/2783129.

Ofsted (2019) School Report: The Olive School, Birmingham (25–26 June). Available at: https://files.ofsted.gov.uk/v1/file/50095180.

Ofsted (2021) Guidance: Education Inspection Framework (23 July). Available at: https://www.gov.uk/government/publications/education-inspection-framework/education-inspection-framework.

Theobald, Katy (2018) Is It the System That Needs to Change, or School Leaders?, *Schools Week* (12 May). Available at: https://schoolsweek.co.uk/is-it-the-system-that-needs-to-change-or-school-leaders.

Part III
Policy Implications: What Can Be Learnt from Birmingham's Experience?

Chapter 12

Lessons for contemporary urban school leadership: where the rubber meets the road

Colin Diamond

> Not everything that can be counted counts, and not everything that counts can be counted.

William Bruce Cameron (1963)

Since arriving in Birmingham in 2014, I have got to know many school leaders well, especially those who have contributed to this book. In my various roles as deputy commissioner for the Department for Education, executive director of education for Birmingham City Council and currently as professor of educational leadership at the University of Birmingham, we have grown together during turbulent times.

Interactions have varied according to our roles at the time. As deputy commissioner for the Department for Education, my main job was to get the Birmingham Improvement Plan mobilised, which relied heavily on the good will, moral purpose and commitment of local school leaders. Azita Zohhadi, Adrian Packer, Sajid Gulzar, Bev Mabey, Herminder Channa and Mufti Hamid Patel personified what Birmingham brought to the table. There are many others like them who contributed to the city's improvement journey, not least Kamal Hanif who described his leadership journey in Chapter 2.

As executive director of education, a major shift of role was required. Relationships between school leaders and their local authorities had been changing since the advent of the local management of schools and have been transformed since the arrival of Michael Gove's academisation policy in 2010. Many of the powers and most of the funding now rest with schools. However, local authorities retain a wide range of duties from early years sufficiency and quality through to 14–19 planning.

As director, I always wanted to be visible and accessible to school leaders in order to add value to what they were doing on the front line. This involved everything from ceremonial duties at prize-giving evenings through to chasing up safeguarding concerns, inspecting flood damage and visiting schools every week. School leaders knew that I was there as a backstop if things could not be progressed through the normal officer channels. All of the leaders in this book knew that their aspirations and concerns – ranging from long-term plans to create more joined-up child and adolescent mental health services provision with health colleagues through to worries about a caretaker misusing CCTV footage – would be taken seriously.

As professor of educational leadership, I turned to these authentic and successful school leaders to share their knowledge and experience with master's students. The Education Leadership Academy at the University of Birmingham co-designs, co-creates and co-delivers its programmes, blending deep research with excellent leadership practice. Feedback from the students indicates that they value highly the input and presence of the strong school leaders co-delivering the programme. They bring alive the research and learning.

Six years of working with these school leaders has provided plenty of time to reflect on how they took on major challenges and transformed schools caught up in a national education crisis into calm, successful, well-governed and well-led organisations. When I asked them to contribute to the master's leadership programme at the university, they told me it was the first time they had set out exactly how they had approached turning their schools around. This is a key point. They had all followed their professional instincts and engaged without hesitation, knowing that they were taking on extraordinarily challenged and damaged schools. However, their leadership experience with these schools was not being captured or shared beyond their own organisations. The hard-won lessons were locked away and valuable professional capital which could benefit other leaders was not documented and disseminated. School-led systems depend on feedback from effective leaders – and in a pressure cooker like the east end of Birmingham, such learning is indispensable.

School improvement post-Trojan Horse

First seek to understand, then to be understood.

Stephen Covey (2020)

So, how do we understand the contribution of school leaders to school improvement universally, and then in the particular context of Birmingham post-Trojan Horse? Are they one and the same thing? Are leaders' behaviours drawn from the same basic repertoire and customised and adapted as Leithwood et al. (2019) imply, or are new approaches required? Is a different emphasis or set of priorities required when working in the inner cities? The robust leadership style captured by Carter and McInerney (2020), with the aphorism 'The standard you walk past, is the standard you accept', is surely applicable in any education leadership setting.[1] Yet, the need to dig deep and establish trust within the complex, polysemic communities of East Birmingham and other similar inner-city areas is not so obvious in the calmer towns and shires of England. The intersectional factors at play in multicultural, multi-faith urban communities require education leaders to first understand them and then engage with them.

From an academic perspective, there is a huge range of material to draw upon when analysing leaders' approaches. At the Education Leadership Academy, we start by asking, 'What does good look like?' The characteristics of an effective school, as captured by Hargreaves and Fullan (2012), are rarely disputed:

- A clear and shared focus.

- High standards and expectations for all pupils.

- Effective school leadership.

- High levels of collaboration and communication.

- Curriculum, instruction and assessments aligned with national standards.

- Frequent monitoring of learning and teaching.

- Focused professional development.

---

1 General David Hurley, Governor-General of Australia, reportedly first made this remark – see https://www. pm.gov.au/media/press-statement-canberra.

◾ Supportive learning environment.

◾ High level of family and community involvement.

The eternal question, given the swathes of meta-research backing up Hargreaves and Fullan's list above, is: why do almost identical schools perform so differently whether in Birmingham, Bath or Brisbane? Why do you know the moment you walk through the front door of school A that it is a vibrant learning community, whereas school B, just down the road, feels flat and dispiriting as you sign in? This is invariably reflected in outcomes, with learners' progress and attainment soaring in school A, whilst their peers in school B are flatlining by comparison. The simple answer to these differences lies in the quality of a school's leadership, which is allied to strong governance.

Figure 12.1 shows the main elements that we explore in the Leadership for School Improvement module on the master's programme at the University of Birmingham.[2] The key content is taught via seminars led by a mixture of academics and practitioners, with the core of them leading schools and multi-academy trusts in Birmingham.

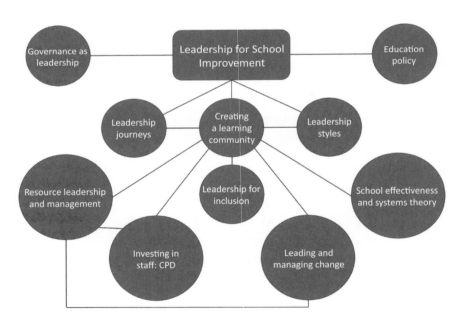

Figure 12.1. Leadership for School Improvement module diagram

2   See https://www.birmingham.ac.uk/postgraduate/courses/taught/edu/educational-leadership.aspx.

When teaching the module, we introduce classic texts, including Kenneth Leithwood's 'Seven Strong Claims about Successful School Leadership' (Leithwood et al., 2008, 2019) and Viviane Robinson's research (Robinson et al., 2009; Robinson, 2011, 2017). Both Leithwood and Robinson have accumulated knowledge about 'what works' over many years. Although we know from 'Seven Strong Claims about Successful School Leadership Revisited' (Leithwood et al., 2019) that the importance and impact of some of the claims have shifted since 2008, the primacy of effective leadership remains unchallenged – second only to the quality of teaching in terms of impact.

We explore the centrality of, and relationship between, effective leadership and high levels of investment in staff through the work of Robinson and Harris and Muijs (2005). To secure sustainable improvements in learner achievement, leaders' energies must be focused on developing teaching and learning in the classroom. It sounds so obvious, but it was not always at the forefront of leadership research or thinking. However, a decade-long focus on exploring the effectiveness of distributed leadership models and the emergence of the concept of teacher leadership (Wallace, 2002) has created a deeper understanding of the golden thread between the leader and how they influence what happens to the learners in the classroom.

We also explore in depth the leadership of change with Fullan's enduring wisdom to guide us – for example, *Change Forces: Probing the Depths of Educational Reform* (1993) and, most recently, *Leading in a Culture of Change* (2020). There can be no impactful leadership without effective change leadership and management. All leaders need to initiate and secure change. There is no standing still in any school or organisation lest they slip backwards.

Leaders' understanding of their schools' context and culture is critical (Leithwood and Jantzi, 2000; MacNeil et al., 2009). We fuse together the direct experience of leaders like Sajid Gulzar in condensing the lessons from five different primary schools (two of which were directly impacted by Trojan Horse) with theories of change, including John Kotter (1996) and Steve Munby's (2019) reworking of the sigmoid curve, which originates with Charles Handy (1995).

The list below is a good example of how practice meets theory on the course, as Gulzar sets out in his strategic approach to leading change:

- Make it safe – site, child protection, health and safety, fire.

- Start with the 'why' – mission and moral purpose.

- Gathering intelligence – open-door policy.

- Clear expectations – establishing the rules of engagement.

- Balancing support with accountability.

- Relationships – starting a movement.

- Communication (staff and parents).

- Fighting many battles on many fronts – leadership resilience.

- All leading to the beginnings of a change in culture.

A wealth of references could be attached to each of these bullet points, but for successful school leaders, including Gulzar, that doesn't really matter because their actions are primarily driven by moral purpose and informed by the local context and the actors with whom they engage. As one of my students wrote in an assignment, 'School leader A was adopting classic theory of change approaches in moving her school forward without realising it.'

We build on established research, with books written by practitioners within education – for example, *Head Strong* by Dame Sally Coates (2015), in which she identifies the main components in her leadership journey at Burlington Danes Academy, West London. In *The Thinking School* (2019), Kulvarn Atwal writes about implementation of a workplace learning culture at the primary schools he leads in North East London. And, from York, John Tomsett writes about why love is a vital ingredient for him as a school leader in *This Much I Know about Love Over Fear* (2015). Munby's high-altitude leadership journey is captured in his book, *Imperfect Leadership: A Book for Leaders Who Know They Don't Know It All* (2019), which has humility at its core and provides an antidote to the macho 'hero leader' narrative. We also go way beyond the world of education leadership to draw on global practice, such as Ronald Heifetz and Marty Linsky's *Leadership on the Line* (2002) with its provenance in decades of experience across corporate, public and non-governmental organisation spheres. We even stray, perhaps controversially, into the military by exploring General Colin Powell's *A Leadership Primer* (2006); yes, 'Being responsible sometimes means pissing people off', whether you are in a corporation, regiment or school.

The following quotation summarises why good leadership is so important:

> Our conclusion from this evidence as a whole is that leadership has very significant effects on the quality of school organisation and on pupil learning. *As far as we are all aware, there is not a single documented case of a school successfully turning around its pupil achievement trajectory in the absence of talented leadership.* One explanation for this is that leadership serves as a catalyst for unleashing the potential capacities that already exist in the organisation. (Leithwood et al. 2008, p. 5; my emphasis)

We understand that the practice of school leadership is influenced by the education policy and system that surrounds it. As Beatriz Pont (2020) summarises neatly in her review of school leadership policy reforms, leadership plays a central part in the implementation of new public management agendas: 'The role of school leaders has evolved in response to changing governance trends, from management, through accountability and now into professionalism.' In England, as the role of the school has been narrowed by government policy away from community engagement and towards a 'direct instruction in a knowledge-rich curriculum' model (Claxton, 2021, p. xx), so we have seen the emergence of a more technocratic form of school leadership.

In this model, narrow technical educational expertise is valued above what some authors refer to as 'generic leadership' (Barker and Rees, 2020), which ascribes to leaders a much broader role. Whilst acknowledging that school leadership is complex, they champion the 'expert model', which is founded in a knowledge-rich approach (of course!). Moreover, in the quest to develop school leadership, the challenges that all leaders face are defined as 'persistent problems' to be overcome. In other words, leadership becomes a 'negative hypothesis' dogged by difficulties rather than a set of challenges to be overcome in a learning community. For example, the 'persistent problem' of managing an efficient and effective organisation could be drawn from any corporate training manual.

How relevant is this narrow approach to urban leadership? What weight should be attached to it? Is a more limited definition helpful in the light of the six leadership journeys captured in Part II of this book? Arguably, prior to the COVID-19 pandemic, the answer was no. Now, with much more evidence on the re-emergence of a broader role for schools and leaders which celebrates deeper engagement with their communities (Harris and Jones, 2020; Netolicky, 2020), it is a resounding no. The rise of managerialism in education policy and systems has had a profound impact on leaders' behaviours over the last decade. Right now, they are not aging well.

Education policy in England has shifted attention away from urban education leadership per se and towards a narrow expert model, which is considered applicable in any setting (Barker and Rees, 2020). This is part of a policy that explicitly rejects the 'soft bigotry of low expectations' (DfE and Gove, 2013), which allegedly patronised disadvantaged pupils, mainly in cities, over many decades. Former Secretary of State for Education Nicky Morgan spoke of a 'one nation' approach, which would level up achievement by abandoning approaches aimed at understanding and engaging with deprived communities. She also wanted to 'slay' low expectations in the name of 'social justice' and reverse the New Labour policies which allegedly sought to 'level everyone down to the bottom' (DfE and Morgan, 2015).

A generation's worth of careful research into raising standards in urban communities was discredited incrementally, and the characteristics of urban education leadership associated with successful outcomes were deliberately ignored. As the National College for School Leadership (NSCL) identified:

> It is impossible to isolate the classroom from the influence of home and community, to create an oasis of learning inside a desert of ambition. Teachers' ability to do their job – and their satisfaction from the job – depends on the engagement of families with the school.

> Urban schools, therefore, can be victims of a wider legacy of the neglect and alienation of whole communities, making them front line targets of crime, vandalism and aggression. Schools have also, at times, contributed to this legacy by forging relationships of authority, hierarchy and dependency with communities. Schools can be forbidding institutions to some parents, conditioned by their own schooling experience. (NCSL, 2009, p. 5)

Therefore, in such intense circumstances, and in order to develop a cadre of school leaders who had the maximum chance of succeeding, NCSL asked: what exactly does it take to survive and thrive in this environment? The outcomes of this research identified very similar traits and dispositions, as set out in the NCSL's *A Model of School Leadership in Challenging Urban Environment* (2009).

Mick Waters turned this into forward-facing tasks. He writes: 'Managerialism is that sense of being busy and decisive, highly organised and structured, clear about objectives and outputs whilst simultaneously losing sight of the underlying values of being community led.' He continues: 'If we want school leaders to be part of a self-improving school system, we shouldn't treat them as branch managers ... Our community of parents must become partners, not customers' (Waters, 2020, pp. 36, 40).

Waters sees the tasks for head teachers and principals as follows:

- Hold on to what matters – the things you said at interview about changing lives, equipping young people for their futures, shaping society and changing the world.

- Resist the pressure to become too managerial and 'feed the machine' of accountability that others drive.

- Require of 'system leaders' the support they profess to offer, and remind them when they deviate from the agreed support.

- Stand by teachers and others who work with children, literally. This means being close to wherever the learning is taking place: in classrooms, workshops, laboratories and gymnasiums. The closer we are to the action, the more influence is possible. And stand by them metaphorically too – by recognizing how systems have become managerial constructs. (Waters, 2020, p. 36)

There is a relationship here with the characteristics of successful leaders in schools that have been serving White working-class schools, as identified by Mongon and Chapman (2008). In summary, and in line with Leithwood et al.'s (2008, 2019) overall conclusions, 'the leaders in these schools appeared to follow the basic strategies, or very close variations, used by most successful school leaders'. However, 'these leaders appeared to draw on three characteristics which ... can be labelled as intelligences' (Mongon and Chapman, 2008, pp. 1–2). They were:

- Contextual intelligence – demonstrating a profound respect for the context in which they worked 'without ever patronising it'.

- Professional intelligence – defined here with a particular emphasis on nurturing teamwork 'on which ... excellent standards of teaching and learning are dependent'.

- Social intelligence – described as leaders' sensitivity to the 'emotional state of their pupils and colleagues' which guided their own actions.

Additionally, they displayed a deep rapport with people and a strong desire to nurture team and community.

These characteristics resonate strongly with the stories in Part II, where the leaders dug deep locally and were committed to building trust and bridging communities.

So where does this leave what we have learnt from our six leaders in Birmingham? What distinguishes their contributions?

We can start with the words of Louise Stoll (1999, p. 3): 'The ultimate goal of school improvement must be to enhance students' progress, achievement and development, to prepare them for the changing world – the bottom line.' These experienced leaders have made this happen through a combination of adaptive leadership and pragmatic interpretation of government education policy from a secure base in the community and driven by a passion for Birmingham's children.

They don't seek 'oven-ready' or 'quick-bake' solutions to turning schools around and are not obsessed with data. They build relationships with the communities served by their schools and create an enduring social contract which, in most cases, precludes the need for exclusions. They work as equals with their communities and are a long way from the policies endorsed by the Department for Education's behaviour tsar, who supports schools that punish children for rolling their eyes and questioning decisions (Busby, 2019). The behaviour control regimes advocated by many contemporary school leaders, and implemented with the laudable aim of creating safe schools in which to teach and learn, are grounded in the breakdown of relationships and trust between schools and the challenged communities they serve. They are implemented – or rather imposed upon pupils – in the name of 'we know what's best' and 'we set the rules'. Negotiation is out. Imposition is the name of the game.

Those scenarios are a long way from the school improvement journeys chronicled here, and that were explicitly rejected by Herminder Channa when interviewed by *The Guardian* in 2020: 'The behaviour is a reaction to something that has gone on and so it's important to understand what caused it' (Lightfoot, 2020). They are not particularly influenced by education writing, but are all durable, resilient and successful urban school leaders. They are not attached to either side of the crass, binary 'progressive' vs 'traditionalist' debate which dominates much of education social media. As Brian Lightman, the distinguished former head teacher and general secretary of the Association of School and College Leaders once tweeted, 'I don't recognise myself here.' These leaders defy simplistic categorisation and classification.

Their leadership journeys all began years before the impact of the Academies Act 2010, which was designed to fragment the English education system (West and Wolfe, 2018; Ainscow and Salokangas, 2020). Many school leaders have become heads and senior leadership team members during the hyper-accountability regime that exists currently in English schools. It emerged during the New Labour years when increased investment in education was twinned with higher levels of accountability than hitherto (see, for example, Hill, 2002). The coalition and Conservative governments reduced investment in schools whilst ramping up accountability. Colloquially, this is best expressed as a regime that is obsessed with the mandatory weighing of the pig without really considering the healthiness or welfare of the animal.

Having read their chapters, worked with them in a variety of roles over seven years and listened to them deliver lectures at the university on topics including leadership journeys, leading change, school improvement and continuing professional development, there are common factors to our leaders' success (see Figure 12.2). There are over 450 state schools in Birmingham, and what follows in this chapter is typical of school leaders in the city. Sir Tim Brighouse (2015) has talked of 'finding the gaps in the hedge'. Many school leaders in Birmingham were never too impressed by the national policy hedge, with all the constraints, fads and exhortations that have been introduced into English education policy since 2010. National education policy informs school leaders' actions, but it doesn't drive them and it has never provided the moral and ethical compass for their work. The origins of how they lead their schools lies much deeper in an education culture founded on understanding and working with the communities they serve.

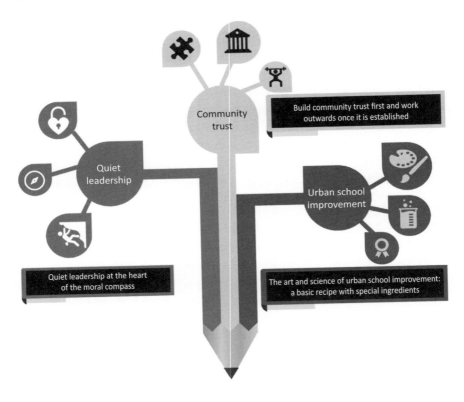

Figure 12.2. Three characteristics of urban leadership

Quiet leadership at the heart of the moral compass

What struck me on first meeting head teachers in Birmingham on school visits and at events organised to talk about Trojan Horse was (a) their embarrassment about Trojan Horse and despair that the slow-motion car crash had been allowed to happen in the first place, and (b) their deep commitment to the city and desire to be part of the solution. No head teacher in the city refused when asked to step up and immerse themselves in dysfunctional schools and traumatised communities. Beneath that willingness to roll up their sleeves and pitch in to long-standing 'stuck' schools is a lack of ego and concern for self.

Christian Schiller – an educationalist who fought in the First World War, survived injury, was awarded the Military Cross and went on to become a government primary education inspector – truly understood the concepts of service and humility. He said that quiet leadership was derived from an involvement in which one's own ego is lost in concern for others, and there is a complete absence of any desire to impress with one's own self (Schiller, 1979). This is the norm. Head teachers who pursue selfish ends are rare in the inner cities because it requires collective energy to move schools forward. Insularity is frowned upon and those acting in obvious self-interest are viewed suspiciously by most head teachers.

When I visit a school, my final question to the head teacher is: 'Who looks after you?' I rarely hear answers that make me feel they are looking after themselves. Mentors, coaches and chairs of governors rarely come into the conversation. Rather, something is muttered about being 'okay', the family and quite often the cat. I am not endorsing this lack of self-care or well-being, but simply observing that it is typical of many school leaders who carry on stoically and deserve more support.

The standard leadership typographies, so popular in leadership literature, take us some of the way in analysing the six leaders in Part II. Bush and Glover's (2003) baseline theory provides the platform for understanding and analysis. Updated in 2014, their conclusion – 'the concept of management has been joined, or superseded, by the language of leadership but the activities undertaken by principals and senior staff resist such labels' (Bush and Glover, 2014) is apposite here.

We find a rich brew of leadership styles at play. Their behaviours and characteristics can be found in several chapters of Steve Munby's (2019) *Imperfect Leadership*. They have taken on leading change with its pitfalls and non-linear, rollercoaster versions of the sigmoid curve. And there are strong elements of servant leadership threaded across the six leadership journeys (Greenleaf, 1977). As Herminder Channa writes in Chapter 10, 'For me, leadership is rooted in the understanding that we are here to serve selflessly, without reward or recognition.'

Closely related is the brand of emotionally literate and learning-focused leadership described by Kulvarn Atwal in *The Thinking School* (2019). For Atwal, leadership is about a constant curiosity to gain new knowledge to be the best teaching assistant, teacher or leader, with every decision in school analysed through its impact on how the children learn best. He stresses the affective domain in his leadership of schools in North East London. This is pure urban gold, and has a strong resonance with Azita Zohhadi (Chapter 6) and Adrian Packer (Chapter 7). In a seminar on emotionally literate leaders for students at the University of Birmingham's Education Leadership Academy, Atwal (2020) outlines the qualities that are important universally and critical for success in city communities:

- **Kindness:** Leaders show respect, generosity of spirit, understanding and consistency.

- **Justice:** Leaders have a sense of fairness and their actions reflect their values and beliefs.

- **Service:** Leaders are conscientious and have a sense of duty and moral purpose.

- **Courage**: Leaders are courageous in their decision-making in the best interests of children.

- **Optimism:** Leaders are positive and cheer others on.

- **Inclusive:** Leaders believe in the learning and development of all children and adults.

Finally, Heifetz and Linksy (2017, p. 13) crystallise the environment that our leaders found themselves in post-Trojan Horse:

> Every day, people have problems for which they do, in fact, have the necessary know-how and procedures. We call these technical problems. But there is a whole host of problems that are not amenable to authoritative expertise or standard operating procedures. They cannot be solved by someone who provides answers from on high. We call these adaptive challenges because they require experiments, new discoveries and adjustments from numerous places in the organisation or community.

For Adrian Packer, Herminder Channa, Sajid Gulzar and Bev Mabey, who took over schools damaged in the name of Trojan Horse, there was no roadmap and each situation required numerous rounds of adaptive change before stability was secured. This process took several years and was a non-linear journey that consisted of endless renegotiation, repositioning, readjustments and infinite patience whilst rebuilding trust.

Build community trust first and work outwards once it is established

A common feature in the school improvement journeys described in this book is that trust between the community and school had been eroded by Trojan Horse. Local communities found it hard to understand what was happening as there was a rapid turnover in school staff, new head teachers arrived, Ofsted inspectors visited frequently and key sections of the national media portrayed events in a decidedly Islamophobic fashion. As Herminder Channa says in Chapter 10, 'parents and carers ... educationalists and operational staff ... were left feeling hurt, angry and confused about the decline of their school'. There was a 'dislocation' between the school and its community.

It was a priority for the new head teachers to listen to parents and pupils, find out their hopes for the future and fears about how Trojan Horse may have blighted their children's education, and what they really wanted from school. For Channa, 'That was my starting point.' Pupil voice had all too often been absent and invisible, so Adrian Packer made it a priority to capture their experiences via an in-house documentary: 'They talk about us a lot. Why don't they try to talk with us?'

What did the parents want? Was there anything exceptional here? Was it a socially conservative Muslim education with opportunities to pray during the day? No. As all the school leaders here explained, the parents wanted to trust their chosen school to deliver a good education. Sajid Gulzar (Chapter 8) writes of 'a general consensus ... for a decent education'. Channa's parents wanted 'excellent educational provision' and, understandably, were 'exasperated' by the quality of education they had been receiving. Gulzar notes that having worked with the Highfield community for four years, if there were any extremist elements within the parent body, they were yet to surface.

There are many parallels with the journey of Hunslet Moor Primary School in South Leeds. Its community was riven by the 7/7 bomb attacks in London when it was discovered that the attackers were from the local neighbourhood of Beeston. Head teacher Narinda Gill has described how the school moved forward from those grim events and how 'education can be used as a tool to engage and raise the aspirations of a diverse community' (Gill and Darley, 2018, p. 16). This work necessarily preceded the establishment of understanding and the setting of the standards agenda.

Washwood Heath Secondary School had been working to build strong community relationships for over a decade when Ofsted's Trojan Horse inspection team arrived. It had deep community roots and strong governance, which enabled it to develop an outward-facing curriculum that was rich in the arts and confident about teaching sex and relationships content without contention. School leaders were able to utilise all of that experience to pick up the pieces at Saltley School and integrate it into the newly formed Washwood Heath Multi-Academy Trust. The tradition of working with arts organisations like Stan's Cafe theatre company enabled rapid progress, with cross-curricular projects that took their pupils into the cultural heart of the city, presenting their work at the Reparatory Theatre. For Bev Mabey (Chapter 9) at Washwood Heath, community engagement ran deep, with a premium placed on community safety partnerships which were seen as a natural extension of the role of the school.

Azita Zohhadi built strong links between Nelson Mandela Primary School and the Royal Shakespeare Company. The Ladypool Road community came to the evening productions of *A Comedy of Errors*, *The Merchant of Venice*, *Julius Caesar* and *The Tempest* in big numbers, with many in the audience exposed to Shakespeare for the first time.

For the other established schools in this book, they started from a very low baseline. Herminder Channa coaxed her school community to look beyond the local area and to make that short bus journey from Small Heath into the stunning municipal jewels in the city centre. Most of her pupils had never felt confident enough to venture into the Library of Birmingham or Symphony Hall. Many rarely left their postcode.

Packer's natural professional disposition was to build partnerships with arts and sports organisations, given his career to date at the BRIT School and Everton Free School. Initially, he needed to rein back external partnership work because so much internal relationship-building was required at Park View. But he recognised how 'culturally introspective' many of the pupils were at Park View – they had been deprived of a 'fully rounded education as a result of the emphasis on academic outcomes'.

To counter this legacy and to take the pupils beyond their postcodes, he initiated a series of partnerships with organisations such as the Lawn Tennis Association. He also established a Combined Cadet Force at Rockwood Academy to create connections between the local community and the armed forces; a statement that says, 'We are part of mainstream British society.' The most publicly visible manifestation of Packer and CORE Education Trust reaching out from the east end of Birmingham to wider society is Echo Eternal, a commemorative arts engagement programme inspired by Holocaust survivors' testimonies.

The art and science of urban school improvement: a basic recipe with special ingredients

The RRSA [Rights Respecting School Award] framework shapes the ethos of Cherry Orchard Primary School and unifies pupils, parents and a community. Through our RRSA ethos, pupils develop a stronger sense of the need to act for global justice and have a stronger understanding of their rights.

Cherry Orchard Primary School, Birmingham[3]

Prior to the eruption of Trojan Horse in 2013, Sir Michael Wilshaw already had Birmingham in his sights. Children's services had been judged inadequate for a decade. However, with customary tact and diplomacy, and taking a swipe at the council's leadership, he said that 'Birmingham was one of the worst places to grow up in the developed world'. Warming to his topic, he added that the city was a 'rotten borough' and 'an absolute disgrace', which needed attention as a matter of urgency (Doughty, 2013). In 2015, a Fox News commentator informed the world that 'In Britain there are not just "no-go zones", there are actually cities like Birmingham that are totally Muslim, where non-Muslims just simply don't go in' (see Sehmer, 2015).

Meanwhile, Trojan Horse had led to a plethora of Islamophobic media coverage, as Reza Gholami points out in Chapter 14. Prevent was being

---

3   See https://www.cherryorchard.bham.sch.uk/page/?title=RRSA&pid=41.

rolled out post-Trojan Horse alongside the imperative to teach so-called 'fundamental British values'. The result was further chaos and confusion. Which way should school leaders and governors jump? Would they pass the equivalent of a latter-day Tebbit loyalty test supervised by Ofsted if they did not display enough Union Jacks?[4] Was the answer to make multiple Prevent referrals and play it safe with orthodox school improvement techniques? Wilshaw was never far away, and he spooked head teachers by sharing his gloomy prognostications that Trojan Horse issues could reappear anytime soon in Birmingham (TES, 2016). He was right, but for the wrong reasons. Trojan Horse activities to undermine school leaders had been purged from inside state schools, so the centre of gravity shifted to outside the school gates (see the introduction to Chapter 2).

In the event, it was a combination of recognisable school turnaround methods combined with the creative use of the United Nations Children's Fund (UNICEF) Rights Respecting Schools Award (RRSA) that has influenced curriculum and pedagogy across Birmingham. In 2015, Razia Butt, Birmingham City Council's resilience officer, visited Park View School (soon to be renamed Rockwood Academy) to review safeguarding procedures and find out how safeguarding was experienced by pupils in the school. She met with the school council and heard how the pupils felt misrepresented in the media, and that what was described was not reflective of their experience of their school or communities. Razia introduced them to the United Nations Convention on the Rights of the Child (UNCRC) – because it belongs to all children and protects their right to faith, culture, language and heritage – and the associated RRSA. This led to the council approaching UNICEF UK to investigate whether the RRSA could be used to address the pupils' trauma (see Chapter 6 for more on this).

Trojan Horse had infused many schools and their host communities with division and polarisation. There were no conventional cohesion or integration strategies available that could offer resolution. Something new was needed through which a multiplicity of perspectives could coexist, something that belonged to all children and would provide a golden thread between them all. The UNCRC represents that universal platform; Article 14 on freedom of thought, belief and religion and Article 30, which addresses children in minority or indigenous groups, were particularly relevant. However, many of the articles drew immediate empathetic

---

4   Norman Tebbit came under fire for the 'cricket test' which implied that the loyalty of British Asians could be determined by which side they cheered for in international cricket matches (see Fisher, 1990).

responses from the pupils at Park View. They empowered and conferred 'common rights [which] give people leverage for action' (Davies, 2014, p. 211). The events of 2014 were one chapter in a long saga of producing a 'distorted knowledge of the other' (Said, 1979, p. 6); 9/11 and 7/7 had led to earlier outbreaks of Islamophobia in the country. Whilst newly created curriculum content could address the specifics of these dreadful events, a vacuum nationally – as a result of the downgrading of anti-racist education and a jingoistic version of Prevent – would only serve to exacerbate tensions.

Clearly, something had clicked between the pupils and what the RRSA brought to the table in Birmingham post-Trojan Horse. Nationally, the award is recognised for putting children's rights at the heart of school policy and practice. Across the UK, 1.6 million children were attending a Rights Respecting School in 2019 and around 5,000 schools were working through the award.[5] Knowledge about and empowerment through children's rights are central to the teaching of the RRSA. Children develop self-esteem, learn about their own rights and how to exercise them, create a culture of trust in their schools and, ultimately, become members of the global community.

By 2017, 249 schools in the city had registered to become Rights Respecting. Some ninety-six schools had achieved Bronze, seventy-five had achieved Silver and five schools had achieved Gold.[6] The great majority of awards had been made between 2015 and 2017, including the first nursery school in the country to secure the award, Gracelands. Head teachers swiftly recognised the value of the RRSA, with its humanist language and accessibility to all sections of the city's communities. Birmingham's unique approach to strengthening safeguarding in schools by addressing the roots of identity and belonging via the RRSA has made a clear impact, as UNICEF's 2017 data shows:

> Analysis of feedback from 75 Birmingham schools who have achieved Silver or Gold since 2016 identifies that:
>
> ▪ 98% of headteachers believe that the Rights Respecting Schools Award (RRSA) has had a positive impact on relationships and behaviour

---

5   See https://www.unicef.org.uk/rights-respecting-schools/the-rrsa/impact-of-rrsa.
6   See https://www.birmingham.gov.uk/blog/school-nb/post/151/15-february-2019.

- 96% of headteachers considered that the RRSA impacted on children and young people's positive attitudes to diversity & overcoming prejudices

- 95% of headteachers considered that working on the RRSA improved children's and young people's respect for themselves and others

- 92% of headteachers considered that the Award contributed to children and young people being more engaged in their learning

- 78% of headteachers stated that the RRSA has had a positive impact on reducing exclusions and bullying.[7]

Each year, prior to COVID-19, the local authority brought together pupils from across the city for a celebration of RRSA learning at the Repertory Theatre. It was a glorious occasion: enjoyment and achievement in equal measure. Presentations ranged from young pupils showing they understood what the rights meant, through to mature theatre from teenagers dealing with themes such as sexual exploitation and trafficking. No conventional subject boundaries were necessary as learning was built around the UNCRC and transcended the traditionalist national curriculum grid.

An urban school improvement model heavily influenced by context

There's no secret or magic formula: clear expectations, culture, relationships and hard work.

**Sajid Gulzar, University of Birmingham Education
Leadership Academy seminar (2020)**

A more recognisable turnaround approach was set out by Sajid Gulzar when he led a seminar on school improvement at the university in 2019. His keys to success (see list below) can be applied in most situations where new leadership is brought to bear on a school that has lost its way. He has home-grown most of the leaders who were deployed across the

---

7   See https://www.birmingham.gov.uk/blog/school-nb/post/151/15-february-2019.

primary schools that joined the Prince Albert Community Trust and made sure they brought outstanding classroom practice steeped in the values of the trust:

- Clear vision.

- High expectations.

- Quality continuing professional development.

- Relentless focus on improvement rooted in a clear moral purpose.

- Building momentum.

- Relationships – keep working at them.

- Celebrate your successes no matter how small.

- Resilience – take nothing personally.

- Inner circle.

Gulzar's exposition of how to lead a school out of trouble has the core elements identified by Robinson (2009): applying deep educational knowledge (he served the city's schools over many years), solving complex problems and building relational trust (a quality best experienced when observing Gulzar and his leadership team at work in their schools where there is a palpable sense of family and belonging). The Prince Albert trust has become a strong community of learners, where adult learning is valued as highly as children's learning in the quest for excellence. Moral purpose lights up the journey.

It is a short step from how the Prince Albert trust operates to the creation of a dynamic learning community with its learning-focused leadership, which was conceptualised and created by Kulvarn Atwal in his seminal *The Thinking School* (2019). He is an education leader who took the findings from his doctoral research into the workplace where he created a dynamic learning community. In a seminar for the university's Leadership for School Improvement programme in 2021, Atwal described the key characteristics as:

- Research-based practice.

- Every decision analysed in terms of its impact on children's learning.

- Teacher choice in learning contextualised to meet the children's needs.

- Collaborative planning and continuous professional learning.

- Coaching for all staff.

- Peer learning and lesson study.

- Non-judgemental lesson observations.

The impact of this learning-focused leadership is extraordinary, with Atwal's urban schools in North East London soaring on every metric available and a remarkably stable staff group who just don't want to leave. (His two schools spent no more than £28 on recruitment between 2012 and 2020.) His approach is notable because it is so different from the expert managerialist model which so many contemporary authors embrace (see, for example, Barker and Rees, 2020). There is plenty of evidence beyond the narrow English government-endorsed view of what works well in urban schools. Atwal's work is a prime example. And that takes us to his neighbours in East London where Peter Hyman and fellow founders Oli de Botton and Ed Fidoe created School 21, which is the polar opposite of those schools lionised by government ministers (DfE and Gibb, 2017).

The curriculum at School 21 is driven by the belief that young people need a fundamentally different approach to standard curricular and pedagogical models in order to prepare them for adult life. Learning is balanced between activities that promote academic success (head), develop character and well-being (heart) and generate ideas and problem-solving (hand). Its values of humanity, community, excellence, openness and responsibility underpin everything in the school. It has an outward focus with real-world learning partners in the community. Ofsted inspectors said of the leaders: 'they strongly believe that education should be done differently so that all children, including those who battle against the odds, have a chance to succeed in the 21st century' (Ofsted, 2014, p. 6). Outstanding grades across the board are evidence of how successful School 21 has become since opening in 2012.

From the schools in Birmingham's east end through to their sister schools in East and North East London, we can see that leaders are addressing the low achievement of generations of children by fusing together well-recognised and well-researched school improvement techniques, an unshakeable commitment to community and innovative approaches that shift them through the gears from surviving to thriving. These urban leaders don't seek out or depend on central government policy initiatives to drive their curriculum because they have already identified what works well for a sustainable future.

Takeaways for urban school leaders

- Don't follow national education policy encyclicals slavishly: they are not designed to take account of the environment in which urban leaders work. Be selective, adopt and adapt according to what your school needs.

- Roots to grow and wings to fly. Sustainable success in urban leadership is built on understanding and respecting the community your school serves. Seek to understand your community's culture and aspirations before being understood yourself.

- UNICEF's RRSA will infuse your curriculum with learning that brings out the best in children in multi-faith and multi-ethnic schools. Its impact has been proven many times over.

- Learn from those who are just ahead of you and be a magpie: the examples in Part II and in this chapter provide rich sources to inspire and inform your leadership journey. Then write your own story.

- Create a learning community and be explicit about it. Learning communities – with their restless quest for innovation and excellence – are the best guarantors of sustained school improvement.

- YNWA – you must never work alone (an adaptation of 'You'll Never Walk Alone' for urban school leaders). Those head teachers who peel off from the group lose their way quickly. All the leaders in this book are well-networked and look outwards constantly.

- Create a network of professional support that works for you. It is likely to be a combination of mentors, coaches, near neighbours and fellow travellers who will be there for you. Without this, there is a major risk that you will take things home and the proverbial cat might get it.

▪ Distributed leadership is paramount for those leading schools in challenging urban environments. If that was true pre-COVID-19, it should be a mandatory element of any leadership development programme now.

▪ School improvement is non-linear. Work on three-year trends and don't be browbeaten by those who appear to display an obsessive interest in micro-trends in data. Many of them have never worked in settings like yours.

▪ Look after yourself by appointing those who will be better than you one day. Bring them on, nurture them, watch them add value to your school and grieve a little when they become head teachers and principals themselves. Celebrate quietly (because this is the highest accolade and recognition of your influence as a leader), regroup and move on to the next chapter in your journey.

References

Ainscow, Mel and Salokangas, Maija (2020) The English School Reforms: Competition, Innovation and Fragmentation. In Michelle Jones and Alma Harris (eds), *Leading and Transforming Education Systems: Evidence, Insights, Critique and Reflections* (Education in the Asia-Pacific Region: Issues, Concerns and Prospects series, vol. 52). Singapore: Springer, pp. 61–76.

Atwal, Kulvarn (2019) *The Thinking School: Developing a Dynamic Learning Community*. Woodbridge: John Catt Educational.

Atwal, Kulvarn (2020) School Leadership During COVID-19: Perspectives from the Front Line [online seminar], Education Leadership Academy, University of Birmingham (15 June). Available at: https://www.birmingham.ac.uk/schools/education/ela/events/2020/school-leadership-during-covid-19.aspx.

Barker, Jennifer and Rees, Tom (2020) What is School Leadership? In Stuart Lock (ed.), *The researchED Guide to Leadership: An Evidence-Informed Guide for Teachers*. Woodbridge: John Catt Educational, pp. 23–43.

Brighouse, Tim (2015) Seizing the Agenda: 'Finding the Gaps in the Hedge' [video]. Speech at Whole Education sixth annual conference, 2 December. Available at: https://www.youtube.com/watch?v=lGUV5-NG8V8.

Busby, Eleanor (2019) School Behaviour Tsar Endorses Detention Regime That Punishes Pupils for Rolling Their Eyes, *The Independent* (14 October). Available at: https://www.independent.co.uk/news/education/education-news/detention-school-tom-bennett-discipline-rolling-eyes-zero-tolerance-twitter-a9155191.html.

Bush, Tony and Glover, Derek (2003) *School Leadership: Concepts and Evidence.* Nottingham: National College for School Leadership. Available at: https://dera.ioe.ac.uk/5119/14/dok217-eng-School_Leadership_Concepts_and_Evidence_Redacted.pdf.

Bush, Tony and Glover, Derek (2014) School Leadership Models: What Do We Know?, *School Leadership & Management*, 34(5): 553–571. Available at: https://www.researchgate.net/publication/271904669_School_leadership_models_What_do_we_know/link/572f5aaa08ae3736095c195f/download.

Cameron, William B. (1963) *Informal Sociology: A Casual Introduction to Sociological Thinking.* New York: Random House.

Carter, David and McInerney, Laura (2020) *Leading Academy Trusts: Why Some Fail, But Most Don't.* Woodbridge: John Catt Educational.

Claxton, Guy (2021) *The Future of Teaching: And the Myths That Hold It Back.* Abingdon and New York: Routledge.

Coates, Sally (2015) *Head Strong: 11 Lessons of School Leadership.* Woodbridge: John Catt Educational.

Covey, Stephen (2020) *The 7 Habits of Highly Effective People: Powerful Lessons in Personal Change*, rev. edn. New York: Simon & Schuster.

Davies, Lynn (2014) *Unsafe Gods: Security, Secularism and Schooling.* London: Trentham Books.

Department for Education (DfE) and Gibb, Nick (2017) Nick Gibb: England's Education Reforms. Speech delivered at the Centre for Independent Studies, Sydney, Australia, 11 April. Available at: https://www.gov.uk/government/speeches/nick-gibb-englands-education-reforms.

Department for Education (DfE) and Gove, Michael (2013) The Civil Rights Struggle of Our Time. Speech to the Mayor of London's Education Conference, City Hall, London, 22 November. Available at: https://www.gov.uk/government/speeches/the-civil-rights-struggle-of-our-time.

Department for Education (DfE) and Morgan, Nicky (2015) Nicky Morgan: One Nation Education. Speech delivered at Policy Exchange, London, 3 November. Available at: https://www.gov.uk/government/speeches/nicky-morgan-one-nation-education.

Doughty, Steve (2013) Bad Parents Are to Blame for Society's Ills, Says Ofsted Chief: Sir Michael Wilshaw Attacks 'Hollowed Out and Fragmented Families', *Daily Mail* (16 October). Available at: https://www.dailymail.co.uk/news/article-2462110/Sir-Michael-Wilshaw-attacks-hollowed-fragmented-families.html.

Fisher, Dan (1990) Split Between Britain, U.S. Seen as 'Inevitable': Foreign Policy: The Conservative Party Chairman Fears That a 'Less European' America Will Provide the Wedge [interview with Norman Tebbit], *Los Angeles Times* (19 April). Available at: https://www.latimes.com/archives/la-xpm-1990-04-19-mn-2009-story.html.

Fullan, Michael (1993) *Change Forces: Probing the Depths of Educational Reform.* Hove: Psychology Press.

Fullan, Michael (2020) *Leading in a Culture of Change.* San Francisco, CA: Jossey-Bass.

Gill, Narinder and Darley, Hannah (2018) *Creating Change in Urban Settings*. Norwich: Singular Publishing.

Greenleaf, Robert K. (1977) *Servant Leadership: A Journey into the Nature of Legitimate Power and Greatness*. New York: Paulist Press.

Handy, Charles (1995) *The Empty Raincoat: Making Sense of the Future*. London: Arrow Books.

Hargreaves, Andy and Fullan, Michael (2012) *Professional Capital: Transforming Teaching in Every School*. Abingdon and New York: Routledge.

Harris, Alma (2004) Successful Leadership in Schools Facing Challenging Circumstances: No Panaceas or Promises. In Janet H. Chrispeels (ed.), *Learning to Lead Together: The Promise and Challenge of Sharing Leadership*. Thousand Oaks, CA: Sage, pp. 282–304.

Harris, Alma and Jones, Michelle (2020) COVID 19 – School Leadership in Disruptive Times, *School Leadership & Management*, 40(4): 243–247. Available at: https://doi.org/10.1080/13632434.2020.1811479.

Harris, Alma and Muijs, Daniel (2005) *Improving Schools Through Teacher Leadership*. Maidenhead: Open University Press.

Heifetz, Ronald A. and Linsky, Marty (2002) *Leadership on the Line: Staying Alive through the Dangers of Leading*. Boston, MA: Harvard Business School Press.

Heifetz, Ronald A. and Linsky, Marty (2017) *Leadership on the Line: Staying Alive Through the Dangers of Change*, rev. edn. Boston, MA: Harvard Business Review Press.

Hill, Dave (2002) The Third Way and Education: New Labour, the Dominance of Neo-Liberal Global Capital in European Education Policies, and the Growth of Inequality. Paper delivered at the European Conference on Educational Research, University of Lisbon, 11–14 September. Available at: http://www.ieps.org.uk/media/1041/hill2002a.pdf.

Kotter, John P. (1996) *Leading Change*. Boston, MA: Harvard Business School Press.

Leithwood, Kenneth; Harris, Alma; and Hopkins, David (2008) Seven Strong Claims About Successful School Leadership, *School Leadership & Management*, 28(1): 27–42. DOI:10.1080/13632430701800060.

Leithwood, Kenneth; Harris, Alma; and Hopkins, David (2019) Seven Strong Claims About Successful School Leadership Revisited, *School Leadership & Management*, 40(1): 5–22. DOI:10.1080/13632434.2019.1596077.

Leithwood, Kenneth and Jantzi, Doris (2000) The Effects of Transformational Leadership on Organizational Conditions and Student Engagement with School, *Journal of Educational Administration*, 38(2): 112–129. DOI:10.1108/09578230010320064.

Leithwood, Kenneth; Jantzi, Doris; and Steinbach, Rosanne (1999) *Changing Leadership for Changing Times*. Buckingham: Open University Press.

Lightfoot, Liz (2020) Headteacher Who Healed a Birmingham 'Trojan Horse' School: 'We Did It with Love', *The Guardian* (24 October).

Available at: https://www.theguardian.com/education/2020/oct/24/headteacher-who-healed-a-birmingham-trojan-horse-school-we-did-it-with-love.

Lock, Stuart (ed.) (2020) *The researchED Guide to Leadership: An Evidence-Informed Guide for Teachers*. Woodbridge: John Catt Educational.

MacNeil, Angus J.; Prater, Doris L.; and Busch, Steve (2009) The Effects of School Culture and Climate on Student Achievement, *International Journal of Leadership in Education*, 12(1): 73–84. DOI:10.1080/13603120701576241.

Mongon, Denis and Chapman, Christopher (2008) *Successful Leadership for Promoting the Achievement of White Working Class Pupils*. Nottingham: National College for School Leadership. Available at: http://www.educationengland.org.uk/documents/pdfs/2008-nut-ncsl.pdf.

Munby, Steve (2019) *Imperfect Leadership: A Book for Leaders Who Know They Don't Know It All*. Carmarthen: Crown House Publishing.

National College for School Leadership (NCSL) (2009) *A Model of School Leadership in Challenging Urban Environments*. Available at: https://dera.ioe.ac.uk/5276/7/download_id%3D17300%26filename%3Dmodel-of-school-leadership-in-challenging-urban-environments_Redacted.pdf.

Netolicky, Deborah M. (2020) School Leadership During a Pandemic: Navigating Tensions, *Journal of Professional Capital and Community*, 5(3/4): 391–395. Available at: https://doi.org/10.1108/JPCC-05-2020-0017.

Ofsted (2014) School Report: School 21 (17–18 June). Available at: https://files.ofsted.gov.uk/v1/file/2405308.

Pont, Beatriz (2020) A Literature Review of School Leadership Policy Reforms, *European Journal of Education Research, Development and Policy*, 55(2): 154–168. Available at: https://doi.org/10.1111/ejed.12398.

Powell, Colin (2006) *A Leadership Primer*. United States: Department of the Army. Available at: https://www.hsdl.org/?abstract&did=467329.

Robinson, Viviane (2011) *Student-Centered Leadership*. San Francisco, CA: John Wiley & Sons.

Robinson, Viviane (2017) *Reduce Change to Increase Improvement*. Thousand Oaks, CA: Corwin Press.

Robinson, Viviane; Hohepa, Margie; and Lloyd, Claire (2009) *School Leadership and Student Outcomes: Identifying What Works and Why Best Evidence Synthesis Iteration (BES)*. Wellington: Ministry of Education. Available at: https://www.researchgate.net/publication/242493851_School_Leadership_and_Student_Outcomes_Identifying_What_Works_and_Why_Best_Evidence_Synthesis_Iteration_BES/citation/download.

Said, Edward W. (1979) *Orientalism*. New York: Vintage Books.

Schiller, Christian (1979) *Christian Schiller in His Own Words*, ed. Christopher Griffin-Beale. London: A&C Black.

Sehmer, Alexander (2015) Fox News 'Birmingham is No-Go Zone for Non-Muslims' Comment Found in Violation of Broadcasting Code, *The Independent* (21 September). Available at: https://www.independent.co.uk/news/uk/home-news/

fox-news-birmingham-is-a-nogo-zone-for-nonmuslims-comment-found-in-violation-of-broadcasting-code-10510953.html.

Stoll, Louise (1999) Realising Our Potential: Understanding and Developing Capacity for Lasting Improvement, *School Effectiveness and School Improvement*, 10(4): 503–532. DOI:10.1076/sesi.10.4.503.3494.

TES (2016) Trojan Horse Issues Could Reappear in Birmingham Schools, Sir Michael Wilshaw Warns (11 December). Available at: https://www.tes.com/magazine/archive/trojan-horse-issues-could-reappear-birmingham-schools-sir-michael-wilshaw-warns.

Tomsett, John (2015) *This Much I Know about Love Over Fear: Creating a Culture of Truly Great Teaching*. Carmarthen: Crown House Publishing.

United Nations Children's Fund (UNICEF) A Summary of the UN Convention on the Rights of the Child. Available at: https://downloads.unicef.org.uk/wp-content/uploads/2019/10/UNCRC_summary-1_1.pdf.

Wallace, Mike (2002) Modelling Distributed Leadership and Management Effectiveness: Primary School Senior Management Teams in England and Wales, *School Effectiveness and School Improvement*, 13(2): 163–186. DOI:10.1076/sesi.13.2.163.3433.

Waters, Mick (2020) Towards a Compassionate School System. In Maurice I. Coles with Bill Gent (eds), *Education for Survival: The Pedagogy of Compassion*. London: University College London Institute of Education Press, pp. 27–43.

West, Anne and Wolfe, David (2018) Academies, the School System in England and a Vision for the Future. Clare Market Papers No. 23. Available at: http://eprints.lse.ac.uk/88240/1/Academies%20Vision%20Report%202%20JUNE.pdf.

Chapter 13

Opposition to LGBT awareness teaching: no outsiders, but what was it like on the inside?

Joy Warmington

Introduction

Introducing mandatory relationships and sex education (RSE) into English schools was always going to be controversial and provoke strong reactions. When the government consulted with the public, 40% of the responses were from people of faith. Overall, 58% of respondents disagreed with the content of relationships education in primary schools and there was considerable opposition to teaching about lesbian, gay, bisexual, transgender and queer (LGBTQ) relationships (Diamond, 2019a). Socially conservative Christian, Jewish and Muslim parents made their opinions known. The government seemed to think things would somehow sort themselves out and head teachers could navigate their own path. The Department for Education was unwilling to discuss how the guidance would play out in complex multi-faith, multi-ethnic schools and communities.

In Birmingham, there was a prolonged period of protests outside two primary schools: Anderton Park (which was maintained by the local authority) and Parkfield (which was an academy with direct accountability to the Department for Education). In the case of Anderton Park, the council secured a temporary injunction banning protestors as they were disrupting the pupils' education. The High Court later turned it into a permanent exclusion zone in order to enable what the judge termed 'lawful' teaching to continue (Dickens, 2019). Away from the media spotlight, whilst having sought judicial remedy to stop the protests, the council worked with its partners to produce an equalities toolkit to support schools in teaching relationships education (Birmingham City Council, 2018).

Events took a different turn at Parkfield: government officials attempted to engage at a local level with mixed results. Things were not working between the school and a minority of parents who challenged the introduction of mandatory RSE. The 'long screwdriver' approach from central government was insufficiently tuned into local community realities. Razia Butt, Birmingham City Council's resilience adviser, knew that brap (formerly Birmingham Race Action Partnership) had a long and successful track record through its application and development of deep democracy 'processwork' training. She asked brap to facilitate a meeting between the parents and the school, which led to an agreement for talks to take place and the protests to stop in the meantime. Teaching of the No Outsiders programme was suspended temporarily and subsequently modified.[1] Three months of destructive protests were ended thanks to the engagement of brap, demonstrating the critical importance of local, community-based contributions and the necessity of skilled processwork (a form of process-oriented psychology).

An Ofsted inspection in February 2019 had fully validated Parkfield's leadership, quality of safeguarding and curriculum, noting that 'The school provides support to several schools, especially for the teaching of mathematics, British values, personal, social, health and economic (PSHE) education and equalities, and spiritual, moral, social and cultural (SMSC) education' (Ofsted, 2019, p. 2). Almost all the parents who completed the Ofsted inspection questionnaire and met inspectors were happy with the school.

> However, *a very small, but vocal, minority of parents* are not clear about the school's vision, policies and practice. This group of parents feel that staff do not sufficiently listen to their concerns. Their view is that the PSHE education and equalities curriculum focuses disproportionately on lesbian, gay and bisexual issues and that this work is not taught in an age-appropriate manner. Inspectors found no evidence that this is the case. (Ofsted, 2019, p. 3; my emphasis)

Significantly, the school was advised to 'Further develop [its] engagement with parents, so that all parents have a clear understanding of the school's policies and procedures, and the curriculum content and how it is taught' (p. 4).

---

1   See https://no-outsiders.com.

So, a resolution – of sorts – to the ugly, disturbing protests was secured, but at no small cost to the schools directly involved. Both were over-exposed as a result of an education policy that gave head teachers and governors the responsibility to interpret contentious legislation in the light of growing signs of opposition from faith communities. As schools minister Nick Gibb told the House of Commons when discussing Parkfield, 'it is a matter for the school itself to decide on the curriculum ... When the school has decided on what it wants to teach and when, it will have the full support and backing of the Department for Education and Ministers.'[2] Lawyer Nazir Afzal, who attempted to mediate at Anderton Park, suggested that teachers were being left isolated by the failings of what he called a 'cowardly Government unwilling to be explicit' about what the law on equality and human rights required schools to do (Haynes, 2019). Afzal also made the link with Trojan Horse and referred to the enduring 'pain' within the Muslim community as a result of the way it was handled.

Perhaps it is also apposite to observe that there was recent history of 'community' activism designed to undermine school leaders who were disapproved of. The difference between the years leading up to 2014 and the landscape in 2019 was that the subversion of head teachers via entryism into governing bodies was no longer possible, so activists focused on mobilising outside the school gates (Diamond, 2019). The most visible signs were the nasty protests; the less visible activities were attempts to discredit school leaders via multiple spurious complaints to Ofsted. The negative reaction to the introduction of compulsory RSE in primary schools had the potential to spread across England. In the event, it was mainly restricted to two schools in the heart of Trojan Horse territory – a stone's throw from where the Park View Brotherhood, with their homophobic WhatsApp messages, operated.

The mainstream media was forthright in condemning the protests but equally critical of the government for its hands-off approach. The Commission for Countering Extremism commissioner, Sara Khan, made a plea for Birmingham's schools to be protected from 'mob rule' (Ford, 2019), whilst the *TES* carried a piece with long quotations from Excelsior Multi Academy Trust CEO (and former Parkfield head teacher) Hazel Pulley and Chair of Trustees Pinky Jain (George, 2019).

---

2   Hansard, HC Deb. vol. 663, col. 709 (16 July 2019). Available at: https://hansard.parliament.
    uk/commons/2019-07-16/debates/CCBB6740-9E01-4CE1-B688-B30ECD61E39A/
    RelationshipEducationInSchools.

The European Court of Human Rights has dismissed religious challenges to rights-based sex education as long as the programmes did not criticise religious beliefs. The United Nations special rapporteur clarified that 'With regard to the freedom to manifest one's religion or belief, both the positive and the negative aspects of that freedom must be equally ensured, i.e. the freedom to express one's conviction as well [as] the freedom not to be exposed to any pressure' (Bielefeldt and UNHRC, 2010, p. 18). Somewhere between the international jurisdictions and head teachers in Birmingham, the transmission chain had broken down, resulting in confusion and uncertainty, with most schools seeking a way forward that met the new requirements on RSE without gratuitously upsetting faith communities. On the ground, the language used to describe those who reasonably asked questions about the teaching of LGBTQ awareness was hostile and offensive. Parents were labelled 'homophobic' and 'bigoted' – accusations they strenuously denied.

In a national vacuum, much depended on local leadership. On the front line, brap secured the agreement which brought to an end the protests outside the school, whilst a dialogue between school and parents was established. CEO of brap, Joy Warmington, writes in this chapter: 'As one protected characteristic cannot be used as a means to override the rights of another, how can the explicit rights of opposing parties both be accommodated?' The meetings she mediated were a crucible in which these issues played out. She concludes that schools need to develop a more nuanced view of the Equality Act 2010, where protected characteristics must be taught in a way that is mindful of the power relations in society, lest it becomes an anodyne nod towards the law. In relation to diversity, she advocates an approach that creates the security wherein children can disagree well rather than create an artificial consensus. And on those apparently contentious books recommended by No Outsiders and widely used in primary schools, she recommends greater exploration of the meaning behind the stories.

Prior to the Parkfield dispute, brap had engaged with the public sector for many years; its work embraced inner-city schools, communities, the police, government agencies, local authorities and voluntary agencies. Brap produced a paper on competing equality claims over a decade ago (Afridi and Warmington, 2010) and has been acutely aware of the potential for new legislation to ignite disagreement. An investment in process-orientated psychology has helped brap to work with the levels of anger, dissent and indifference they encountered on all sides at Parkfield.

Away from the front line, the city council worked with school leaders, governors and the University of Birmingham. Deborah Youdell, professor of education at the university and known for her work on identity-based claims, shifted the discourse towards the public duty elements of the Equality Act and the centrality of 'fostering good relations between people who share a protected characteristic and people who do not share it' (PowerPoint presentation to Birmingham primary head teachers, 2019). She argues that in schools committed to equalities, developing relationships within communities should come first – ahead of pedagogies, institutional practices and curriculum. At a deeper level, it is important to acknowledge the agonism that exists in pluralistic environments, such as those in which many schools operate, where the values of groups don't necessarily align and require a safe space to talk about such things. Fundamentally, her message is rooted in the importance of schools practising, as opposed to just teaching, 'thick democracy', which requires good levels of self-awareness and criticality amongst those working in communities where there is always a risk of tension between protected characteristics (Youdell, 2011).

In Part II, Azita Zohhadi wrote of the significance of the Rights Respecting Schools Award at Nelson Mandela Primary School. She endorsed Birmingham City Council's equalities toolkit[3] when it was launched in 2020 because it 'aligns fully with the UNICEF Rights Respecting Schools programme; both firmly rooted in building respect and appreciation for diversity and all aspects of equality. The approach strongly embraces openness through the consultation process, giving parents, children and staff a platform to discuss, challenge and listen' (quoted in Birmingham City Council, 2020). Nelson Mandela School, under her leadership, embodied the characteristics and behaviours that were advocated by Youdell and brought into the heart of Alum Rock's community by Joy Warmington.

Colin Diamond

---

3   See https://www.birmingham.gov.uk/info/20014/schools_and_learning/2198/
     birmingham_approach_to_relationships_and_health_education_in_primary_schools.

Opposition to LGBT awareness teaching: no outsiders, but what was it like on the inside?

Joy Warmington

Protesting parents

This chapter reflects on brap's experiences in helping to mediate the dispute between Parkfield Community School, Birmingham City Council and representatives of parents at the school who protested against the teaching of the No Outsiders programme to their children.

The No Outsiders project was developed by Andrew Moffatt, who at the time was an assistant head teacher at Parkfield Community School in Birmingham. The aim was to inform children about equality and British values, whilst also recognising and celebrating difference and diversity.

The dispute began in earnest in January 2019, and at its height resulted in parents (mostly Muslim) withdrawing their children from classes and angry demonstrators protesting outside the school. Parents' objections centred on their children being educated about same-sex relationships. In addition to believing the No Outsiders curriculum to be inappropriate, they were angry that the school had undertaken no prior consultation with parents in relation to how it would be taught. Parents objected specifically on the grounds that No Outsiders promoted and normalised gay relationships, was not age-appropriate and was in contradiction of parents' religious views. Parents insisted that their views were not homophobic, and they appreciated that their children needed to understand about different relationships, but they felt this should be done at an older age when they were less likely to be 'confused'.

brap, a national equalities and human rights charity based in Birmingham, was approached by Birmingham City Council's resilience team in February 2019 and asked to chair a meeting between parent representatives and senior staff from the school, with a view to initiating productive conversations between the two parties.

The school's view was that the programme delivered on its responsibility to teach the Equality Act 2010. From the school's perspective, No Outsiders had been running for a number of years without any concerns. Moreover, it considered that consultation with parents about the programme had taken place some three years earlier. Communication between the school and parents had since broken down for a number of reasons. The protests outside the school had become increasingly visceral and there were claims of school staff being threatened and abused. As the protests deepened, other groups of protestors also became actively involved in support of the parents and it became increasingly difficult for the school to know to whom they could talk.

In the six years leading up to 2021, members of the brap team have been training in a method called processwork or process-oriented psychology — a multicultural, multi-level awareness practice designed to support more meaningful human interactions and relationship-building.[4] The technique is considered especially helpful in conflict situations. brap has been developing skills in processwork and practising its application as part of a toolkit of interventions to support our agenda of furthering equality and human rights. As the technique is fluid and can be applied in systems, large groups and organisational contexts (where the technique is sometimes referred to as deep democracy[5]), there was an opportunity to explore how the method could be employed to create further engagement between the school and parents.

All disputes are polarised. They bring with them those who vehemently believe that one party is right and the other wrong. In most disputes, the majority or consensus voice pronounces judgement. The media portrayal of such conflicts is rarely objective and usually gives more voice to one side of the argument over the other. In this case, it was the parents who were vilified: they were portrayed as unreasonable, unlawful, undemocratic, violent and homophobic. Staff at the school were viewed as the victims of the dispute, and portrayed as reasonable, upholding of British values and protectors of equality — including the rights of the LGBT community. As the dispute escalated, each party lobbied for their version of 'right'.

brap's involvement began with a request from the resilience team at Birmingham City Council that we facilitate a meeting between the

---

4   The processwork method was developed by Arnold Mindell – see http://www.aamindell.net/process-work.
5   See http://www.aamindell.net/worldwork.

school and parents on 6 February 2019. At this point, previous discussions between the school and parents had broken down. What was distinctive about this first meeting was the lack of parental attendance. It was attended by two imams (who had no previous connection with the school), two parents, six members of the school leadership team, representatives from the council's resilience team and regional schools commissioners.

It was an uncomfortable meeting, primarily because there was little conversation between the two parties. The school simply stated and restated its viewpoint; the role of those in attendance was to listen and comply. It became apparent to me why communication between the school and parents had broken down: it was because it had never really existed in the first place.

What emerged from the meeting was a need to engage in the complexity of the debate and to recognise and respond to the issues presented by both sides. Power and control were also unhelpful ingredients threaded throughout the relationships between parents and school. Crudely put, schools are accustomed to being listened to and obeyed. Parkfield school enjoyed good scholastic results and was used to having the respect of parents. It was challenged by this group of individuals whom it no longer knew and with whom it didn't agree. Parents were terrified of the authority and privilege exerted by the school. They had little understanding of the curriculum they were opposed to and were relatively ill-equipped to engage in the debate.

In any dispute, it is often hard to see where your allegiances as a mediator lie. Not noticing this can make it impossible to mediate effectively. In this instance, the role of parents and their views had already been cast – they had been vilified as being unreasonable, aggressive, undemocratic and homophobic. On the other side was the school – an outstanding school in a poor area of Birmingham, which was portrayed as having committed and dedicated staff who were unprepared for the parents' reaction. Furthermore, the media and school community were vocal in support of a school that was defending the Equality Act and teaching about different types of families as part of its curriculum.

But nothing is clear-cut.

The Equality Act 2010

The Equality Act is a silent player in this dispute but one that needs to be named more explicitly. It is often assumed that the law is neutral. It isn't; it conveys beliefs and values. In the case of the Equality Act, it compels organisations that are funded by the public purse to recognise and respond positively to address discrimination experienced by groups that are described by the Act as having 'protected characteristics'.[6] These include age, disability, gender reassignment, marriage and civil partnership, pregnancy and maternity, race, religion or belief, sex and sexual orientation.

In *Managing Competing Equality Claims* (Afridi and Warmington, 2010), brap had already begun to think through, research and reference real scenarios where people with different protected characteristics were making competing equality claims using the law. We predicted that there would be cases in the future where a belief in the law and what it protects would clash with the beliefs of other parties and the protections they also believed were afforded to them under the Act. A lack of understanding about the limitations of the Equality Act is central to this dispute. As one protected characteristic cannot be used as a means to override the rights of another, how can the explicit rights of opposing parties both be accommodated?

The dispute

What becomes clearer as you begin to study and work with deep democracy methodology is how much we gain by going towards conflict rather than steering away from it. I am not suggesting that we should advocate war, but I am suggesting that we can often prevent large-scale distress if we recognise the signs of conflict and engage early on. We tend to assume that peace is the opposite of conflict and that lack of conflict is a good thing. What history tells us, however, is that conflict is frequently preceded by signs of distress – signals we ignore because we believe that if we focus on them, or try to address them, it will only make things worse. We confuse lack of outward conflict as a sign of peace. We also ignore the feelings generated by conflict, focusing instead on trying to keep arguments logical. How people feel is often much, if not the whole, of a conflict, rather than a small part of it that can be swept under the

---

6   See https://www.legislation.gov.uk/ukpga/2010/15/contents/enacted.

carpet. Presuming to 'solve' conflict without recognising the feelings and hurt underneath invariably does make things worse.

Whether or not you agree with their views, parents felt hurt by the school, and opportunities had been missed earlier in the dispute to engage with that hurt. This didn't mean agreeing with them, but it did mean listening to them, understanding their views and, most importantly, being prepared to take them seriously. Instead, parents felt dismissed by the school, and the school felt that it had nothing to answer or atone for. By taking the righteous path, the school was able to play both victim and perpetrator at the same time. At this early stage, had there been a moment of pause when those in power held themselves to account and behaved more democratically, there was a possibility that the dispute could have travelled another course. However, hindsight is invariably of limited use.

Using the Equality Act as a lever to win this argument was always going to entail skating on thin ice. Both parties assumed that the Act would offer them protection and justification under the law. The parents believed that their religious beliefs must be adhered to, and the school believed that its duty to fulfil its obligations under the Equality Act, including the teaching of different types of family relationships, was being delivered through the No Outsiders programme.

brap's first full-on session with parents took place on 20 March 2019, when thirty-three parents attended a meeting held in a hall adjacent to the school. The meeting was also attended by six school representatives, two educational advisers and three regional schools commissioners. In fact, this event can scarcely be described as a meeting. It quickly descended into a shouting match: parents (who felt misinterpreted and silenced) attempted to relay their concerns and demand compliance from brap (in our role as mediators). There was little listening going on from either side. The main concern of each party was presenting its own beliefs and its own view of what it saw as right.

Our skills in processwork helped us to roll with the punches and resist the urge to control the meeting. This enabled us to work towards agreeing some skeleton ground rules for further engagement – most importantly, that both parties acknowledge the need for future meetings if there was to be any meaningful prospect of working towards a positive outcome. By the end of that session the following agreements had been secured: from the school, that teaching of the No Outsiders programme would be suspended whilst talks between parents and school took place; and from the parents, the cessation of demonstrations outside the school.

This chapter isn't intended to be an account of all the meetings that took place between March and June 2019. Suffice it to say that with each meeting, we (as facilitators) found each side of the argument becoming clearer to us, but we also observed each side becoming more entrenched in its own position. Our biggest regret is that we couldn't help the school and parents to forge more equitable relationships, which might have helped them to see each other as human beings first rather than as opponents. Had this been possible, it might have led to an entirely different outcome.

In short, parents stopped protesting outside the school and the school presented parents with a revised equality programme called No Outsiders in the Faith Community. Within it, there were some concessions to parents' concerns regarding the types of books being used as teaching materials and the age at which parts of the programme were introduced to children. Some parents permanently withdrew their children from the school – around thirty in total, which was something of a relief given that at the height of the protest in March 2019 up to 600 children had been withdrawn from lessons for a day.

It could be argued that revising an equalities curriculum so that it reflects the requirements of parents with religious views does offer a way forward in respect of introducing the concept of 'different families' into communities where strongly held religious views inhibit the understanding and acceptance of non-traditional family units. But it is by no means clear that this is what happened, nor that wider and more generally applicable lessons have been drawn from the Parkfield school experience. From September 2020, relationships education has been compulsory in primary schools and relationships and sex education compulsory in secondary schools.

Reflections

One of the reasons that the Parkfield school situation was subject to such intense national scrutiny is because it was a microcosm of wider national tensions. Parents (mostly of the Muslim faith) were central to this dispute, but it would be naive to think that it is only Muslim parents who object to the teaching of LGBT relationships in schools. It would also be naive to assume that this issue has been solved.

At the heart of the dispute was the challenge of hearing opposing views – both those that contradict our own and those with which we vehemently disagree. It is not easy to work in this space. However, not to learn the importance of engaging with views we find oppositional is a disaster and can have potentially serious social consequences.

Whilst it is now the duty of schools to teach RSE, the practice is still open to scrutiny. In communities that disagree with the idea of different types of families, how will this be introduced without further opposition? The diversity that is now the norm in many communities is also subject to scrutiny, with many believing that it is the cause of competing conceptions of fairness and justice. Some would argue that diverse communities are only beneficial if they believe as we do and practise the laws of the land. That's right, I hear you say: they are here and should abide by our laws. But 'our laws' don't always have a positive impact on these communities, even those drafted with the specific intention of doing so. And many in these communities grow up and are still disadvantaged by religious and race discrimination, but not many of us are protesting about that.

No one in this dispute wanted children from LGBT communities to be treated unfairly. No one intended to cause distress. But what the Parkfield school affair shows us is that, despite the best of intentions, enforcing the law doesn't necessarily lay the foundations for fairness. It may be the correct thing to do, but it is also a last resort. And here it was a last resort tried as a first resort, and without other efforts that could have enabled both school and parents to communicate on a more positive and human basis.

It also shows us that legislation is a blunt instrument and that simply stating the law doesn't necessarily help. It doesn't create opportunities for understanding, it doesn't foster debate, it doesn't help us (as individuals, colleagues or communities) to navigate complex issues and, perhaps most importantly, it doesn't help us to have better relationships, more understanding or greater tolerance. (I use the term 'tolerance' advisedly. I dislike it because it sets the bar very low; if tolerance is the best we can hope for then we are all doomed. I use it here in the strict Cambridge Dictionary sense of 'willingness to accept behaviour and beliefs that are different from your own, although you might not agree with or approve of them'.[7]) In the case of protected characteristics under the law, when one protected characteristic comes up against another, elevating one view can only be achieved at the expense of the other.

And there is another question that must be asked – a question that has not been posed frequently or loudly enough: what of the children's views and feelings in the midst of such a public conflict? Is the example of bitterly divided for-and-against protests in which hundreds of people vent their anger and anxiety the best example we can offer to our young people? Is this how we want them to resolve the conflicts and disputes that will be an inevitable part of their lives as our society becomes even more diverse and complex? As James Baldwin (1961, p. 60) observes, 'Children have never been very good at listening to their elders, but they have never failed to imitate them.'

Leadership takeaways

- **Not all differences are the same.** We need to reflect on how we teach/expose children to multiculturalism and the Equality Act 2010. Many schools explore these issues as part of the PSHE curriculum. Our expectation is that if children explore many beliefs alongside one another, this will help them to understand more about society and see these beliefs as having an equal place in our world. Unfortunately, we live in a society where beliefs do not have equal value. Children know, as we do, that Eurocentric beliefs are privileged in our society, and whilst we might think this is appropriate (we are in the UK, after all), this construct of what is 'right' and 'wrong' comes from a place which has vilified the cultures and practices of others and still continues to do so to this day. Working with parents and children from other cultures is not just about multicultural practice; it must also be about recognising the power of the educator and the system this power sits within.

- **Belief in diversity.** Schools have the opportunity to teach children how to live with difference. They can demonstrate that everyone has the right to their existence, and that this right should not deny the existence of others. This means exemplifying and demonstrating

---

7   See https://dictionary.cambridge.org/dictionary/english/tolerance.

a genuine belief in diversity. However, our greatest efforts are often spent in trying to get people to agree, on the basis that agreement will promote belonging; indeed, that agreement is the same as belonging. This contradicts our supposed belief in the benefits of diversity. Diversity requires us to be open to debate. It requires us to welcome disagreement. It requires us to understand how we can disagree well – and still get along. Neither the curriculum nor the law have much space for this more nuanced and interpersonal approach. The satisfaction of being right may feed our egos, but it doesn't nourish our relationships or our ability to navigate conflict and competing rights. Winning is not transformative.

■ **More than resources.** One of the root causes of the disagreement between parents and school in this affair was the No Outsiders programme. Much of the emphasis was on books, educational resources and lesson plans, and in which year group it was appropriate to use them. Much less emphasis was placed on how schools and society more generally might help children to think beyond the constructs and attitudes we have bequeathed them – the tools we use to discriminate against others. For example, how do we encourage children to think beyond race and the idea of different races? How do we enable children to question gender constructs? This is not about books; it is about the skills of teachers and their own understanding of equality. Very little resource has been put into this. Teachers need help and support to become more than just storytellers; to become instead those who can help children to question the stories they have been told.

References

Afridi, Asif and Warmington, Joy (2010) *Managing Competing Equality Claims: A Paper for the Equality and Diversity Forum*. London: Equality and Diversity Forum. Available at: https://www.equallyours.org.uk/wp-content/uploads/2010/08/EDF_Competing-Equality-ClaimsFeb11.pdf.

Baldwin, James (1961) Fifth Avenue, Uptown: A Letter from Harlem. In *Nobody Knows My Name: More Notes of a Native Son*. New York: Dial Press, pp. 56–71.

Birmingham City Council (2018) *We're All Different But Equal: An Equality, Diversity and Cohesion Framework for Schools in Birmingham*. Available at: https://www.birmingham.gov.uk/downloads/download/2226/equalities_and_cohesion_toolkit_all_equal_all_different.

Birmingham City Council (2020) Equalities Toolkit to Help All Children Feel Valued and Respected [press release] (6 July).

Available at: https://www.birmingham.gov.uk/news/article/659/ equalities_toolkit_to_help_all_children_feel_valued_and_respected.

Diamond, Colin (2019) There is a Way Out of the Schools LGBT Protest Mess – But Ministers Need to Get Behind It, *The Guardian* (6 August). Available at: https://www.theguardian.com/education/2019/aug/06/ way-out-of-schools-protest-mess-birmingham-trojan-horse.

Diamond, Colin (2020) Everyone Must Have a Say in the Future of Education, *TES* (15 May). Available at: https://www.tes.com/magazine/archive/ everyone-must-have-say-future-education.

Dickens, John (2019) High Court Grants Permanent Exclusion Zone at School in LGBT Teaching Row, *Schools Week* (26 November). Available at: https://schoolsweek.co.uk/ high-court-grants-permanent-exclusion-zone-at-school-in-lgbt-teaching-row.

Ford, Richard (2019) Protect Birmingham Schools from Mob Opposed to LGBT Lessons, Says Counterterror Chief, *The Times* (15 July). Available at: https://www.thetimes.co.uk/article/ schools-need-protection-against-mob-opposed-to-gay-lessons-gdn59gs9l.

George, Martin (2019) Long Read: Life in the Academy Rocked By LGBT Protests, *TES* (20 July). Available at: https://web.archive.org/web/20210314185016/https://www. tes.com/news/long-read-life-academy-rocked-lgbt-protests.

Haynes, Jane (2019) 'Cowardly Government' Blamed for Breakdown of Anderton Park Protest Peace Talks, *Birmingham Mail* (30 May). Available at: https://www.birminghammail.co.uk/news/midlands-news/ cowardly-government-blamed-breakdown-anderton-16351301.

Bielefeldt, Heiner and United Nations Human Rights Council (UNHRC) (2010) Report of the Special Rapporteur on Freedom of Religion or Belief (15 December). Available at: https://www2.ohchr.org/english/bodies/hrcouncil/docs/16session/A-HRC-16-53.pdf.

Ofsted (2019) No Formal Designation Inspection of Parkfield Community School (13 February). Available at: https://files.ofsted.gov.uk/v1/file/50062382.

Youdell, Deborah (2011) *School Trouble: Identity, Power and Politics in Education.* Abingdon and New York: Routledge.

Chapter 14

Reflections on the impact and legacy of Trojan Horse: an intersectional view

Reza Gholami

Introduction

This chapter digs deep into themes that recur throughout the book and offers an intersectional analysis which broadens our understanding of the factors at play in Birmingham's schools and its communities. The underachievement of Muslim pupils in Birmingham (and nationally), set out clearly by Tom Perry in Chapter 4, is nuanced by discussing it in the context of the intersection of race and faith and with the wider wrap of gender and socio-economic status. Two threads drive Reza Gholami's arguments: the damaging policy implications of Trojan Horse and the need for Muslimness not to be subsumed within ethnic analysis. He debates the identification of Islam as a barrier to educational progress per se. How sadly ironic, as Karamat Iqbal explained in Chapter 3, that first-generation migrants from Kashmir brought with them a huge respect for education, which embraced *taleem* (knowledge) and *tehzeeb* (culture) with teachers revered as *roohani* (spiritual) parents. Aspiration was supressed by the school system with its inbuilt institutional racism (see Chapter 2 by Kamal Hanif), and it has taken an extraordinary effort from school leaders to overcome structural inequalities against the odds. Part II illustrates how this can be achieved by capturing the hopes, ambitions and talents of these predominantly Birmingham Muslim communities.

The rites of passage growing up as a member of the Pakistani community from childhood to senior professional status within the education community – as described by Sajid Gulzar, Kamal Hanif and Karamat Iqbal – are echoed in the social tightrope they walked, with a judgement on whether they were a 'good' or 'bad' Muslim never far away. At a more visceral level, it was not about the relatively safe havens of school and college, but rather a case of survival in the streets and avoiding Birmingham City football ground on match days when things could get overtly hostile.

Gholami watched Trojan Horse explode in the national media and describes here how it can be located in the longer term saga (broadly from 9/11 onwards) which ramped up a climate of Islamophobia in the West. How the original community cohesion programmes in the first decade of the twenty-first century became tools which monitored Islamic extremism with counter-terrorism legislation created in the wake of Trojan Horse events. And how national mainstream media displayed banner headlines which overwhelmingly pointed towards the supposed Islamic extremist elements of Trojan Horse rather than deficiencies in school governance.

Gholami asks whether an interpretation of Trojan Horse as a 'drab and technical' episode of inept governance at the hands of some school governors would have been front page news; he rightly points out that there are thousands of schools where poor governance has not challenged inadequate leadership. As I mention in the introduction to Chapter 5 by Emma Knights, in Birmingham alone there were several high-profile incidents of academies being judged by Ofsted to require special measures around the same time as Trojan Horse, which attracted passing local media interest at most. However, as I explore in Chapter 1, largely drawing on the city council's own investigation into Trojan Horse and using Adderley Primary School as a case study, the activities of a small group of Muslim governors went way beyond acceptable standards and led to several competent head teachers being forced to leave their posts.

There was an agenda that is traceable back to the model of education deemed suitable for young Muslims growing up in England as set out in *Towards Greater Understanding: Meeting the Needs of Muslim Pupils in State Schools* (Muslim Council of Britain, 2007), with its advice on halal food, dress code, collective worship and so on. It was greeted by one tabloid newspaper as containing 'Taliban-style demands' (with respect to hopes for individual shower cubicles for pupils – outrageous!) (Alam, 2007). Its advice was well-intended and invitational. Unfortunately, the material was used subsequently in a confrontational and damaging way at a time when schools were adjusting to higher levels of autonomy, which conferred greater responsibility on governors and less monitoring from middle-tier local authorities.

Successive iterations of government policy since 2014 have skated above the level of debate required to engage with the complex, intersectional issues thrown into sharp relief by Trojan Horse. Joy Warmington's chapter (13), which shares insights from her engagement with the dispute about lesbian, gay, bisexual, transgender and queer awareness teaching at Parkfield Community School, provides an example of how the vacuum at a national level left schools over-exposed to community pressures, with no script or advice to guide them through the inevitable dissonance between two of the protected characteristics in the Equality Act 2010 – faith and sexual orientation. In short, a one-dimensional interpretation of the law with insufficient guidance on handling intersectional tensions was always going to lead to more headlines which would portray Muslims (mainly parents in this case) negatively.

Organisations like SINCE 9/11, which have produced curriculum materials aimed at enabling pupils to understand the origins of 9/11 and, critically, how to avoid such terrible events in the future, have found it hard to get traction in schools.[1] Such innovative, cross-curricular models have been further marginalised by the latest content-heavy GCSE courses and are often relegated to the ritual of an annual assembly. The most recent report commissioned by SINCE 9/11 (Taylor et al., 2021) contains recommendations couched in positive language – for example, the importance of schools enacting anti-discrimination policies consistently and of developing critical literacy skills *across the curriculum*. It recognises that pupils and teachers need support when navigating the intersectional territory that any form of extremism invariably throws up.

Adopting Gholami's conceptual framework would be a worthy addition to school and education policy creation and would signpost a way for practitioners through issues that no future-facing curriculum should ignore. Without safe spaces to learn about these issues in the public domain (as we have seen during the pandemic), young people's discourse is driven from classroom to bedroom and from safe school content towards the unregulated plains of the internet and social media.

Colin Diamond

1   See https://since911.com.

Reflections on the impact and legacy of Trojan Horse: an intersectional view

Reza Gholami

My context

I am not writing this chapter as someone who has had any direct involvement with the events that have come to be known as the Trojan Horse affair. In fact, when Trojan Horse was happening in 2014, I had not even spent any significant amount of time in the city of Birmingham. I am writing this as an observer – a highly interested, if somewhat distant, one. My interest in Trojan Horse had (and continues to have) two sources. On the one hand, I was watching the events unfold as a Muslim immigrant: I was born in Iran but grew up in various Western countries before permanently settling in the UK in 2001. In this position, the West's increasing demonisation of Islam and Muslims post-9/11 has affected me and my family and friends personally. Trojan Horse was something of a milestone event in this context, as I will discuss later. On the other hand, I also observed Trojan Horse as a researcher and analyst interested in Islamophobia and education. The ideas I share in this chapter straddle both these positions, and I hope to offer something of analytical value through my reflections.

The on-the-ground events of Trojan Horse touched many lives in many distinct ways; there were various stakeholders and commentators, each with their version of events and each identifying 'culprits'. These experiences and voices are all important, as many chapters in this book explore. But I will not get tangled up in all of that – my distant observer status affords me that privilege in a way that is perhaps impossible for those more directly involved. My broad argument is, rather, that Trojan Horse implicates a series of pivotal issues in what being British and Muslim has come to mean today in the post-9/11 world.

Chief amongst these is the fact that Trojan Horse was a key fulcrum between discourses that problematised, even vilified, Muslims and Muslimness, and that vilification finding a comfortable space in Britain's legal and policy structures. This is a serious claim, and I am not the first to make it, but it is a claim that deserves attention if we are to reach a comprehensive understanding of Trojan Horse.

Moreover, what makes the whole saga important beyond Birmingham is the fact that Trojan Horse was a narrative – a long-running story about Muslimness, Britishness, security, values and the integrity of the education system. In this vein, I have been amazed (and frankly disturbed) by how the dominant narrative of Trojan Horse could be so easily constructed and gather near-unstoppable momentum; how nuances and contestations, and in some cases a lack of evidence, could be seemingly sidestepped by powerful players with relative ease; and how it led to significant changes in Britain's policy landscape and thus affected the lives of millions of citizens. Seen from this perspective, Trojan Horse is about much more than what happened in Birmingham in 2014. It allows a unique glimpse into the machinations of Britain's politics of difference, as well as the ways in which the education system has become the preferred site for the enactment of that politics.

From these broader points, this chapter makes two specific arguments about Muslim students in Britain today. Firstly, Trojan Horse was central in creating what I have described elsewhere as an Islamophobic educational discourse (Gholami, 2017). That is, post-Trojan Horse it has become quite easy for non-Muslims to imagine and talk about Islam and education as almost mutually exclusive categories and to think of Muslim people as somehow 'anti-education' or an educational 'lost cause'. In turn, this has helped to rationalise and formalise the singling out of Muslim students and the shutting down of 'undesirable' expressions of Muslimness via the Prevent agenda. However, such a discourse has no basis in reality, which leads to my second argument.

Where Muslim students in Birmingham and beyond are underperforming educationally, there is a complex set of circumstances at play that must be understood in an intersectional manner. Intersectionality refers here to examining multiple vectors of disadvantage – such as race, class and gender – as intertwining factors. However, it also requires a closer examination of the concept of Islamophobia itself, which I contend has become too closely aligned with race/racism at the expense of questions of religion and religiosity. Drawing upon Kimberlé Crenshaw's (1991) seminal work on structural, political and representational intersectionality, I will conclude the chapter by examining what lessons we can learn from an intersectional analysis of the impact and legacy of the Trojan Horse affair.

Trojan Horse – a story about extremism?

One of the most fascinating aspects of Trojan Horse is how easily it became predominantly a story about Islamist extremism, even after official investigations had found no evidence to that effect. The reasons for this relate both to entrenched representations of Islam and Muslims in the West and to the specific events of Trojan Horse itself. Allow me to briefly explore these.

Most news stories about Muslims in Western countries seem to be stories about extremism and terrorism, so much so that Muslim respondents in a number of research contexts have recently been commenting to me about the sad irony that it has taken the COVID-19 pandemic to hear positive media stories about Muslim doctors and nurses being lifesavers, as well as humanising stories about the vulnerability of some Muslim people to the coronavirus. That the post-9/11 media and political landscape of the West is openly hostile to Muslims and Islam is by now well-established knowledge (see, *inter alia*, Poole, 2002; Kassimeris and Jackson, 2011; Sian et al., 2013). Even at the time of writing (October 2020), following terrorist attacks in France, French President Emmanuel Macron has been far more interested in blaming what he sees as Muslims' 'separatism' and Islam's 'global crisis' than in addressing the many factors in French society that draw young people of all backgrounds towards extremist movements (see Abbas, 2020; see also Panjwani et al., 2018). Nor is there much debate about retaliatory forms of right-wing extremism, such as two Muslim women being called 'dirty Arabs' and repeatedly stabbed by a White extremist under the Eiffel Tower less than a week after the murder of the French schoolteacher Samuel Paty in October 2020 (France 24, 2020).

The point I am making is that there exists a well-entrenched discourse in Western media and politics that feels entitled to associate Islam and Muslims en masse with extremism and terrorism. It does so with impunity and without much regard for the astounding diversity of the people who may describe themselves as Muslim or, indeed, for the social and economic challenges they often face as second-class citizens in their own (Western) countries. And it does so in a way that is disproportionate, not to mention silent, about the power imbalances that animate such representations. As Mamdani (2002) explained in the wake of 9/11, Western Muslims have been divided up into categories of 'good' and 'bad' Muslim

– categories that they themselves have had no say in defining and which reflect the West's dominant notions of history, culture, theology and secularism. As such, a criminal act committed by someone claiming (or perceived) to be Muslim is more than just a crime committed by a citizen/civilian; it is a crime committed by a 'bad' Muslim and thus works to demonstrate the innate 'un-Western-ness' of Western Muslims and the supposed unbridgeable cultural chasm that exists between Islam and the West. It is not a great leap from there to the idea that anyone who doesn't 'do Islam' in a way that is deemed acceptable to dominant Western sensibilities may be classed as a 'bad' Muslim and potentially an extremist.

Given the existence of such a discourse, by 2014 the stage was set for Trojan Horse to take on the media and political life in the way that it did. However, the specific events surrounding the saga itself are also significant in that they helped to catapult Trojan Horse into a sphere where it would be truly politically seismic. The basic timeline of Trojan Horse (following receipt of the anonymous letter by Birmingham City Council) holds some interesting clues about why and how this happened:

- 2 March: *The Sunday Times* published its influential 'Trojan Horse' article titled 'Islamist Plot to Take Over Schools' (Kerbaj and Griffiths, 2014). The article's lead author Richard Kerbaj was a security correspondent.

- 5 March–1 May: twenty-one Birmingham schools were investigated by Ofsted. Five schools were placed in special measures.

- 14 April: Birmingham City Council commissioned its own investigation led by Ian Kershaw.

- 15 April: Michael Gove (then education secretary) appointed Peter Clarke to lead a national inquiry. Clark was the former head of counter-terrorism at Scotland Yard.

The official investigations by Ofsted, Kershaw and Clarke into the Trojan Horse allegations were clear that they had found no evidence of extremist activities at the schools in question. They also pointed out that the whole issue concerned a very small number of individuals at a very small number of schools. All this was public knowledge and is even spelled out on the UK Parliament website.[2] Kershaw and Clarke did point towards

---

2   See https://publications.parliament.uk/pa/cm201415/cmselect/cmeduc/473/47304.htm. See also House of Commons Education Committee (2015).

a narrowly defined conservative form of Sunni Islam that had become dominant in a few schools and which did not, in their view, adequately promote British values or challenge the extremist views of others. Ofsted, on the other hand, alleged a slew of leadership and governance issues at the schools in question, such as mismanagement of funds, bullying, conflict of interest and so on. Therefore, judging only by the official findings, at worst Trojan Horse was a case of a handful of conservative Muslim individuals (specifically one conservative Muslim individual) in positions of leadership who were being accused of potentially mismanaging their schools.

But this was a far cry from the way the story was covered by the national press. I still recall vividly the first time I read the above-mentioned *Sunday Times* article. It sent shivers down my spine. The piece opened with: 'An apparent plot by Muslim fundamentalists to destabilise and take over state schools in England …' Given the Islamophobic context I have described, I remember thinking at the time that printing this sentence was akin to lighting a match near a house that has been doused in petrol. One may or may not cause a fire but the chances are certainly very high, and at any rate it is a hugely irresponsible thing to do. The suggestion that 'Muslim fundamentalists' were planning to take over 'English state schools' sounds imminently threatening at a national level.

And what was the evidence? The leaked Trojan Horse letter – the veracity of which has always been in question. The article was clearly more interested in grabbing national attention than providing context, nuance and, above all, solid evidence. It went on to say that the letter appeared to have been written by 'disaffected Muslims'. This is a highly problematic and contemptuous choice of language. The implication in that phrase is that Islam and Muslims are by default in the wrong; that they are un-British and always prone to un-British and unsavoury behaviour. However, some Muslims have the good fortune of 'seeing the light', as it were, and realise the error of their religion's ways. These Muslims become disaffected and warn the rest of us against the dangers of Islam.

Subsequent national coverage did not improve even after the official investigations had reported. In 2016, Sara Cannizzaro and I published a paper that studied the press coverage of Trojan Horse following the publication of Ofsted's (2014) advice note. We found that only 38.5% of Trojan Horse coverage focused on the issue of 'poor governance', whereas 61.5% of the reporting was devoted to 'Islamist extremism' – clearly, biased press coverage backed up by very little evidence. What seemed to be happening, in our view, was that the story was being wilfully steered in a certain direction by the government and the right-wing papers, which we believed was evident not just in the press coverage but also in the appointment of Peter Clarke. It seemed as if a decision had been made that Trojan Horse was going to emphasise the 'Islamist issue' first and foremost.

This is the process that Hall et al. (1978) described many years ago through the concept of 'primary institutional definers', whereby a narrative is produced by powerful players which provides the initial framing of a news story. These institutional players set the tone and define the key issues and the parameters of the debate. As such, they also force others to enter the debate on their terms and to describe the issues in their way. For example, in the samples we studied, *The Guardian* (a left-wing broadsheet) was the only paper that reported more evidence of poor governance. It also pointed out that Park View (the school at the centre of Trojan Horse) was an academy and thus exempt from teaching the national curriculum, and that this was fully in line with the government's aggressive academisation agenda and crypto-privatisation of the public education system. But it simply did not have enough power to turn the narrative and had little choice but to engage with the story from within the framework of an 'Islamist plot'. Thus, from the outset, Trojan Horse became primarily a story about Islamist extremism and was used to exemplify everything that is wrong with having an 'uncontrolled' Muslim population and, in particular, having Muslims in positions of educational influence.

It is also important to note that *all* of the Trojan Horse allegations have always been contested. In fact, as Holmwood and O'Toole (2018) meticulously demonstrate, the story of Park View was until 2014 one of spectacular success, having been transformed from one of the worst-performing schools in the country to being rated outstanding by Ofsted and singled out as exemplary; a school serving one of the most deprived areas of England but managing to support three quarters of its students to achieve the highest grades and have excellent prospects. Similarly, the man at the centre of Trojan Horse, Tahir Alam – clearly identified by the Clarke Report (2014) as the main culprit and banned for life from educational leadership – could in this narrative be seen as an inspirational leader able to recognise and respond to the needs of the local community.[3] After all, the GCSE success rates at Park View when he became governor of the school in 1997 stood at only 4%, and Alam himself had always challenged the dominant narratives (see Abbas, 2017). But these facts and nuances were glaringly absent in the press coverage and government discourse, which seemed hell-bent on 'protecting' the public from a supposedly imminent Islamist threat. Meanwhile, the personal and professional lives of many school staff caught up in Trojan Horse have been irreparably damaged (see Holmwood and O'Toole, 2018).

Values, policy and the 'soul of the nation'

In drawing attention to media narratives, Hall et al. (1978) make a bigger argument about the criminalisation of non-White people during times of economic crisis. In short, by demonising ethnic/racial minorities, the White elite, who are responsible for causing economic crises, deflect attention away from themselves and focus the anger of the disenfranchised majority upon racially minoritised groups. I think such an analysis only partially lends itself to the Trojan Horse news story. It is true that in 2014 Britain was in the throes of an agonising programme of austerity politics, which itself was the result of the 2008 global credit crisis. But although I am sure that the bankers and their friends in government would much prefer the media's focus to be on 'the Muslims' than on them, nonetheless, the credit crunch and austerity measures did receive a great deal of public attention. The political expediency and sheer force of the Trojan Horse story becomes fully clear when we consider another set of policy shifts that was underway at the time. At stake in these shifts was, arguably, the soul of the nation – its values, its politics of difference and the state's reach into its key institutions.

Put bluntly, Trojan Horse helped to clear the ground for the government's counter-extremism policy, Prevent, to become statutory. It made Prevent seem totally rational, indeed necessary; not many people were going to question Prevent after Trojan Horse, which was held up as a grim example of the dangers of not keeping tabs on Muslims. Before Trojan Horse, the government had signalled that it wanted to centralise Prevent and extend its reach, but in 2014 Prevent was not yet statutory. This happened more

---

3   See also the BBC Radio 4 documentary, *The Corrections*, examining these issues (Fidgen, 2020).

or less immediately after Trojan Horse, as the Counter Terrorism and Security Act came into law in February 2015.

In May 2015, a new Extremism Bill was announced in the Queen's Speech targeting potentially extremist behaviour that fell below the threshold of the Counter Terrorism and Security Act. This was an overt move in the direction of fighting extremist ideologies (Dawson and Godec, 2017, p. 21). Although the Bill itself proved too controversial to become law – not least because it proposed sweeping new powers for the authorities to censor and shut down whatever they perceived as extremist behaviour – it did, nonetheless, signal a clear direction of travel for counter-extremism policy and revealed its spirit, which was, arguably, present in subsequent policy-making and continues to be so.

The final piece in the jigsaw was introduced in October 2015 in the form of the Counter-Extremism Strategy, which was aimed at what it called 'extremist entryism' – the idea that extremists can gain access to public institutions. This document explicitly cited the Clarke report into the Trojan Horse affair (HM Government, 2015, p. 13). In this way, the Prevent policy, via the Trojan Horse episode, shifted its focus away from tackling violent extremism to simply 'countering extremism' (Holmwood and O'Toole, 2018, p. 55). Crucially, this involved mobilising public sector employees and placing citizens in a pre-crime category to predict whether someone's thought or behaviour today means they might become a terrorist in the future.

There can be no doubt that Britain's Muslim population had always been at the receiving end of these policy manoeuvres, which, interestingly, pivoted on the central concept of fundamental British values. After the so-called 'race riots' in northern English cities in 2001, which the Cantle Report (2004) blamed on the 'self-segregation' of ethnic minority (mostly Muslim) communities, the Labour government at the time responded with its politics of 'community cohesion', suggesting that Britain's social fabric itself was under threat from ethnic minorities living 'parallel lives'.[4] This led to some changes in policy (e.g. the introduction of the citizenship test) and generally paved the way for a less benign attitude towards multiculturalism. However, in the post-9/11 climate, and particularly following the 7/7 London bombings in 2005, successive British governments went further.

---

4   A surprisingly similar narrative is being used by French President Emmanuel Macron at the time of writing.

On the one hand, the discourse of 'ethnic minorities' (South Asians, Pakistanis, etc.) had since 2001 gradually changed to one focusing more intently on Islam, Muslims and the Muslim community. But more importantly, under Tony Blair and Gordon Brown, the Labour government dovetailed Prevent with its community cohesion agenda. As Conservative Prime Minister David Cameron would later emphasise, the idea was that the putative self-segregation of Muslims would lead to their radicalisation and thus to extremist and terrorist acts. This narrative had the backing of other influential public figures, such as the former head of the Commission for Racial Equality, Trevor Phillips, who warned that multiculturalism meant Britain was at risk of 'sleepwalking to segregation' (*The Guardian*, 2005). It goes without saying that Muslim people were specially mentioned in these discourses (see Finney and Simpson, 2009). It is also interesting to note that the 2008 Prevent documents mention building cohesion overtly, and that until 2011, Prevent was administered both by the Home Office and the Department for Communities and Local Government. Creating cohesive communities had in effect become a programme for preventing home-grown Islamist terrorism.

A major problem with this approach is that, of course, not all home-grown terrorism is Islamist in nature. In fact, the latest government figures show that in its obsession with Muslims, Prevent has failed to tackle an exponential rise in far-right extremism, making it the biggest terrorist threat the UK faces currently (Dearden, 2019; Home Office, 2019). But an equally important problem is that 'Islamist' is a somewhat deceptive concept in the counter-terrorism discourse. Judging by the way the policy has unfolded over the years, 'Islamism' doesn't refer only to the sorts of activities we would associate with al-Qaida and Islamic State of Iraq and Syria (ISIS); it could just as easily refer to any type of activity that is *perceived* by the UK majority to be (1) Islamic and (2) suspicious, unpalatable or simply too different.

Nowhere is the problematisation and securitisation of Muslims in general more visible than in Prevent identifying as 'priority areas' parts of the country with a Muslim population of more than 5%. This was a core part of the provenance of Prevent, and although it is no longer an explicit feature, it has planted the seeds for and nurtured the idea that a mere Muslim presence is a possible security risk. Under Prevent, areas with a larger than average Muslim concentration became seen as potential hotbeds of radicalisation and extremism, and the idea of British values, delivered in a neat policy package, was seen as the antidote for the particularism of Muslim religious values. Incidentally, all the schools embroiled in the Trojan Horse saga were situated in exactly such areas. It is quite clear, then, that regardless of what any individual politician might claim, the dominant policy and discursive forces at play have created a separation between 'Britishness' and 'Muslimness', and identified the latter as potentially threatening to the former.

At the intersection of religion, race and education

In the climate described above, the advent of the Trojan Horse affair had two educational implications. Firstly, in clearing the ground for Prevent becoming a legal duty, Trojan Horse distinctly identified the education system as an institution warranting particular surveillance (to date, the education system has been responsible for the majority of referrals under Prevent). Secondly, any reference to Muslims in education or Muslim education (however broadly defined) took on a range of non-educational connotations and could be 'reasonably' associated with extremism and terrorism. As I have shown elsewhere (Gholami, 2017), this discourse has serious educational ramifications for British people of Muslim backgrounds. For starters, it masks some highly innovative and transformative forms of education for which Britain's Muslim communities are responsible (Gholami, 2017). But, more pertinent to this chapter, the casting of Muslims in a negative educational light takes attention away from the intersectional and systemic disadvantages that Muslim children and young people often have to battle through to secure their futures. This is a discourse that relies on racist and colonialist tropes around Islam as an archaic, irrational, inimical, sexist ... religion, which means that its adherents must be equally prone to irrationality and violence.

As such, so the narrative goes, wider society should not be surprised if Muslim children underperform educationally or if Muslim educationalists want to turn schools into arenas of extremism; Muslims are, for all intents and purposes, an educational lost cause and in many cases probably opposed to a 'proper' education altogether. Examples of this sort of representation abound (see Gholami, 2017): to give just one here, Shackle (2017) points out that in one of its articles about Trojan Horse, *The Spectator* used a picture of child with a Qur'an in one hand and a sword in the other, under the caption 'taught to hate'. Such an image does not describe any aspect of the empirical reality of today's Britain, yet it is considered an acceptable way of depicting the educational attitudes of some 3.3 million Muslims in the UK.

Of course, there is a legitimate concern that the extremely conservative, or simply the loudest and most overbearing, people in a given community may impose themselves on others and try to hijack or define the identity of that community. Wider society must guard against this and defend the principles of equality and social justice. But, as we have seen, the Trojan Horse saga was decidedly *not* about that concern; it simply worked to further vilify and ostracise British Muslims by portraying them as Islamist plotters. The concerns raised over an 'aggressive Islamic ethos' at Park View (Clarke, 2014, p. 96) also need qualification (the disturbing behaviour of a handful of individuals notwithstanding): given that the school served a predominantly Muslim neighbourhood, the school's Islamic ethos was neither strange nor illegal. In fact, the law makes provision for exactly these situations by allowing schools to apply to change the legally required daily act of collective worship of a 'Christian character'[5] to reflect the faith of the majority of the school community; Park View had done this. And let us not forget that the UK does not have a secular education system. The Islamic ethos of the school is to be seen in this context, as Shackle (2017) also highlights. The teachers she interviewed said that religion was a positive force used to boost performance and build a sense of community – for instance, fasting was sometimes used as a way to mentally prepare for an exam. However, the media twisted this to say that students were being forced to fast.

We must also unpack some of the inconsistencies in the accusations of poor governance. For even if we accept Ofsted's assessment, then issues of poor governance and leadership are professional educational issues, not Islamist or extremist ones. According to Ofsted's (2020) own figures, currently 14% of schools in England are judged either to require improvement or to be inadequate. To be sure, this refers to thousands of schools up and down the country, no doubt many of them with the same kinds of problems identified at the Birmingham schools.[6] The big difference

---

5   As set out in Schedule 20 of the School Standards and Framework Act 1998 – see https://www. legislation.gov.uk/ukpga/1998/31/schedule/20/enacted.

6   According to UK government figures, in 2019 there were 27,212 primary and secondary state schools in England – see https://www.compare-school-performance.service.gov.uk/schools-by-type?step=default&table=schools&region=all-england&for=secondary.

is that the vast majority of 'problem schools' are not situated in areas with a large Muslim population, and their leaders are White, middle-class individuals – only around 3% of UK head teachers are Black, Asian and minority ethnic (BAME) (Johnson, 2017). Yet, the thought of anyone raising questions about extremism in these schools or alleging that students are being poorly prepared for life in today's Britain is all but laughable, albeit it may actually be true.[7]

In my view, this is a major effect of the Islamophobic discourse of education: as perverse as it may sound, the dominant discourse does not allow Muslims to simply make 'normal' or professional mistakes. Mismanaging a school is a serious matter, but it is a technical, professional matter – and, in light of the figures quoted here, a relatively common matter in the field of education. However, dealing with the Birmingham issue purely from an educational angle would be to humanise the Muslim leaders at the schools in question; it would be to admit that, just like the rest of us, they too are capable of making professional errors; and it would be, of course, to acknowledge them as qualified, trained professionals to begin with. It is hard to imagine the sort of policy shifts described earlier happening on the back of such a drab and technical story.

The final issue to unpack here follows from the point raised above about the Islamophobic discourse masking Muslim educational excellence as well as the barriers Muslim children and young people have to overcome to succeed educationally. Looking at Birmingham's attainment data (see Perry – Chapter 4 in this volume), it is easy to conclude that Muslim children are low achievers, and that Trojan Horse has not had much of an effect on this chronically bleak educational picture. However, Perry himself warns that we must be wary of 'ecological fallacy' and resist the temptation of inferring something about individuals from large statistical datasets. I agree wholeheartedly. But I also think we need to shine a light on what such data hide from view. National datasets subsume religiosity under the category of ethnicity, despite the fact that the two characteristics are protected separately under the Equality Act 2010.

Firstly, this is problematic because the elision of religion assumes that the challenges faced by Muslim students can be wholly addressed through an anti-racist agenda; in other words, that Islamophobia is adequately definable as a form of racism, which is in fact how it is officially defined in

---

7   See, for example, Turner (2017) and Telegraph (2018).

the UK. But as I demonstrate elsewhere (Gholami, 2021), Islamophobia comprises a religious dimension that must be at least partially separated from race for analytical and policy-making purposes. This is an intersectional positioning at the nexus of race and religion. From this perspective, the changing of a school's ethos to an Islamic one to respond to the needs of a local community actually makes sense – it works in the interests of educational equity. And if some stakeholders have concerns over the way in which an individual leader (e.g. Tahir Alam) or a group of leaders is operating, then the response should be to deal with those individuals. It should not be to castigate Muslims en masse, make Prevent and fundamental British values a legal duty, and totally transform the ethos of the school in question. This is all the more important in light of evidence that a 'normal' school ethos and fundamental British values are reflective of what Vincent (2018) describes as de-theologised Christian values. From an intersectional position, then, the Trojan Horse response was disproportionate and inappropriate.

Secondly, the national data also conceal the ongoing impact of the Trojan Horse episode and the government and media response to it. This is because the most significant ongoing impact is ineffable in numerical terms. Shackle (2017) interviewed a former Park View student, Muneeza, who said: 'If I apply for a job, I'm always worried they'll see where I went to school and think: is she an extremist?' This captures the point I am trying to make here about the devastating legacy of Trojan Horse. In addition to the disadvantages arising from their non-White and working-class positions, the Muslim young people embroiled in Trojan Horse have to contend with debilitating Islamophobia as a result of their perceived religious identity and its association with extremism. And, because of the sort of national attention Trojan Horse received, the same can be said of thousands of young Muslims up and down the country.

Interestingly, the UK's Higher Education Statistics Agency recently published for the first time student attainment data by religious identity which showed that Muslims are by far the lowest attaining group of university students (Advance HE, 2020). Relevant government departments, British universities, the National Union of Students and a host of research projects all agree that racism and Islamophobia play a central role in this attainment (or awarding) deficit (Gholami, 2021). More generally, there is plenty of evidence that Islamophobic hate crimes have increased exponentially since Trojan Horse. Although this rise cannot be attributed to Trojan Horse alone, but links to a range of issues, including the rise of ISIS and the Brexit vote, Trojan Horse is cited as a significant factor.[8] But the problem with measuring such issues through statistics alone is that significance takes on a very different meaning in the numbers game – one that is largely dismissive of the experiences of people like Muneeza.

Conclusion: framing the intersectional agenda

It is hopefully clear by now that the sort of argument I have been making in this chapter ushers us in the direction of an intersectional (and mixed-method) analysis. Kimberlé Crenshaw (1991) distinguishes between three types (or aspects) of intersectionality: structural, political and representational. I think these can be usefully applied to the Trojan Horse saga as a way for us to learn broader lessons about Islamophobia, education and the politics of difference in Britain. I will conclude the chapter by briefly discussing these.

Structural intersectionality is, in essence, about the necessity for social structures (e.g. laws and policies) to operate in full recognition of intersectional identities. As we have seen, the government and media response to the widely discredited Trojan Horse letter was problematic, to say the least. A structurally intersectional approach would have been far more sensitive to the particular plight of Muslims in the context of widespread Islamophobia in post-9/11 Britain. It would have recognised – in line with the state's own education policy – that the education system has provisions to serve a diverse population in an equitable manner. Thus, a fundamental British values zero-sum game is likely to be counterproductive, not to mention opposed to the principles of equality and social justice.

I am astonished at the structural contradictions that Trojan Horse has thrown light upon: there are policies and political discourses that are committed to equality, inclusion, evidence-led deliberation, protecting citizens, social mobility, closing BAME attainment gaps and so forth. Yet, at the same time, the government and the media can take a security-driven, at best paranoid, at worst Islamophobic approach to an issue like Trojan Horse whose long-term effects fly in the face of those admirable commitments. Whatever may have been happening at the hands of a

---

8   See, for example, Marsh (2018) and TellMAMA (2014).

few individuals in a few Birmingham schools, Trojan Horse became about far deeper questions around the soul of the nation, as I suggested earlier; it was about the state asserting its authority as the primary arbiter of an 'acceptable' Islam and its place in Britain; and it was about creating the legal space in which ideas of (im)proper Islam could be defined and distinguished from 'British' values. A structurally intersectional approach would prevent such a response by having enough checks and balances to ensure that the various parts of the political machinery are in meaning-ful dialogue about intersectional identities – that they are level-headed, consistent, socially engaged and work to guarantee equity for minoritised groups.

Political intersectionality refers to the need for intersectional subjects to understand that they may at any given moment straddle multiple and competing political agendas. Crenshaw (1991) discusses how women of colour may be implicated simultaneously in anti-racist and feminist agendas, but this can lead to intersectional disempowerment because anti-racism is often dominated by Black men and feminism by White women. This certainly holds true for non-White Muslim women too. But for British Muslims generally, even those who do not practise Islam devoutly and may not even identify as Muslim, there is a need to under-stand that anti-racist and BAME-equality agendas – with the best of intentions – cannot fully address the issues of Islamophobia.

As I have argued elsewhere (Gholami, 2021), this is partly because the concept of Islamophobia is itself too closely aligned to race/racism. What is missing from race/BAME agendas is due regard for what Ghaffar-Kucher (2012) has called 'religification', which importantly accounts for the process of ascription of religious identity on Muslims – that is, having 'Muslimness' thrust upon one by others regardless of actual religiosity and often at the expense of other identity positions. If we have learnt anything from the Trojan Horse episode, it is that Muslimness is defined in a generally Islamophobic socio-political atmosphere and is now all too easily associated with notions of extremism and terrorism in addition to the aforementioned colonialist tropes. As such, I would argue that it behoves everyone, but especially people of Muslim backgrounds (even if they are secular or simply 'look Muslim'), to take a political stance against not just the racial but also the religious aspects of Islamophobia.

Finally, representational intersectionality refers to the ways in which the dominant, often stereotypical, cultural imagery of minoritised groups is used to justify their differential treatment. Crenshaw (1991, p. 1286) gives the example of 2 Live Crew, a Black American rap group who were arrested and tried on charges of obscenity in Florida in 1990. The media debate revolved around the glorification of misogyny and sexual violence against women in popular music, and there is no doubt that 2 Live Crew's lyrics are disturbingly misogynistic. However, Crenshaw highlights the hypocrisy in that plenty of White artists, such as Madonna, have produced similarly obscene lyrics and live performances but have never even been criticised, let alone arrested. This demonstrates the racism that animates dominant representations of Black men. For Crenshaw, therefore, it is imperative that the feminists who rightly decry misogyny should also acknowledge the role of racist stereotypes, just as anti-racists cannot focus solely on racism in the 2 Live Crew case.

We have seen how the dominant post-9/11 representation of Muslims took over the Trojan Horse affair and changed it from an educational issue into one about a 'jihadist plot'. I have argued that whereas problems around school governance and leadership are relatively common in England, Muslim school leaders are never allowed to be *just* educational professionals; their mistakes make them potential Jihadi plotters and Salafist extremists – a national security threat. At the same time, anti-racist, BAME-equality and anti-poverty agendas represent some Muslim children as educational underachievers in need of support, just as they show some Muslims to be 'disaffected' and thus ready to be welcomed back into the mainstream. In this way, the problems that Muslim students face are dissociated from the fact that they encounter these problems *as a result of their being Muslim*, and wider society can continue to peddle its Islamophobic representations and policies whilst appearing to help the 'good Muslims'. An intersectional approach would be cognisant of the representational inconsistencies involved in these processes – that is, Muslim children depicted solely as BAME, which references an equally racist representation of chronically failing but deserving non-White children. Meanwhile, their Muslimness can be used whenever expedient to mark them out as dangerous jihadists.

There is a great deal more to be said about all of the issues raised in this chapter, including the intersectional framework, which space has permitted me to set out only cursorily here. What is clear, however, is that beyond the nitty-gritty issues that were happening on the ground, and which the various chapters in this volume have shed light upon, Trojan Horse was an event of immense magnitude and its legacy continues to be a significant one. It would be incredibly naive to think that the damages for which Trojan Horse is responsible can be somehow undone, especially when we look upon what is today a very different policy landscape. However, I believe we ought to be willing to recognise those harms and learn lessons from them, and I hope I have made a small contribution towards that aim.

References

Abbas, Tahir (2017) The 'Trojan Horse' Plot and the Fear of Muslim Power in British State Schools, *Journal of Muslim Minority Affairs*, 37(4): 426–441. DOI:10.1080/13602 004.2017.1313974.

Abbas, Tahir (2020) Bigotry, Intolerance, and Revenge: The Vicious Cycle of Islamophobia and Radicalisation in France (31 October). Available at: https:// tahirabbas.medium.com/bigotry-intolerance-and-revenge-the-vicious-cycle-of-islamophobia-and-radicalisation-in-france-660422c58737.

Advance HE (2020) Research Insight: Religion and Belief in UK Higher Education. Available at: https://www.advance-he.ac.uk/knowledge-hub/research-insight-religion-and-belief-uk-higher-education.

Alam, Tahir (2007) An Agenda for Integration, *The Guardian (Opinion Education)* (28 February). Available at: https://www.theguardian.com/commentisfree/2007/feb/28/tahiralam.

Cannizzaro, Sara and Gholami, Reza (2016) The Devil Is *Not* in the Detail: Representational Absence and Stereotyping in the 'Trojan Horse' News Story, *Race Ethnicity and Education*, 21(1): 15–19. DOI:10.1080/13613324.2016.1195350.

Cantle, Ted (2001) *Community Cohesion: A Report of the Independent Review Team* [Cantle Report]. London: Home Office. Available at: https://tedcantle.co.uk/pdf/communitycohesion%20cantlereport.pdf.

Cantle, Ted (2004) *The End of Parallel Lives? The Report of the Community Cohesion Panel* [2nd Cantle Report]. London: Home Office. Available at: http://www.tedcantle. co.uk/publications/012%20The%20end%20of%20parallel%20lives%20the%202nd%20 Cantle%20Report%20Home%20Off.pdf.

Clarke, Peter (2014) *Report into Allegations Concerning Birmingham Schools Arising from the 'Trojan Horse' Letter* (HC 576). Available at: https://assets.publishing.service. gov.uk/government/uploads/system/uploads/attachment_data/file/340526/HC_576_ accessible_-.pdf.

Crenshaw, Kimberlé (1991) Mapping the Margins: Intersectionality, Identity Politics, and Violence Against Women of Color, *Stanford Law Review*, 43(6): 1241–1299. DOI:10.2307/1229039.

Dawson, Joanna and Godec, Samantha (2017) *Counter-Extremism Policy: An Overview*. House of Commons Library Briefing Paper No. 7238 (23 June). Available at: https:// commonslibrary.parliament.uk/research-briefings/cbp-7238.

Dearden, Lizzie (2019) Number of Far-Right Referrals to Counter-Extremism Programme Hits Record High, *The Independent* (19 December). Available at: https://www.independent.co.uk/news/uk/home-news/far-right-extremists-programme-prevent-counter-terrorism-record-a9253016.html.

Fidgen, Jo (2020) *The Corrections: Trojan Horse – The Kingpin* [audio], BBC Radio 4 (13 November).

Finney, Nissa and Simpson, Ludi (2009) *Sleepwalking to Segregation? Challenging Myths About Race and Migration.* Bristol: Policy Press.

France 24 (2020) Two French Women Charged Over 'Racist' Stabbing of Veiled Muslim Women (22 October). Available at: https://www.france24.com/en/live-news/20201022-two-french-women-charged-over-racist-stabbing-of-veiled-muslim-women.

Ghaffar-Kucher, Ameena (2012) The Religification of Pakistani-American Youth, *American Educational Research Journal*, 49(1): 30–52. DOI:10.3102/0002831211414858.

Gholami, Reza (2017) Beyond Myths of 'Muslim Education': A Case Study of Two Iranian Schools in London, *Oxford Review of Education*, 43(5): 566–579. DOI:10.1080/03054985.2017.1352352.

Gholami, Reza (2021) Critical Race Theory and Islamophobia: Challenging Inequity in Higher Education, *Race Ethnicity and Education*, 24(3): 319–337. DOI:10.1080/13613324.2021.1879770.

Guardian, The (2005) Britain 'Sleepwalking to Segregation' (19 September). Available at: https://www.theguardian.com/world/2005/sep/19/race.socialexclusion.

Hall, Stuart; Critcher, Chas; Jefferson, Tony; Clarke, John; and Roberts, Brian (1978) *Policing the Crisis: Mugging, the State, and Law and Order.* London: Macmillan.

HM Government (2008) *The Prevent Strategy: A Guide for Local Partners in England.* Available at: https://webarchive.nationalarchives.gov.uk/ukgwa/20130123124929/http://www.education.gov.uk/publications/eOrderingDownload/Prevent_Strategy.pdf.

HM Government (2015) *Counter-Extremism Strategy* (Cm 9148). Available at: https://www.gov.uk/government/publications/counter-extremism-strategy.

Holmwood, John and O'Toole, Therese (2018) *Countering Extremism in British Schools: The Truth about the Birmingham Trojan Horse Affair.* Bristol: Policy Press.

Home Office (2019) Individuals Referred To and Supported Through the Prevent Programme, England and Wales, April 2018 to March 2019. Available at: https://assets.publishing.service.gov.uk/government/uploads/system/uploads/attachment_data/file/853646/individuals-referred-supported-prevent-programme-apr2018-mar2019-hosb3219.pdf.

House of Commons Education Committee (2015) *Extremism in Schools: The Trojan Horse Affair. Seventh Report of Session 2014–15* (HC 473). Available at: https://dera.ioe.ac.uk/22429/1/9780215084200.pdf.

Johnson, Lauri (2017) The Lives and Identities of UK Black and South Asian Headteachers: Metaphors of Leadership, *Educational Management Administration & Leadership,* 45(5): 842–862. DOI:10.1177/1741143217717279.

Kassimeris, George and Jackson, Leonie (2011) The West, the Rest, and the 'War on Terror': Representation of Muslims in Neoconservative Media Discourse, *Contemporary Politics*, 17(1): 19–33. DOI:10.1080/13569775.2011.552684.

Kerbaj, Richard and Griffiths, Sian (2014) Islamist Plot to Take Over Schools: Leaked Papers Reveal an Alleged Plan to Target Ailing Schools, Force Out Heads and Convert Classes to Islamic Principles, *Sunday Times* (2 March). Available at: https://www.thetimes.co.uk/article/islamist-plot-to-take-over-schools-655mhbw0vtc.

Kershaw, Ian (2014) *Investigation Report: Trojan Horse Letter* [Kershaw Report]. Available at: https://www.birmingham.gov.uk/downloads/file/1579/investigation_report_trojan_horse_letter_the_kershaw_report.

Mamdani, Mahmood (2002) Good Muslim, Bad Muslim: A Political Perspective on Culture and Terrorism, *American Anthropologist*, 104(3): 766–775. DOI:10.1525/aa.2002.104.3.766.

Marsh, Sarah (2018) Record Number of Anti-Muslim Attacks Reported in UK Last Year, *The Guardian* (20 July). Available at: https://www.theguardian.com/uk-news/2018/jul/20/record-number-anti-muslim-attacks-reported-uk-2017.

Muslim Council of Britain (2007) *Towards Greater Understanding: Meeting the Needs of Muslim Pupils in State Schools. Information and Guidance for Schools.* Available at: http://www.muslimparents.org.uk/app/download/5777027680/MCBSchoolGuidance.pdf.

Ofsted (2014) Advice Notes on Academies and Maintained Schools in Birmingham. Advice Notes from Sir Michael Wilshaw HMCI to the Secretary of State for Education on School Inspections in Birmingham (9 June, updated 8 July 2016). Available at: https://www.gov.uk/government/publications/advice-note-on-academies-and-maintained-schools-in-birmingham.

Panjwani, Farid; Revell, Lynn; Gholami, Reza; and Diboll, Mike (2018) *Education and Extremisms: Rethinking Liberal Pedagogies in the Contemporary World*. Abingdon and New York: Routledge.

Poole, Elizabeth (2002) *Reporting Islam: Media Representations of British Muslims*. London: I.B. Tauris.

Shackle, Samira (2017) Trojan Horse: The Real Story Behind the Fake 'Islamic Plot' to Take Over Schools, *The Guardian* (1 September). Available at: https://www.theguardian.com/world/2017/sep/01/trojan-horse-the-real-story-behind-the-fake-islamic-plot-to-take-over-schools.

Sian, Katy; Law, Ian; and Sayyid, Salman (2013) The Limits of Representation: Muslims and the News Media. In Katy Sian, Ian Law and Salman Sayyid (eds), *Racism, Governance and Public Policy: Beyond Human Rights*. Abingdon and New York: Routledge, pp. 80–116.

Taylor, Becky; Mills, Martin; Elwick, Alex; Pillinger, Claire; Gronland, Gemma; Hayward, Jeremy; Hextall, Ian; and Panjwani, Farid (2021) *Addressing Extremism Through the Classroom. A Research Report from the Centre for Teachers & Teaching Research.* London: UCL Institute of Education. Available at: https://discovery.ucl.ac.uk/id/eprint/10133809.

Telegraph, The (2018) Religious Extremists Use Schools to 'Isolate and Segregate' Children and Brainwash Minds, Ofsted Chief Warns (1 February). Available at: https://www.telegraph.co.uk/news/2018/02/01/ religious-extremists-use-schools-isolate-segregate-children.

TellMAMA (2014) Anti-Muslim Hate Crimes, 2012–2014 in London: An Analysis of the Situation (11 November). Available at: https://tellmamauk.org/ anti-muslim-hate-crimes-2012-2014-in-london-an-analysis-of-the-situation.

Turner, Camilla (2017) Church of England Headteacher Hits Out at Parents Who Forced 'Extremist' Christian Group Out of the School, *The Telegraph* (17 October). Available at: https://www.telegraph.co.uk/education/2017/10/17/ church-england-headteacher-hits-parents-forced-extremist-christian.

Vincent, Carol (2018) Civic Virtue and Values Teaching in a 'Post-Secular' World, *Theory and Research in Education*, 16(2): 226–243. DOI:10.1177/147787851877412.

Chapter 15

Trojan Horse and aspiring Asian leaders: the impact on development programmes intended to change the face and heart of leadership

Rosemary Campbell-Stephens

Introduction

Rosemary Campbell-Stephens has been involved with initiatives to create a more diverse leadership cadre in English schools for many years. She developed Investing in Diversity (IiD), a leadership programme funded through the London Challenge and delivered through UCL's Institute of Education, at a time when education policy recognised the importance of enabling more leaders to emerge from the Global Majority community. This priority was backed with significant resources. Research indicated its impact on the self-confidence and perceptions of 'empowerment' of the course participants (Johnson and Campbell-Stephens, 2010). The IiD programme ran from 2003 to 2011; initial indications, over the first three to four years, were that the numbers of Black and other Global Majority middle leaders in London significantly increased by several hundred. In some London boroughs, senior leaders at assistant head, deputy head and head teacher level doubled. When the initial funding focused on secondary schools was extended to primary, there was particular success in the sector, led by two outstanding primary head teachers.

By the time Trojan Horse engulfed education in Birmingham and the shock waves reverberated nationally, education policy drivers had changed and the centre of gravity of leadership development moved away from the National College for Teaching and Leadership, which was scaled back and eventually disbanded in 2018. Much of the urban education work of the original National College for School Leadership, its predecessor organisation, had already been dropped, including the London Challenge methodology.

Campbell-Stephens does not pull her punches; she tells it as she sees it. I first met her at a head teachers' meeting in the midst of the Trojan Horse crisis when she challenged Birmingham City Council's chief officers on the absence of Global Majority representation at the top table. How could that be so, she asked, when we were dealing with events that deeply involved schools in Birmingham's South Asian, Muslim-majority communities? As Karamat Iqbal explores in Chapter 3, the council has long undershot its targets for recruitment from the Pakistani community in particular, and at the most senior officer levels it remains a largely White affair. In this chapter, Campbell-Stephens has written directly about the negative impact of those events in 2014 and 2015 on leadership development for those aspiring to be education leaders.

The narrative takes us beyond the important question, 'Why doesn't my head teacher look like me?' It starts from the recognition that simply recruiting more Global Majority leaders does little, of itself, to address the underlying issues as England wrestles with its colonial history and struggles to define equity and social justice. In Chapter 4, Tom Perry nailed the centrality of social disadvantage and then, alarmingly, highlighted the long-term underachievement of most Global Majority pupils over the decade leading up to Trojan Horse.

Campbell-Stephens' leadership development work in Yorkshire was hit by the negative impact of Trojan Horse, with some participants feeling a dual stigma because of their ethnicity and religion, and reappraising downwards their chances of securing the most senior roles. Her latest book (Campbell-Stephens, 2021) develops further the underlying discourse in this chapter, with customary challenges to readers. She argues for a shift from 'tolerating' Global Majority leaders to empowering them to be authentic, truly representing their communities rather than feeling compelled to assimilate within mainstream leadership culture.

The national and local data reveal that we remain far from any kind of representative balance between the communities that inner-city schools serve, with their White pupil minorities and White school leaders. Birmingham City Council's (2021) data on its maintained schools shows that 81% of primary head teachers and 62% of secondary head teachers are White, whilst White pupils constitute less than a third of the overall school population (see also Chapter 16). The BAME Headteachers and Senior Leaders Forum in Birmingham continues the spirit of that work going back to the early years of this century, and has attracted a modest amount of Department for Education funding for its programmes. The journey continues with input from two of the school leaders who have written about their own leadership stories in this book. Examples of success are to be celebrated, but there is a long road ahead before we reach anything like the right levels of Global Majority representation in our school leadership teams.

Colin Diamond

Trojan Horse and aspiring Asian leaders: the impact on development programmes intended to change the face and heart of leadership

Rosemary Campbell-Stephens

[It is] as though our lives have no meaning, no depth without the white gaze. And I have spent my entire writing life trying to make sure that the white gaze was not the dominant one in any of my books.

Toni Morrison[1]

Efforts to diversify the leadership of educational institutions should beg several fundamental questions beyond those of representation – amongst them, leadership for what purpose and in whose interests? Does having a more diverse leadership in itself change anything? What difference does it make if the training and professional socialisation that Black and other Global Majority[2] educators receive, the institutional culture of which they become a part, and the systems and processes they operate are identical to that of their White counterparts? These and other fundamental discourses with progressive anti-racist educators such as Professor Gus John, which I joined as a young teacher back in the early 1980s, shaped my approach to leadership development decades later.

Investing in Diversity (IiD) (Campbell-Stephens, 2009) formed in 2003 at the Institute of Education, University College London, was a government-funded, colour and race-conscious, self-defined, Black-led twelve-month leadership development programme. We rejected the

---

1   See https://www.youtube.com/watch?v=SHHHL31bFPA.
2   I started to use the term 'Global Majority' in 2003. It is a more accurate collective term for those routinely described as 'minorities' as they are in fact the majority, the largest demographic of the world, in terms of population. When I need to be specific about a particular group, I will use terminology such as 'Black and Global Majority', which serves to avoid homogenisation without negatively 'othering'. 'Global Majority' is both empowering and inclusive. 'Minority' often carries and perpetuates negative connotations. The term 'people of colour' centres whiteness as the default. The use of the term 'minorities' serves to minoritise both those so described and the issues pertaining to them.

White gaze[3] of the revered institutions that we were in; their dismissal or patronising 'tolerance' of us ironically provided exactly the right environment to thrive. The intention was to develop networks of school leaders who would challenge structural inequity and racism within the education system. At the start, IiD enjoyed high-level government support from the then newly created position of minister for London schools, first held by Stephen Twigg MP. IiD London ran successfully for eight years between 2003 and 2011 as part of the highly successful London Challenge initiative (Hutchings et al., 2012; Baars et al., 2014) and continued to receive support from Minister of State for Education Lord Adonis.

IiD targeted experienced Black and Global Majority educators who aspired to be leaders but were under-represented in London schools. From inception, the approach was prefaced on the proposition that the call for more leaders from diverse backgrounds should be accompanied by the creation of professional space for those leaders to lead successfully, by using their difference to make a difference. The aim was to build a community of Black and Global Majority educators who not only looked like the communities they served but were authentic in co-creating school leadership focused on equity and social justice, thereby addressing the concerns of their communities. IiD challenged the notion that under-representation had anything to do with lack of intellectual capacity, confidence or competence. Amongst the organisations we worked closely with was the Muslim Teachers Association; members of the association's leadership, who were long-term associates, formed part of IiD's core team.

The programme aimed to increase the number of middle- and senior-level leaders, initially in London secondary schools but subsequently included the primary sector. Instead of reducing the representation discourse to recruiting aspirant leaders from under-represented groups, the programme's stated philosophy and curriculum went beyond a colour-blind perspective. The understanding that people brought who they were, culturally and ideologically, to their leadership identity was the foundation on which IiD and the many programmes that it inspired was built. In fact, for many participants, their cultural identity was not only for the first time positively foregrounded and embraced as an asset, but legitimised within their professional identity. It provided an opportunity for Black and other Global Majority educators to reflect on who they are and

---

3   Toni Morrison's (1999) beautifully crafted novel *The Bluest Eye* is a complete exercise in resisting the White gaze.

what they potentially bring by way of additionality and challenge to the leadership space. Far from the deficit model that implied their under-representation was due to what they lacked when compared to their White counterparts, IiD focused on encouraging Black and Global Majority educators, who so identified, to acknowledge and embrace the values they bring to their teaching and leadership function.

The intention, therefore, was not merely to have more diverse educators in leadership positions, but by their presence to change the arena in which leadership took place and reconstruct narratives. IiD participants were encouraged to confront, amongst other things, the effects of systemic racism – for them, their students and the communities they served. IiD intentionally empowered a more diverse leadership to play their unique part in, where possible, working alongside White allies to change the trajectory of those students who had traditionally been failed by the system. They had to be personally as well as professionally invested.

It was March 2014. The UK's national security threat level was raised from substantial to severe. The official threat level related to developments in Syria and Iraq and the perceived growing power of al-Qaida associated groups. An overhaul of the Home Office's counter-terrorism strategy was being called for by some government ministers. The overhaul led to the Prevent strategy being published in 2011, which was intended to stop young people from being sucked into extremist ideology. It specifically profiled young Muslims to prevent them from becoming radicalised and travelling overseas to fight for the Islamic State of Iraq and Syria (ISIS) or al-Qaida groups.

The Trojan Horse affair was used by government to get the Prevent strategy on the statute books (DfE, 2015). It took a dark and sinister tone when the Department for Education decided to appoint a former national head of counter-terrorism to investigate several schools in Birmingham. What began as concerns about matters of school governance immediately became politicised and escalated because of the Muslim demographic. Muslim youngsters, their teachers, governors and parents were suddenly under suspicion, as well as, in the case of the students at least, being seen as vulnerable.

The hostile environment created had rapid and severe implications for Muslims in Birmingham. Let us be clear: Trojan Horse ruined some people's lives – from the teachers who were hounded out of the profession, to the families and colleagues who were investigated and were now indefinitely on the radar of the Security Services, to students whose life chances were destroyed by placing previously outstanding schools in special measures. Muslim students and educators learnt at a stroke how vulnerable their 'model minority' status was as Asians in the UK and how British systems and values could crush them. If ever there was a platform for radicalising an entire demographic, Trojan Horse and the Prevent strategy provided a blueprint. The Trojan Horse affair changed everything. The highly politicised context in which we found ourselves due to the Trojan Horse operation in Birmingham spread across the country like wildfire. The implications for leadership development focused on diversifying school leadership could not be ignored because of the forensic focus that the system now had on Muslim students and those of whatever background who educated them.

The Yorkshire and Humber Diverse Leaders Programme, a sister programme to IiD London and Leeds, had been running successfully for several years. Funding secured through the National College for Teaching and Leadership (NCTL) paid for a suite of programmes targeted at Global Majority educators, mostly though not exclusively South Asian. This was due to their under-representation at the school leadership level in the region. A Diverse Leaders Steering Group was set up. Participants on the Diverse Leaders programmes were principally young Muslim educators. The trainers and mentors forged a partnership between the original core team who ran IiD London and then Leeds, working with the relatively newly formed steering group. The leadership development programmes that the regional steering group ran in collaboration with, amongst others, Teaching Schools and Carnegie Leaders in Learning, built on the bold but tried-and-tested principles, methods and structure of IiD. Not only were we rejecting deficit narratives of difference and otherness, but acknowledging and challenging systemic barriers to progression for Muslim educators, such as Islamophobia. We had to confront the reality that the model minority status enjoyed by some South Asian communities in the UK, enabling their educators to be apolitical, was not enjoyed by the majority of South Asian Muslims. They were stigmatised by their religion as well as their ethnicity.

In the education system in the Yorkshire and Humber region, as across the country, particularly at the leadership level, Global Majority teaching talent was not typically being spotted, planned for, nurtured, retained or grown. Leadership development remained stubbornly generic and determinedly colour blind, with the focus on what educators didn't have instead of seriously engaging with the systemic barriers that Global Majority educators faced. There was a determination within the suite of development programmes offered by the Diverse Leaders Steering Group, like the IiD programme before them, to create safe spaces to speak about what Professor Paul Miller (2020) describes as 'the politics of knowledge', systemic racism and Islamophobia.

At one level, it would be impossible to have a discourse about diverse leaders leading differently if we were unwilling to confront what we wanted this new generation of leaders to be able to play their part in dismantling – the emphasis being on playing their part. At another more practical level, we acknowledged colleagues' lived experience and developed resilience in those individuals to weather the storm, while enabling them to cause change to happen. We wanted participants in these programmes to bring themselves, their values and their lived experience to the process, and to feel empowered to build professional networks and communities alongside the skills, attributes and attitudes required to navigate the spaces within which they worked – all while remaining relatively sane.

The importance of connecting with their communities, without being perceived through the White gaze as only being able to connect with the communities from which they came, was part of the unwritten curriculum. The contradiction of being within a system but not being of that system was a well-trodden road for Black educators. Not taking the default position of being the spokesperson for all Asian communities, while knowing when it is imperative to speak because no one else will, are subtle forms of leadership with which Global Majority educators have to contend. The collision at the intersection of class, race, religion and gender tend to be ignored in generic leadership programmes.

Trust became a significant issue and sensitivities were running extremely high during the storm that was Trojan Horse. For some, to turn up and sign up for such programmes could bring you under suspicion. We felt a moral obligation to be cognisant of the realities facing our colleagues. This included providing coaching for those individuals who were directly affected by the Trojan Horse affair as well as signposting others to legal counsel. Muslim communities in general felt feared and were fearful. Muslims were under attack in a relentless and sensationalising press. Government and the opposition were outdoing each other in seemingly being more hard line in quelling the perceived threat from within.

Educators in schools anywhere in England with a similar demographic to those under investigation in Birmingham now felt not only under constant pressure and surveillance but also under threat.

It set development programmes back years as ambitious young Asian educators, many of whom were male, grappled with unapologetically embracing their identity. In seeking the development and support they needed now more than ever, would they be drawing unwanted attention to themselves when they should be keeping their heads down and under the wire? Being a bearded Asian man or an Asian woman who chose to cover, irrespective of the area in which you worked or the ethnicity or religion of your students, took on a whole new political significance. Many decided to sacrifice career progression to present physically and culturally as Muslim. Others assimilated to the extent that their skin colour and name would allow. Some, unable to secure leadership positions or receive the scaffolding and support for career progression through the UK system, left the country and headed for countries like the United Arab Emirates and cities like Dubai.

Lessons learnt

Language matters. Global Majority is both an empowering term and a position to adopt.

The government defined 'extremism' in the Prevent strategy as, amongst other things, 'vocal or active opposition to fundamental British values'; British values were said to include 'mutual respect and tolerance of different faiths and beliefs' (DfE, 2015, p. 5). It was on the basis of a group's faith and beliefs that sections of the Muslim community in Birmingham were targeted during the Trojan Horse affair. Being young and Muslim could identify you as at risk of becoming radicalised while simultaneously posing a potential terrorist threat to other Britons. The Prevent strategy talked about Islamist extremists in Muslim-majority countries, creating a narrative of 'them' and 'us', while ignoring the unmistakable message that UK policy and practice was sending to British Muslims in places like Birmingham and Bradford about belonging and 'them' and 'us'. Trojan Horse never quite squared that circle.

The way in which the Trojan Horse affair was sensationalised in the media was recklessly irresponsible. The overwhelming silence from White counterparts who were not directly involved in the Trojan Horse affair, and what that said about a collective willingness to be complicit in their condemnation of colleagues through silence, was unconscionable. The lack of empathy for fellow educators who worked in the targeted schools was nothing short of shameful. The accused educators found no recourse or protection from their professional associations. The relief of some Black colleagues that the spotlight was off the Black community for a change was embarrassing.

Trojan Horse marked an immediate shift away from policies of community cohesion and towards the Prevent strategy against extremism. Neoliberalism allowed this to happen with minimal challenge from anywhere. It took nothing more than an unauthenticated, anonymous letter, later identified as a hoax, sent to a local council and leaked to the press, alleging a conspiracy to trigger swift government action that was both wrong and strong. A dangerous precedent was set.

At IiD, we were able to mobilise support relatively quickly. Ecosystems of networks that cohorts of our trainees had sustained beyond the taught leadership programmes over the years helped to provide some refuge and minimise the isolation, loneliness and misplaced shame felt by some of our targeted colleagues. The affair reminded Global Majority people that the demonisation that plays into existing deeply held beliefs about the 'other' can be instantly weaponised by the state. Muslims as folk-devils were not new; what was new, however, was the categorising of young British people as being both at risk of segregation and simultaneously vulnerable to radicalisation, thereby posing a threat to their country. Islam became the main threat – to them and to their acceptance in British society.

Institutions such as the NCTL and Ofsted were in the invidious position of respectively overseeing the investigation of teachers for professional misconduct and placing schools previously ranked as outstanding into special measures. Both government authorities, in their handling of these situations, lost credibility and any semblance of moral authority they might have had with those under investigation during the Trojan Horse affair. West Midlands Police, to its credit on this occasion, handed the matter back to Birmingham City Council as no criminal offences were found.

The Trojan Horse affair undoubtedly set back the work that was being done on increasing diversity in school leadership, particularly within the Asian Muslim community, and halted the work planned to encourage more Muslims into the profession. It coincided with, if not contributed to, the unseemly haste away from a focus and funding for racial diversity in leadership to a redirection to other areas of inequality, namely gender and to a lesser extent disability. At IiD, we were in favour of broadening the portfolio of work to focus more explicitly on other areas of diversity, particularly disability, but to pretend that the job on race had been done – in the face of such a significant setback as the Trojan Horse affair – was disingenuous.

The work on getting more Black and Global Majority educators into positions of leadership became increasingly marginalised and unsupported at a national level. Insipid lip service from within the new NCTL leadership was now barely being paid to the efforts of the diversity associates they had inherited. Funding for diversity was diverted without so much as a conversation, often to White head teachers and Teaching School alliances led by White people who had no experience or indeed real interest in diversifying leadership. It didn't matter whether they met recruitment targets or the quality of the experience they were offering, they were guaranteed to receive diversity funding with minimum levels of scrutiny or expectations in terms of deliverables. Some head teachers were embarrassed by being 'invited' to apply for diversity funds for which others had to make a strong case. Most had to call on the three diversity associates left for the entire country to develop programmes for them in areas with little demonstrable need. Others just spent the money.

The new hierarchy at the NCTL was deafeningly silent on the Trojan Horse affair; it was as if it never happened. The implications for Muslim educators and students or for diversity, succession planning, equity and race were that they all ceased to be part of the NCTL narrative going forward. A courageous leadership moment was squandered, as was the opportunity to rebuild trust between entities such as NCTL and Muslim teachers. There was no political will in 2014 to address institutionalised, systemic racism or other forms of discrimination. Indeed, we had even lost the language to discuss issues of race and religious discrimination, which had been airbrushed out of discourse through the language of 'diversity' and 'inclusion', and difference had been stigmatised through the discursive process of 'otherness'.[4] Inequality was so deeply entrenched within the system that it had become normalised.

At the time of writing, in the light of Black Lives Matter, some institutions are beginning to talk about decolonising their thinking, but how far are they prepared to go? Indeed, the language is much less coded than in 2014, and at least more of the participants in the conversation are White people. A critical challenge that will require courage is an honest analysis of the extent to which Britain's colonial and imperial past exemplifies British values. Given that history, and what it clearly and repeatedly says about past and current relationships between White people, Black people and other people of the Global Majority, it is unclear where the incentive is for the White establishment to change. Are Black and other Global Majority people seen as a threat to British values if they bring their authentic selves to the table? Can British values be anti-racist when Britain is based on racist beliefs about the 'other', is in denial about how it came to be 'Great Britain' and then transitioned to 'Little Britain' in a globalised world?

Diversity too needs to be scrutinised, critiqued and challenged. Did Trojan Horse expose internal, colourism, class and caste-isms within Black and Brown communities? Do we know the weight of the impact of Trojan Horse on Pakistani Muslim communities in Birmingham? Were other Muslim communities complicit in their silence? At a time when places of learning are more diverse than ever, and the inequity is completely exposed, we need spaces for Black and Global Majority educators and leaders where our presence in that space is not questioned. In fact, the converse ought to be true: our absence from those spaces should be challenged. How can Birmingham, the largest local authority in Europe with amongst the fastest-growing young Global Majority population, have a school leadership demographic that relegates Black and Global Majority people to percentages that can be counted on a couple of fingers? We don't only want better representation, we want to change the narrative and the praxis by foregrounding the difference we bring and make. Our presence should not be conditional on us assimilating to the point of oblivion, but society can render you invisible as a Global Majority if you will insist on being yourself.

---

4   See Jean-François Staszak (2008) Other/Otherness. In Noel Castree, Rob Kitchin, Nigel Thrift, Mike
     Crang and Mona Domosh (eds), *International Encyclopedia of Human Geography*. Amsterdam: Elsevier
     BV. Available at: https://www.unige.ch/sciencessociete/ geo/files/3214/4464/7634/OtherOtherness.pdf.

Until Britain comes to terms with its colonial and imperialistic roots, its history and its truth, it will always be haunted by it. The imperialist footprint around the globe, and the bearing this has on its present and world events such as Black Lives Matter, are critical. Britain will never be able to embrace difference until it can hold a mirror up to itself.

References

Baars, Sam; Bernardes, Eleanor; Elwick, Alex; Malortie, Abigail; McAleavy, Tony; McInerney, Laura; Menzies, Loic; and Riggall, Anna (2014) *Lessons from London Schools: Investigating the Success*. Reading and London: Centre for London/CfBT Education Trust. Available at: https://www.centreforlondon.org/wp-content/uploads/2016/08/Lessons-from-London-Schools.pdf.

Birmingham City Council (2021) The Latest Ethnicity Breakdown of Senior Leaders (Assistant/Deputy Heads/Principals and Separately Heads/Principals) in Birmingham State Schools Broken Down into Maintained Schools and Academies and Free Schools [Freedom of Information Act request] (21 August). Ref: 27615143.

Campbell-Stephens, Rosemary (2009) Investing in Diversity: Changing the Face (and the Heart) of Educational Leadership, *School Leadership & Management*, 29(3): 321–331. DOI:10.1080/13632430902793726.

Campbell-Stephens, Rosemary (2021) *Educational Leadership and the Global Majority: Decolonising Narratives*. Cham, Switzerland: Palgrave Macmillan.

Department for Education (DfE) (2015) *The Prevent Duty: Departmental Advice for Schools and Childcare Providers* (June). Available at: https://www.gov.uk/government/publications/protecting-children-from-radicalisation-the-prevent-duty.

Hutchings, Merryn; Greenwood, Charley; Hollingworth, Sumi; Mansaray, Ayo; Rose, Anthea; Minty, Sarah; and Glass, Katie (2012) *Evaluation of the City Challenge Programme*. London: Institute for Policy Studies in Education, London Metropolitan University. Available at: https://www.gov.uk/government/publications/evaluation-of-the-city-challenge-programme.

Johnson, Lauri and Campbell-Stephens, Rosemary (2010) Investing in Diversity in London Schools: Leadership Preparation for Black and Global Majority Educators, *Urban Education*, 45(6): 840–870. DOI:10.1177/0042085910384353.

Miller, Paul (2020) Race Discrimination, the Politics of Knowledge, and Cultural Inequality in England. In Rosemary Papa (ed.), *Handbook on Promoting Social Justice in Education*, 1st edn. London: Springer, pp. 1913–1934.

Morrison, Toni (1994) *The Bluest Eye*. London: Vintage.

Staszak, Jean-François (2008) Other/Otherness. In Noel Castree, Rob Kitchin, Nigel Thrift, Mike Crang and Mona Domosh (eds), *International Encyclopedia of Human Geography*. Amsterdam: Elsevier BV. Available at: https://www.unige.ch/sciences-societe/geo/files/3214/4464/7634/OtherOtherness.pdf.

Chapter 16
Urban education policy: it takes a city to raise a child

Colin Diamond

> The conception of education as a social process and function has no definite meaning until we define the kind of society we have in mind.
>
> John Dewey, *Democracy and Education* (1916)

A passionate and compassionate city: an incubator for education excellence

Birmingham, England's second largest city, has been at the forefront of educational practice several times over the last 250 years with episodes of intellectual and innovatory brilliance. From the days of the Lunar Society in the late eighteenth century, when Birmingham was the world's equivalent of Silicon Valley, through to being recognised as the best local education authority in England (Ofsted 2002), the importance of place and identity has shone through.

When Forster's Elementary Education Act was passed in 1870, Birmingham was the first city in England to establish a school board and levy funds to open schools for children aged 5–13. Joseph Chamberlain, who was already working to establish free primary education for children in Birmingham ahead of the 1870 Act, became a city councillor in 1869. By 1873, he had become Birmingham's mayor and embarked on a massive programme to provide civic amenities, including more schools, libraries and parks. In 1900, the University of Birmingham became England's first civic (or redbrick) university where students from all religions and backgrounds were accepted on an equal basis. Joseph Chamberlain was its first chancellor. Today, as the metropolis has begun its post-manufacturing regeneration, symbolised by its stunning civic plaza, iconic new city centre buildings and preparation for HS2 and the Commonwealth Games

2022, visitors are surprised by the quality and vibrancy of what they find. That is a long way from Tolkien's inspiration for Mordor – those vistas of a smoky, black hell that he saw growing up in Birmingham in the 1930s.

Birmingham's educational capital was highly regarded in England at the turn of this century when its local education authority, led by Sir Tim Brighouse and team, received powerful accolades from Ofsted for demonstrating how achievement could be improved in gravity-defying fashion (Ofsted, 2002; see also Chapter 1). All of this had been possible because there was a united education system in the city and local education authorities had the powers and resources to drive forward school improvement. Schools already had a high degree of autonomy and financial delegation as a result of the policies introduced by the Education Reform Act 1988, but at that time, during the 1990s and early 2000s, the pendulum had not swung entirely in their direction. That happened as a result of the Academies Act 2010, which led to the destruction of a unified civic education system, in spite of the evidence that with good leadership standards could be raised by using school improvement strategies at scale across urban areas (see Brighouse and Woods, 2008, 2013; Woods, 2020).

The consequences of the Academies Act 2010 continue to unfold. Whilst he was shadow secretary of state, Michael Gove was busy formulating plans that would transfer power to schools and parents in a post-bureaucratic landscape where freedom and choice would shine like lodestars: 'We want to see a radical shift in power – away from the educational establishment – from Whitehall and the bureaucratic organisations it sponsors – and down towards, schools and parents. We want, crucially, to see heads and teachers given greater freedom from bureaucracy and parents given more control over their children's education' (Gove, 2009).

The Academies Act received Royal Assent on 27 July 2010. With the brakes off, the progressive lowering of the bar on academy conversions from 2010, the over-expansion of several leading national multi-academy trusts (which subsequently needed asset stripping, to use the appropriate metaphor) and a blinkered approach to anything worthy in the maintained sector, chaos was unleashed. When the pin was pulled on the Trojan Horse letter in 2013, this provided an early stress test for the new order as freedom and choice looked to have gifted schools into the hands of extremists. Not quite the sunlit uplands Gove had predicted.

Academisation, the advent of free schools and the incremental emas-culation of local authorities' education roles has not led to an overall improvement in the effectiveness of the system in England per se.[1] However, the influence of the Academies Act on all aspects of educa-tion leadership and governance has been profound.[2] At the time of writing, the government continues to push its plans in which multi-acad-emy trusts occupy the system's centre of gravity (Carr, 2021a), in spite of the fact that 61% of schools remain maintained by local authorities and seemingly unimpressed by the so-called academy freedoms (HM Government, 2021). The Schools White Paper has pledged to finish the job by creating 'a stronger and fairer school system' in which all schools will be in 'a strong multi academy trust or with plans to join or form one' (HM Government, 2022, p. 47).

Neoliberal ideology, managerialism and centralisation continue to drive forward English education policy and evidence is cherry-picked to sup-port its advancement. The key components of market ideology (choice, competition and freedom – exemplified by the neologism of the 'free school') are currently shaping the English school system. This is classic Hayek (1986) theory let loose into the heartlands of education, with the inevitable outcome that players in the system will game its rules.

For example, Liam Nolan's expensive double-salary leadership of the Perry Beeches Academy Trust led to all of its schools being re-brokered and Nolan himself being barred from teaching and managing any inde-pendent school or academy (Roberts, 2020). His unethical behaviour, found to be challenging by his peers ahead of academisation, knew no bounds once freed from any notion of local authority control and exhib-ited many features of the 'dark side' of leadership (Sam, 2020). More broadly, introducing a quasi-market into the state education system in a large city with severe inequalities, which require a joined-up response from all local government agencies, can be described as at best irrespon-sible and at worst dangerous. Greany (2020; my emphasis) reported that 'the process and impact of "middle tier" disintermediation is uneven [in England] and often fraught, with significant implications for place-based *coherence, equity and legitimacy'*.

---

1   See Thomson (2020) for a thorough and disturbing discussion of this crucial topic, especially ch. 6 ('The Effects of Effectiveness').
2   For a superb overview see Earley and Greany (2017).

So, how can education policy be formulated to take account of the urban environment and the needs of its communities? To what extent should governors and leaders be able to build education and social capital within a broader framework of social justice and equity, and focus their energies and creativity beyond their own gates?

As we have seen in Part II, following the round of Trojan Horse Ofsted inspections, a mixture of school leaders (some from existing multi-academy trusts, others needing to establish multi-academy trusts to be eligible to sponsor schools in special measures and many others from the maintained sector) found their way through the policy maze. As senior, road-tested leaders they have 'middled out' change, collaborating around shared agendas in the gap left by a weakened local authority (Munby and Fullan, 2016). They have created educational and social capital by forging new organisations that resemble community-based fortresses after the power and influence of the city state waned.

There is no doubt that Ark, Prince Albert Community Trust, CORE, Washwood Heath and Star are successful at filling that void, along with a mixture of maintained school partnerships, as Azita Zohhadi captured when describing the importance of her local primary forum (see Chapter 6). Urban school leaders are generally pragmatic, not allied ideologically to particular government policies and want the best for their schools. They will always strive to make local and national policy rules work in their own situation and context. The question here is how national policy can be adapted to enable urban leaders in multi-faith, multiracial and economically challenged communities to become ever more effective and not feel that they are working against the grain, hindered by perverse incentives and a seeming lack of willingness to recognise their landscape? The recommendations below are aimed at national and local policy-makers, based on examples of what has worked or is working well in Birmingham.

Recommendations to advance urban education policy

1. Resolve the middle-tier question so that the English Core Cities have education governance and structures that are co-terminus with their boundaries

In 2014, ministers at the Department for Education puzzled over maps of East Birmingham which plotted the twenty-one schools inspected by Ofsted in the Trojan Horse round and showed the other academies that existed in the area at that time. The only solution they could contemplate was to engage the capacity of locally based academy chains. Of course, the map was incomplete as it excluded all the maintained schools, regardless of the fact that many of them were judged outstanding. This illustrates the inherent bias and delimiting elements in government policy. The education capital of Birmingham's maintained schools was marginalised as if it counted for nothing. In the event, governors and leaders emerged from the maintained sector to combine with local multi-academy trusts in order to make progress.

As the number of academies and free schools grew in England, the Department for Education introduced eight regional schools commissioners (RSCs) to oversee the programme (House of Commons Education Committee, 2016, p. 18). In all but one region (the South West), the RSCs' areas were variations on the former government office regions, no doubt designed to introduce a contrived element of innovation and to chop up London between three jurisdictions. After all, it would not do to replicate systems that had been dismantled just a few years earlier and had been described by then Cabinet minister Eric Pickles as 'agents of Whitehall to intervene and interfere in localities' in the regions (BBC News, 2010). The newly appointed West Midlands RSC, a successful secondary head teacher, suddenly had a major role in determining the future of schools from the south bank of the River Mersey to the Welsh border, including the Black Country and Birmingham. Would this model work across sixteen local authority areas as diverse as Herefordshire and Coventry? What did it have to offer a city with over 450 state schools and a rich, distinctive education history?

As the debate on the middle tier began, greater numbers of academies were opening and the secretary of state for education was winding down and then removing the education services grant in 2017, which had previously paid for local authorities' school improvement work. (See, for example, the Department for Education's reconfiguration of the education services grant (DfE, 2014) and a statement about its removal obtained via a Freedom of Information Act request.[3]) Former education secretary David Blunkett argued that around eighty commissioners should be created and each city should have its own schools commissioner to work alongside the director of children's services and other agencies (Adams and Belger, 2014). Blunkett's argument was rejected and Birmingham became part of a wider RSC region far removed from its identity and an office based in another city.

More radical options have countenanced almost complete removal of the role of local authorities in education and the turbocharging of multi-academy trusts 'to embrace cutting-edge quality informed by the best research' (Cruddas, 2019, cited in Thomson, 2020, p. 40). This approach would not just 'hollow out' the middle tier, it would reinforce the notion that multi-academy trusts do all the interesting curriculum development work and refining of pedagogy, whilst the local authorities pick up the pieces. After all, who really wants to sort out the difficult stuff around special needs, permanent exclusions, elective home education, early years sufficiency and quality, ensuring a child has a school place and so on? Breaking that connection would lead to a two-tier state system where multi-academy trust leaders and governors are excused from any wider social responsibility beyond their immediate boundaries.

During the early days of the COVID-19 pandemic, some multi-academy trust leaders questioned in public whether they actually had to pay any attention to what their local authority directors of public health and directors of children's services were requiring them to do. Such behaviour, whilst unusual, illustrates the effect of ten years of education policy designed to weaken the links between multi-academy trusts and anything other than the RSC office. The EDSK report *Trust Issues: How to Bring Academies and Maintained Schools into a Unified State School System* avows the need for simplicity, collaboration, coherence and transparency in what it describes as a 'fragmented and incoherent education system, with little sign of improvement on either front' (Richmond, 2019,

---

3   See https://www.whatdotheyknow.com/request/what_replaces_the_removal_of_edu.

p. 1). However, its recommendations appear to be at odds with the virtuous characteristics advocated across the system. For example, under 'collaboration' head teachers would be given the power to operate as 'independent state schools' which would put them in a private orbit (p. 5). Under 'coherence', the eight RSCs are replaced by thirty-five 'Local Schools Commissioners' (p. 6) who would turn school planning into a procurement process akin to a bagatelle with zero local roots. Once again, local authorities become lenders of last resort in the challenging interface between education and wider children's welfare and safeguarding duties. The aim of the Schools White Paper, that all schools will provide a 'high quality and inclusive education' for all and a 'clear role for every part of the school system' (HM Government, 2022, p. 43), is laudable. It remains to be seen how this latest statement of academisation policy will be enacted.

A Birmingham RSC (or regional director, as of 2022) operating within the city area and having co-terminosity with the director of children's services would be more efficient and effective than the current model. Operational decisions about the future of vulnerable schools and academies, the supply of school places, real-time quality assurance and an overview of independent schools would be unified in one place rather than being shuffled between local and central government agencies. Advice from leaders and governors would be sourced from within the city rather than provided by those based in villages in rural counties where they have no experience of the inner-city environment.

2. Create local systems that enable the co-construction and co-delivery of school improvement that benefit all city schools

The current mishmash of maintained and academy schools, laced with the complicated interface between local authority school improvement duties as set out in the *Schools Causing Concern* guidance (DfE, 2020b), is a recipe for muddle. The inconvenient truth is that since the arrival of the Academies Act 2010 we have seen significant numbers of academies crashing into special measures (476 between 2013 and 2019) and insufficient sponsors coming forward to pick up these 'orphan schools' (Dickens, 2019). There have been many cases of multi-academy trusts growing too rapidly, not adding value to schools forced into sponsorship and being mired in abuses of power by leaders and trustees (see, for example, Stephen Ball's (2018) brilliant lecture on the incoherence of the current system).

The challenges of what amounts to a big experiment in the multi-academy trust governance model are captured well by the National Governance Association, which asks pertinent questions about the amount of power in the hands of a few people and whether local tiers of governance are being used meaningfully (Collins et al., 2021). The reality is that a mixed-economy education ecosystem with high levels of delegation requires strong coordination at middle-tier and central government levels. In cities, where the intersectional elements of class, socio-economic status, faith, gender and race continually interweave and throw up new dynamics, full cooperation and collaboration between all senior players is required to hold things together and make progress.

In 2015, an education improvement group was established to unite education stakeholders in Birmingham. Its membership drew together senior colleagues from the Birmingham Education Partnership (BEP), city council, Department for Education (with representatives from the RSC office and, as required, the due diligence and counter-terrorism group) and Birmingham Schools Forum leaders from all phases. This group was able to be proactive, sharing data, information and intelligence about schools of all stripes – both state and independent with input about elective home education patterns and provision – knowing that each stakeholder had access to different sources of information. For example, attendance and exclusions data, which is often a bellwether on effective leadership and governance, was held in real time by the local authority but with a major lag before it reached the Department for Education and Ofsted. Support for vulnerable schools was brokered by combinations of agencies including BEP, the city council and the RSC office. This model was commended by Sir David Carter during his tenure as the national schools commissioner. At the biannual Birmingham stocktake meeting, he observed that all Core Cities in England should have this culture and practice.

School improvement is more than the sum of its individual parts; focusing on individual schools or local groupings of schools misses the big picture. In Chapter 4, Tom Perry analysed exactly what was happening to pupil attainment in the city across a decade using information from the Office for National Statistics and revealed the performance of different ethnic groups.

In summary, the city's own data analysis reveals that it continues to track the improvements in national performance, with some strong features amongst pupils entitled to free school meals and sixth-form pupils who achieve higher than the national average across all the main attainment measures for A levels. A level performance is largely driven by the large sixth forms in the city's eight grammar schools (Birmingham City Council, 2019a). This is a long way from what had been possible when schools were united in a values-driven civic education system that transcended received wisdom about overcoming disadvantage.

Elsewhere, the policy lessons and learning from the London Challenge programme, with its provenance in Birmingham and its co-existence with the National College for School Leadership, showed unequivocally that school improvement at scale is possible in a capital city. An evidence-based and research-literate theory of action emerged drawing on the powerhouses of Michael Fullan and David Hargreaves. Its principles acknowledged the importance of moral, knowledge, social and organisational capital in underpinning its strategy (Woods, 2020). The long-term success and sustainability of the London Challenge are indisputable and could usefully inform post-pandemic education policy.

3. An urban school curriculum model

When David Hargreaves wrote his seminal *The Challenge for the Comprehensive School: Culture, Curriculum and Community* (1982), he asked profound questions about the role of the comprehensive school in relation to wider society. He argued that until there was agreement about the nature of society for which comprehensive schools were preparing their pupils, their purpose could not be defined. In words that proved to be remarkably prescient when considering the relationship between schools and society today, he said:

> So far we have considered a number of themes of significance to contemporary society and education: the persisting damage that school does to the dignity of many school pupils, especially those from working-class homes; the erosion of working-class culture and community; the preservation of and dominant emphasis given to the cognitive-intellectual domain in the school curriculum; the growth of the cult of individualism and the failure of the school to make its proper contribution to social solidarity in society. In all these matters comprehensive re-organization has promoted little

change for the better and even made matters worse. (Hargreaves, 1982, p. 113)

This was written before the Thatcher government's reforms, culminating in the Education Reform Act 1988 that paved the way for today's model, which is infused with central control and hyper-accountability. As mentioned in my discussion of leadership journeys in Chapter 12, the role of schools has been narrowed by waves of education policy that have deliberately divorced them from their civic roots (although in all six cases in Part II, the leaders have recognised the importance of their community anchors and constantly pushed outwards). Centralisation is not compatible with strong urban identity when the panopticon surveys all schools in the country through the same, conformist lens. And neither is the fundamental British values wallpaper, drafted in the wake of Trojan Horse, which evokes a vague sense of nationalism and places those not truly 'British' on the margins: a latter-day exhumation of the Tebbit test incorporated into statute.

Certain urban role-model schools are celebrated relentlessly by government to demonstrate that, with the strictest of behaviour regimes, direct instruction, knowledge-rich pedagogy delivered using the techniques proselytised by those who follow Teach Like a Champion[4] approaches and uber-controlling methods such as SLANT (sit up, listen, ask and answer questions, nod your head, track the teacher), the cycle of chronic underachievement can be broken. It would be churlish to criticise the huge efforts of those who work in such schools and to ignore their successes. However, there are deep concerns about the authoritarian nature of such an education. 'It's our way or the highway' is the stark message at the Michaela Community School (Carr, 2018), where its principal, Katharine Birbalsingh, celebrates the dubious accolade of being 'the strictest school in Britain'. As David Buckingham (2020) writes with reference to its ultra-conservative curriculum: 'This is not the curriculum of a modern country, confident and secure of its place in the wider world. It is the curriculum of Little Britain. It gazes not forwards and outwards, but backwards and inwards. Welcome to the curriculum of Brexit.'

This is a far cry from the leadership and teaching models shared in Part II of this book. They have more in common with the pedagogies (note the plural) found in School 21 in London's Docklands. And what does

---

4   See https://teachlikeachampion.com.

such a narrow approach have to offer when reflecting on the conundrums thrown up by the challenges of teaching lesbian, gay, bisexual, transgender, queer and others (LGBTQ+) awareness in primary schools or the questions that arise when discussing the intersectional issues in that space between socially conservative faith and young women's independence? None of the above can be 'taught' in an overtly authoritarian mode; rather, they require a range of resources and methods and skilled teachers who are immersed in and understand their local cultures. Finally, if there is fear within a Black family that natural hairstyles can lead to exclusion from school, what are the messages to their community? The post-colonial intersection will remain barbed and tangled until government is willing to recognise its existence, let alone actually do something about it other than whitewashing.

The following examples are drawn from successful initiatives across Birmingham's schools and education communities of purpose. They are all ingredients that can add value and complement the orthodox curriculum to be found anywhere in English schools. For urban schools, I suggest that they are incorporated into local and national policy.

The United Nations Children's Fund's Rights Respecting Schools Award

Schools across the UK work with United Nations Children's Fund (UNICEF) and place different emphases on how working towards the Rights Respecting Schools Award (RRSA) contributes to children and young people's broad development, well beyond the standard subject boundaries. It may be children's rights in Scotland and Wales or children's health in Camden and Wandsworth. UNICEF UK has researched its theory of change and demonstrated impact for children and whole-school communities. The most recent survey runs up to schools across the UK participating in 2019 (UNICEF, 2020). The positive impact on children learning about their rights, how to exercise them, engendering a culture of respect across the school community and developing a shared sense of community and belonging is incontestable. Given the urgency of the climate crisis, possibly the most valuable outcome is children embracing global citizenship and believing they can change the world for the better.

Birmingham started from a different position in 2014 (as described in Chapter 12). It needed a way to strengthen safeguarding in schools that was not driven by the Prevent duty, with all of its negative connotations for Muslim communities, in particular. An approach was required that was cognisant of structural intersectionality and recognised the identities of communities and families rather than trampling on them with a crude central government tool. Starting small, the RRSA quickly became popular with schools in the city because of its universal, humanist language, which afforded pupils the opportunity to learn about themselves and how to remain safe and secure in the diverse urban mix. The United Nations Convention on the Rights of the Child (UNCRC) (UNICEF, 1989) offered a viewing platform where a multiplicity of perspectives could coexist; something that could belong to all children.

A decolonised curriculum

Harper Bell Seventh-Day Adventist primary school has been on its own improvement journey led by Nigel Oram, one of the few Black male head teachers in the city. Several years ago, the school was struggling on all fronts with low numbers of pupils and poor outcomes. It is now thriving, with Ofsted (2019, p. 1) reporting: 'Pupils' spiritual, moral, social and cultural development is very well supported. In their day-to-day learning, pupils develop a secure understanding of respect and why celebrating diversity is important.' The school unashamedly promotes a knowledge-rich culture, ensures its young pupils are focused on the importance of work in adult life and is explicit about the goal of university in a community where this is unknown territory for most families.

The school makes this work by adapting the national curriculum requirements so it is laden with an understanding of Black history, culture and important historical characters (as Figure 16.1 illustrates). The impact on attainment (and parental satisfaction) is impressive, and the school has moved from requiring special measures in 2013 to a strong good in 2019. The mission is clear and is summed up in this quotation often attributed to Marcus Garvey: 'A people without the knowledge of their past history, origin and culture is like a tree without roots.' Young people growing up in the inner cities need to be able to identify with their cultures and understand their histories to be fully paid-up members of adult society.

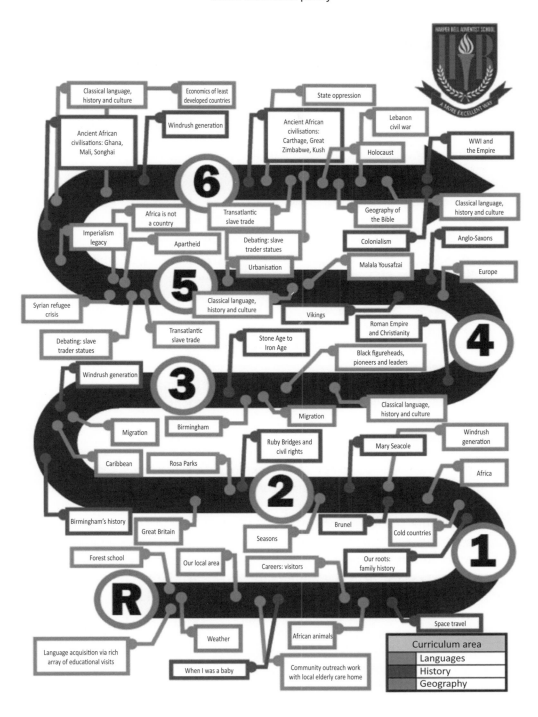

Figure 16.1. Our curriculum – faith, aspirations and cultural heritage. With permission from Nigel Oram, head teacher and Phil Hynan, deputy head teacher, Harper Bell Seventh-day Adventist Primary School

A multi-faith locally agreed RE syllabus

The Birmingham Standing Advisory Council for Religious Education (SACRE) was one of the few local organisations to emerge with credit from Ian Kershaw's (2014, p. 15) report: 'It is our view that Birmingham SACRE has undertaken its responsibilities in advising on a locally agreed syllabus with due diligence and sensitive care in meeting the needs of a variety of young people from a wide range of world religions.' I refer to it here because the role of religious education teaching, given all that happened during Trojan Horse and the wider growth of extremist and intolerant views in English society, has become more important than ever. The Birmingham City Council agreed syllabus, which is based on twenty-four dispositions that are valued by all the major faiths, is well-regarded nationally.[5] Locally, it binds together maintained schools, it has been adopted by free schools and academies are encouraged to do so when they leave local authority control. In an era of fragmented school structures, which can introduce artificial boundaries and divisions, SACRE remains a city-wide force that unifies schools within a multi-faith community.

Health, relationships and sex education teaching models produced by the city for the city

In 2019, the government consulted on the introduction of mandatory health, relationships and sex education (RSE) in all UK schools (state and independent) from 2020. In Birmingham, the proposals led to unseemly and aggressive protests outside two primary schools. Both have been longstanding champions of teaching their pupils about LGBTQ+ awareness. Parkfield Community School used the No Outsiders materials produced by its assistant head teacher, Andy Moffatt.[6] The protests went on for weeks in spite of many attempts to mediate from central and local government, causing enormous disruption and distress. The protests were almost universally condemned, yet this episode exposed deep fault lines between some primary schools and their community about teaching on the sensitive subject of RSE (Diamond, 2019). It was apparent that locally sourced teaching materials were needed in the absence of any guidelines from central government, which placed all the responsibility on head teachers and governors to decide what to teach and how. The

---

5   See https://www.faithmakesadifference.co.uk/landing#node-66.
6   See https://no-outsiders.com.

obvious place to start in Birmingham was the RRSA which had already been adopted by over 250 schools in the city.

Learning about the 54 children's rights is a sound basis upon which young people can grow towards making informed choices about their own lives. The UNCRC and its articles are silent on sexuality (although clear about sexual exploitation), but rich on freedom of thought and association and the right to education that embraces all faiths and none. LGBTQ+ awareness can be incorporated by building in dialogue around mutual respect and care for children from all kinds of families. The council worked with local primary schools to update the equalities toolkit (Birmingham City Council, 2018b) and produce a standalone resource for RSE (Birmingham City Council, 2020).

This foregrounded the importance of consultation with governors and families in establishing a shared understanding of what is involved, particularly in the light of the misinformation that had been peddled during the protests. The guidance contains lesson plans and resources from reception to Year 6, based on appropriate levels of understanding and a clear division between mandatory relationships education and optional sex education lessons. These provide a baseline that all primary schools can use confidently, knowing they were produced by teachers working in similar communities. This place-based creation of learning resources obviates the pressures that are felt by local schools and provides a shared language and understanding of the pedagogy within a local context.

A repertoire of pedagogies that recognise the centrality of art, drama, music and sport

> All children, and especially urban children, need the arts if they are to thrive and blossom to their full potentials. (Creedon, 2011, p. 36)

We have seen how our school leaders placed a premium on arts and creativity to raise pupil and family awareness of the broader cultural horizons in the city, getting them beyond their postcode and immediate community to experience what Birmingham and the region has to offer. Azita Zohhadi recognised the importance of regular visits from the Royal Shakespeare Company to her school in order to expose families to adapted versions of the plays. Adrian Packer (Chapter 7) placed huge emphasis on secondary pupils learning about the Holocaust through participation in the

Echo Eternal exhibitions and productions. He also broke new ground with CORE pupils joining Wimbledon every year. At Eden Boys' School, the pupils contributed to global poetry and song competitions with the Never Such Innocence charity and attended the launch of the competition from Birmingham's Council House in 2017.[7]

The new schools in the city established by Sir Mufti Hamid Patel's Tauheedul charitable trust (now Star Academies) (see Chapter 11) were outward-facing from the start, as he realised the need to bridge communities. Few schools make a greater contribution than Eden Boys', with its regular events that involve the pupils serving the community, which confers a sense of responsibility to others and a commitment to charitable endeavours. These areas of school life offer modes of learning that go beyond conventional classroom activities, widen pupils' horizons and plant aspirational seeds which influence how they view their place in society.

Many studies have confirmed the benefits of the arts for those growing up in cities. Cognitive research shows that well-structured music and arts education programmes enhance the emotional well-being of children, including their readiness for learning. They also reduce stress and negative social behaviours (Teplin et al., 2002, cited in Creedon, 2011). Integrating the arts with other subjects can contribute towards developing an emotionally positive social disposition within young people. Artist residency programmes, like Stan's Cafe at Saltley and the Royal Shakespeare Company at Nelson Mandela, partnered with teachers in curricular projects to reduce stress and promote learning. At a deeper level, studies have affirmed that such programmes help young people to develop social capital and strengthen their sense of agency (Hampshire and Matthijsse, 2010).

The most rounded understanding of the importance of participation in school drama productions, whether in a leading role or backstage, comes from David Hargreaves (1982, ch. 5) and his discussion of the curriculum and the community. He recognised that the full benefits would only be achieved when the school faced outwards and shared its accomplishments with parents, neighbours and local dignitaries. Where there were options for all pupils to join in, often those with less obvious academic prowess in the classroom shone in the production; they found

---

7   See https://www.neversuchinnocence.com.

themselves. The drama productions developed skills, honed talent and showcased in an authentic way what the collective efforts of the school could muster.

In the early 1980s, the culture of individualism – with heavy cognitive load content to match – was already militating against whole-school events, and drama teachers found themselves hemmed in by timetabling constraints. The opportunities for inner-city educators to explore individuality through the creative arts – with the potential for empowerment and strengthening the sense of self, as opposed to furthering the predominant emphasis on competitive individualism – were limited. In inner-city schools, where the majority of school leavers were predestined to go into traditional, low-skilled or semi-skilled employment, this was the norm. In the third decade of the twenty-first century, with a radically different economic and employment structure, those educated in cities can benefit from combining a strong understanding of self with impressive qualifications to move into employment, the next stage of education or training.

Access to arts services driven by equity and inclusion

The Birmingham Music Service weighed anchor from Birmingham City Council in 2013 and moved into a new community interest company. It has since thrived, working with over 90% of schools in the city during a decade in which music has been downgraded as a result of being excluded from the philistine English Baccalaureate (DfE, 2019), which contains no performing arts subjects. The community interest company directors are values-driven and have put affordable instrument tuition, free loans and ensembles at the core of the Music Service's delivery model in the city. It would have been easy to operate a market-driven model and cater mainly for those families who can afford instrument tuition in the more affluent areas of the city; in fact, exactly the opposite happens.

The Music Service analyses the city's youth population through the lenses of free school meal entitlement and special educational needs and disabilities (SEND). This enables them to track and target schools with higher social economic needs and steer music tutors into these areas. Building on this approach are initiatives aimed at the twenty-seven special schools whose populations have extremely high levels of socio-economic deprivation. Additionally, the service works with Birmingham Virtual School for children who are in the care of the city.[8] Year 4 children in care receive one-to-one thirty-minute weekly instrument lessons and there are plans to extend that up the age range.

4. A balanced scorecard with an international flavour

How can everything above be recorded and celebrated so that it becomes a formal record of what these schools and their pupils are achieving? The list below is derived from what Sir Tim Brighouse shared at the Priestley Lecture in 2019 and expanded for the purposes of this chapter. The narrow measurement of school performance in England, with its emphasis on testing and exams, is cheap and convenient. It mirrors the dominant policy ideology that results matter above all else, even though the system is predicated on 'failing' a large percentage of pupils at 16. According to which data you select, between a quarter and a third of pupils are not achieving 'strong' GCSE passes. This is compounded by the attainment gap. Teach First research revealed that nationally in 2019, 45% of pupils from economically disadvantaged homes achieved a standard GCSE pass in English and maths compared with 72% of non-economically disadvantaged pupils (Starkey-Midha, 2020, p. 4).

The balanced scorecard model is designed to make sure that all functions of a school are captured, giving a rounded picture of everything achieved and experienced by its pupils and read alongside the headline attainment data. It would include, for example:

- Progress made in graded tests and exams in skills and knowledge specified in the national curriculum, assessed and moderated locally and validated regionally.

- Inclusion data with local, statistical neighbour and national comparisons for attendance and exclusions.

- Attitudes and motivation as assessed by using one of the many surveys (e.g. Keele[9]) available for this purpose.

- Well-being using the methodology employed by UNICEF's (2021) latest research into what shapes child well-being in rich countries.

---

8   See https://www.birmingham.gov.uk/bvs.
9   See https://www.edsrs.org.uk.

- Participation in the school's sporting, performing and expressive arts opportunities.

- Pupil destinations after the end of participation in education and the data for those who are not in employment, education or training (NEET).

- Community contributions made by pupils, including volunteering activities via school, family or other organisations.

And, for the broader position of the school and its professional development looking outwards beyond English norms, a regular stocktake using the Organisation for Economic Co-operation and Development's Teaching and Learning International Survey lines of enquiry would be included.[10] This is the largest international survey examining teaching and learning environments in forty-eight education systems across all continents. As the pressure for norming towards centrally ordained standards grows and a generation of teachers and leaders are socialised into the post-2010 Academies Act version of education, such international perspectives on the health of schools become vital.

5. An inspection system that takes account of the realities of inner-city schools and addresses the real risks

Her Majesty's Chief Inspector (HMCI) Amanda Spielman has consistently denied it is 'unfair' that so-called deprived schools are more likely to receive lower grades than those in more affluent areas (Carr, 2021b). Her logic is understandable to a point: the current Ofsted school inspection system is based on a simplistic version of what constitutes 'high standards', regardless of a school's context. If value-added performance were built into the model, the number of schools with advantaged intakes judged to be outstanding would halve. Conversely, the number of schools with disadvantaged intakes judged outstanding would double (Hutchinson, 2016).

This model is deeply flawed. There are profound differences between schools serving socially and economically challenged areas, mostly to be found in cities, and those serving relatively comfortable communities. In the tougher areas, school leaders dig deeper into their communities, they are more empathetic, adapt constantly and transform lives against

---

10   See https://www.oecd.org/education/talis.

the odds every day. Such commitment is way beyond outstanding. Sub-judgements on leadership and management may reflect inspectors' recognition of these leaders' contributions, but ultimately it is the overall judgement that schools have to live with.

The current Ofsted model is viewed as an instrument of surveillance and a disincentive to those drawn to working in inner-city schools, rather than as a source of improvement or development. It has the power to make or destroy a leader's career, with the odds stacked in favour of negative outcomes. A recent Association of School and College Leaders survey reported that 88% of school leaders believed the current inspection system did not report the performance of schools and colleges consistently, fairly and accurately. Only 10% of those surveyed wanted the current graded judgement model to be retained, adding that poor judgements make it all the harder to recruit and retain staff and also impacts on pupil numbers (Bettsworth, 2020). This is a double jeopardy for inner-city schools and contributes to a cycle of poor judgements, which leads to destabilisation, which leads to even worse judgements. Surely, the opposite of a compassionate and constructive education system.

In 2015, I argued to senior Her Majesty's Inspectors (HMIs) that the risks in Birmingham had shifted away from state schools following the changes made to governance in the wake of Trojan Horse. The largest risks could now be found in the twilight zones of elective home education, recently established independent schools, unlawful 'schools' and the unregulated sector, which includes all manner of supplementary educational activities. A specialist HMI team was created to investigate the unlawful 'schools' that purported to provide an education to parents who in many cases had told the local authority that they were home-educating their children. Working in cooperation with the local children's services and the police to gain entry, a number of these establishments were visited. They were often found to be wholly unsafe: adults lacking Disclosure and Barring Service checks and appropriate qualifications; cramped, dangerous and unsanitary accommodation; and impossibly poor teaching (Titheradge, 2018). The inspectors made the right calls and told the proprietors that the Department for Education would be informed of their activities, which were probably illegal, but had no powers to close them. So, the most vulnerable of children continued to be denied a good education and were put at risk of being exposed to teaching that would fail them.

Finally, elective home education has been growing in Birmingham for a number of years, in common with the overall growth in England (Birmingham City Council, 2016). In spite of numbers exceeding 80,000 nationally, with a 38% increase as a result of the pandemic, the Department for Education does not collect data. It relies on local authorities to monitor the position and the Association of Directors of Children's Services to survey the national picture (ADCS, 2020). Reasons for parents choosing to educate their children at home include what are termed philosophical or lifestyle reasons, which include a preference for socially conservative religious norms. The reality is that many of these children in Birmingham are educated in 'tuition centres' – that is, unregistered, illegal schools operating below the council's radar. This is intensively problematic because, whilst local authorities have a duty to establish whether a suitable education is being provided, they do not have a role in monitoring its quality.

There are also high levels of vulnerability in the population, including SEND and safeguarding concerns. The House of Commons Education Committee (2021) recommended that a statutory register is introduced for children out of school as part of a package which includes supporting children with SEND, assessment of what constitutes a 'suitable education', better data on outcomes and fairer access to examinations. All fine recommendations but nothing more than that unless the Department for Education delegates the necessary powers and duties to local authorities and Ofsted.

In summary, the government's default position on inspection is based on a framework predicated on one size fits all, penalises inner-city schools and doesn't attach sufficient importance to the areas of highest risk, including the independent sector, elective home education and unlawful schooling.

6. Customised leadership development programmes: 'my head teacher doesn't look like me'

If schools cannot be the gatekeeper for equity and diversity, then suffer the children. They have no chance to believe in a meritocratic working life.

Kausor Amin-Ali[11]

---

11 Kausor Amin-Ali, FRSA FCCT is a school leader and author, who was reflecting in a speech on the lack of Black, Asian and minority ethnic representation in senior echelons of the English education system.

In Chapter 2, Kamal Hanif described his struggles to be taken seriously as a potential school leader in the early days and the continuing struggles he has endured. In Chapter 15, Rosemary Campbell-Stephens portrayed the damage done to aspiring Asian school leaders through the handling of Trojan Horse. Recent national workforce data reveals that White British people made up 88.6% of nursery and primary school teachers, 82.2% of secondary school teachers and 86.1% of special school teachers. At senior leadership level (head teachers and deputies), there has been an increase in the percentage of White British teachers achieving promotion compared to the total number within the group. At headship level, all Black, Asian and minority ethnic (BAME) groups are significantly under-represented, with the poorest representation amongst Bangladeshi, Black African and Pakistani groups (DfE, 2020a). If faith is combined with ethnicity, then Muslim groups are the least well represented, perhaps reflecting a post-Trojan Horse legacy of the sort that Campbell-Stephens explores.

The Birmingham data in relation to maintained schools is deeply worrying because it reveals the stark disconnect between the city's population and the profile of its education leaders. In 2011, 57.9% of the adult population in Birmingham was White, 26.6% Asian (with Pakistanis being the largest group at 13.5%) and Black people constituted 8.9% (Birmingham City Council, 2013). When we look at school data, we see the changing dynamics within the young population. By 2017, the numbers of eligible pupils for Key Stage 2 results showed that White British children were 31.4% (and any other White background 3%), Pakistani 25%, Black African 7.3% and Bangladeshi 6%. In short, pupils from Global Majority communities constituted over 66% of the Year 6 population according to the 2017 examinations and assessments (Birmingham City Council, 2018a), and school leaders, taking the maintained head teachers as a representative sample, were around 12% (see Table 16.1).

Table 16.1. Leadership data (head teachers, deputies and assistant heads) in Birmingham (not including academies), 2021

	Asian or Asian British	Black or Black British	Mixed	Other	Unknown	White	Grand total
Number	59.75	28.52	8.3	4	131.69	614.45	846.71
Percentage	7	3	1	0.5	16	73	

Source: Birmingham City Council [Freedom of Information request] (2021)

Vieler-Porter (2019) looked at the picture across England, surveying 152 local authorities and interviewing twenty-two leaders from the BAME community. His research (founded in critical race theory) dived into the undercurrents of low expectations, awareness of position, pressures arising from 'the need to be better' and 'third rail' career issues connected with racism, bringing them to the surface. He concluded that none of this was chance or coincidence: the system is designed to perpetuate the hegemony of the White male leader and exclude BAME usurpers.

There can be no doubt that becoming a BAME education leader is an uphill struggle. As Ava Sturridge-Packer, a first-generation Windrush primary head teacher, has said in public on many occasions, she felt the pressure as a representative of the Black community, encountered racist obstacles at every turn and always knew that if she got it wrong there would be no second chance (Staufenberg, 2020). She contrasted this with the seemingly endless ability of some White leaders to airbrush their curriculum vitae after catastrophic episodes of running schools into the buffers. The glass ceiling was invisible yet tangible. The make-up of those mainly White appointment panels meant that, consciously or unconsciously, they veered towards the 'safe' option of the candidate that looked like them. In her early career, this was a professionally nuanced version of the landlord's sign stating 'No Blacks'.

Talent management and career progression for BAME leaders in urban schools, where their position as role models has enormous impact on pupils' aspirations, has been largely ignored by successive governments in England in this century. The latest Wallace Foundation research from the United States reinforces our knowledge of the impact that effective principals have on student learning and recognises the additional payoff that BAME leaders have for both students and staff as representatives of their communities (Grissom et al., 2021). Principals were found to have substantially large effects way beyond achievement in the student population, notably in reducing absence and exclusions, and in motivating staff to perform better and stay longer in their schools. Diversity amongst the principal population was reported to be growing, but was being outpaced by changes within the student population – exactly the same position as in Birmingham and England overall.

As a White ally, I have been privileged to work with the BAME Headteachers and Senior Leaders Forum in Birmingham, the first organisation that the Education Leadership Academy partnered with in 2018. The forum provides a safe and supportive space for aspiring and established leaders to work together via networking, meetings and residentials. Its anteced- ents lay in many similar projects launched by the city council that had prospered temporarily, benefited a generation of new leaders and then floundered in the wake of anodyne national education policy and a reduc- tion in the local authority's education resources.

There is little research into the impact of such initiatives over time. However, empirically we can see that the lived experience of BAME leaders raises many questions about lack of penetration into the highest levels of leadership and the perception that only the toughest and most resilient make it through in a world where White people hold the high cards (see Miller and Callender, 2019). It is time for those programmes that aim to encourage, develop and deliver a larger generation of BAME education leaders to be mainstreamed. For years they have relied on piecemeal and poorly funded initiatives which have lacked sustainability. Policy has been wilfully blind to any recognition of representational inter- sectionality, failing to see the way in which BAME leadership has often been stereotyped and marginalised for convenience rather than studying the facts. The longer many children can say 'my head teacher doesn't look like me', the poorer the chances that they will themselves be the education leaders of the future.

*

In conclusion, over 100 years ago, Dewey identified that you cannot be sure of the purpose of education until you have understood the nature of society that is sought by the state. Since the 1980s, successive gov- ernments have recognised that the quality of education in English cities was not good enough and many schools would not pass that most basic of tests: would you send your own children there? However, few govern- ments have sought policy rooted in the evidence of what really works over time. When Estelle Morris announced the headlines of the London Challenge in 2002, it marked a radical shift. She brought together a team that had experience of successfully implementing school improvement at scale, gave them the time to create an effective operating model and provided significant resources (Kidson and Norris, 2011). It worked.

I attended a Department for Education conference for senior civil serv- ants in 2011. Jon Coles, the department's original lead official and by then director general for schools and education standards, shared with us the impact of the London Challenge – an impressive tour de force. It was axed that same year by Michael Gove, and the policy lessons were consigned to filing cabinets in Sanctuary Buildings.

References

Adams, Richard and Belger, Tom (2014) David Blunkett Attacks 'Nonsense' Oversight System for Academies, *The Guardian* (2 July). Available at: https://www.theguardian.com/education/2014/jul/02/david-blunkett-oversight-academies-schools.

Association of Directors of Children's Services (ADCS) (2020) *Elective Home Education Survey 2020* (November). Available at: https://adcs.org.uk/assets/documentation/ADCS_EHE_Survey_2020_FINALweb.pdf.

Ball, Stephen (2018) The Tragedy of State Education in England: Reluctance, Compromise and Muddle – A System in Disarray, *Journal of the British Academy*, 6: 207–238. Available at: https://doi.org/10.5871/jba/006.207.

BBC News (2010) Regional Government Offices Face Axe (22 July). Available at: https://www.bbc.co.uk/news/uk-politics-10728140.

Bettsworth, Richard (2020) Improving Ofsted Inspections: Results of a Survey Conducted by the Association of School and College Leaders [press release] (March). Available at: https://www.ascl.org.uk/ASCL/media/ASCL/News/Press%20releases/Ofsted-survey-analysis-March-2020.pdf.

Birmingham City Council (2013) *2011 Census: Birmingham Population and Migration Topic Report* (October). Available at: https://www.birmingham.gov.uk/downloads/file/9742/2011_birmingham_population_and_migration_topic_report.

Birmingham City Council (2016) *Report to the Education and Vulnerable Children Overview and Scrutiny Committee* (January). Available at: https://birmingham.cmis.uk.com/Birmingham/Document.ashx?czJKcaeAi5tUFL1DTL2UE4zNRBcoShgo=SgUIin EO3fxHprm19qe4uAuclvp4luDvyydlWi9z4WqXCViz0osG9w%3D%3D&rUzwRPf%2BZ3 zd4E7Ikn8Lyw%3D%3D=pwRE6AGJFLDNlh225F5QMaQWCtPHwdhUfCZ%2FLUQzgA2 uL5jNRG4jdQ%3D%3D&mCTIbCubSFf.

Birmingham City Council (2018a) *Annual Education Performance Report: 2017 Examinations and Assessments* (March). Available at: https://www.birmingham.gov.uk/downloads/file/6318/annual_education_performance_report_2017.

Birmingham City Council (2018b) *We're All Different But Equal: An Equality, Diversity and Cohesion Framework for Schools in Birmingham*. Available at: https://www.birmingham.gov.uk/downloads/download/2226/equalities_and_cohesion_toolkit_all_equal_all_different.

Birmingham City Council (2019a) Educational Outcome Dashboards: Birmingham and Constituency Level. 2018 Examinations and Assessments (Revised) (March). Available at: https://tinyurl.com/5aw8pw5e.

Birmingham City Council (2019b) Noticeboard (15 February). Available at: https://www.birmingham.gov.uk/blog/school-nb/post/151/15-february-2019/#UNICEF.

Birmingham City Council (2020) *The Birmingham Approach to Relationships and Health Education in Primary Schools*. Available at: https://www.birmingham.gov.uk/downloads/file/16430/rshe_primary_schools.

Brighouse, Tim (2019) The English Schooling System – Yesterday, Today But Especially Tomorrow: A Baker's Dozen of Essential Changes Towards a Fairer Deal for Everyone. The Priestley Lecture. Delivered at the University of Birmingham, 26 June. Available at: https://www.oxfordschoolofthought.org/blog/strongthe-english-schooling-system-yesterday-today-but-especially-tomorrowstrong#sdfootnote1anc.

Brighouse, Tim and Woods, David (2008) *What Makes a Good School Now?* London: Bloomsbury Education.

Brighouse, Tim and Woods, David (2013) *The A–Z of School Improvement: Principles and Practice*. London: Bloomsbury Education.

Buckingham, David (2020) The Curriculum of Brexit: Culture, Education and Power the Michaela Way [blog] (12 December). Available at: https://davidbuckingham.net/2020/12/12/the-curriculum-of-brexit-culture-education-and-power-the-michaela-way.

Carr, Flora (2018) What It's Like to Study at the Strictest School in Britain, *TIME* (20 April). Available at: https://time.com/5232857/michaela-britains-strictest-school.

Carr, James (2021a) Speed Read: Williamson's 7 Policies to Revive the Academies Drive, *Schools Week* (28 April). Available at: https://schoolsweek.co.uk/speed-read-williamsons-7-policies-to-revive-the-academies-drive.

Carr, James (2021b) Spielman: It's Not Unfair Deprived Schools Get Lower Grades, *Schools Week* (25 June). Available at: https://schoolsweek.co.uk/spielman-its-not-unfair-deprived-schools-get-lower-grades.

Collins, Clare; Henson, Sam; and Knights, Emma (2021) *MATs Moving Forward: The Power of Governance* (March). Birmingham: National Governance Association. Available at: https://www.nga.org.uk/getmedia/e32677ee-ce8d-49b8-bc68-356073ea5913/Moving-MATs-30pp-Report-(March-2021)-AW.pdf.

Creedon, Dennis W. (2011) Fight the Stress of Urban Education with the ARTS, *Phi Delta Kappan*, 92(6): 34–36. DOI:10.1177/003172171109200607.

Cruddas, Leora (2019) Academisation: It's Time for the Final Stage of Reform, *TES* (14 May). Available at: https://www.tes.com/magazine/archive/academisation-its-time-final-stage-reform.

Department for Education (DfE) (2014) The Education Services Grant: Statement of Final Arrangements for 2015 to 2016 (July). Available at: https://www.gov.uk/government/publications/education-services-grant-2015-to-2016.

Department for Education (DfE) (2019) Guidance: English Baccalaureate (EBacc) (updated 20 August). Available at: https://www.gov.uk/government/publications/english-baccalaureate-ebacc/english-baccalaureate-ebacc.

Department for Education (DfE) (2020a) National Statistics: School Workforce in England: November 2019. Available at: https://www.gov.uk/government/statistics/school-workforce-in-england-november-2019.

Department for Education (DfE) (2020b) Schools Causing Concern: Guidance for Local Authorities and Regional Schools Commissioners on How to Work with Schools to Support Improvements to Educational Performance, and on Using Their Intervention Powers (September). Available at: https://www.gov.uk/government/publications/schools-causing-concern--2.

Dewey, John (1916) *Democracy and Education: An Introduction to the Philosophy of Education*. New York: Macmillan.

Diamond, Colin (2019) There Is a Way Out of the Schools LGBT Protest Mess – But Ministers Need to Get Behind It, *The Guardian* (6 August). Available at: https://www.theguardian.com/education/2019/aug/06/way-out-of-schools-protest-mess-birmingham-trojan-horse.

Dickens, John (2019) Failing Academies 'Left in Limbo' as Lack of Sponsors Causes 'Bottleneck', *Schools Week* (8 November). Available at: https://schoolsweek.co.uk/failing-academies-left-in-limbo-as-lack-of-sponsors-causes-bottleneck.

Earley, Peter, and Greany, Toby (eds) (2017) *School Leadership and Education System Reform*. London: Bloomsbury Academic.

Gove, Michael (2009) A Comprehensive Programme for State Education [speech] (6 November). Available at: https://conservative-speeches.sayit.mysociety.org/speech/601248.

Greany, Toby (2020) Place-Based Governance and Leadership in Decentralised School Systems: Evidence from England, *Journal of Education Policy*, 37(2): 247–268. Available at: https://doi.org/10.1080/02680939.2020.1792554.

Grissom, Jason; Egalite, Anna; and Lindsay, Constance (2021) *How Principals Affect Students and Schools: A Systematic Synthesis of Two Decades of Research*. New York: Wallace Foundation. Available at: http://www.wallacefoundation.org/principalsynthesis.

Hampshire, Katherine and Matthijsse, Mathilde (2010) Can Arts Projects Improve Young People's Wellbeing? A Social Capital Approach, *Social Science & Medicine*, 71(4): 708–716. DOI:10.1016/j.socscimed.2010.05.015.

Hargreaves, David H. (1982) *Challenge for the Comprehensive School: Culture, Curriculum and Community*. London: Routledge & Kegan Paul.

Hayek, Friedrich A. von (1986) *The Road to Serfdom*. London: Ark Paperbacks.

HM Government (2021) Academic Year 2020/21: Schools, Pupils and their Characteristics. Available at: https://explore-education-statistics.service.gov.uk/find-statistics/school-pupils-and-their-characteristics.

HM Government (2022) *Opportunity for All: Strong Schools with Great Teachers for Your Child* [White Paper] (March). Available at: https://assets.publishing.service.gov.uk/government/uploads/system/uploads/attachment_data/file/1063602/Opportunity_for_all_strong_schools_with_great_teachers_for_your_child__print_version_.pdf.

House of Commons Education Committee (2016) *The Role of Regional Schools Commissioners: First Report of Session 2015–16* (HC 401). Available at: https://publications.parliament.uk/pa/cm201516/cmselect/cmeduc/401/401.pdf.

House of Commons Education Committee (2021) *Strengthening Home Education: Third Report of Session 2021–22* (HC 84). Available at: https://committees.parliament.uk/publications/6974/documents/72808/default.

Hutchinson, Jo (2016) *School Inspection in England: Is There Room to Improve?* London: Education Policy Institute. Available at: https://epi.org.uk/wp-content/uploads/2018/01/school-inspection-in-england-web.pdf.

Kershaw, Ian (2014) *Investigation Report: Trojan Horse Letter* [Kershaw Report]. Available at: https://www.birmingham.gov.uk/downloads/file/1579/investigation_report_trojan_horse_letter_the_kershaw_report.

Kidson, Marc and Norris, Emma (2011) *Implementing the London Challenge*. London: Institute for Government. Available at: https://www.instituteforgovernment.org.uk/sites/default/files/publications/Implementing%20the%20London%20Challenge%20-%20final_0.pdf.

Miller, Paul and Callender, Christine (eds) (2019) *Race, Education and Educational Leadership in England: An Integrated Analysis*. London: Bloomsbury Academic.

Munby, Steve and Fullan, Michael (2016) *Inside-Out and Downside-Up: How Leading from the Middle Has the Power to Transform Education Systems. A Think/Action Piece*. Reading: Education Development Trust. Available at: https://www.educationdevelopmenttrust.com/EducationDevelopmentTrust/files/51/51251173-e25d-4b34-80ae-033fcd7685ab.pdf.

Ofsted (2019) School Report: Harper Bell Seventh-Day Adventist School (16–17 July). Available at: https://files.ofsted.gov.uk/v1/file/50109590.

Ofsted (2002) Inspection of Birmingham Local Authority (April). Available at: https://files.ofsted.gov.uk/v1/file/50003646.

Richmond, Tom (2019) *Trust Issues: How to Bring Academies and Maintained Schools into a Unified State School System*. London: EDSK. Available at: https://www.edsk.org/wp-content/uploads/2019/09/Trust-issues.pdf.

Roberts, John (2020) Liam Nolan Barred from Running Academies, *TES* (7 September). Available at: https://www.tes.com/news/liam-nolan-barred-running-academies.

Sam, Cecile H. (2020) What Are the Practices of Unethical Leaders? Exploring How Teachers Experience the 'Dark Side' of Administrative Leadership, *Educational Management Administration & Leadership*, 49(2): 303–320. DOI:10.1177/1741143219898480.

Staufenberg, Jess (2020) Profile: Ava Sturridge-Packer, *Schools Week* (21 January). Available at: https://schoolsweek.co.uk/profile-ava-sturridge-packer.

Starkey-Midha, George (2020) *Building a Fairer Future: Tackling the Attainment Gap in GCSE English and Maths*. London: Teach First. Available at: https://www.teachfirst.org.uk/sites/default/files/2020-08/GCSE%20report%20-%20Building%20a%20fairer%20future..pdf.

Teplin, Linda; Abram, Karen; McClelland, Gary; Dulcan, Mina; and Mericle, Amy (2002) Psychiatric Disorders in Youth in Juvenile Detention, *Archives of General Psychiatry*, 59(2): 1133–1143. DOI:10.1001/archpsyc.59.12.1133.

Thomson, Pat (2020) *School Scandals: Blowing the Whistle on the Corruption of Our Education System*. Bristol: Policy Press.

Titheradge, Noel (2018) Is There a Problem with Unregistered Schools?, *BBC News* (27 February). Available at: https://www.bbc.co.uk/news/education-43170447.amp.

United Nations Children's Fund (UNICEF) (1989) *The United Nations Convention on the Rights of the Child*. Available at: https://downloads.unicef.org.uk/wp-content/uploads/2016/08/unicef-convention-rights-child-uncrc.pdf.

United Nations Children's Fund (UNICEF) (2020) *RRSA Impact: The Evidence. Our Theory of Change.* Available at: https://www.unicef.org.uk/rights-respecting-schools/wp-content/uploads/sites/4/2020/11/RRSA_Evidence-Report_Nov-2020v2.pdf.

United Nations Children's Fund (UNICEF) (2021) *Annual Report 2020: Turning Research into Action for Children and Young People*. Florence: UNICEF Office of Research – Innocenti. Available at: https://www.unicef-irc.org/publications/1198-annual-report-2020.html.

Vieler-Porter, Christopher G. (2019) The Underrepresentation of Black and Minority Ethnic People in the Leadership of Children's Learning: Chance, Coincidence or Design? Unpublished PhD thesis, University of Birmingham. Available at: https://etheses.bham.ac.uk/id/eprint/9643/7/VielerPorter2019PhD.pdf.

Weale, Sally (2021) Schools Minister Rebuffs Calls to Decolonise English Curriculum, *The Guardian* (21 July). Available at: https://www.theguardian.com/education/2021/jul/21/schools-minister-rebuffs-calls-to-decolonise-english-curriculum.

Woods, David (2020) Lessons from 'The London Challenge': A Whole-System Approach to Leadership Development. In Emil Jackson and Andrea Berkeley (eds), *Sustaining Depth and Meaning in School Leadership: Keeping Your Head*, 1st edn. Abingdon and New York: Routledge, pp. 267–284.

Final thoughts

The Moving Finger writes; and having writ,
Moves on: nor all thy Piety nor Wit
Shall lure it back to cancel half a Line,
Nor all thy Tears wash out a Word of it.

Rubáiyát of Omar Khayyám (1859)

The author (or perhaps authors) of the Trojan Horse letter unleashed a chain reaction that had consequences way beyond the backstreets of East Birmingham. Events unfolded rapidly in 2014. Twenty-one schools were inspected and five – including the much celebrated Park View Academy – were judged to require special measures with new governance and leadership mandated. Two major investigations into Trojan Horse were commissioned with the Clarke and Kershaw reports published in July. A commissioner was appointed by the secretary of state for education to oversee the city council's improvement plans. The leader of council, Sir Albert Bore, apologised in public for letting Trojan Horse activities go on for so long in the city for fear of being branded racist (Elkes, 2014). National media whipped up an Islamophobic feeding frenzy and the term 'extremism' was used to loosely describe anything 'Muslim' in Birmingham's schools.

In 2015, the Counter-Terrorism and Security Act, drafted in the wake of Trojan Horse, introduced the duty for all schools to have 'due regard to the need to prevent people from being drawn into terrorism'.[1] The subjective term 'non-violent extremism' was promoted in the lexicon and became another shorthand description for any so-called intolerant educational activities. Internationally, a Fox News commentator decreed that Birmingham was a city where 'non-Muslims just simply don't go', to both the amusement and consternation of its inhabitants (Sehmer, 2015). Was this what the author(s) hoped for?

What were the long-term consequences? As Arthur (2015, pp. 1–2) describes, national education policy had deliberately weakened 'the

---

1   See https://www.legislation.gov.uk/ukpga/2015/6/section/26/enacted.

power of local authorities in favour of the de-regulation of schools together with unintentionally encouraging culturally conservative Muslim leaders with entrepreneurial values effectively to run public schools as private institutions ... these policies have contributed much to the mal-practice found and to the suspicions of "extremism" attributed to the governor leaders of these schools by the press and others.' Government policy had skirted around the interrelationship between its custodianship of academy schools – now under the direct control of the secretary of state – and critical intersectional factors, including faith, collective wor-ship, the curriculum and gender. The pace of academisation required by ministers necessitated the airbrushing out of any complications, and gov-ernment officials had no appetite to probe deeply into the credentials of those seeking to set up vanguard multi-academy trusts, especially in Labour-run cities. 'Due diligence' was rushed through with devastating consequences.

When things unravelled so spectacularly in Birmingham, Ofsted inspectors were only able to work within the parameters of the inspection frame-work. Serious failings in safeguarding, governance and leadership were found and rightly called out. However, Ofsted's modus operandi inevita-bly left others to pick up the pieces. The headlines from both Clarke and Kershaw, that no evidence was found of radicalisation or terrorism, did not calm the waters. As the heavy lifting to make Birmingham's education department fit for purpose once again began, it needed to find new ways of building resilience and trust with schools amidst the chaos.

What could Muslim communities hope for? Education leaders now found it hard to recruit in Muslim-majority schools, Muslims were reluctant to put themselves forward as school governors for fear of being branded as extremists with a Trojan Horse agenda, and, as Adrian Packer observed in Chapter 7, pupils demanded to know why nobody had consulted them about anything. With Birmingham's Muslim population growing rapidly, what was needed were local and national policies that explicitly aimed to tackle what could become irreconcilable differences between communi-ties, not the further ramping up of hostility and suspicion.

It can be argued that there is no rational consensus here because the starting points, political principles and cultural norms within the city would never find universal endorsement (Crowder, 2006). Agonistic pluralism would persist because no amount of deliberation or political process would bind everyone together. How can such differences be harnessed productively? How can we foster resilience in schools (and between school and home) where there are few absolutes and much ambiguity around the interface between culture, faith and education? Did Trojan Horse signify the fissuring of a shallow consensus and point to stresses that will always exist below the surface?

There are longstanding tensions between elements of all faith communities, and in national education policy, but nothing has erupted so spectacularly as Trojan Horse, which led directly to the introduction of anti-terrorist primary legislation. Her Majesty's Chief Inspector had never previously embarked on a narrative about the risks of premature sexualisation as a result of girls in primary schools wearing headscarves until Amanda Spielman controversially weighed in on the subject in 2017 (Adams, 2017a). Celebrated ultra-orthodox Jewish state schools had educated boys and girls separately with no criticism from Ofsted for years, until a state school operating identically in Birmingham, Al-Hijrah, was found guilty of unlawful sex discrimination by the Court of Appeal following an Ofsted inspection that placed it in special measures (Ofsted, 2017).

Such actions from the regulator, inspectorate and judiciary towards Muslims in Birmingham continued to set back progress from the necessary investigations and interventions in 2014. Trojan Horse activities, catalogued so clearly in the Kershaw Report, needed to stop with immediate effect. However, the sense of injustice amongst Muslim communities was exacerbated by the chain reaction to Trojan Horse and the perception of irrationality and disproportionality. Unsurprisingly, many Muslim school leaders felt insecure and demonstrated their support for fundamental British values lest Ofsted found them wanting. In 2017, the National College for Teaching and Leadership's poorly managed attempts to ban five senior leaders from Park View Educational Trust collapsed amidst recriminations from all sides, amplifying feelings of injustice from within the Muslim community (Adams, 2017b).

*

In 2018, I delivered the annual Priestley Lecture at the University of Birmingham. I guess it was my informal job interview ahead of taking up post as chair of educational leadership later that year. It was entitled 'Why Authentic Education Leadership is Needed More Than Ever: The Counterweight to Populism and Extremism'. The headwind of austerity was hitting the city's schools hard: their own spending power was declining and child poverty was growing around them. The side-winds of government education policy were also working against those serving the most challenged and cash-poor communities. The combination of traditional exams, the English Baccalaureate (EBacc), a zero-tolerance behaviour culture and Ofsted's inspection framework were driving schools towards a central government defined managerialist culture. Extremist views were proliferating, with dog-whistle racist politics just beneath the surface of Brexit, the Windrush scandal and the heinous 'Punish a Muslim Day', which generated fear in the city's children (Perraudin, 2018). The job of urban school leaders was being made harder. It had been heading that way for some years:

> In a bygone, deferential age when urban schools knew their place, they turned out hundreds of thousands of young people prepared to make a career in one of the plentiful supply of unskilled and semi-skilled jobs. In those days, the role of headteacher was an easier one than it is today. (Brighouse, 2009, p. 1)

The economic insecurities of a post-industrial society have invalidated many assumptions about the role of schools in preparing young people for adult life. From the early 1980s, when Birmingham lost over 200,000 manufacturing jobs, unemployment and shifting patterns of underemployment reduced certainty and belonging. In communities like Longbridge, former home to the Austin Rover car plant where most school-leavers found employment, what future were schools educating their pupils for? In some parts of the south end of the city there is now third-generation unemployment, with the local economy never having fully recovered from the manufacturing losses. The differences in attainment across the city are stark. In 2018, 31% of pupils in the Longbridge and West Heath ward achieved strong GCSE (grade 9–5) passes in English and maths. Just three miles up the road in relatively affluent Edgbaston ward, the equivalent figure is 74% (Birmingham City Council, 2019).

School attainment data analysed by Tom Perry in Chapter 4 reinforce the link between pupils' socio-economic position and their educational outcomes in Birmingham and nationally: overall, pupils entitled to free school meals have poor attainment from Key Stage 1–4. However, migration into Birmingham has complicated the picture with some ethnic groups thriving whilst others are making slow progress or flatlining. There are distinct profiles for the educational performance of major ethnic groups from across the age range which closely mirror national data. Within those groups, and crucial to our understanding of the background to Trojan Horse, pupils from Pakistani backgrounds show relative improvement, albeit from a low starting point. Progress is evident, although lagging behind, in pupils from Bangladeshi backgrounds, which is outstripping those from Black Caribbean backgrounds. Digging further into the data exposes large differences within constituencies, wards, schools and ethnic groups. The data beg questions that need further research to understand and address. Why, for example, are Black African pupils in Birmingham behind their peers elsewhere? What lies behind the lack in Birmingham of the English as an additional language bonus at Key Stage 4 in the EBacc results we see elsewhere? What are the determinants of the low relative performance of Black Caribbean pupils, and what can be done about it?

In Birmingham's rust belt on the edges of the city where the major manufacturing has long gone, the education data reveals low progress and attainment from predominantly White working-class young people. King Edward's School had a long and proud history of attracting working-class pupils from the south end of the city who have gone on to study at Oxford and Cambridge via the direct grant grammar school route. John Claughton, former chief master, recalled how in the 1970s, even though Birmingham already had a multiracial community, very few Black, Asian and minority ethnic (BAME) pupils gained admission. Now, 90% of applications for the assisted places scheme are from BAME families (many of whom engage private tutors for their children) and virtually none are from White families in Longbridge, which is a few bus stops away. King Edward's has invested heavily in outreach programmes, harnessed aspiration where it was to be found in abundance and worked extra hard in the predominantly White wards to the south and west of the school. The challenge of rekindling education aspiration in former manufacturing communities is as urgent for social cohesion as the work needed within some sections of the BAME community.

In the Priestley Lecture, I spoke of authentic education leadership founded in ethics, service and compassion. It is a leadership rooted in community that looks outwards beyond a reductionist, 'expert' model. Authentic leadership is inclusive of all adults, children and young people in a way that transcends legal definitions and goes far beyond special educational needs and disabilities. It understands that there is a wide range of pedagogies and develops and empowers teachers with agency and professional inquisitiveness. Responsibility is distributed widely.

Such leaders are humble, readily acknowledge their imperfections, seek mentors and coaches, and populate senior teams with colleagues who are better than them. Authentic leadership is resilient and sustainable because of all of these factors. The leaders who were brave enough to write about their own journeys in this book embody many of these characteristics, and their schools bear witness to their effectiveness. It is possible to have high-achieving schools based on a positive culture that stems from ethical, inclusive and moral leadership.

The quest for leadership that asks 'what matters?' before 'what works?' continues. In 2017, the Association of School and College Leaders announced a commission on ethical leadership, reflecting the pressures on leaders and the ever-present need for a moral compass (ASCL, 2019). Since 2018, the National Governance Association's Framework for Ethical Leadership has found strong support in the profession. In the pithy words of Paul Whitehouse, general secretary of the school leaders' union NAHT, 'School leadership is an ethical business. The desire to act first and foremost in the best interests of the whole school community is the base code of a school leader's DNA' (NGA, 2021). Maurice Waters (2020, p. 27) described the characteristics of a compassionate education leader in *Education for Survival: The Pedagogy of Compassion*, drawing on international evidence from New Zealand, Costa Rica and Wales to demonstrate that there is no immutable link between the principles of commerce and education. Education systems can and do perform well beyond the distortions imposed by all-pervasive inspection systems and league tables that ought to have stayed in the sporting arena.

As Andy Hargreaves (2019, p. 17) writes, ethical leadership requires courage and 'fighting for a positive educational and ethical environment together that removes ethical dilemmas between serving the child and complying with the system'. Herminder Channa's values-based leadership of the former Golden Hillock School (renamed as Ark Boulton Academy in 2015) is a powerful case study that demonstrates just what is possible by 'treating students with love and their families with respect', as the antidote to governors' and senior leaders' attempts to 'impose the dictates of a hardline and politicised strand of Sunni Islam' (Lightfoot, 2020). Channa is explicit: 'Teachers at Ark Boulton care with compassion, listen with love and help with humility.' She rejected a zero-tolerance approach to discipline because it was unnecessary and unhelpful. The results speak for themselves: this once struggling school is now heavily oversubscribed and firing on all fronts.

*

The headwinds and side-winds that were buffeting schools in 2018 have been supplemented by even greater challenges in the form of COVID-19, Black Lives Matter and the climate emergency — all events with global reach and consequences that have polarised educational opinion. The English policy response reflects its ideological position that a traditional education system, with recognisable subjects taught well and tested via sit-down exams, is wholly fit for purpose and, apart from the rapid move to online learning and teaching, nothing really needs to change. This position has many supporters who have become senior professionals during this era and have much invested in its continuation. However, there are growing numbers who question this approach. As the founders of School 21 observe, there is 'a shared belief that education must be done differently if we are to prepare young people properly for the world they are going into'.[2] Rehashing a twentieth-century education model with antecedents visible from the nineteenth is surely not appropriate any longer. But it takes courage to innovate in the current policy environment because the pressures and elephant traps in the English system are immense.

The mission of Big Education, where Peter Hyman is co-director, is explicit about bringing together those 'who know there is something wrong with our education system. And want to help to put it right. In place of a narrow, exam-focused system we want something that is more expansive. In place of massive inequalities, we want a system that nurtures the potential of every child from every background.'[3] Meena Kumari Wood and Nick Haddon's Secondary Curriculum Transformed: Enabling All to Achieve (2020) is a fine example of transforming these aims into practice as it is centred on extensive school-based research and evidence. It argues for a new blend of skills, subjects and assessment tools which will reduce the high level of marginalisation experienced by so many young people. A system designed to fail around a third of secondary pupils has built-in wastage that would never be tolerated in any other serious industry. Urban school leaders and governors in Birmingham and other cities are all too familiar with this inbuilt tension.

---

2   See https://www.school21.org.uk/our-story.
3   See https://bigeducation.org.

Urban education leadership has been an undervalued and under-researched domain in England in recent years. Contrast this with the picture in Australia, Canada, Europe and the United States where urban education centres prosper in universities because the importance of understanding and improving cities' schools is a central platform. I hope this book will act as a catalyst to generate more interest and research into what really works best and how to develop the next generation of leaders. As the Wallace Foundation research (Grissom et al., 2021) reminds us, the impact of those leaders goes way beyond conventional metrics. They galvanise special achievements by harnessing the social and education capital within their communities. The Education Leadership Academy at the University of Birmingham, with its fellows of practice, will ensure that urban education remains at the heart of our teaching and research.

And finally ...

When I was director of education, I had the honour of being asked to attend many prize-giving celebrations in Birmingham. One evening stays with me. At Bordersley Green Girls' School, which has a mainly Muslim pupil population, almost 85% of whom have English as an additional language, the former Year 13 pupils returned in numbers to hear their commendations read out and receive their prizes in a hall packed with family members. Many of them had already taken up university places across a range of subjects. In medicine and healthcare, we had undergraduate doctors, pharmacists, nurses and therapists who would go on to make up the backbone of the NHS. We had good numbers of young women studying science, technology, engineering and mathematics. Almost all of their grandparents, and many of their parents, had not taken any qualifications at school. None of their grandmothers and mothers had the opportunity to study at A level and go to university. The family pride was enormous. Traditions were being challenged and glass ceilings broken. The experience of the young women at Bordersley Green exemplifies what is good about education in inner-city Birmingham. They are the role models for the next generation of British Asian women, showing what is possible through study irrespective of background. Long may that continue.

References

Adams, Richard (2017a) Inspectors to Question Primary School Girls Who Wear Hijab, *The Guardian* (19 November). Available at: https://www.theguardian.com/education/2017/nov/19/school-inspectors-to-question-primary-school-girls-who-wear-hijab.

Adams, Richard (2017b) Trojan Horse Affair: Remaining Disciplinary Proceedings Dropped, *The Guardian* (28 July). Available at: http://www.theguardian.com/education/2017/jul/28/trojan-horse-affair-remaining-disciplinary-proceedings-dropped-teachers-birmingham-schools.

Arthur, James (2015) Extremism and Neo-Liberal Education Policy: A Contextual Critique of the Trojan Horse Affair in Birmingham Schools, *British Journal of Educational Studies*, 63(3): 311–328. DOI:10.1080/00071005.2015.1069258.

Association of School and College Leaders (ASCL) (2019) *Navigating the Educational Moral Maze: The Final Report of the Ethical Leadership Commission*. Available at: https://www.ascl.org.uk/ASCL/media/ASCL/Our%20view/Campaigns/Navigating-the-educational-moral-maze.pdf.

Birmingham City Council (2019) Educational Outcome Dashboards: Birmingham and Constituency Level. 2018 Examinations and Assessments (Revised) (March). Available at: https://tinyurl.com/5aw8pw5e.

Brighouse, Tim (2009) Foreword. In *National College for School Leadership, A Model of School Leadership in Challenging Urban Environments*. Available at: https://dera.ioe.ac.uk/5276/7/download_id%3D17300%26filename%3Dmodel-of-school-leadership-in-challenging-urban-environments_Redacted.pdf.

Clarke, Peter (2014) *Report into Allegations Concerning Birmingham Schools Arising from the 'Trojan Horse' Letter* (HC 576). Available at: https://assets.publishing.service.gov.uk/government/uploads/system/uploads/attachment_data/file/340526/HC_576_accessible_-.pdf.

Crowder, George (2006) Chantal Mouffe's Agonistic Democracy. Paper presented to the Australasian Political Studies Association conference, University of Newcastle, 25–27 September. Available at: http://blog.ub.ac.id/irfan11/files/2013/02/Chantal-Mouffes-Agonistic-Democracy-oleh-George-Crowder.pdf.

Diamond, Colin (2018) Why Authentic Education Leadership is Needed More Than Ever: The Counterweight to Populism and Extremism. The Priestley Lecture. Delivered at the University of Birmingham, 25 April.

Elkes, Neil (2014) 'We're Sorry' Council Leader Admits Staff Ignored Trojan Horse Issue for 'Fear of Being Accused of Racism', *Birmingham Mail* (18 June). Available at: https://www.birminghammail.co.uk/news/midlands-news/birmingham-mail-trojan-horse-investigation-7456936.

Hargreaves, Andy (2019) Leadership Ethics, Inequality and Identity, *Principal Connections*, 23(1): 14–17. Available at: http://www.andyhargreaves.com/uploads/5/2/9/2/5292616/andy_hargreaves_pdf__4_.pdf.

Kershaw, Ian (2014) *Investigation Report: Trojan Horse Letter* [Kershaw Report]. Available at: https://www.birmingham.gov.uk/downloads/file/1579/ investigation_report_trojan_horse_letter_the_kershaw_report.

Khayyám, Omar (1859) *Rubáiyát of Omar Khayyám*, tr. Edward FitzGerald. London: Bernard Quaritch. Available at: https://www.gutenberg.org/files/246/246.txt.

Lightfoot, Liz (2020) Headteacher Who Healed a Birmingham 'Trojan Horse' School: 'We Did It with Love', *The Guardian* (24 October). Available at: https://www.theguardian.com/education/2020/oct/24/ headteacher-who-healed-a-birmingham-trojan-horse-school-we-did-it-with-love.

National Governance Association (NGA) (2021) Sector Leaders Respond to Framework for Ethical Leadership in Education Report [press release] (11 February). Available at: https://www.nga.org.uk/News/NGA-News/February-2021/Sector-leaders-respond-to-Framework-for-Ethical-Le.aspx.

Ofsted (2017) School Report: Al-Hijrah School (28–29 March). Available at: https:// files.ofsted.gov.uk/v1/file/2684137.

Perraudin, Frances (2018) UK Charity Urges Vigilance After 'Punish a Muslim Day' Letters, *The Guardian* (11 March). Available at: https://www.theguardian.com/ uk-news/2018/mar/11/uk-charity-urges-vigilance-after-punish-a-muslim-day-letters.

Sehmer, Alexander (2015) Fox News 'Birmingham is No-Go Zone for Non-Muslims' Comment Found in Violation of Broadcasting Code, *The Independent* (21 September). Available at: https://www.independent.co.uk/news/uk/home-news/ fox-news-birmingham-is-a-nogo-zone-for-nonmuslims-comment-found-in-violation-of-broadcasting-code-10510953.html.

Waters, Mick. (2020) Towards a Compassionate School System. In Maurice I. Coles with Bill Gent (eds), *Education for Survival: The Pedagogy of Compassion*. London: University College London Institute of Education Press, pp. 27–43.

Wood, Meena K. and Haddon, Nick (2020) *Secondary Curriculum Transformed: Enabling All to Achieve*. Abingdon and New York: Routledge.

Postscript 2021

When we met in Imran's Restaurant on Ladypool Road to plan this book in 2019, little could we imagine what was about to befall the world. Black Swan events – those that impact catastrophically on all aspects of society – are, by definition, rare. The world is experiencing two of them right now in the shape of a pandemic and the climate emergency, as well as the fall-out of the murder of George Floyd, which led directly to the Black Lives Matter movement, jaggedly refocusing attention on institutional racism. With geopolitics remaining so profoundly unequal, the impact of such events will always hit the poorest and most vulnerable communities the hardest.

England locked down late, which resulted in many thousands of avoidable deaths. Inner-city communities were disproportionately affected. David Miliband (2020) has called it 'the age of impunity'. No matter how badly senior politicians performed in England, they appeared untouchable. The secretary of state for education, recently knighted and now Sir Gavin Williamson, generated derision from education leaders when he threatened schools with legal action as they sought to keep everyone safe in December 2020, weeks ahead of a coherent national lockdown policy. School leaders have described the 2020/2021 academic year as the most stressful ever, with the number one stressor, extraordinarily, the Department for Education. The social contract between school leaders and the state was wilfully abused and there are no immediate signs of trust being rebuilt (Thompson, 2021).

However, the Department for Education was catapulted into the digital age by COVID-19 and the necessity to take online learning seriously. The hackneyed obsessions with Latin as the breakthrough language for the twenty-first century and proscribing the use of mobile phones anywhere near a school building were temporarily laid aside as Williamson invested £300,000 to pump-prime Oak National Academy in April 2020 (Diamond, 2020). Prior to the pandemic just a handful of officials were working on digital education; suddenly it became the number one priority. Within weeks, the Oak initiative had taken off, produced by teachers for teachers, with thousands of online lessons available. It has prospered subsequently, and could become the digital backbone of a national curriculum if education policy continues in the direction of one size fits all.

Schools rapidly adapted to the COVID-19 environment, staying open throughout the early stages for the children of key workers. Since then they have responded brilliantly to closures, bubbles, medical testing, online learning and assessing pupils in lieu of examinations. Ela McSorley, principal of Ark Victoria Academy in Small Heath, told a university seminar how she and her staff had called at every pupil's home to conduct safe-and-well checks and provide advice about benefits, accessing the health service and general well-being. This scenario was repeated by thousands of schools. For families with little English in the household, contact with teachers was a lifeline. Existing relations with the community were extended and tempered by teachers going those extra miles.

Government policy remains largely indifferent to the consequences of the climate emergency and the provenance of Black Lives Matter. Secondary school pupils have been motivated by Greta Thunberg's *Skolstrejk för klimatet* and walked out of lessons to join the protest, yet there is no interest in mainstreaming the subject. The official response to Black Lives Matter – which saw thousands of young people marching peacefully through Birmingham city centre – was the Sewell Report (2021), which denied the existence of institutional racism and, in the view of Doreen Lawrence (Baroness Lawrence of Clarendon), condoned the continuation of racist behaviour (Syal, 2021).

Cities are by definition founded by immigrants, whether forced out of rural Worcestershire by the Enclosure Acts in the nineteenth century as the first Industrial Revolution demanded labour in the factories and mills, through to the Windrush generation and Mirpuri migration. More recently, asylum seekers and economic migrants have arrived in Birmingham from Afghanistan, Eritrea, Somalia, Syria and Yemen. Such patterns are set to continue with the ongoing economic, climate and political drivers. Birmingham declared itself a city of sanctuary in 2015, reflecting its history and continued commitment to welcome refugees and asylum seekers. Education has led the way. A few years back, I visited a primary school in Druids Heath, a tough area of the city, and watched some young Syrian children playing in the reception class. They had been in England for just a few months after enduring war in their home country and suffering trauma on their journey to the UK, but they were clearly well settled and starting to thrive. Such things occur right across all of our cities, with schools often providing the anchor for newly arrived citizens.

Birmingham's education leaders and governors have not stood still in the midst of the uncertainty. A few examples from our authors: Sajid Gulzar opened Prince Albert High School in September 2021 with the aim of offering secondary education to all of the Prince Albert Community Trust primary graduates. Herminder Channa is now an executive principal with Ark and sharing her successful school improvement strategies beyond Birmingham. Hamid Patel became the first mufti to be knighted for his services to education in the Queen's Birthday Honours in 2021. He has taken Star Academies, with its Blackburn roots, into partnership with Eton College, demonstrating even higher aspiration for his pupils. Azita Zohhadi retired from headship at Nelson Mandela and is now working closely with the Compassionate Education Foundation and is a member of ukactive Kids Council.

Are there new mantras to learn about urban education leadership in the light of the events of the last two years? Take it as read that change is a constant and distributed leadership is here to stay. Assume that in the digital age connecting and collaborating are more effective than traditional command and control as pedagogy accelerates irreversibly to new platforms. Accept that schools' pivotal role in the community will be a key building block in the recovery from COVID-19. All these ingredients will be factored into continuing professional development and learning programmes and will be integral to leadership development. And, underneath all of this, the machinery of government will plough on – assuming we can get back to 'normal' sometime soon.

The pressures on cities to absorb inward migration will increase for the foreseeable future. Humanity is in an existential crisis as a result of rapid global heating, population expansion and unsustainable behaviours. People will flow into the cities to find security as large areas become uninhabitable and the gap between rich and poor nations widens. Post-colonial wars will continue to displace millions. Afghanistan has fallen to the Taliban again and Russia has invaded Ukraine.

Trojan Horse was one attempt to hold on to an old order born of migration from rural Pakistan. It was never going to succeed because cities invariably move forward to create new realities that blend the old with the new. Compassionate city schools will continue to provide learning that enables generations of immigrants to belong and succeed. No new mantras are needed. The moral compass will guide us, as ever.

References

Diamond, Colin (2020) Everyone Must Have a Say in the Future of Education, *TES* (15 May). Available at: https://www.tes.com/magazine/archive/everyone-must-have-say-future-education.

Miliband, David (2020) Welcome to the Age of Impunity. Speech to the World Economic Forum, Davos-Klosters, Switzerland, 24 January. Available at: https://www.rescue.org/press-release/welcome-age-impunity-david-milibands-world-economic-forum-speech.

Sewell, Tony (2021) *Commission on Race and Ethnic Disparities: The Report* [Sewell Report]. Available at: https://www.gov.uk/government/publications/the-report-of-the-commission-on-race-and-ethnic-disparities.

Syal, Rajeev (2021) Doreen Lawrence Says No 10 Report Gives 'Racists the Green Light', *The Guardian* (1 April). Available at: https://www.theguardian.com/world/2021/apr/01/doreen-lawrence-says-no-10-report-gives-racists-the-green-light.

Thompson, Pat (2021) Survey Results: School Leaders' Experiences, *School Leaders' Work and Well Being* (6 July). Available at: https://schoolleadersworkandwellbeing.com/2021/07/06/a-crisis-in-school-leadership.

Zephaniah, Benjamin (2000) We Refugees. In *Wicked World!* London: Puffin.